D0765366

Inhibition in Cognition

INHIBITION
in Cognition

Edited by

**David S. Gorfein and
Colin M. MacLeod**

American Psychological Association
Washington, DC

Copyright © 2007 by the American Psychological Association. All rights reserved. Except as permitted under the United States Copyright Act of 1976, no part of this publication may be reproduced or distributed in any form or by any means, including, but not limited to, the process of scanning and digitization, or stored in a database or retrieval system, without the prior written permission of the publisher.

Published by
American Psychological Association
750 First Street, NE
Washington, DC 20002
www.apa.org

To order
APA Order Department
P.O. Box 92984
Washington, DC 20090-2984
Tel: (800) 374-2721
Direct: (202) 336-5510
Fax: (202) 336-5502
TDD/TTY: (202) 336-6123
Online: www.apa.org/books/
E-mail: order@apa.org

In the U.K., Europe, Africa, and the Middle East,
copies may be ordered from
American Psychological Association
3 Henrietta Street
Covent Garden, London
WC2E 8LU England

Typeset in New Century Schoolbook by World Composition Services, Inc., Sterling, VA

Printer: Sheridan Books, Ann Arbor, MI
Cover Designer: Scribe Typography, Port Townsend, WA
Technical/Production Editor: Harriet Kaplan

The opinions and statements published are the responsibility of the authors, and such opinions and statements do not necessarily represent the policies of the American Psychological Association.

Library of Congress Cataloging-in-Publication Data

Inhibition in cognition / edited by David S. Gorfein and Colin M. MacLeod.
        p. cm. — (Decade of behavior)
    Includes bibliographical references and index.
    ISBN-13: 978-1-59147-930-7
    ISBN-10: 1-59147-930-4
    1. Cognition. 2. Inhibition. I. Gorfein, David S. II. MacLeod, Colin M.

    BF323.148154   2007
    153—dc22   2007002957

British Library Cataloguing-in-Publication Data
A CIP record is available from the British Library.

Printed in the United States of America
First Edition

APA Science Volumes

Attribution and Social Interaction: The Legacy of Edward E. Jones

Best Methods for the Analysis of Change: Recent Advances, Unanswered Questions, Future Directions

Cardiovascular Reactivity to Psychological Stress and Disease

The Challenge in Mathematics and Science Education: Psychology's Response

Changing Employment Relations: Behavioral and Social Perspectives

Children Exposed to Marital Violence: Theory, Research, and Applied Issues

Cognition: Conceptual and Methodological Issues

Cognitive Bases of Musical Communication

Cognitive Dissonance: Progress on a Pivotal Theory in Social Psychology

Conceptualization and Measurement of Organism–Environment Interaction

Converging Operations in the Study of Visual Selective Attention

Creative Thought: An Investigation of Conceptual Structures and Processes

Developmental Psychoacoustics

Diversity in Work Teams: Research Paradigms for a Changing Workplace

Emotion and Culture: Empirical Studies of Mutual Influence

Emotion, Disclosure, and Health

Evolving Explanations of Development: Ecological Approaches to Organism–Environment Systems

Examining Lives in Context: Perspectives on the Ecology of Human Development

Global Prospects for Education: Development, Culture, and Schooling

Hostility, Coping, and Health

Measuring Patient Changes in Mood, Anxiety, and Personality Disorders: Toward a Core Battery

Occasion Setting: Associative Learning and Cognition in Animals

Organ Donation and Transplantation: Psychological and Behavioral Factors

APA Decade of Behavior Volumes

Contents

Contributors

Michael C. Anderson, University of Oregon, Eugene
David A. Balota, Washington University, St. Louis, MO
Vincent R. Brown, Hofstra University, Hempstead, NY
Deborah M. Burke, Pomona College, Claremont, CA
Laurie Carr, Michigan State University, East Lansing
Thomas H. Carr, Michigan State University, East Lansing
Holly M. Chalk, Wake Forest University, Winston–Salem, NC
Dale Dagenbach, Wake Forest University, Winston–Salem, NC
Peter J. Duquette, Wake Forest University, Winston–Salem, NC
Randall W. Engle, Georgia Institute of Technology, Atlanta
Mark E. Faust, University of North Carolina, Charlotte
David S. Gorfein, University of Texas, Arlington
A. Cris Hamilton, University of Pennsylvania, Philadelphia
Lynn Hasher, University of Toronto, Toronto, Ontario, Canada
Richard P. Heitz, Georgia Institute of Technology, Atlanta
John M. Henderson, University of Edinburgh, Edinburgh, Scotland
Robert S. E. Hurley, Northwestern University, Chicago, IL
Daniel S. Levine, University of Texas, Arlington
Benjamin J. Levy, University of Oregon, Eugene
Cindy Lustig, University of Michigan, Ann Arbor
Colin M. MacLeod, University of Waterloo, Waterloo, Ontario, Canada
Michelle Martel, Michigan State University, East Lansing
Randi C. Martin, Rice University, Houston, TX
Ulrich Mayr, University of Oregon, Eugene
David Menzer, Weill Graduate School of Medical Sciences, Cornell
    University, New York, NY
Britain A. Mills, Cornell University, Ithaca, NY
W. Trammell Neill, State University of New York at Albany
Joel T. Nigg, Michigan State University, East Lansing
Gabrielle Osborne, Claremont Graduate University, Claremont, CA
Thomas S. Redick, Georgia Institute of Technology, Atlanta
Valerie F. Reyna, Cornell University, Ithaca, NY
Melinda Rupard, North Carolina State University, Raleigh
Rose T. Zacks, Michigan State University, East Lansing

Series Foreword

In early 1988, the American Psychological Association (APA) Science Director-ate began its sponsorship of what would become an exceptionally successful activity in support of psychological science—the APA Scientific Conferences program. This program has showcased some of the most important topics in psychological science and has provided a forum for collaboration among many leading figures in the field.

The program has inspired a series of books that have presented cutting-edge work in all areas of psychology. At the turn of the millennium, the series was renamed the Decade of Behavior Series to help advance the goals of this important initiative. The Decade of Behavior is a major interdisciplinary campaign designed to promote the contributions of the behavioral and social sciences to our most important societal challenges in the decade leading up to 2010. Although a key goal has been to inform the public about these scientific contributions, other activities have been designed to encourage and further collaboration among scientists. Hence, the series that was the "APA Science Series" has continued as the "Decade of Behavior Series." This represents one element in APA's efforts to promote the Decade of Behavior initiative as one of its endorsing organizations. For additional information about the Decade of Behavior, please visit http://www.decadeofbehavior.org.

Over the course of the past years, the Science Conference and Decade of Behavior Series has allowed psychological scientists to share and explore cutting-edge findings in psychology. The APA Science Directorate looks forward to continuing this successful program and to sponsoring other conferences and books in the years ahead. This series has been so successful that we have chosen to extend it to include books that, although they do not arise from conferences, report with the same high quality of scholarship on the latest research.

We are pleased that this important contribution to the literature was supported in part by the Decade of Behavior program. Congratulations to the editors and contributors of this volume on their sterling effort.

Steven J. Breckler, PhD
Executive Director for Science

Virginia E. Holt
Assistant Executive Director for Science

Preface

Historians of psychology have often been struck by the enormous impact of the *zeitgeist* (the spirit of the times) on current research. It was therefore not too surprising that when David S. Gorfein attended a professional meeting shortly after editing a volume reviewing the role of suppression and inhibition mechanisms in the processing of ambiguous words,[1] his attention was immediately called to a recent review chapter on the role of inhibition in attention and memory.[2] A brief meeting with the senior author of that chapter, Colin MacLeod, led to a swap of chapters and to the subsequent joint conclusion that the ubiquity of the debate over inhibition across the field of cognition warranted a more formal discussion of the topic. The last extensive presentations on the subject—edited volumes by Dagenbach and Carr[3] and by Dempster and Brainerd[4]—had been published more than a decade before, and a great deal of relevant research and theorizing had happened in the interim. We agreed that cognitive psychology in general could benefit from bringing together leading researchers in the field to discuss the concept of cognitive inhibition and what might (and might not) constitute evidence of its role in processing.

The timeliness of the discussion was confirmed by the enthusiastic response to our call for a conference. We sought representatives of the breadth of cognitive psychology—performance, memory, language, and decision making—and of the applications of this research to normal aging, as well as pathology and psychopathology. Almost all who were invited accepted our invitation, which ultimately led to a thoroughgoing discussion by a group of influential and dedicated scholars. Attendees from North America and Europe told us that they were excited by the discussion and had been led to think much more deeply about the place of inhibition in cognition.

The conference was held March 4 and 5, 2005, at the University of Texas at Arlington. A significant part of the funding was provided by a grant from the Board of Scientific Affairs of the American Psychological Association, generously supplemented by the University of Texas at Arlington. The Metroplex Institute for Neural Dynamics provided additional funds to make possible a

[1] Gorfein, D. S. (Ed.). (2001). *On the consequences of meaning selection: Perspectives on resolving lexical ambiguity*. Washington, DC: American Psychological Association.

[2] MacLeod, C. M., Dodd, M. C., Sheard, E. D., Wilson, D. E., & Bibi, U. (2003). In opposition to inhibition. In B. H. Ross (Ed.), *The psychology of learning and motivation* (Vol. 43, pp. 163–214). San Diego, CA: Academic Press.

[3] Dagenbach, D., & Carr, T. H. (Eds.). (1994). *Inhibitory processes in attention, memory, and language*. San Diego, CA: Academic Press.

[4] Dempster, F. N., & Brainerd, C. J. (Eds.). (1995). *Interference and inhibition in cognition*. San Diego, CA: Academic Press.

postconference workshop devoted to the utility of formal modeling, particularly with reference to inhibitory constructs, in the explication of cognitive processes.

This volume is the result of the always stimulating—and sometimes heated—discussion that the conference generated. It was a terrific conference, the kind of focused, smaller conference where there is time for lots of discussion between the formal talks and in the hallways and over dinners. As editors, we are convinced that each of the authors of the chapters in this volume benefited from the discussion and that the book both represents their individual research programs and theorizing and simultaneously provides an overview of the questions addressed and the different perspectives offered. The authors also served as the reviewers of the other chapters, so there was further discussion of the concepts as the chapters were reviewed and edited. We believe that this volume could readily form the basis for a graduate seminar in cognitive processes and that it will be of considerable interest to investigators of cognitive skills and processes and likely to researchers beyond cognition as well.

Acknowledgments

In a volume such as this, it is difficult to do full justice to the contributions of all those who helped make it possible. Foremost, of course, are our colleagues the chapter authors, who first presented their ideas to a critical audience of their peers. Later, they faced the difficult task of saying what they wanted to say in a limited space in print and of responding to externally imposed deadlines. Many of the authors also served as reviewers for the work of their fellow authors, always a challenging task. In addition to the author–reviewers, several outside reviewers provided their helpful perspectives, including James Bartlett, Karl-Heinz Bäuml, James Erickson, and Susan Kemper. Our development editor at the American Psychological Association (APA), Genevieve Gill, along with two anonymous reviewers selected by APA, contributed important insights as well. We also thank APA Books staff members Lansing Hays, senior acquisition editor, and Harriet Kaplan, production editor, for their work on this project.

The volume benefited immensely from the funding provided by APA's Science Directorate to bring the authors together to discuss their views. Additional funding was provided by the University of Texas at Arlington (UTA). The Office of Research and the College of Science contributed. Paul Paulus, Dean of Science, helped in welcoming the guests to UTA. Harriett Amster contributed by entertaining a busload of guests in her home. Daniel Levine arranged for the Metroplex Institute of Neural Dynamics to provide supplemental funding for a workshop on the modeling of cognitive processes.

The editors especially acknowledge the many contributions of Denise Arellano, a doctoral candidate at UTA, who took full charge of the logistics of the meetings attended by the participants and our guests. Denise literally made sure that even the buses ran on time, thereby freeing us to concentrate fully on the many fruitful discussions that the gathering produced. We are grateful to her.

Part I

Introduction

1

The Concept of Inhibition in Cognition

Colin M. MacLeod

Everyone knows what inhibition is—and that creates a very real problem. The idea is so ingrained that it is difficult to discuss it as a scientific concept without contamination from existing world knowledge. Yet discussing it is exactly what cognitive scientists have been attempting to do with renewed vigor in the recent past, owing to at least three factors: the growth of cognitive neuroscience, developments in cognitive modeling, and newly described cognitive phenomena. Beginning with the phenomenon of negative priming (for reviews, see Fox, 1995; May, Kane, & Hasher, 1995; Tipper, 2001) and spurred by two influential books that appeared in quick succession just over a decade ago (Dagenbach & Carr, 1994; Dempster & Brainerd, 1995), interest in cognitive inhibition grew. Of course, the desire to mesh cognition with neuroscience also has provided a powerful impetus for understanding the place of inhibition in the current conceptualization of mind and brain. This interest is well illustrated by the inclusion of inhibition as one of only 16 core concepts in a recent effort to grapple with concepts—free of empirical research findings—that are fundamental to memory (Roediger, Dudai, & Fitzpatrick, in press).

This chapter is intended as a broad introduction to the concept of inhibition in cognition and consequently to this book as a whole. For this reason, I take no strong stand on the value of the concept (although I have expressed a skeptical point of view elsewhere; see MacLeod, in press; MacLeod, Dodd, Sheard, Wilson, & Bibi, 2003). In this chapter, the goal is to set out the issues involved in the empirical study and theoretical understanding of the concept of inhibition as it applies to the operation of cognition. So I begin with what this chapter is and is not about. This chapter is not about the neural concept of inhibition: It is accepted that neurons certainly can inhibit each other. This chapter also is not about the physical–response concept of inhibition: It is

Preparation of this chapter was supported by Discovery Grant A7459 from the Natural Sciences and Engineering Research Council of Canada. I greatly appreciate discussions with my colleagues Ori Friedman and Steve Spencer and with my friend Kevin Dunbar about the research described in the first part of the chapter. I also thank Nigel Gopie and Kathleen Hourihan for their careful, helpful comments.

accepted that actions can be initiated and then cancelled (Logan & Cowan, 1984), although the extent to which these two domains of inhibition relate to each other remains to be established. This chapter is about the concept of *cognitive inhibition*—the idea that mental processes or representations can be inhibited.

Cognitive and Neural Inhibition: Two Separate Worlds

There is one aspect of this preliminary framing that must be highlighted. The unassailable evidence for the existence of neural inhibition should be seen as in no way speaking to whether cognitive inhibition exists or, if it exists, to the form or forms that it might take: These are simply different levels of analysis that share a label, which may be responsible for more confusion than clarity. Indeed, neural inhibition at the conceptual level is likely not unitary. Cohen (1993), for example, distinguished four types of neural inhibition, each composed of a variety of neural components. Should all of these inform thinking about cognitive inhibition? Should there be four kinds of cognitive inhibition? These questions are meant to illustrate one of the problems in trying to draw a direct analogy between neural and cognitive inhibition; they are not meant to suggest that such analysis should not be undertaken or that it is doomed to fail. Rather, they are meant to encourage more concerted efforts with respect to the evidentiary and/or logical arguments for or against symmetry across levels of analysis.

With the goal of focusing attention on *cognitive* inhibition, I take one strong stand here. I strongly disagree with the common view, as stated in one of the most influential modern articles on cognitive inhibition, that

> the existence of such inhibitory mechanisms in the functional architecture of cognition seems both plausible and necessary: plausible because the substrate on which that architecture operates—the brain—uses both excitatory and inhibitory processes to perform neural computation, and necessary because computational analyses show that inhibitory mechanisms are critical for maintaining stability in neuronal networks. (Anderson & Spellman, 1995, p. 68)

Trying to force these two levels of analysis to fit together so that they can share a common term is unlikely to help advance understanding of either, a point that was made a long time ago (Breese, 1899). Indeed, it is noteworthy that even Anderson and Spellman (1995) chose to set aside one of the hallmark features of neural inhibition—its brief duration—in their argument for a much longer lasting cognitive inhibition, saying, "The strong assumption that cognitive inhibition should follow the characteristics of individual neurons receiving a single inhibitory input . . . is likely to be far too simple" (p. 95).

To reiterate, then, this chapter is about the cognitive or mental concept of inhibition, also variously called *repression*, *suppression*, or *restraining* (and sometimes even *blocking*, although *blocking* appears to have a different meaning for most investigators). For excellent histories of ideas concerning inhibition, the reader should consult S. Diamond, Balvin, and Diamond (1963) and particularly the more recent treatment by Smith (1992). As a point of departure, *The Oxford English Dictionary* (1989) lists four meanings for *inhibition*. The first two relate to the societal or legal prohibition senses and so are not relevant here. The remaining two relate to the physiological and psychological senses, consistent with the admonishment (MacLeod, in press; MacLeod et al., 2003) to keep these two senses distinct.

Focusing just on cognitive inhibition, the active ingredients appear to be primarily two: mental withholding and reduced performance. The former is an inference from the latter, reflecting a confusion that pervades the literature. In cognition, inhibition is sometimes a measurable phenomenon, sometimes a theory about the cause of that phenomenon, and often both. As always, it is a bad idea to name a phenomenon using the label for one of the possible theories that might explain it. This is not to claim that that theory is wrong, but to urge avoidance of confusion. Inhibition may—or may not—play a key role in explaining (aspects of) cognition: That is what this book is about, with the aim of considering the variety of perspectives.

A Definition of Cognitive Inhibition

How might *inhibition* be defined from a cognitive standpoint? Given its strong standing in the vernacular, the term often is not defined at all. To remedy that common oversight, I propose the following definition: *Cognitive inhibition is the stopping or overriding of a mental process, in whole or in part, with or without intention.* The mental process so influenced might be selective attention or memory retrieval or a host of other cognitive processes. Typically, this influence would not be to eradicate or entirely prevent some process from occurring but rather to slow it down or reduce its probability of taking place (relative to some neutral baseline condition or situation). Inhibition could be applied as an act of will, or it could be more automatic, perhaps as a by-product of another cognitive process. Two other features might be considered relevant: recovery and reactivity. In the present context, *recovery* means that inhibition could be permanent or could be transitory, subject to (perhaps complete) lifting under specified conditions. *Reactivity* means that inhibition may be applied to the extent that it is required under the circumstances (i.e., it may not be all or none), an idea that goes back to Wundt (1902) but one that if not embedded in a formal theory may give too much flexibility to the concept.

Because inhibition is so rarely explicitly defined, my definition is certain to be challenged, but at least it provides a starting point. Indeed, some of the confusion apparent in the literature could be eliminated if each investigator would explicitly define what he or she means by inhibition. My strong sense is that this practice would quickly demonstrate that the term has a wide range of meanings and that at the very least, some kind of framework for a theory of inhibition is required. The definitions offered in chapters 6, 8, 9, and 14 of this volume help to underscore this point. In this regard, attempts at offering empirical criteria for the demonstration of inhibition (e.g., Anderson & Bjork,

1994) should certainly be encouraged, a point that is amplified later in this chapter.

Cognitive Inhibition Beyond Cognition

The concept of cognitive inhibition in mainstream cognitive psychology is permeating all of the other traditional areas of psychological inquiry as well (e.g., developmental, social, clinical). This concept—sometimes it is more of a meta-concept—is a powerful one and hence a seductive one. For this reason, it is useful to illustrate this broader research perspective before homing in on mainstream cognitive research. Certainly, the tasks and approaches developed within cognitive psychology, as well as the theoretical principles to which those tasks and approaches become linked, are influential not just in the study of cognition but throughout the discipline. In the next sections I illustrate several subareas, each with a single study, although numerous other published studies could have been selected.

Developmental Psychology

O. Friedman and Leslie (2004) explained children's performance in the false belief task as relying on a critical inhibitory process (for related ideas, see Carlson & Moses, 2001; Russell, Mauthner, Sharpe, & Tidswell, 1991). In a variation on the standard version of this task, children are told about a girl, Sally, who sees two boxes, one red and one blue, and then sees a frog placed under the red box. After Sally leaves the room, the children see the frog moved under the blue box. The critical question asked of the children is where Sally thinks the frog is or where Sally will look for the frog. Given that Sally did not see the frog switch boxes, the correct answer is the red box (where the frog initially was) and the incorrect answer is the blue box (where the frog now actually is). Somewhere between ages 3 and 4, children shift from the incorrect to the correct answer (for a review, see Wellman, Cross, & Watson, 2001)—from relying on what they themselves saw to taking the perspective of what Sally knows.

O. Friedman and Leslie (2004) argued that the inhibition of competitors is fundamental to the selection among alternative beliefs, akin to the selection-by-inhibition explanation of negative priming in the attention literature (for a review, see Tipper, 2001). They theorized that for children to succeed, the most salient box—the blue one, because that is where the children know the frog actually is—must be inhibited. What the 4-year-old can do that the 3-year-old cannot is successfully apply the inhibition. O. Friedman and Leslie went on to provide an elegant test of their inhibition theory in a considerably more complex version of the false belief task, but describing this would take us too far afield. They concluded that "competent reasoning about beliefs depends on the development of inhibitory control" (p. 552). This emphasis on inhibition in understanding development is not unique to O. Friedman and Leslie (see, e.g., Bull & Scerif, 2001; A. Diamond, Kirkham, & Amso, 2002; Wilson & Kipp, 1998; see also chap. 13, this volume).

Social Psychology

A major question in social psychology is what causes a stereotype to come to mind (activation) and to influence one's impression (application) when one comes in contact with a member of the stereotype-relevant group. Kunda and Spencer (2003) proposed that the activation of stereotypes is driven by three goals. First is the goal of comprehension—simplifying and understanding the situation. Second is the goal of self-enhancement—the nurturing of self-esteem. Third is the goal of avoiding prejudice—either to see oneself as egalitarian or to comply with egalitarian social norms. The comprehension and self-enhancement goals function similarly: As the strength of the goal increases, often the likelihood of stereotype activation and application increases as well. The stereotype simplifies interpretation of the situation and maintains or even enhances self-esteem.

What makes the Kunda and Spencer (2003) framework unique is the emphasis on inhibition. They argued that it is also possible that a stronger goal will lead to inhibiting the stereotype. So for comprehension, when information about the specific individual is available, it may be better to inhibit the stereotype and instead use the individuating information. For self-esteem, if one is motivated to form a positive impression of an individual, it may be better to inhibit the (negative) stereotype. In the case of the goal of avoiding prejudice, the primary process may in fact be inhibitory, acting to suppress the negative stereotypic information. Kunda and Spencer suggested that the application of inhibition may be cognitively demanding and may become more likely to fail as cognitive resource demands increase. Such an emphasis on inhibition in understanding social processes is not unique to Kunda and Spencer (see, e.g., Beer, Heerey, Keltner, Scabini, & Knight, 2003; Förster, Liberman, & Higgins, 2005; Shah, Friedman, & Kruglanski, 2002; von Hippel & Gonsalkorale, 2005; see also chap. 7, this volume).

Clinical and Personality Psychology

Many illustrations are possible in the domain of clinical and personality psychology, but I describe only one. Wood, Mathews, and Dalgleish (2001) asked subjects who were either high or low in trait anxiety to make decisions on each trial about whether a single target word was or was not related to the sentence that preceded it. Sentences were constructed in pairs, differing only in the final word, an example being "At the party she had some punch/wine," where the first of the two possible final words was a homograph. The task was to determine whether the probe word *fist* was semantically related to the sentence. The answer should have been no in both cases, but critically, *fist* is related to the other sense of the homograph *punch*. Therefore, failure to suppress that other sense would slow rejection of *fist*. The prediction was that such a failure to inhibit would be more likely in high-anxiety subjects.

In their first experiment, Wood et al. (2001) found that all subjects were faster to reject the probe *fist* in response to *wine* than to *punch* but that there was no effect of anxiety level. This finding might seem to conflict with their prediction, but in their second experiment, when subjects were under higher cognitive load because they had to rehearse a set of digits during task performance, the pattern changed. Anxious subjects showed a pattern suggesting a general impairment of inhibitory processing. Wood et al. concluded that "anxiety-prone individuals have a deficit in tasks requiring the inhibition of currently irrelevant meanings" but that this impairment "may be revealed only when task-related control strategies are limited by mental load" (p. 176). This emphasis on inhibition in understanding personality and abnormal behavior is not unique to Wood et al. (see, e.g., Bohne, Keuthen, Tuschen-Caffier, & Wilhelm, 2005; Dorahy, Middleton, & Irwin, 2005; Kuhl & Kazén, 1999; see also chaps. 10, 11, and 13, this volume).

Behavioral Neuroscience

Colvin, Dunbar, and Grafman (2001) contrasted patients with frontal lobe lesions with normal subjects performing a water jug task (Luchins, 1942). In the version of the task that they used, subjects had to manipulate three jugs with known capacities (A = 8 units, B = 5 units, C = 3 units) to reach a specified goal state (A = 4 units, B = 4 units, C = 0 units). Patients, particularly those with left dorsolateral prefrontal lesions, performed poorly, especially when they had to make a counterintuitive move—one that resulted in a step back from the goal state and therefore was not predicted by a simple means–end analysis without planning. In particular, patients tended to prefer to go back to an earlier state rather than to make a counterintuitive move. Colvin et al. argued that intact functioning of the left dorsolateral prefrontal region is necessary in part for "the inhibition of a response generated by an adopted problem-solving strategy" (p. 1138). Of course, this emphasis on inhibition in understanding behavior from a neuroscientific perspective is certainly not unique to Colvin et al. (see, e.g., Amos, 2000; Durston et al., 2002; Gazzaley, Cooney, Rissman, & D'Esposito, 2005) and is in fact very much in the zeitgeist in this domain.

Inhibition in Cognition

In the preceding section, the goal was to indicate the breadth and current impact of the concept of inhibition as an explanatory element in traditionally recognized subdomains of psychology other than cognition. Much of this impact can be placed at the doorstep of cognition, in that the tasks and explanations in these domains have often been modified from cognitive antecedents. Let us turn now to cognition itself, where the growth of explanations involving inhibition has been dramatic in the past 25 to 30 years since research on negative priming began to lead the charge.

All of the illustrations in the preceding section are instances where cognitive inhibition has been proposed as a key mechanism in explaining observed behavior. It is fair to say that the concept is by now ubiquitous, having been applied to, among other cognitive activities, action, language, meaning, memory, perception, responding, thought, and working memory. Without doubt, it is a compelling idea, one that lends considerable power to theory—not to mention the seductive draw of the neural analogy. It seems, in fact, that cognitive inhibition *has* to exist: In James's (1890) words, "Inhibition is a *vera causa*, of that there can be no doubt" (p. 67). Even more to the point is what Mercier (quoted in Smith, 1992) said a couple of years earlier, in 1888: "If [inhibition] did not exist it would be necessary to invent it" (p. 21).

In the early days of psychology, the concept of inhibition was prevalent and influential (e.g., Breese, 1899; Pillsbury, 1908; Wundt, 1902). However, it largely disappeared as a theoretical entity in the face of behaviorism and even through the early growth of cognitive psychology, relegated to terms describing empirical phenomena such as *conditioned inhibition* and *proactive inhibition*. Then, about 30 years ago, it began to reappear with theoretical impact in research on the phenomenon initially given several names (e.g., *distractor suppression*) but ultimately called *negative priming* (Lowe, 1979; Neill, 1977; Tipper, 1985). Wundt (1902) had argued that to attend to one of several simultaneous stimuli, the others had to be inhibited. This idea was revived to explain negative priming, and a strong paradigm–theory linkage quickly developed.

Attention

In negative priming experiments, each trial typically involves two stimuli, one to be attended and one to be ignored. If the ignored stimulus on one trial becomes the target stimulus on the next trial, responding to it is slower than would have been the case if the previous trial were completely unrelated. The argument originally put forward by Neill (1977; for an updated view, see chap. 4, this volume) and championed by Tipper (1985, 2001) was that the ignored stimulus was inhibited to permit the target stimulus to control responding. Then, when that ignored stimulus itself became the target, the inhibition just applied to it had to be overcome for it to control responding, and this process took additional time.

This apparently simple task, with its intuitively appealing explanation, was quickly followed in the attention literature by the phenomenon of inhibition of return (Posner & Cohen, 1984). The prototypical procedure consists of three outline boxes with subjects instructed to fixate on the center box and to move only their attention (not their eyes) during the trial. Then one of the two peripheral boxes brightens, drawing attention to that cued location despite the cue not being informative. Shortly thereafter, a target appears. When the time between cue and target is brief, target detection is faster at the cued location— the intuitive pattern of automatic capturing of attention by the cue. However, when the cue–target interval is longer than 300 milliseconds, detection is slower at the cued location. As the term *inhibition of return* was intended to suggest, attention may be inhibited from reorienting back to the cued location, resulting in delayed or slower processing there (e.g., Rafal, Egly, & Rhodes, 1994; Reuter-Lorenz, Jha, & Rosenquist, 1996).

Much research has followed in which inhibition has been proposed to play a key role in attentional processing (e.g., task switching in Allport, Styles, &

Hsieh, 1994; visual marking in Watson & Humphreys, 1997; see also chaps. 2–4, this volume). The nature of that role, however, appears to be broad, leading to the question of what these various forms of inhibition have in common. Are there common processes or at least a small set of crucial processes? Such a limitation would seem to be important for the concept of attentional inhibition to be coherent and parsimonious. Efforts have been made to address this question. Thus, Rafal and Henik (1994) distinguished three inhibitory processes. The first is inhibition of responding to signals at unattended locations, the kind of process involved in spatial versions of negative priming. The second is endogenous inhibition of reflexes, more akin to stopping a prepotent response. The third is reflexive inhibition of the detection of subsequent signals, the kind of process involved in inhibition of return. The glue that links these processes together as inhibition remains elusive, but that certainly does not mean that such a linkage cannot or will not be accomplished as research progresses.

Turning to the neural level, there is also evidence consistent with attentional inhibition operating at intermediate levels of cortical processing, in visual area V4 and in TEO (the posterior portion of the inferior temporal cortex). Attention may work in a push–pull fashion to promote processing of what is attended and to inhibit processing of what is unattended (for a review, see Kastner & Pinsk, 2004). This push–pull idea is also familiar as *center-surround* and goes by other names as well. The extent to which this idea relates directly to cognitive inhibition must be clarified, but the connection is unquestionably appealing.

Memory

The employment of inhibition as an explanatory tool is no less prominent in memory than it is in attention. This emphasis began with the work of Hasher and Zacks (1988; see also chap. 8, this volume) focusing on the cognitive costs associated with aging and bridging the attention–memory gap. Like Rafal and Henik (1994), Hasher and Zacks described three components of inhibition, all seen as influencing the optimal operation of working memory (via attention): (a) control of the specific information that enters working memory, (b) control of the information that is deleted from working memory, and (c) prevention of possibly relevant but incorrect responses from being executed. Their argument, based on an extended series of studies, is that older people do not execute these functions as well as younger people because older people do not inhibit as well. Their research program has made a concerted effort to characterize these proposed processes, and their account has been influential (for review and commentary, see Burke, 1997; McDowd, 1997; for other views, see chaps. 9 and 10, this volume). The Hasher and Zacks inhibition-based account of aging has not been without critics, however: As Charlot and Feyereisen (2005) concluded in their review concerning executive control and prefrontal cortex, "The changes tied to cognitive aging in the domain of episodic memory cannot be uniquely explained by a deficit in inhibition" (p. 349, my translation).

Next to the work of Hasher and Zacks (1988), the most visible work arguing for inhibitory processes in memory is that of Anderson and colleagues (Anderson, 2005; Anderson & Green, 2001; Anderson & Spellman, 1995). Anderson and Spellman (1995) had subjects learn an initial list of category–instance word pairs and then practice half of the items in half of the categories. They found that the unpracticed half of a category was actually more poorly remembered than a corresponding half from a category in which no items were practiced. Moreover, not only were the unpracticed items less accessible from their studied cues, they were also less accessible from independent semantically related probes. It appeared that these unpracticed items had become generally less accessible, a pattern consistent with their representations having been inhibited.

Anderson and Green (2001) went on to develop a clever variation on this paradigm that they referred to as the "think/no think" paradigm. After studying a list of pairs, participants were asked to try not to think of a previously studied word when provided with a cue that had been studied with that word. Having tried not to think of a word resulted in poorer recall than in the control condition, where studied pairs were neither thought of nor suppressed. Moreover, the target word was also less likely to be recalled to a semantic cue that had not been studied: It appeared that the target word itself, not just the studied pair, was inhibited as a result of not thinking about it. This cue independence has been seen by Anderson and Green as the strongest evidence of inhibition being involved in memory.

There are many other illustrations of inhibitory accounts applied to memory phenomena. Anderson (2005) pointed to the related paradigm of directed forgetting (for a review, see MacLeod, 1998), in which it has been argued (Basden, Basden, & Gargano, 1993) that when the first half of a list is followed by an instruction to forget, it is more poorly remembered than the second, to-be-remembered half of the list because it has been inhibited. Similarly, when subjects are provided with a partial set of members of a studied list to aid the retrieval of the remainder, this typically hurts rather than helps performance— the part-list cuing effect (Slamecka, 1968). Bäuml and Aslan (2006) argued that this effect is, at least under certain conditions, due to inhibition of retrieval. There are certainly plenty of other illustrations of memory phenomena held to be at least in part attributable to inhibition (see, e.g., Brown, Zoccoli, & Leahy, 2005; Racsmány & Conway, 2006; Veling & van Knippenberg, 2004).

In the memory literature, another way of examining inhibition has been prominent—that of individual differences. Two different approaches have been taken—that of Engle and his colleagues and that of N. P. Friedman, Miyake, and their colleagues. Engle and his colleagues (Conway & Engle, 1994; Engle, Conway, Tuholski, & Shisler, 1995; Kane & Engle, 2000) put forth a perspective related to that of Hasher and Zacks (1988) in that it also emphasizes attentional resources and working memory, although Engle's emphasis on general capacity distinguishes his view from theirs. Conway and Engle (1994) argued that a major source of individual differences in cognitive ability is the capacity of working memory and that these individual differences result from variation in attentional resources that in turn produce "differences in the ability to inhibit or suppress irrelevant information" (p. 354). The impact of these differences should be evident in controlled tasks requiring attention but not in more automatic tasks. Redick, Heitz, and Engle (chap. 7, this volume) have carried forward this work.

N. P. Friedman, Miyake, and their colleagues (N. P. Friedman & Miyake, 2004; Miyake, Friedman, Emerson, Witzki, & Howerter, 2000) have taken the more psychometric approach of seeking patterns of correlations between cognitive measures. Thus, when N. P. Friedman and Miyake (2004) directed this approach to examining inhibition, they administered an extensive battery of tasks, several of which were seen as markers for each of three key inhibitory abilities: prepotent response inhibition (e.g., Stroop task, stop signal task), resistance to distractor interference (e.g., Eriksen flanker task, word naming with distraction), and resistance to proactive interference (e.g., Brown–Peterson task, cued recall task). Via structural equation modeling, they found the first two inhibitory abilities to be closely related but the third to be clearly separate, suggesting to them that the overall "trait" of inhibition was not unified. More recent work (N. P. Friedman et al., 2006) has suggested that, unlike updating working memory, which is related to intelligence, inhibiting prepotent responses (and shifting mental sets) is not.

Turning to the neural level, again multiple approaches have been taken. Hamilton and Martin (2005; see also chap. 12, this volume) presented a case study of a participant with left inferior frontal damage in which the pattern of task dissociation across a series of inhibition tasks seemed incompatible with a single shared neural substrate. Their work simultaneously supports that of Miyake et al. (2000) and N. P. Friedman and Miyake (2004)—in showing dissociations across proposed inhibitory abilities—and conflicts with it—in showing dissociations within abilities that the Miyake group held to be single abilities. Hamilton and Martin suggested that one fruitful direction to pursue would be to consider that variations might hinge not on common brain areas but rather on common patterns of neurotransmitters, such as dopamine and norepinephrine, which may influence how different brain areas operate. The puzzle of the diversity of brain areas involved in some ability might then be resolved by the commonality in the neurotransmitters affecting these areas. This is an intriguing idea, although it also highlights the fact that cognitive neurotopology may be even more complicated than currently viewed.

Gazzaley et al. (2005) used functional magnetic resonance imaging (fMRI) to examine how aging affects what they saw as a goal-driven mechanism in support of attention and memory that enhances and suppresses the processing of sensory information. On each trial, participants watched two faces and two scenes in random order and tried to remember one type of stimulus or the other for a subsequent recognition test; the control was passive viewing without the memory instruction. Like younger adults, older adults showed enhanced cortical activity for task-relevant representations; unlike younger adults, older adults were deficient in suppression of cortical activity for task-irrelevant representations. Gazzaley et al. saw their results as indicating that the inhibitory function was deficient in the older subjects but that the enhancement function was unaffected by aging, which fits nicely with the Hasher and Zacks (1988) theory (although Gazzaley et al. did note that their results could reflect excitation and inhibition or simply different levels of excitation, an issue that is at present difficult to resolve in fMRI research).

Anderson et al. (2004), also using fMRI, investigated neural activity in the Anderson and Green (2001) think/no think paradigm. They first reported obtaining the same behavioral data pattern as reported by Anderson and Green—poorer memory for no-think items both in response to their studied cues and, importantly, in response to independent probes. Neural differences were evident in reduced hippocampal activation and increased dorsolateral prefrontal activation for the no-think items. They saw their results as supporting the existence of active cognitive inhibition at the neural level. Thus, there have recently been a number of quite concerted efforts to demonstrate brain parallels of cognitive inhibition in memory. This domain of research is likely to be very influential in determining the role of inhibition in cognitive processing.

Beyond Attention and Memory

In the domain of intelligence, where presumably cognitive processes are assembled and orchestrated, inhibition has also been proposed to be a fundamental component. Dempster (1991) reviewed the relation between measures of intelligence and of inhibition across a broad age range and concluded that "intelligence cannot be understood without reference to inhibitory processes" (p. 157). Although at odds with the conclusions of N. P. Friedman, Miyake, and their colleagues (N. P. Friedman & Miyake, 2004; Miyake et al., 2000), Dempster's conclusion is consistent with the findings of Salthouse, Atkinson, and Berish (2003) that in older adults, measures of inhibition correlated well with measures of fluid intelligence (although Salthouse et al. were not convinced that inhibition represented a distinct executive control function).

There is no way to do justice to the breadth and diversity of cognitive research invoking inhibition as an explanatory construct. So, like the preceding discussion of research outside cognition, this survey has been only cursory, the goal being to illustrate some of the key areas across cognition where inhibition has played a central role in the explanation of empirical findings. That role continues to grow. In the remainder of this chapter, the goal shifts to consideration of the concept of inhibition as an explanatory entity in cognition and to identifying some of the questions that must be addressed.

Four Conceptual Issues

The following section outlines in brief form four of the key issues related to understanding cognitive inhibition as a theoretical construct: definition, relation to neural inhibition, relation to interference, and measurement and the baseline problem.

Definition

When applied to cognition, the term *inhibition* definitely does not have a consistent meaning. Many scholars have recognized this, as two recent quotes and a less recent one demonstrate. Conway and Engle (1994) said, "Unfortunately, the term *inhibition* is a nebulous one that connotes a multitude of meanings" (p. 368); N. P. Friedman and Miyake (2004) similarly observed, "These results suggest that the term inhibition has been overextended and that researchers need to be more specific when discussing and measuring inhibition-related functions" (p. 101). Slipping back a century, Breese (1899) said, "Inhibition is a term which has been used to designate all kinds of mental conflict, hesitation and arrest" (p. 14). The first charge for theorists, then, is to provide their own meaningful definition of the term so that it can be compared with other definitions, permitting debate about the "proper" definition of the term and what it entails. In my reading of the literature, the default is to not define the term and to assume that all researchers share the same meaning. They do not. It is for this reason that I offered a possible definition early in this chapter.[1]

Relation to Neural Inhibition

At the outset of this chapter and elsewhere (MacLeod, in press; MacLeod et al., 2003), I have argued that there is no necessary relation between cognitive inhibition and neural inhibition. These are different levels of analysis, and my speculation is that theorists will ultimately abandon the desire to force these two conceptual entities to become one. Just as activation in cognition is supported at the neural level by the coordination of excitation and inhibition, the same is likely to be true of inhibition in cognition should researchers choose to incorporate cognitive inhibition in explaining aspects of performance. I hasten to note that rejecting this link in no way impugns the concept of cognitive inhibition: I am not arguing that cognitive inhibition cannot be theoretically useful (or empirically demonstrated) if it is not directly linked to neural inhibition. I am arguing, in fact, the contrary—that determining the value of the concept of cognitive inhibition will be a more attainable goal if researchers avoid the confusion of trying to relate it to its nominal counterpart in the nervous system.

Relation to Interference

It is not uncommon now, nor was it in the past, to use the terms *interference* and *inhibition* interchangeably; indeed, Stroop (1935) noted this tendency in the first sentence of his famous article. But this practice unquestionably results in misunderstanding. Instead, it would be preferable to reserve the term *interference* for an empirical phenomenon in which performance decreases (relative to a suitable baseline) because of processing of some at least nominally irrelevant information. Then the term *inhibition* would be preserved as one theoretical mechanism that could potentially explain that interference. Yoking these

---

[1]Also to be handled with caution is the term *cognitive control*, which has crept into widespread usage and of which inhibition is often characterized as a subset. What *cognitive control* means is also in need of more rigorous definition and consideration; otherwise, it is in danger of meaning nothing more specific than *processing* or even *cognition*.

two terms tends to wed the interpretation to the phenomenon. MacLeod et al. (2003) addressed this point in more detail, and Klein and Taylor (1994) put it very well: "There is a danger of circularity whereby investigators attribute interference effects to inhibition and subsequently define inhibition on the basis of behavioral interference" (p. 146).

Measurement and the Baseline Problem

Even the term *interference* can be theoretical, implying a competition between two stimuli or two dimensions of a stimulus. For this reason, at the empirical level, the terms *cost* and *benefit* seem preferable, reflecting a deviation from some neutral condition that must then be explained (see Jonides & Mack, 1984; Posner, 1978). An observed cost might or might not be attributable to inhibition (or indeed to interference). However, this consideration pushes the problem back a level empirically, and it is an important level to consider. Observing an empirical cost in performance hinges on the neutral condition used. As always, one of the greatest problems faced by the experimental psychologist is selecting the appropriate neutral condition from the myriad possibilities. It is problematic to assume that a deflection below baseline is a straightforward reflection of inhibition, both because the baseline is always subject to debate and because other mechanisms could be solely responsible, or jointly responsible with inhibition, for the observed cost.

Five Conceptual Questions

Many of the conceptual issues that have been raised in this chapter and will be raised throughout this volume apply to other concepts in cognition just as they apply to cognitive inhibition. In holding cognitive inhibition to a high standard, my intention is not that it should be singled out in that regard. What follows is a set of questions that need to be addressed with respect to inhibition as a theoretical mechanism in cognition; these questions are, of course, not restricted to inhibition.

Use of the Concept

First, how is the concept of inhibition being used inside and outside cognition? Much of this chapter has been devoted to illustrating the use of inhibition as a theoretical mechanism both in cognition and in psychology more broadly, so a beginning has been made on this question at least at one level. However, there is another way to answer this question—in terms of the overall use of the concept. The answer is, in a word, broadly. Inhibition appears to mean different things to different investigators and theorists. Perhaps inhibition is the superordinate for a set of inhibitory subordinates, but if so, this taxonomy is in need of considerable development. The fact that the use of the term is so broad has implications for researchers' thinking about the concept and leads directly to the second question.

The Idea of a Domain-General Central Concept

Second, is there a "domain-general" central concept? The issue is whether there is conceptual coherence within and across domains—whether there is a core concept of inhibition. The analysis in this chapter (see also MacLeod, in press; MacLeod et al., 2003) suggests that inhibition at present is not a coherent theoretical entity. Once again, I note that this is in no way the death knell for the concept of cognitive inhibition. In fact, there is some agreement: Generally, the blocking sense of inhibition is not being invoked; it is, rather, the suppression (or restraint) sense that is emphasized. How that suppression operates is not well defined in many cases, however. As a result, inhibition is a concept in the same way as encoding or retrieval are concepts—at too high a level to have value as an actual processing explanation. Of course, one could certainly argue that a central concept is not necessary (or perhaps even important) and that inhibition is still a useful concept in cognition, albeit one in need of refining.

In this regard, there have been efforts to capture what is meant by inhibition, including the work of Hasher and Zacks (1988) and Rafal and Henik (1994) discussed earlier in this chapter. As another instance, Nigg (2000) proposed four kinds of inhibition, three related to cognition—executive inhibition, automatic inhibition of attention, and motivational inhibition—and the fourth more tied to psychopathological variation in these cognitive kinds of inhibition. His "executive inhibition" includes controlling inhibition due to competition, suppressing irrelevant information, and suppressing highly likely responses, all reminiscent of the three types of inhibition put forth by Hasher and Zacks. A fourth type listed under "executive inhibition" by Nigg—suppressing reflexive saccades—when coupled with the two types that he lists under "automatic inhibition of attention"—suppressing recently examined stimuli and suppressing unattended information—closely resemble the set suggested by Rafal and Henik (1994).

This convergence of theory is clearly good, linked as it is to a strong empirical base. Such efforts certainly help researchers to think about the concept, although it is reasonable to keep in mind the caution by N. P. Friedman and Miyake (2004) that "theories positing inhibition as a unifying mechanism or theme may be overly ambitious" (p. 128). What is needed is a convergence of empirical findings on each of the multiple kinds of inhibition—a goal that researchers are vigorously pursuing—as well as a theory, ideally a formal theory, specifying how to link these kinds of inhibition together and what it is that they share that makes them all inhibition.

Criteria for Behavioral Evidence

Third, what criteria must behavioral evidence fulfill to justify a claim of having demonstrated inhibition? This question is one to be emphasized, given that empirical phenomena involving behavioral costs are the wellspring of heightened interest in inhibition as an explanatory mechanism. I have suggested (MacLeod, in press) that only two criteria have been identified. The first is a reversal from a benefit to a cost over a short period of time, as in inhibition of return in the attention literature, but there is ongoing debate as to whether inhibition actually plays a role in inhibition of return (see, e.g., MacLeod et al., 2003). The second criterion is a cost associated with an independent cue, as in the retrieval-induced forgetting and think/no think paradigms from the memory literature; I will consider this more in a moment. One might also include a third index—the switch in instructional status from being ignored to being attended, as in negative priming—but that, too, has been questioned as diagnostic of inhibition (see, e.g., Egner & Hirsch, 2005; MacLeod et al., 2003; Neill & Mathis, 1998). Although certainly useful at this juncture, these criteria are neither definitive nor sufficient.

The independent cue is so far the most compelling criterion for demonstrating that an effect is attributable to inhibition. Certainly, Anderson and his collaborators replicated the effect in numerous studies using both the retrieval-induced forgetting and think/no think paradigms (for reviews, see, e.g., Anderson, 2003, 2005; see also chap. 5, this volume). Other laboratories (e.g., Camp, Pecher, & Schmidt, 2005; Saunders & MacLeod, 2006) also have replicated the effect in retrieval-induced forgetting, but others have not (e.g., Williams & Zacks, 2001). Although there are as yet no published replications by other laboratories of inhibition to independent cues in the think/no think paradigm (but see Bergström, Richardson-Klavehn, & de Fockert, 2006), there is again a failure to replicate (Bulevich, Roediger, Balota, & Butler, in press). The meaning of these limitations should be a focus of ongoing research given the present centrality of the independent cue criterion for inhibition.

One of the goals of theorizing in providing a guide to empirical research must be to set out criteria for a behavioral phenomenon to be seen as involving inhibition. What would be especially praiseworthy would be a set of criteria that could each be applied to a given empirical phenomenon, providing conceptual convergence. Although the extant research has focused heavily on the independent cue evidence, Anderson and his colleagues have made a concerted effort to identify other criteria (see Anderson, 2003; Anderson & Bjork, 1994; see also chap. 5, this volume). Still, it would be most impressive to see further efforts and to have these jointly lead to a set of well-tested and widely accepted criteria. Finally, testing well-specified models is, as always, a most promising avenue for ascertaining the viability of concepts such as inhibition, because implemented models require that these concepts be rigorously specified (see, e.g., chaps. 6 and 14, this volume).

Accounting for Other Phenomena

Fourth, what does inhibition account for that is not or cannot be explained by other existing processes or mechanisms? This can certainly be read as a loaded question. My intention, however, is to point out that researchers need to carefully consider other possible mechanisms, particularly those already carrying substantial theoretical loads elsewhere, whenever they consider inhibition as a possible explanation. Of course, this admonition must be a two-way street and serves to highlight that inhibition should also be given fair consideration when other explanations of behavioral costs are being considered. Generality and parsimony have their place in this evaluation.

Another factor that warrants consideration in this evaluation is whether there are any "hidden layers" in an explanation. In the case of inhibition, the idea sometimes depends on an inlaid resource/capacity theory, which is itself often vague (for more on this issue, see, e.g., Hasher & Zacks, 1988; Logan & Zbrodoff, 1999; McDowd, 1997). It is important, therefore, to examine carefully the assumptions underlying an account in terms of inhibition. Adding inhibition to activation provides a powerful—possibly too powerful—theoretical framework, which may well be capable of explaining any observed pattern of data as well as its opposite. It often is difficult to enumerate the free parameters, but it is important to do so. Ultimately, only formal models are likely to be successful in this regard, so it is important to develop these in the context of inhibition. Again, inhibition is no more to be criticized than are many other cognitive constructs, but its ubiquity demands concise theory.

Plausible Alternatives

Finally, what are (some of) the plausible alternatives to inhibition? The previous question feeds directly into this last question: If not inhibition, then what? Inhibition seems to fit certain phenomena—negative priming and inhibition of return spring to mind—exceptionally well, and the list could certainly be longer. Are there mechanisms with equivalent span and intuitive appeal that provide worthy theoretical adversaries? At the level of any individual research project or even at the level of a single phenomenon, there no doubt are, and this returns us to the third and fourth questions. More globally, however, are there processing accounts that can do the same theoretical work as inhibition?

In the context of negative priming, Neill (see, e.g., Neill & Mathis, 1998) argued for what he described as an episodic retrieval view, a view derived from Logan's (1988, 2002) instance theory of automaticity. The idea is that people routinely check their memory for relevant information that might help with current processing. This checking is usually beneficial, reducing reliance on working out algorithms. Instead, the information provided by memory can simply be used to determine what to do in the present. Sometimes, however, especially in the creative tasks that cognitive psychology is known for developing, the information from memory conflicts with the information presently in the world, demanding resolution of this conflict. Making such a decision takes additional time, and so there is a behavioral cost.

In negative priming, memory indicates that this stimulus should not be responded to (because of its fate on the previous trial), whereas the perceptual display indicates that this stimulus is the response-relevant target (on the current trial). Resolving this conflict takes time that manifests as a cost. Thus, under this episodic view, it is not the inhibition of the previously ignored stimulus that slows its current processing, which is the most common explanation of negative priming. Evidence exists that favors this "automatic retrieval plus conflict resolution" (e.g., Egner & Hirsch, 2005; MacLeod, Chiappe, & Fox, 2002), although there is certainly evidence consistent with the inhibition account as well (see, e.g., Tipper, 2001).

As always, it is important to recognize the competing accounts and then to put them to critical test. It may also be that these two accounts are both correct, but for different situations. If this possibility can be convincingly shown, it would help researchers to understand the limitations of both sets of processes. The same applies to other possible theoretical framings that also handle the patterns captured by inhibition and by episodic retrieval and that may come forward as the empirical basis and conceptual understanding deepen.

Conclusion

Inhibition at the cognitive level is a powerful theoretical construct. It has come into widespread usage in the past quarter century in part because of this power and in part because of its apparent linkage to its neural cognate. One purpose of this chapter has been to illustrate this wide usage; another purpose has been to question the value of the neural linkage. The main purpose of this chapter, however, has been to set out the issues that researchers need to grapple with as they try to ascertain the utility of inhibition—and its competitors—in explaining the operation of the cognitive system (see also chap. 15, this volume). The success of this goal hinges on more explicit definition and better criteria, on the development of more formal theorizing about inhibition, and on the discovery of new phenomena that call for inhibitory mechanisms. As the rest of this book ably demonstrates, this work is well under way. Researchers will undoubtedly learn a great deal more about the place of inhibition in cognition over the next decade.

References

Allport, D. A., Styles, E. A., & Hsieh, S. (1994). Shifting intentional set: Exploring the dynamic control of tasks. In C. Umiltà & M. Moscovitch (Eds.), *Attention and performance* (Vol. 15, pp. 421–452). Cambridge, MA: MIT Press.

Amos, A. (2000). A computational model of information processing in the frontal cortex and basal ganglia. *Journal of Cognitive Neuroscience, 12,* 505–519.

Anderson, M. C. (2003). Rethinking interference theory: Executive control and the mechanisms of forgetting. *Journal of Memory and Language, 49,* 415–445.

Anderson, M. C. (2005). The role of inhibitory control in forgetting unwanted memories: A consideration of three methods. In N. Ohta, C. M. MacLeod, & B. Uttl (Eds.), *Dynamic cognitive processes* (pp. 159–189). Tokyo: Springer-Verlag.

Anderson, M. C., & Bjork, R. A. (1994). Mechanisms of inhibition in long-term memory: A new taxonomy. In D. Dagenbach & T. H. Carr (Eds.), *Inhibitory processes in attention, memory, and language* (pp. 265–325). San Diego, CA: Academic Press.

Anderson, M. C., & Green, C. (2001, March 15). Suppressing unwanted memories by executive control. *Nature, 410,* 366–369.

Anderson, M. C., Ochsner, K. N., Kuhl, B., Cooper, J., Robertson, E., Gabrieli, S. W., et al. (2004, January 9). Neural systems underlying the suppression of unwanted memories. *Science, 303,* 232–235.

Anderson, M. C., & Spellman, B. A. (1995). On the status of inhibitory mechanisms in cognition: Memory retrieval as a model case. *Psychological Review, 102,* 68–100.

Basden, B. H., Basden, D. R., & Gargano, G. J. (1993). Directed forgetting in implicit and explicit memory tests: A comparison of methods. *Journal of Experimental Psychology: Learning, Memory, and Cognition, 19,* 603–616.

Bäuml, K., & Aslan, A. (2006). Part-list cuing can be transient and lasting: The role of encoding. *Journal of Experimental Psychology: Learning, Memory, and Cognition, 32,* 33–43.

Beer, J. S., Heerey, E. A., Keltner, D., Scabini, D., & Knight, R. T. (2003). The regulatory function of self-conscious emotion: Insights from patients with orbitofrontal damage. *Journal of Personality and Social Psychology, 85,* 594–604.

Bergström, Z., Richardson-Klavehn, A., & de Fockert, J. (2006, July). *Electrophysiological correlates of thought-substitution and thought-suppression strategies in the think / no-think task.* Paper presented at the Fourth International Conference on Memory, Sydney, Australia.

Bohne, A., Keuthen, N. J., Tuschen-Caffier, B., & Wilhelm, S. (2005). Cognitive inhibition in trichotillomania and obsessive–compulsive disorder. *Behaviour Research and Therapy, 43,* 923–942.

Breese, B. B. (1899). On inhibition. *Psychological Monographs, 3,* 1–65.

Brown, A. S., Zoccoli, S. L., & Leahy, M. M. (2005). Cumulating retrieval inhibition in semantic and lexical domains. *Journal of Experimental Psychology: Learning, Memory, and Cognition, 31,* 496–507.

Bulevich, J. B., Roediger, H. L., III, Balota, D. A., & Butler, A. C. (in press). Failures to find suppression of episodic memories in the think/no-think paradigm. *Memory & Cognition.*

Bull, R., & Scerif, G. (2001). Executive functioning as a predictor of children's mathematics ability: Shifting, inhibition, and working memory. *Developmental Neuropsychology, 19,* 273–293.

Burke, D. M. (1997). Language, aging, and inhibitory deficits: Evaluation of a theory. *Journals of Gerontology: Series B. Psychological Sciences and Social Sciences, 52,* P254–P264.

Camp, G., Pecher, D., & Schmidt, H. G. (2005). Retrieval-induced forgetting in implicit memory tests: The role of test awareness. *Psychonomic Bulletin & Review, 12,* 490–494.

Carlson, S. M., & Moses, L. J. (2001). Individual differences in inhibitory control and children's theory of mind. *Child Development, 72,* 1032–1053.

Charlot, V., & Feyereisen, P. (2005). Mémoire épisodique et deficit d'inhibition au cours de vieillissement cognitif: Un examen de l'hypothèse frontale [Episodic memory and inhibition deficit in cognitive aging: An examination of the frontal hypothesis]. *L'Année Psychologique, 105,* 323–357.

Cohen, R. A. (1993). Neural mechanisms of attention. In R. A. Cohen (Ed.), *The neuropsychology of attention* (pp. 145–176). New York: Plenum Press.

Colvin, M. K., Dunbar, K., & Grafman, J. (2001). The effects of frontal lobe lesions on goal achievement in the water jug task. *Journal of Cognitive Neuroscience, 13,* 1129–1147.

Conway, A. R. A., & Engle, R. W. (1994). Working memory and retrieval: A resource-dependent inhibition model. *Journal of Experimental Psychology: General, 123,* 354–373.

Dagenbach, D., & Carr, T. H. (Eds.). (1994). *Inhibitory processes in attention, memory, and language.* San Diego, CA: Academic Press.

Dempster, F. N. (1991). Inhibitory processes: A neglected dimension of intelligence. *Intelligence, 15,* 157–173.

Dempster, F. N., & Brainerd, C. J. (Eds.). (1995). *Interference and inhibition in cognition.* San Diego, CA: Academic Press.

Diamond, A., Kirkham, N. Z., & Amso, D. (2002). Conditions under which young children can hold two rules in mind and inhibit a prepotent response. *Developmental Psychology, 38,* 352–362.

Diamond, S., Balvin, R. S., & Diamond, F. R. (1963). *Inhibition and choice: A neurobehavioral approach to problems of plasticity in behavior.* New York: Harper Row.

Dorahy, M. J., Middleton, W., & Irwin, H. J. (2005). The effect of emotional context on cognitive inhibition and attentional processing in dissociative identity disorder. *Behaviour Research and Therapy, 43,* 555–568.

Durston, S., Thomas, K. M., Yang, Y., Ulug, A. M., Zimmerman, R., & Casey, B. J. (2002). A neural basis for development of inhibitory control. *Developmental Science, 5,* 9–16.

Egner, T., & Hirsch, J. (2005). Where memory meets attention: Neural substrates of negative priming. *Journal of Cognitive Neuroscience, 17,* 1774–1784.

Engle, R. W., Conway, A. R. A., Tuholski, S. W., & Shisler, R. J. (1995). A resource account of inhibition. *Psychological Science, 6,* 122–125.

Förster, J., Liberman, N., & Higgins, E. T. (2005). Accessibility from active and fulfilled goals. *Journal of Experimental Social Psychology, 41,* 220–239.

Fox, E. (1995). Negative priming from ignored distractors in visual selection: A review. *Psychonomic Bulletin & Review, 2,* 145–173.

Friedman, N. P., & Miyake, A. (2004). The relations among inhibition and interference control functions: A latent-variable analysis. *Journal of Experimental Psychology: General, 133,* 101–135.

Friedman, N. P., Miyake, A., Corley, R. P., Young, S. E., DeFries, J. C., & Hewitt, J. K. (2006). Not all executive functions are related to intelligence. *Psychological Science, 17,* 172–179.

Friedman, O., & Leslie, A. M. (2004). Mechanisms of belief–desire reasoning: Inhibition and bias. *Psychological Science, 15,* 547–552.

Gazzaley, A., Cooney, J. W., Rissman, J., & D'Esposito, M. (2005). Top-down suppression deficit underlies working memory impairment in normal aging. *Nature Neuroscience, 8,* 1298–1300.

Hamilton, A. C., & Martin, R. C. (2005). Dissociations among tasks involving inhibition: A single-case study. *Cognitive, Affective, & Behavioral Neuroscience, 5,* 1–13.

Hasher, L., & Zacks, R. T. (1988). Working memory, comprehension, and aging: A review and a new view. In G. H. Bower (Ed.), *The psychology of learning and motivation* (pp. 193–225). New York: Academic Press.

James, W. (1890). *The principles of psychology.* New York: Henry Holt.

Jonides, J., & Mack, R. (1984). On the cost and benefit of cost and benefit. *Psychological Bulletin, 96,* 29–44.

Kane, M. J., & Engle, R. W. (2000). Working-memory capacity, proactive interference, and divided attention: Limits on long-term memory retrieval. *Journal of Experimental Psychology: Learning, Memory, and Cognition, 26,* 336–358.

Kastner, S., & Pinsk, M. A. (2004). Visual attention as a multilevel selection process. *Cognitive, Affective, and Behavioral Neuroscience, 4,* 483–500.

Klein, R. M., & Taylor, T. L. (1994). Categories of cognitive inhibition with reference to attention. In D. Dagenbach & T. H. Carr (Eds.), *Inhibitory processes in attention, memory, and language* (pp. 113–150). San Diego, CA: Academic Press.

Kuhl, J., & Kazén, M. (1999). Volitional facilitation of difficult intentions: Joint activation of intention memory and positive affect removes Stroop interference. *Journal of Experimental Psychology: General, 128,* 382–399.

Kunda, Z., & Spencer, S. J. (2003). When do stereotypes come to mind and when do they color judgment? A goal-based theoretical framework for stereotype activation and application. *Psychological Bulletin, 129,* 522–544.

Logan, G. D. (1988). Toward an instance theory of automatization. *Psychological Review, 95,* 492–527.

Logan, G. D. (2002). An instance theory of attention and memory. *Psychological Review, 109,* 376–400.

Logan, G. D., & Cowan, W. B. (1984). On the ability to inhibit thought and action: A theory of an act of control. *Psychological Review, 91,* 295–327.

Logan, G. D., & Zbrodoff, N. J. (1999). Selection for cognition: Cognitive constraints on visual spatial attention. *Visual Cognition, 6,* 55–81.

Lowe, D. G. (1979). Strategies, context, and the mechanism of response inhibition. *Memory & Cognition, 7,* 382–389.

Luchins, A. S. (1942). Mechanization in problem solving. *Psychological Monographs, 54*(Whole No. 248).

MacLeod, C. M. (1998). Directed forgetting. In J. M. Golding & C. M. MacLeod (Eds.), *Intentional forgetting: Interdisciplinary approaches* (pp. 1–57). Mahwah, NJ: Erlbaum.

MacLeod, C. M. (in press). Inhibition: Elusive or illusion? In H. L. Roediger III, Y. Dudai, & S. M. Fitzpatrick (Eds.), *Science of memory: Concepts.* Oxford, England: Oxford University Press.

MacLeod, C. M., Chiappe, D. L., & Fox, E. (2002). The crucial roles of stimulus identity and stimulus matching in negative priming. *Psychonomic Bulletin & Review, 9,* 521–528.

MacLeod, C. M., Dodd, M. D., Sheard, E. D., Wilson, D. E., & Bibi, U. (2003). In opposition to inhibition. In B. H. Ross (Ed.), *The psychology of learning and motivation* (Vol. 43, pp. 163–214). San Diego, CA: Academic Press.

May, C. P., Kane, M. J., & Hasher, L. (1995). Determinants of negative priming. *Psychological Bulletin, 118,* 35–54.

McDowd, J. M. (1997). Inhibition in attention and aging. *Journals of Gerontology: Series B. Psychological Sciences and Social Sciences, 52,* P265–P273.

Miyake, A., Friedman, N. P., Emerson, M. J., Witzki, A. H., & Howerter, A. (2000). The unity and diversity of executive functions and their contributions to complex "frontal lobe" tasks: A latent variable analysis. *Cognitive Psychology, 41,* 49–100.

Neill, W. T. (1977). Inhibitory and facilitatory processes in attention. *Journal of Experimental Psychology: Human Perception and Performance, 3,* 444–450.

Neill, W. T., & Mathis, K. M. (1998). Transfer-inappropriate processing: Negative priming and related phenomena. In D. L. Medin (Ed.), *The psychology of learning and motivation: Advances in research and theory* (Vol. 38, pp. 1–44). San Diego, CA: Academic Press.

Nigg, J. T. (2000). On inhibition/disinhibition in developmental psychopathology: Views from cognitive and personality psychology and a working inhibition hypothesis. *Psychological Bulletin, 126,* 220–246.

The Oxford English dictionary (2nd ed.). (1989). New York: Oxford University Press.

Pillsbury, W. B. (1908). *Attention.* New York: Macmillan.

Posner, M. I. (1978). *Chronometric explorations of mind.* Oxford, England: Erlbaum.

Posner, M. I., & Cohen, Y. (1984). Components of visual orienting. In D. Bouma & D. Bonwhuis (Eds.), *Attention and performance* (Vol. 10, pp. 531–566). Hillsdale, NJ: Erlbaum.

Racsmány, M., & Conway, M. A. (2006). Episodic inhibition. *Journal of Experimental Psychology: Learning, Memory, and Cognition, 32,* 44–57.

Rafal, R., Egly, R., & Rhodes, D. (1994). Effects of inhibition of return on voluntary and visually guided saccades. *Canadian Journal of Experimental Psychology, 48,* 284–300.

Rafal, R., & Henik, A. (1994). The neurology of inhibition: Integrating controlled and automatic processes. In D. Dagenbach & T. H. Carr (Eds.), *Inhibitory processes in attention, memory, and language* (pp. 1–51). San Diego, CA: Academic Press.

Reuter-Lorenz, P. A., Jha, A. P., & Rosenquist, J. N. (1996). What is inhibited in inhibition of return? *Journal of Experimental Psychology: Human Perception and Performance, 22,* 367–378.

Roediger, H. L., III, Dudai, Y., & Fitzpatrick, S. M. (in press). *Science of memory: Concepts.* Oxford, England: Oxford University Press.

Russell, J., Mauthner, N., Sharpe, S., & Tidswell, T. (1991). The "windows task" as a measure of strategic deception in preschoolers and autistic subjects. *British Journal of Developmental Psychology, 9,* 331–349.

Salthouse, T. A., Atkinson, T. M., & Berish, D. E. (2003). Executive functioning as a potential mediator of age-related cognitive decline in normal adults. *Journal of Experimental Psychology: General, 132,* 566–594.

Saunders, J., & MacLeod, M. D. (2006). Can inhibition resolve retrieval competition through the control of spreading activation? *Memory & Cognition, 34,* 307–322.

Shah, J. Y., Friedman, R., & Kruglanski, A. W. (2002). Forgetting all else: On the antecedents and consequences of goal shielding. *Journal of Personality and Social Psychology, 83,* 1261–1280.

Slamecka, N. J. (1968). An examination of trace storage in free recall. *Journal of Experimental Psychology, 76,* 504–513.

Smith, R. (1992). *Inhibition: History and meaning in the sciences of mind and brain.* Berkeley: University of California Press.

Stroop, J. R. (1935). Studies of interference in serial verbal reactions. *Journal of Experimental Psychology, 18,* 643–662.

Tipper, S. P. (1985). The negative priming effect: Inhibitory priming by ignored objects. *Quarterly Journal of Experimental Psychology, 37A,* 571–590.

Tipper, S. P. (2001). Does negative priming reflect inhibitory mechanisms? A review and integration of conflicting views. *Quarterly Journal of Experimental Psychology, 54A,* 321–343.

Veling, H., & van Knippenberg, A. (2004). Remembering can cause inhibition: Retrieval-induced inhibition as cue independent process. *Journal of Experimental Psychology: Learning, Memory, and Cognition, 30,* 315–318.

von Hippel, W., & Gonsalkorale, K. (2005). "That is bloody revolting!" Inhibitory control of thoughts better left unsaid. *Psychological Science, 16,* 497–500.

Watson, D. G., & Humphreys, G. W. (1997). Visual marking: Prioritizing selection for new objects by top-down attentional inhibition of old objects. *Psychological Review, 104,* 90–122.

Wellman, H. M., Cross, D., & Watson, J. (2001). Meta-analysis of theory of mind development: The truth about false-belief. *Child Development, 72,* 655–684.

Williams, C. C., & Zacks, R. T. (2001). Is retrieval-induced forgetting an inhibitory process? *American Journal of Psychology, 114,* 329–354.

Wilson, S. P., & Kipp, K. (1998). The development of efficient inhibition: Evidence from directed-forgetting tasks. *Developmental Review, 18,* 86–123.

Wood, J., Mathews, A., & Dalgleish, T. (2001). Anxiety and cognitive inhibition. *Emotion, 1,* 166–181.

Wundt, W. (1902). *Grundzüge der physiologischen Psychologie* [Principles of physiological psychology] (5th ed.). Leipzig, Germany: Engelmann.

Part II

Attention and Performance

2

Inhibition of Task Sets

Ulrich Mayr

Does the human cognitive system use inhibition to resolve conflict between competing representations? This is the question addressed in one way or another in most of the contributions to this volume. On a theoretical or neural level, there are interesting arguments on both sides of the inhibition debate (see Dagenbach & Carr, 1994). However, attempts to address the inhibition question empirically have been marred by difficulties. Often, empirical patterns that look like inhibition invite an array of noninhibitory explanations (e.g., chap. 1, this volume). Nevertheless, ultimately it is only through empirical evidence that researchers will be able to settle the question of whether cognitive inhibition exists. In this chapter, I summarize some attempts to trace cognitive inhibition in the context of executive selection among competing task sets. I begin by providing some reasons for why the domain of task-set selection may be particularly well suited for finding an empirical, behavioral-level signature of inhibition. I present the lag-2 repetition paradigm (sometimes also referred to as the *backward inhibition paradigm*) as the basic experimental tool to trace task-set inhibition, as well as some of the basic characteristics of task-set inhibition that have been revealed using this paradigm. Then, I discuss at some length how researchers can deal with possible alternative, noninhibitory interpretations. Finally, I present some new findings from mostly ongoing projects about the neural implementation and associative learning aspects of task-set inhibition.

Why Inhibition During Task-Set Selection?

A task set can be thought of as the constellation of attentional settings that allow an individual to perform one among several tasks that are potentially possible in a given situation. For example, a simple task used in some experiments requires subjects to localize a deviant object on a given stimulus dimension (see Figure 2.1). In this case, the task set would represent the dimension (e.g., color) and ensure an attentional configuration that gives increased weight to processing information from that dimension. Empirical evidence pointing to the existence of task sets comes from the simple finding that when task sets need to change from one trial to the next, there is a time cost (i.e., the so-called

Bottom-Up Control:

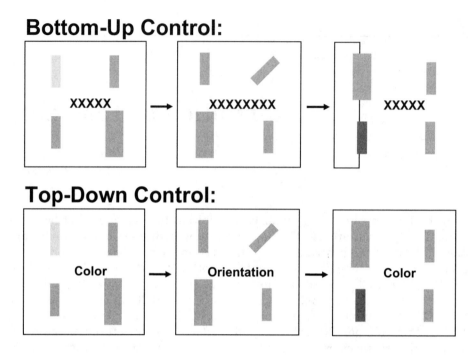

Top-Down Control:

Figure 2.1.   Sample displays for a lag-2 repetition and a lag-2 change sequence.

"switch cost"; Monsell, 2003) irrespective of whether specific dimensional values or response parameters change.

Task sets can be triggered in a bottom-up manner. For example, when one steps into the kitchen in the morning, one usually does not have to intentionally gear one's cognitive system toward brewing coffee and making breakfast. Rather, the general context and environmental cues activate the appropriate configuration of processes. Although such bottom-up task-set priming is generally useful, it is also one important reason why people need to be able to exert top-down control on task-set selection: Only through top-down task-set control can one arrive at a stable behavioral pattern in a situation in which the environment triggers multiple possible task sets.

For example, because of a looming grant deadline, one may decide to stop all activities such as Web surfing and e-mailing that may otherwise be prompted by sitting in front of the computer. In such situations, a top-down selected set is necessary to maintain a coherent stream of goal-directed activity in the face of constant reminders of other possible activities. Another important reason for top-down task-set control is that sometimes an already firmly established, and thus fully activated, task set needs to be replaced by an alternative task set. These two different demands on task-set selection—maintenance in the face of competition and the need to flexibly replace a task set with an alternative task set—are difficult to align with each other, a fact that is sometimes referred to as the *stability–flexibility dilemma* (e.g., Goschke, 2000). To achieve behavioral stability in the face of interference, strongly activated task sets are needed. However, strongly activated task sets should also be particularly difficult to get rid of once the time for change has come. Theoretically, a mechanism that inhibits the no-longer-relevant task may provide a solution to this dilemma. Just as one dares speed on a bicycle only when there are functioning brakes in place, the cognitive system may be able to afford full task-set endorsement only because inhibition allows clearing the slate when a new task set becomes necessary. Occam's razor may advise against invoking extra mechanisms, such as inhibition. However, arguably, if there is a place for a special, inhibitory mechanism, flexible task-set control may be a prime candidate to look for it.

A second reason why task-set inhibition may be a particularly promising domain in which to look for cognitive inhibition is related to the methodological challenge of finding unambiguous evidence for inhibition. Evidence for inhibition typically comes in the form of some kind of change in performance (usually a decrement) in response to a stimulus that at some earlier time was supposedly a target of inhibition (e.g., Tipper & Cranston, 1985). However, data patterns of this general type are open to noninhibitory explanations based on the assumption of proactive interference between ways of dealing with a certain stimulus in the recent past (e.g., not to respond to it) and the currently required way of dealing with that same stimulus (e.g., to respond to it; Neill, 1997). Importantly, a hallmark of such memory influences is their specificity. That is, the greater the similarity between the initial suppression–encoding situation and the response–retrieval situation, the greater these influences should be. Standard inhibitory paradigms allow little variation in stimulus aspects, simply because inhibition is usually supposed to be targeted at a specific stimulus representation. However, task sets are by definition abstract and therefore not bound to any specific stimulus situation. This fact opens up much-needed degrees of freedom to manipulate the similarity between past and present selection instances. Later in this chapter, I show how this freedom allows researchers to establish inhibitory phenomena that are less susceptible to the proactive-interference argument.

The Lag-2 Repetition Paradigm

How can one find an empirical indication of inhibition at the level of task sets? The basic idea is simple and rests on two assumptions: First, abandoning a task set to switch to a new one goes along with inhibition of the abandoned task set, and second, inhibition renders the task-set representation less available for some time. If this is the case, then it should be relatively difficult to return to a recently abandoned task set. Figure 2.1 shows how my laboratory implemented this basic idea using the deviant-detection paradigm. For each trial, one task of three or four possible tasks is cued using a verbal task label. The critical lag-2 repetition sequence is one in which subjects might be cued from the color to the orientation task set and then back to color. Theoretically, inhibition should be needed to go from color to orientation. Assuming that inhibition decays gradually but at a relatively slow pace, this task set should still be inhibited. It therefore should be more difficult to select than the third-position task from a control sequence that had been abandoned less recently and therefore had more time to recover from inhibition (see Figure 2.1).

In most implementations of this paradigm, lag-2 repetition and lag-2 change sequences were established by selecting tasks randomly on a trial-by-trial basis and then categorizing task triples post hoc into the critical categories. In the initial article that introduced this paradigm, results did in fact show a slowing of response times on the third trial of a lag-2 repetition sequence relative to control sequences of about 20 to 50 milliseconds (Mayr & Keele, 2000). Subsequently, this basic result has been replicated numerous times across different labs (e.g., Arbuthnott & Frank, 2000; Dreher & Berman, 2002; Hübner, Dreisbach, Haider, & Kluwe, 2003; Schuch & Koch, 2003; Mayr, 2002), suggesting that it is a robust phenomenon in task-selection situations. Certainly, an interesting aspect of this phenomenon is that activation-only theories should have a hard time explaining why activating a representation should render it less accessible for subsequent selection. In contrast, this is exactly what one would expect if inhibition were critical during task-set selection. However, before accepting that this effect is in fact associated with inhibition, one needs to explore its characteristics to see whether it behaves as one would expect from an inhibitory process that is in the service of flexible task-set control.

Characteristics of the Lag-2 Repetition Cost

The initial demonstration of the lag-2 repetition cost in Mayr and Keele (2000) was with simple perceptual sets, which may raise the question to what degree this is a general effect that can also be found for more complex task sets or sets that are not bound to perceptual dimensions. In recent years, the effect has been found for more complex perceptual tasks (Mayr, 2001), tasks requiring semantic judgments about digits (e.g., Schuch & Koch, 2003), and tasks that require applying different spatial response rules to invariant stimulus aspects (Mayr, 2002; see also chap. 3, this volume). Thus, currently there is little reason to assume that the lag-2 repetition cost is bound to certain stimulus or response characteristics or to certain domains of processing.

An even more important theoretical question is to what degree the lag-2 repetition cost is actually associated with abstract representations rather than with specific stimulus characteristics. Mayr and Keele (2000) addressed this question using the deviant-detection paradigm. For each possible dimension, deviations from the standard object, a stationary blue vertical line, could occur in two ways. For example, the object could be tilted either 45 degrees to the left or to the right with regard to the orientation dimension or it could be dyed either cyan or purple on the color dimension. This method allowed the authors to test the degree to which the lag-2 repetition effect survived lag-2 changes in the dimensional value. Across five different experiments, they found no statistically reliable influence of value changes on the lag-2 repetition effect.

Similarly, we could look at the degree to which lag-2 repetitions versus changes in location and response affected the lag-2 repetition effect. For example, on a lag-2 repetition of the color task, the critical color deviant might occur in the upper left corner on the lag-2 trial and either in the same location or in a different location on the probe trial. Again, we found no statistically reliable influence of this variable. If anything, there was a numerical reduction of the lag-2 repetition cost for lag-2 response repetitions. We will return to the possible role of lag-2 response repetitions in a later section discussing possible alternative interpretations of the lag-2 repetition cost. For now, the fact that this effect was not reliably modulated by repetitions versus changes in specific stimulus and response aspects suggests that it is in fact bound to the level of abstract task sets rather than to the level of stimulus-specific implementations of a particular task.

A core assumption is that task-set inhibition serves top-down selection of task sets. In other words, one should see the lag-2 repetition cost only when subjects are actually selecting task sets in a top-down manner but not when tasks are primed bottom-up. Mayr and Keele (2000) tested this assumption using a variant of the deviant-detection paradigm. Again, subjects had to locate deviants on three possible dimensions (color, orientation, and movement). Each display contained one deviant on one of these dimensions. Unlike the preceding experiments, the distractor deviant was of a different kind—namely, size. In each display, one rectangle was substantially larger than the rectangle object. However, object size was never one of the cued dimensions (see Figure 2.2). This setup allowed the comparison of two different conditions. In the top-down condition, subjects received valid precues about the next relevant dimension, just as in the preceding experiments. In the bottom-up condition, they only saw noninformative letter strings as cues. Given that there was only one deviant from one of the three "legal" dimensions in each display, the adequate response could be selected even without prior task-set information. However, our hope was that inclusion of the irrelevant size deviant would make response selection sufficiently hard to motivate subjects to use the precue in the top-down condition.

In fact, we found that overall, subjects performed reliably faster in the top-down than in the bottom-up condition, suggesting that they did in fact make use of the task cues. As predicted, there was no lag-2 repetition cost in the bottom-up condition. However, there was a reliable, although very small (7-millisecond), lag-2 repetition cost in the top-down condition. The small size of this effect is not surprising, given that there was really no need for subjects to use top-down control. In fact, for each individual subject, one can use the difference score between the top-down and the bottom-up condition as an indicator of top-down control effort. Figure 2.3 shows the scatter plot underlying the correlation between this variable and the lag-2 repetition cost; for subjects with large top-down selection costs, the lag-2 repetition cost was substantial, but the lag-2 repetition cost was basically nonexistent for subjects with zero or negative top-down effect. Thus, just as one would expect if task-set inhibition aids between-task conflict resolution during top-down task-set selection, the lag-2 repetition cost occurred only when subjects actually engaged in top-down task-set control.

Does the fact that the lag-2 repetition cost is tied to top-down task selection necessarily imply that it is also under top-down control? In Experiment 4, Mayr

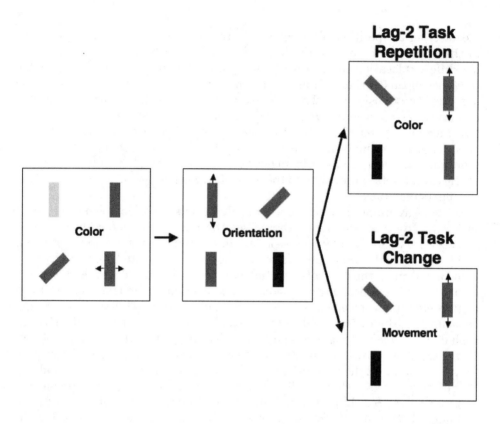

Figure 2.2. Sample displays for top-down and bottom-up lag-2 repetition sequence used in Mayr and Keele (2000, Experiment 3). The valid task labels presented in the top-down condition were replaced by meaningless strings of Xs in the bottom-up condition.

and Keele (2000) used, instead of the random cuing procedure, a procedure in which subjects were preinformed about a sequence of four tasks. Specifically, at the beginning of each new sequence of four tasks, they saw a precue listing the entire sequence of four tasks. After studying this precue, the information disappeared, four displays were presented one at a time, and subjects had to execute a response to each one according to the currently relevant memorized task. The first task in the sequence was a filler task (always the size task), whereas in second through fourth positions the lag-2 repetition versus control sequence was implemented (e.g., color–orientation–color vs. movement–orientation–color). Thus, in this case, subjects had foreknowledge about the entire sequence, including knowing that when switching in an inhibition sequence from the second to the third task they would inhibit a task that would become relevant again on Position 4. Nevertheless, we obtained a robust lag-2 repetition effect in this situation. In other words, it seems that task-set inhibition is not affected by foreknowledge and thus is not under top-down control. More likely, task-set inhibition is a mandatory process that may be recruited when a top-down-initiated switch between tasks occurs.

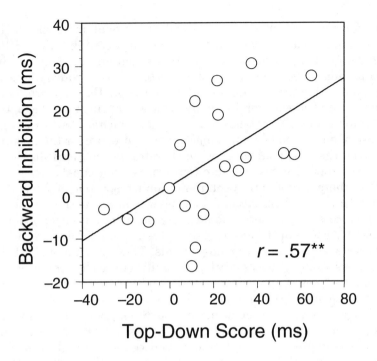

Figure 2.3. Scatter plot showing individual subjects' lag-2 repetition costs as a function of their top-down control score (i.e., mean response time in top-down condition minus mean response time in bottom-up condition; Mayr & Keele, 2000, Experiment 3). **p < .01.

If task-set inhibition aids the resolution of between-task conflict, it should be particularly strong when between-task competition is high. Gade and Koch (2005; see also Mayr & Keele, 2000, Experiment 2) provided interesting evidence in this regard by manipulating the temporal relation between successive trials. For a specific inhibition (or control) sequence, there were two potential transitions: the one between the lag-2 and the lag-1 of the sequence and the one between the lag-1 and the probe trial of the sequence. Inhibition should arise at the transition between the lag-2 and the lag-1 trial. Arguably, inhibition should be particularly important when the task for the lag-1 trial needs to be initiated when the lag-2 task is still highly active. The authors manipulated this aspect by varying the time between the response to the previous task and the cue to the next task randomly on a trial-to-trial basis (while keeping the total time between trials constant; see Meiran, 1996). As expected, inhibition was much stronger for short response–cue intervals (i.e., when the preceding task should still be highly active) than for long intervals. It is important to note that inhibition was dependent only on the response–cue interval between the lag-2 and the lag-1 trial of the sequence (i.e., where inhibition should occur) but not on the interval between the lag-1 and the probe trial of the sequence. This result is highly consistent with the notion that inhibition is recruited in response to between-task competition.

Another recent result seems to provide additional, more specific information about the type of competition that elicits task-set inhibition. Schuch and Koch (2003) used the basic lag-2 repetition situation but combined it with a go/no-go paradigm. On 25% of the trials, a tone was sounded along with the stimulus, indicating that subjects should not execute the response. The critical comparison was between inhibition sequences for which the lag-1 trial task happened to be a no-go trial and sequences for which all trials were go trials. In the case of a lag-1 no-go trial, subjects had to prepare for the task indicated by the cue for the lag-1 trial but then had to refrain from executing the relevant response selection process. If inhibition arises from cue-driven preparation alone, then there should have been inhibition irrespective of the status of the lag-1 trial. However, if inhibition is in some way linked to the actual response-selection process, then there should have been inhibition only for go trial sequences. In fact, robust lag-2 repetition costs were obtained after go trials, but zero costs were found after no-go trials. These results suggest that cue-driven processes may be necessary but not sufficient to elicit inhibition. Rather, only once a task set is applied to a particular stimulus situation is inhibition of the other (competing) task triggered.

Although this is an interesting and surprisingly clean result, there are some open questions. For example, it is not easy to reconcile the fact that inhibition was highly sensitive to the response–cue interval in the Gade and Koch (2005) study when, according to Schuch and Koch (2003), the critical competition takes place only after stimulus presentation. One possibility is that with 25% no-go trials, subjects may encode the cue but not actually use the information to prepare the next task until after they are certain that a response will be required (e.g., Kleinsorge & Gajewski, 2004). When Mayr and Keele (2000) contrasted the role of task cues, they found that inhibition was limited to subjects who actually made use of the cue (see Figures 2.2 and 2.3). In so far unpublished work, my colleagues and I constructed conditions in which there was a greater incentive for preparation even in the case of no-go trials. At least in some of these situations, we have found reliable lag-2 repetition costs. Overall, Schuch and Koch's results suggest that response selection may be one important triggering condition for task-set inhibition. However, an important question requires additional scrutiny: the degree to which it is the only possible trigger or whether merely thinking about an alternative task can also elicit inhibition.

Although it currently is not completely clear what exactly triggers task-set inhibition, some information is available about the level of representation that is the most likely targeted by inhibition. Several authors have argued for a kind of two-component view of task selection (e.g., Mayr & Kliegl, 2003; Rubinstein, Meyer, & Evans, 2001). The first component involves retrieving or activating a symbol-level goal in working memory (e.g., "do the color task"). This may be the most important aspect of what can be achieved after the cue has been presented but before the stimulus appears (i.e., the preparation interval). The second component is the actual configuration that results from applying this goal to a particular stimulus situation. It is not clear how much of this component can be prepared. It seems, however, that it is this component that is targeted through task-set inhibition. One critical result in this regard came from a study by Mayr and Kliegl (2003), who used a paradigm in which two different cues were mapped onto each of three tasks. This paradigm allowed the implementation of lag-2 task repetitions in which the cues either stayed the same or changed. In other experiments reported in this article, the authors demonstrated that a large part of switch costs between tasks arose from a mere change in cue and that this component was specifically sensitive to the cue–stimulus interval. From this result, the authors concluded that the cue-associated switch cost reflects the symbol-level component, whereas the smaller switch-cost component associated with the actual switch in task reflects the change in configuration. Using this paradigm with three different tasks, the authors looked at lag-2 repetition transitions with or without cue changes. Interestingly, a robust lag-2 cost was found for cue changes, suggesting that inhibition is associated with the actual representation that is used to operate on a particular stimulus in a task-congruent manner.

A similar conclusion can be derived from results regarding the dependency of the lag-2 repetition costs on the cue–stimulus interval. If the representation that undergoes inhibition is easily targeted through preparatory activity, then the lag-2 repetition cost can be expected to decrease when there is sufficient time to prepare. However, studies looking at this aspect have regularly found the lag-2 repetition cost to be completely insensitive to this variable (e.g., Mayr & Keele, 2000; Schuch & Koch, 2003). Again, this finding suggests that inhibition targets the actual configuration that is applied to the appearance of the stimulus. It seems possible that this representation, because it is so closely tied to the stimulus, becomes activated only when the stimulus appears and therefore is out of the reach of purely cue-driven preparatory processes (for additional discussion of this aspect, see Mayr & Keele, 2000).

The results that I have reviewed here suggest that the lag-2 repetition cost behaves as one would expect from a process that is tied to top-down task selection and that is geared toward resolving between-task competition. This cost occurs only when top-down control is required and is sensitive to the amount of between-task competition (as indexed through the temporal interval between successive tasks). Although it is tied to top-down control, the lag-2 repetition cost is not itself penetrable through top-down control. It occurs even when it implies inhibiting a task that will be relevant again in the very near future, and once a task is inhibited, preparation does not allow the subject to reverse the inhibition associated with that task. At the same time, important questions remain open regarding the sufficient and necessary conditions for inhibition. Specifically, it will be important to firmly establish whether it is enough for one to think about a new task or whether one has to execute a new task to accomplish inhibition of the preceding task.

Noninhibitory Explanations of the Lag-2 Repetition Cost

Three different types of noninhibitory explanations of the lag-2 repetition cost need to be considered: (a) sequential expectancies, (b) activation of likely successor tasks, and (c) instance-based episodic priming. Whereas the first two are specific to the lag-2 repetition effect, the third explanation is of more general importance, because it has also been applied rather successfully in the context of other inhibitory paradigms.

Sequential Expectancies

When people are asked to make random, sequential choices, they usually deviate in a predictable manner from randomness. For example, in the case of binary choices, they tend to produce a higher rate of alternations than random choice would imply (i.e., the gambler's fallacy). The typical explanation for this behavior is that people use a representativeness-within-small-runs heuristic. In other words, they try to produce short sequences that "look" representative. In binary-choice cases, they would favor a sequence such as ABA over AAA, even though both triples are, of course, equally likely. Applying this to the lag-2 repetition paradigm, where subjects need to select among three different tasks, one might expect them to favor an ABC over an ABA sequence, simply because only the first kind involves all possible tasks and therefore may seem more representative. If subjects actually entertain such sequential expectancies, the lag-2 repetition effect may arise from an expectancy violation rather than task-set inhibition.

Two results, however, speak against such an interpretation of the lag-2 repetition effect, both of them mentioned in the preceding section. The first is that the inhibition effect is not affected by the duration of the preparatory interval. If the lag-2 repetition effect is driven by a sequential expectancy, why would such an expectancy not be overruled, or at least attenuated, by a cue-induced 100% valid expectancy about the task to come? The same argument holds for the second relevant result, that the lag-2 repetition cost is found even when subjects have complete foreknowledge about an upcoming sequence of tasks. It seems hard to explain how sequential expectancies could develop about a sequence of tasks for which a complete plan exists.

Activation of Likely Successor Tasks

Usually, the lag-2 repetition cost is assessed in a situation with 100% task switches, done to maximize the occurrence of the relevant inhibition or control triples. However, it is possible that this method may lead subjects to actively prepare after each task (e.g., color) for the two now potentially relevant tasks (orientation or movement). Thus, both tasks are now preactivated, but only one of them—for example, the movement task—will actually be used on the next trial. The orientation task, having been prepared but still unused, may continue to be residually active, which could give this task a slight edge in case it needs to be selected on the following trial (which would serve as probe trial of a lag-2 nonrepetition sequence). As a result, performance on the third trial of a control sequence (color–movement–orientation) might be faster than on the third trial of a lag-2 repetition sequence (color–movement–color). Obviously, this explanation of the lag-2 repetition cost requires no assumption about inhibition. However, as with the sequential expectancy account, it is also based on expectancies. Therefore, all of the counterarguments against the sequential expectancies account are also relevant in this case.

In addition, there are two other results that speak against this particular account. First, if this account were correct, one would expect that the lag-2 repetition cost should be particularly large when there is plenty of time between the response to the lag-2 trial and the task cue for the lag-1 trial so that the critical activation pattern can develop. However, as I reported in the previous section, the lag-2 repetition cost is at its maximum precisely when the time between the response to the lag-2 trial and the cue to the lag-1 trial is very short (Gade & Koch, 2005). Second, there are a number of studies in which transition probabilities between tasks were balanced (e.g., Arbuthnott & Frank, 2000; Dreher & Berman, 2002; Mayr & Keele, 2000). In such a situation, there is little reason to assume that subjects prepare for task changes. Nevertheless, robust lag-2 repetition costs usually can be found even in these situations.

Instance-Based Episodic Priming

Instance-based episodic priming is in many ways the most interesting and probably also the most challenging noninhibitory account. It is interesting both because it arises from a well-founded theory on the interplay between attention and memory (i.e., instance theory; Logan, 1988) and because versions of it have been applied to other inhibitory phenomena (e.g., chap. 4, this volume). The account basically holds that each selection episode is encoded into memory as a specific instance. Such "memory snapshots" may contain all selection-relevant parameters, such as the stimulus location, the values on the relevant dimension, and possibly also the locations and values of distractor objects. When, on one of the following trials, the stimulus situation happens to match in some way the encoded episode, then it is automatically retrieved. In some cases, automatic retrieval might help performance on this trial, in particular if there is a complete match between the encoded selection parameters and the currently required selection parameters. At other times, when the match is incomplete, a mismatch cost may arise. For example, the negative-priming effect can be explained in terms of episodic, instance-based priming: When subjects try to ignore a distractor object on the prime trial, the resulting memory trace may include a no-go tag that becomes associated with the representation of that object. This memory trace would then produce proactive interference when, on the probe trial, a response has to be made to that same object. Results with the negative-priming paradigm have demonstrated that episodic priming effects are clearly one important factor (see chap. 4, this volume).

As an aside, it is interesting to note that from an inhibition theory standpoint, inhibition is exactly what might help prevent unwanted intrusions from earlier selection episodes. This process may have interesting consequences when comparing people who presumably differ in inhibitory control ability (e.g., old and young adults). People with good inhibitory control may be able to remain relatively unaffected by episodic priming effects, and therefore negative priming (or some other inhibitory phenomenon) may actually represent "true" inhibition. In contrast, people with poor inhibitory control may be particularly vulnerable to proactive interference from earlier selection instances. They may therefore show the inhibitory phenomenon, but for the wrong reasons—ironically, exactly because their inhibitory control is poor.

The episodic-priming account is a viable competitor for the inhibitory explanation of the lag-2 repetition cost. For example, if the lag-2 trial of an inhibition sequence requires locating the color deviant (e.g., a pink rectangle in the upper right corner), according to the episodic-priming account, all of these aspects are encoded in the memory instance. If on the probe trial the color task is cued again, the cue may also lead to reactivation of this particular memory instance. However, now the critical deviant may be a purple rectangle in the lower-left corner. Thus, there is a mismatch between the required selection setting and the earlier encoded memory instance, and it is this mismatch that might cause the lag-2 cost.

Although the episodic-priming account rendered the negative-priming paradigm basically useless as a tool to study inhibitory control, there are reasons to believe that the lag-2 priming paradigm may be more resistant to this particular alternative explanation. Given that in the lag-2 priming paradigm, inhibition targets the task-set level rather than the level of specific stimulus or response representations, the researcher is in an excellent position to vary the similarity of stimulus–response aspects across the critical lag-2 repetitions. This consideration is important, because specificity is an important factor that should modulate episodic-priming effects. Thus, if the lag-2 repetition cost actually arises because of the mismatch between a memory instance and the current selection demands, then one should see the cost disappear and even turn into a benefit if one establishes conditions in which the memory instance and the selection needs match.

Mayr and Keele (2000) tried to do exactly that by comparing cases in which potentially critical parameters matched between the lag-2 trial and the probe trial of a lag-2 repetition sequence with cases where there was a mismatch. With regard to the feature value and the location–response aspect, there were no reliable effects. This lack of a clear mismatch effect is not entirely reassuring, because these analyses could focus on only one potentially relevant parameter at a time. It is possible that only a complete match on all parameters would produce a priming benefit and that all other cases might produce a cost (e.g., Hommel, 2004). The deviant-detection paradigm simply involved too much stimulus variability to allow an analysis of all potentially relevant parameters, including their interactions, as well as the most informative case of a complete match on all aspects.

Mayr (2002) therefore used a paradigm in which stimulus variability was greatly reduced. Subjects saw on each trial a circle appearing in one of four corners of a square. Responses were determined by three different spatial transformation rules (horizontal, vertical, and diagonal). For example, for the horizontal rule, a stimulus in the upper-left corner would require a horizontal translation and thus a response in the upper-right corner. Given that there were only four different stimulus positions, 25% of all lag-2 repetition cases involved a complete stimulus match. If episodic priming is in fact responsible for the lag-2 repetition cost, then a benefit for these trials should have been observed. Fortunately for the inhibition view, however, there was a lag-2 repetition cost even in the case of these complete matches. Of course, this result does not speak against the reality of instance-based priming effects in general (see chap. 4, this volume). Together with the results reported in Mayr and Keele (2000; see also Schuch & Koch, 2003), however, there is thus far no evidence that they are behind the lag-2 repetition cost.

To summarize, the lag-2 repetition cost cannot be accounted for in terms of sequential expectancies, activation of likely competitors, or instance-based priming. These findings strengthen the conclusion that the lag-2 repetition cost does in fact reflect inhibition targeted at no-longer-relevant task sets.

Neural-Level Explorations

Aron, Robbins, and Poldrack (2004) recently proposed that an area in the right inferior frontal cortex is critically involved when inhibitory control is used to resolve conflict. This conclusion is based on two results. First, they found that stop-signal time—that is, the time an individual needs to stop an initiated response process—increased linearly and in a quite orderly fashion with the size of the lesion in this region. Second, with the same group of patients, Aron and colleagues also looked at task-switching performance (Aron, Monsell, Sahakian, & Robbins, 2004). They found that patients with right frontal, but not left frontal, lesions showed much-increased error switch costs and somewhat-increased response time switch costs when the switch-trial stimulus was bivalent. They argued that deficient inhibition of the previous task set allowed for an increase in task-set interference after a switch. Although these results are certainly consistent with the claim that right inferior frontal patients have an inhibitory deficit, they are not fully conclusive. The degree to which inhibition proper is involved in the stop-signal procedure is currently not resolved. In fact, the original model simply assumes a race between two independent processes (a go process and a stop process; see Logan & Cowan, 1984). Similarly, the task-switching result could be easily explained in terms of slowed activation of the currently relevant task, which would give the previously relevant task more time to interfere (see Cohen & Dehaene, 1998). In brain-imaging studies, right prefrontal activations are often found in situations of high response conflict (Garavan, Ross, & Stein, 1999; Hazeltine, Poldrack, & Gabrieli, 2000), so maybe this is simply an area that is responsible for response conflict resolution without any necessary implication for inhibitory control.

It would be useful to obtain results with a paradigm that provides a more unambiguous record of inhibitory activity. We therefore compared 7 patients with left prefrontal lesions and 4 with right prefrontal lesions in a task-switching paradigm that allowed us to assess trial-to-trial switch costs, the global costs that emerge when comparing task-switching performance with single-task performance, and the lag-2 repetition cost (Mayr, Diedrichsen, Ivry, & Keele, 2006). We found that the left prefrontal patients showed increased local and global costs. Interestingly, they had increased costs even when stimuli were univalent, suggesting a rather basic deficit in terms of activating the next task set. However, left prefrontal patients showed lag-2 repetition costs that were, if anything, numerically larger than those of control subjects. In contrast, the right prefrontal patients had normal local and global costs but no lag-2 inhibition cost. This result is fully consistent with the hypothesis put forward by Aron, Robbins, and Poldrack (2004) that inhibition is associated with the right prefrontal cortex. However, one aspect of our study was at odds with the Aron, Monsell, et al. (2004) task-switching study: Whereas their right frontal patients had a switching deficit, our patients seemed quite unaffected by the switching demands, despite the fact that they did not show inhibition. If inhibition is involved in switching, shouldn't lack of inhibition lead to greater switch costs? A follow-up experiment provided a hint about what may have been going on. Aron, Monsell, et al. used a paradigm in which subjects worked on the same task for three trials in a row, a situation that allowed strong endorsement of each task. In contrast, to get at the lag-2 repetition effect, we had to use a paradigm in which tasks could change randomly after each trial. Such a procedure probably led to less endorsement of each individual task and therefore also to less need for inhibition to get rid of it on the next trial. In our follow-up experiment, we used a procedure with runs of three tasks between switches (thus promoting full task-set endorsement but no assessment of lag-2 repetition costs). In this situation, the right frontal patients actually did show a trend toward an increased switch cost that, at least in terms of numerical response time effect, was similar in size to the one that Aron, Monsell, et al. (2004) found. This pattern of results suggests that the typical lag-2 repetition paradigm in which tasks change every trial may be well suited to tracking task-set inhibition, but because this paradigm does not encourage full endorsement of each task, it may not be the best paradigm to reveal the effects of an inhibitory deficit on switch costs.

Together, our results and the findings by Aron and colleagues point to the involvement of the right prefrontal cortex in the manifestation of inhibitory control. However, it is also important to point out that so far, these data do not specify what exactly this area is doing. Probably the most straightforward hypothesis is that it is directly involved in initiating inhibition. However, a slightly more complicated model might follow from the premise that prefrontal neurons are primarily involved in representing potentially relevant aspects of the current task environment. Recent neuroimaging findings are of interest in this regard. Using the lag-2 repetition paradigm, Dreher and Berman (2002) obtained a robust increase in right prefrontal activation when subjects had to switch back to the most recently suppressed task set. In other words, the right prefrontal cortex seemed involved in expressing the lag-2 repetition cost when returning to a recently abandoned task but not necessarily at the time when one would expect inhibition to operate (i.e., when switching to Task B in an ABA sequence). One way to interpret these data is by assuming that whereas the left prefrontal cortex implements the selection of a single, coherent task set (e.g., Mayr & Kliegl, 2000, 2003), the right prefrontal cortex maintains a broader context (e.g., Keele, Ivry, Mayr, Hazeltine, & Heuer, 2003). Such a broader context would allow backtracking or monitoring of success across different tasks in multiple-task performance, and it may include a trace of the suppression associated with task sets that had recently been deactivated. Thus, although the right prefrontal cortex may represent the fact that a task has been suppressed, it is not necessarily the origin of the suppression. This interpretation is consistent with recent neuroimaging results reported by Braver, Reynolds, and Donaldson (2003) suggesting that during task-switching blocks, there is sustained activity in the right prefrontal cortex, possibly reflecting the increased load of tracking multiple tasks. In contrast, activity associated with local switch transitions is expressed in the left frontal cortex. One novel prediction derived from this view is that deficits associated with right frontal lesions should become particularly apparent in multitask situations in which task selection occurs in a more self-guided manner (i.e., on the basis of a record of previous task selections; Arrington & Logan, 2004) than when selection is under the control of external cues. Whether the prefrontal cortex actually houses certain control operations or whether it fulfills strictly representational functions is a fundamental question. At least for inhibition, further research on how exactly the right prefrontal cortex contributes to the lag-2 repetition cost should be informative with regard to this important issue.

Limitations and Open Issues

So far, I have emphasized the virtues of the lag-2 repetition cost as an indicator of inhibitory control and what researchers have learned about inhibition using this indicator. However, as with every paradigm, certain shortcomings are worth pointing out, and many things are yet to be learned. In this final section, I highlight some of these issues.

Assessing Aftereffects of Inhibition Versus Assessing Inhibition When It Actually Happens

Basically all known behavioral inhibitory paradigms, including the lag-2 repetition paradigm, try to catch the aftereffect of inhibiting a representation. This fact makes it difficult to study inhibition as it actually occurs. For example, it is precisely for this reason that the exact point during a task switch at which inhibition comes into play has remained elusive (i.e., during the processing of the cue for the lag-1 trial task or during processing of the lag-1 trial stimulus). Similarly, the results of Dreher and Berman (2002) regarding right prefrontal activity associated with the lag-2 repetition cost leave open the question of which brain area is involved with the inhibitory process itself.

Unfortunately, similar ambiguities arise when trying to infer from the lack of a group difference in lag-2 repetition cost that there is no group difference in inhibition. For example, Mayr (2001) found no evidence for a reduced lag-2 repetition cost in older adults, even though a prominent theory states that inhibition is generally reduced in old age (see chap. 8, this volume). The Mayr (2001) result could be interpreted as being inconsistent with the inhibition-deficit view (see chap. 9, this volume). However, given that one cannot observe the inhibitory process itself, but only the aftereffect of this process, it is also possible that although the end product may be equivalent for older and younger adults, it may be much harder (i.e., take much more time) for older adults to arrive at this end product. Thus, future progress in this area hinges on coming up with a paradigm that allows a better way of tracking what is going on during inhibition of a currently unwanted task set. One interesting path that researchers are currently exploring is the use of an analog of Anderson's think/ no think paradigm (Anderson & Green, 2001; see also chap. 5, this volume) in the task-selection domain. This paradigm has proved useful in establishing neural correlates of memory inhibition as it occurs and relating these to the behavioral aftereffects of inhibition (Anderson et al., 2004).

Inhibition and Learning

I have shown that task-set inhibition itself, at least as indexed by the lag-2 repetition cost, is not subject to top-down control. However, this conclusion does not mean that inhibition is immune to contextual factors. All studies using the lag-2 repetition paradigm reviewed this far used either a 100% switch rate or equiprobable transitions between all possible tasks (leading to a 66.6% switch rate for three tasks). Philipp and Koch (2006) recently used lower switch rates (50%) and found that the lag-2 repetition cost disappeared. One interpretation of this result is that the amount of inhibition exerted during task switches is modulated through the general switch rate. In this respect, the amount of inhibition may be a general control parameter that is adjusted according to current context (Philipp & Koch, 2006). However, there is another possibility: Maybe it is not so much the general control context that is critical but rather specific transition probabilities between pairs of tasks.

For example, in a situation with a 100% switch rate, the subject might learn that a particular task (e.g., A) can be followed by all other possible tasks (A to B, A to C) but never by itself. Thus, possibly individual, task-specific inhibitory links are established (i.e., from Task A to Task A) that are ultimately responsible for the lag-2 repetition cost. This model makes two unique predictions: First, if one manipulates between-task transition probabilities such that only particular tasks are never repeated, then one should see lag-2 repetition costs only for these tasks. Second, the ability to establish inhibitory links between task sets should not function only in a self-inhibitory manner. Rather, inhibitory association should evolve between any pair of tasks that never (or only rarely) follow each other. For example, one might construct transition probabilities such that a specific task (e.g., A) is never followed by a specific other task (e.g., B). During the transition from A to a "legal" successor task (e.g., C), Task B is inhibited. If, then, on the next trial, B happens to become relevant, then it should still be in an inhibited state and thus difficult to activate. In recent and partly ongoing work, my colleagues and I have found evidence supporting each of these novel predictions.

At first sight, these results seem to suggest a radical alternative to the idea that I put forward in the introduction to this chapter—namely, that task-set inhibition is an executive control operation that is generally applied when switching from one task to the next. Rather, task-set inhibition may be the result of specific learning experiences that help to sculpt the internal representation of the task space according to current task demands. However, given that this work is relatively recent, it is too early to draw firm conclusions. For example, the fact that specific transition probabilities have been found to modulate the development of inhibitory effects does not rule out the possibility that general control settings (as proposed by Philipp & Koch, 2006) may also play a role. In addition, elsewhere I reviewed results suggesting that lag-2 repetition costs can be observed when the transition to each possible task (including task repetitions) is equally likely (e.g., Mayr, 2002). If inhibition were exclusively tied to unlikely transitions, there would be no reason to expect lag-2 repetition costs in the case of equiprobable transitions. Thus, so far, the existing evidence seems most compatible with the view that lag-2 repetition costs may reflect a general inhibitory process that is modulated by specific (and possibly also general) control demands. Clearly, though, in future work it will be important to further examine the role of specific and general experiences in shaping inhibitory control.

Conclusion

In this chapter, I focused on reviewing the range of empirical findings resulting from the lag-2 repetition paradigm. Despite its fairly recent entry as an experimental paradigm, it has already provided a number of important empirical results regarding the nature of task-set inhibition. As an answer to the main underlying question of this volume—is there cognitive inhibition?—these results suggest a cautious yes. In many ways, the lag-2 repetition cost behaves as one would expect from a mechanism involved in resolving between-task competition, and so far it has proved relatively robust in the face of potential alternative interpretations. At the same time, both the neural-level findings and, in particular, the novel results regarding the relation between associative learning and inhibition suggest new avenues of research that promise important insights into the nature of cognitive inhibition.

References

Anderson, M. C., & Green, C. (2001, March 15). Suppressing unwanted memories by executive control. *Nature, 410,* 366–369.

Anderson, M. C., Ochsner, K. N., Kuhl, B., Cooper, J., Robertson, E., Gabrieli, S. W., et al. (2004, January 9). Neural systems underlying the suppression of unwanted memories. *Science, 303,* 232–235.

Arbuthnott, K. D., & Frank, J. (2000). Trail Making Test, Part B as a measure of executive control: Validation using a set-switching paradigm. *Journal of Clinical and Experimental Neuropsychology, 4,* 518–528.

Aron, A. R., Monsell, S., Sahakian, B. J., & Robbins, T. W. (2004). A componential analysis of task-switching deficits associated with lesions of left and right frontal cortex. *Brain, 127,* 1561–1573.

Aron, A. R., Robbins, T. W., & Poldrack, R. A. (2004). Inhibition and the right inferior frontal cortex. *Trends in Cognitive Sciences, 8,* 170–177.

Arrington, C. M., & Logan, G. D. (2004). The cost of a voluntary task switch. *Psychological Science, 15,* 610–615.

Braver, T., Reynolds, J. R., & Donaldson, D. I. (2003). Neural mechanisms of transient and sustained cognitive control during task switching. *Neuron, 39,* 713–726.

Cohen, L., & Dehaene, S. (1998). Competition between past and present: Assessment and interpretation of verbal perseverations. *Brain, 121,* 1641–1659.

Dagenbach, D., & Carr, T. H. (1994). *Inhibitory processes in attention, memory, and language.* San Diego, CA: Academic Press.

Dreher, J.-C., & Berman, K. F. (2002). Fractionating the neural substrate of cognitive control processes. *Proceedings of the National Academy of Sciences, 99,* 14595–14600.

Gade, M., & Koch, I. (2005). Linking inhibition to activation in the control of task sequences. *Psychonomic Bulletin & Review, 12,* 530–534.

Garavan, H., Ross, T. J., & Stein, E. A. (1999). Right hemispheric dominance of inhibitory control: An event-related functional MRI study. *Proceedings of the National Academy of Sciences, 96,* 8301–8306.

Goschke, T. (2000). Intentional configuration and involuntary persistence in task set switching. In S. Monsell & J. Driver (Eds.), *Control of cognitive processes: Attention and performance* (Vol. 18, pp. 331–355). Cambridge, MA: MIT Press.

Hazeltine, E., Poldrack, R., & Gabrieli, J. D. E. (2000). Neural activation during response competition. *Journal of Cognitive Neuroscience, 12,* 118–129.

Hommel, B. (2004). Event files: Feature binding in and across perception and action. *Trends in Cognitive Sciences, 8,* 494–500.

Hübner, M., Dreisbach, G., Haider, H., & Kluwe, R. H. (2003). Backward inhibition as a means of sequential task control: Evidence for reduction of task competition. *Journal of Experimental Psychology: Learning, Memory, & Cognition, 29,* 289–297.

Keele, S., Ivry, R., Mayr, U., Hazeltine, E., & Heuer, H. (2003). The cognitive and neural architecture of sequence representation. *Psychological Review, 110,* 316–339.

Kleinsorge, T., & Gajewski, P. D. (2004). Preparation for a forthcoming task is sufficient to produce subsequent shift costs. *Psychonomic Bulletin & Review, 11,* 302–306.

Logan, G. D. (1988). Toward an instance theory of automatization. *Psychological Review, 95,* 492–527.

Logan, G. D., & Cowan, W. B. (1984). On the ability to inhibit thought and action: A theory of an act of control. *Psychological Review, 91,* 295–327.

Mayr, U. (2001). Age differences in the selection of mental sets: The role of inhibition, stimulus ambiguity, and response-set overlap. *Psychology and Aging, 16,* 96–109.

Mayr, U. (2002). Inhibition of action rules. *Psychonomic Bulletin & Review, 9,* 93–99.

Mayr, U., Diedrichsen, J., Ivry, R., & Keele, S. (2006). Dissociating task-set selection from task-set inhibition in prefrontal cortex. *Journal of Cognitive Neuroscience, 18,* 14–21.

Mayr, U., & Keele, S. W. (2000). Changing internal constraints on action: The role of backward inhibition. *Journal of Experimental Psychology: General, 129,* 4–26.

Mayr, U., & Kliegl, R. (2000). Task-set switching and long-term memory retrieval. *Journal of Experimental Psychology: Learning, Memory, and Cognition, 26,* 1124–1140.

Mayr, U., & Kliegl, R. (2003). Differential effects of cue changes and task changes on task-set selection costs. *Journal of Experimental Psychology: Learning, Memory, and Cognition, 29,* 362–372.

Meiran, N. (1996). Reconfiguration of processing mode prior to task performance. *Journal of Experimental Psychology: Learning, Memory, and Cognition, 22,* 1423–1442.

Monsell, S. (2003). Task switching. *Trends in Cognitive Sciences, 7,* 134–140.

Neill, W. T. (1997). Episodic retrieval in negative priming and repetition priming. *Journal of Experimental Psychology: Learning, Memory, and Cognition, 23,* 1291–1305.

Philipp, A. M., & Koch, I. (2006). The relation of task inhibition and task repetition in task switching. *European Journal of Cognitive Psychology, 18,* 624–639.

Rubinstein, J., Meyer, E. D., & Evans, J. E. (2001). Executive control of cognitive processes in task switching. *Journal of Experimental Psychology: Human Perception and Performance, 27,* 763–797.

Schuch, S., & Koch, I. (2003). The role of response selection for inhibition of task sets in task shifting. *Journal of Experimental Psychology: Human Perception and Performance, 29,* 92–105.

Tipper, S. P., & Cranston, M. (1985). Selective attention and priming: Inhibitory and facilitatory effects of ignored primes. *Quarterly Journal of Experimental Psychology, 37,* 591–611.

3

Adventures in Inhibition: Plausibly, But Not Certifiably, Inhibitory Processes

Dale Dagenbach, Thomas H. Carr, David Menzer, Peter J. Duquette, Holly M. Chalk, Melinda Rupard, and Robert S. E. Hurley

A number of researchers have argued strenuously in favor of inhibitory processes as a crucial tool for managing cognitive overload in busy information-processing environments. In these accounts, inhibition is used to suppress activated but irrelevant and distracting representations of stimuli, goals, or motor responses that are not appropriate to the currently desired task performance. Other researchers have argued just as strenuously that a concept of active inhibition overreaches the data. Phenomena that might be attributed to active inhibition can be explained by other processes, such as by passively resolving interference by waiting longer for the right information to win out in a competition for highest levels of activation or by deploying attention to facilitate the representations that are relevant but not inhibiting those that are irrelevant.

This is by no means a new debate. Pillsbury (1908), in one of the classic treatments of attention, described three possible theories of selection: Attention might facilitate what is wanted in order to overcome interference, it might inhibit what is not wanted in order to eliminate interference, or it might do both. Pillsbury seemed to prefer the last option—attention does both—but he made clear that the data available at that time could not decide the question. Apparently, things have changed only a little since 1908. Now it is generally agreed that attention facilitates the representations and processing operations toward which it is directed, but debate about the existence of active inhibition continues approximately unabated.

The case for inhibition was well made in some of the conference presentations, but in other situations where inhibition is often invoked, the arguments against it were provocative and worthy of consideration even by inhibition's most stalwart proponents. A few arguments were made that the distinction is unimportant—whether facilitation or inhibition, the end result is differences in activation and accessibility, so the two are simply what mathematicians might call "notation variants" of one another. However, we think this view is wrong and that it is important to try to tell the difference. The present situation seems analogous to that in the literature on serial and parallel processes 15 years ago. Townsend (1990) summarized the difficulties of distinguishing between serial and parallel processes, along with some hopes for advances on that front, in an article entitled "Serial vs. Parallel Processing: Sometimes They Look Like Tweedledum and Tweedledee but They Can (and Should) Be Distinguished." Significant progress has been made toward that end in the intervening years. Inhibitory and noninhibitory mechanisms also may look like Tweedledee and Tweedledum, but they too can and should be distinguished.

Typically, inhibitory mechanisms are invoked to solve difficult cognitive processing problems in which the stimulus to be processed competes with other stimuli possessing qualities that make them especially salient and likely to capture attention and/or decision processes and hence lead performance astray. Theoretically, one way of resolving such a situation is to invoke inhibition of the unattended or unselected information—but if one is to do so, one needs to be able to collect empirical evidence that inhibition has actually occurred. In general, this is the approach that we have followed in this chapter. In the lines of research that we describe, target stimuli or memory representations must be selected or acted on in the face of competition from other highly salient stimuli or representations. In each case, we look for confirmatory evidence consisting of an inhibitory signature left by the selection process: Access to the competing information is shown to be impaired from the act of selection. If this signature is present, then we conclude in favor of inhibition. If this signature is absent, then other ways of resolving interference must be invoked to explain the results.

We first consider evidence from the phenomenon of backward inhibition in task switching. Studies of task switching require participants to perform two or more tasks that are mixed together across trials. On each trial, a cue of some type tells the participant which task to perform; the cue may be the name of the task presented at the start of the trial, an ordered list of task names held in memory, or the stimuli themselves if each task has its own unique stimulus set on which the other task or tasks cannot be performed. Across trials, tasks may repeat in runs of varying length, or they may switch. The most basic fact of this "multitasking life" is switch costs—for any given task, speed and sometimes accuracy of task performance are lower on a switch trial than on a repetition trial. Backward inhibition is manifested in the magnitude of this switch cost, which is greater if the new task has recently been switched away from and now must be chosen again than if it has not been performed for several trials. This evidence of reduced accessibility following selection against a task meets our test, and therefore we offer it as a potential example of an act of inhibition in real-time task performance. Mayr (2002; Mayr & Keele, 2000; see also chap. 2, this volume) has made a convincing case against alternative interpretations. We describe a couple of extensions of what is known about backward inhibition in the following section.

Issues in Backward Inhibition

Research on the control processes that enable adaptive responding to stimuli has yielded a number of interesting insights and accompanying challenges to theory. Among these is the stability–flexibility paradox noted by Mayr and Keele (2000): Because of the multitude of possible responses to stimuli in the environment, relatively stable internal representations of control are required to preserve the coherence of behavior. Conversely, although representations strong enough to prevent inappropriate responding are clearly important, the representations enabling such control also must be flexible enough to allow for fluid switching from one task to another without having overwhelming interference from the earlier task.

Mayr and Keele (2000) proposed that one means of achieving both stable representations and flexible transitions would be to have an inhibitory process, called *backward inhibition,* that suppresses representations of the control settings from the preceding task during intentional task or goal shifts. They then reported results from a series of experiments that were consistent with the existence of such a mechanism. Most generally, this research involved demonstrating that responses were slower with a repetition of a task set from two trials back (lag 2) compared with responses with a task set that had not occurred within the last two trials. The underlying assumptions were that inhibition is applied to the preceding task set at each task switch and that the inhibition dissipates slowly. Experimentally, the consequences cannot be discerned at the point of switching (the lag-1 trial), but looking at the lag-2 trials enables one to assess the inhibition's lingering effects.

In these experiments, participants were presented with arrays of perceptual shapes that could vary along a number of dimensions (e.g., orientation, color, direction of motion). Each dimension could assume different values. One was preassigned to be "neutral" and was never to be responded to, whereas two others were designated "discrepant" or "deviant." On each trial, one dimension was cued as the relevant dimension to monitor, providing the task set for that trial. All but one of the shapes in the array had the neutral value for the relevant dimension; the participants' task was to indicate the location in the display (e.g., top left corner) of the shape that deviated from the neutral value along this relevant dimension. To assess backward inhibition, repetitions of sets from the lag-2 trials were contrasted with nonrepetitions (e.g., a sequence of task sets on successive trials consisting of color–orientation–color vs. a sequence consisting of motion–orientation–color). Backward inhibition was observed across an array of cue–stimulus intervals (CSIs) and response–cue intervals (RCIs), although there was some indication that it decreased with longer RCIs.

Further work by Mayr (2002) addressed whether backward inhibition might be explained in a manner akin to episodic memory retrieval explanations of negative priming. According to such an account, automatic task-set retrieval with a mismatch between the response for a task set on trial n and that same task set on trial $n - 2$ could generate a cost that would appear as backward inhibition. To test this, Mayr conducted an experiment in which a circular stimulus was presented in one of the four corners of the display, and an action rule (horizontal, vertical, or diagonal) indicated the location to which the participant should mentally shift the stimulus before responding by indicating that location. Mayr found evidence for backward inhibition even when both the stimulus configuration and the action rule were the same for n and $n - 2$ trials, where responding should have been facilitated if automatic episodic retrieval effects were occurring. The backward inhibition effect shows the signature characteristic that we defined earlier: reduced accessibility—in this case of a task set—on processing subsequent to an act of selection against that task.

Although it is clear from these studies that backward inhibition may play an important role in cognitive control, many details remain to be worked out. Little is known about its development, and the details of the temporal parameters of its decline once it has been initiated are also uncertain. In addition, the exact stimulus and task properties that elicit backward inhibition and that it affects remain to be fully elucidated. Mayr and Keele (2000) argued that backward inhibition applies to *task-set representations* and defined those as the assemblage of attentional, perceptual, mnemonic, and motor processes involved in the performance of a goal-directed behavior, but experiments to date have looked primarily at effects on perceptual processes.

Backward Inhibition of Response Mappings

One recent study (Menzer & Dagenbach, 2002), somewhat akin to that of Mayr (2002), looked at whether response mappings, another presumed component of task sets, also were inhibited on backward inhibition trials. The first experiment was a conceptual replication of Mayr and Keele (2000) using an array with three locations, and responses using three fingers rather than one, to indicate the location of a target defined by a perceptual dimension cue that changed from trial to trial. In the second experiment, the perceptual dimension was held constant while response mappings (the appropriate finger to press when the target was in a given location) changed from trial to trial. In the third experiment, both the perceptual dimensions and the response mappings switched between trials. As in Mayr and Keele, backward inhibition was assessed at three response–stimulus interval (RSI) and cue–stimulus interval configurations (100 milliseconds and 100 milliseconds, 900 milliseconds and 100 milliseconds, 100 milliseconds and 900 milliseconds) in each experiment to allow insight into the effect of task-set preparation and into its decay once implemented.

In Experiment 1, subjects categorized stimuli according to the perceptual dimensions of size, orientation, and shape. In each dimension, two values were deviant and one value was neutral, and the subject's task was to indicate the location of the stimulus that was deviant on the cued dimension for that trial. Written cues appearing over the top of the stimulus boxes assigned the relevant dimension on each trial, with cue–stimulus onset intervals and response–cue intervals varying between blocks.

Participants repeated practice sets of 20 trials until they were able to attain an accuracy rate of at least 80% in the task. Practice trials were followed

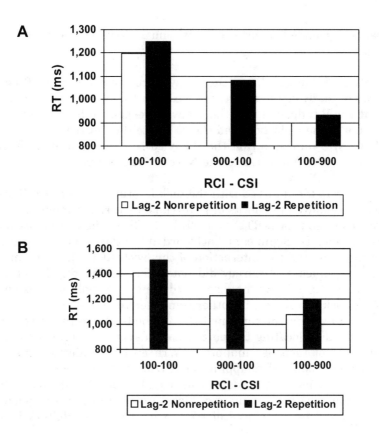

Figure 3.1. Backward inhibition of (A) switching perceptual dimensions and (B) switching response mappings. RT = response time; RCI = response–cue interval; CSI = cue–stimulus interval.

by two sets of six blocks of 94 real trials. Three types of trials were present: control, nonspecific $n - 2$ repetitions, and specific $n - 2$ repetitions. On control trials, the cued stimulus dimension was different than on either of the preceding two trials. On nonspecific $n - 2$ repetitions, the cued stimulus dimension was the same as on the $n - 2$ trial, but the other deviant value was the target. On the specific $n - 2$ repetitions, the cued stimulus dimension was the same as on the $n - 2$ trial, and the deviant target value was also the same.

Mean response times for each RCI–CSI configuration as a function of trial type are shown in Figure 3.1, Panel A. Replicating Mayr and Keele (2000), significant backward inhibition was observed, and it did not interact significantly with the RCI–CSI factor, although there was a suggestion of less backward inhibition with the long (900-millisecond) response–cue interval. No significant differences in accuracy were observed. Thus, Mayr and Keele's basic phenomenon bearing the signature of an inhibitory process was replicated.

The second experiment assessed whether backward inhibition applies to response mappings by varying those between trials. The response mappings were defined as the key presses made to indicate the target's location.

Participants responded using the V, B, and N keys according to the task-cue instruction:

- Pattern A indicated that the V key corresponded to the left box in the frame, the B key to the center box, and the N key to the right box.
- Pattern B indicated that the V key corresponded to the center box, the B key to the right box, and the N key to the left box.
- Pattern C indicated that the V key corresponded to the right box, the B key to the left box, and the N key to the center box.

Participants were familiarized with the task in practice blocks until proficient (80% correct), followed by blocks of real trials as in Experiment 1.

Mean response times (RTs) for each RCI–CSI configuration are shown in Figure 3.1, Panel B. Significant backward inhibition was observed at each RCI–CSI interval, and the interaction of this with RCI–CSI interval was not statistically significant. Accuracy did not differ significantly between conditions. These results indicate that backward inhibition applies to response mappings in the task set along with other components.

The third experiment combined the methods of the first two. The task was now defined as locating the perceptually deviant stimulus and using the appropriate set of response mappings. Written cues indicated the relevant perceptual dimension and mapping for a trial, with dimension or mapping coming first or second on a random basis (e.g., Pattern A = shape, Pattern B = size). Participants were given practice blocks until 80% correct responding was attained, followed by six blocks of trials with the same RCI–CSI intervals as before.

In this case, lag-2 repetitions could take one of three forms: (a) The perceptual dimension, but not the response mapping, could be repeated; (b) the response mapping, but not the perceptual dimension, could be repeated; or (c) both the perceptual and response mapping could be repeated. In the case where only the perceptual dimension or response mapping repeated, the other component did not repeat—that is, it followed an ABC pattern. If tasks are componential, with encoding, decision-making, and response stages maintaining their integrity and independence from one another, it might be expected that these components can be inhibited independently. Under this expectation, we would expect to replicate the results showing backward inhibition of perceptual dimensions observed in Experiment 1, as well as the backward inhibition of response mappings observed in Experiment 2, with these two effects summing together in some way to create a larger backward inhibition effect when both components of the task changed at once. If the backward inhibition mechanism can carry out two inhibition operations at once without loss of effectiveness, then the two effects might simply add when both task components changed. However, if the inhibition mechanism is limited in capacity or can operate on only one task component at a time in serial fashion, then an underadditive pattern might be observed. The results for these three conditions versus control conditions are shown in Figure 3.2.

Obviously, the prediction derived from a simple componential view of how tasks are organized and how backward inhibition might operate on that organi-

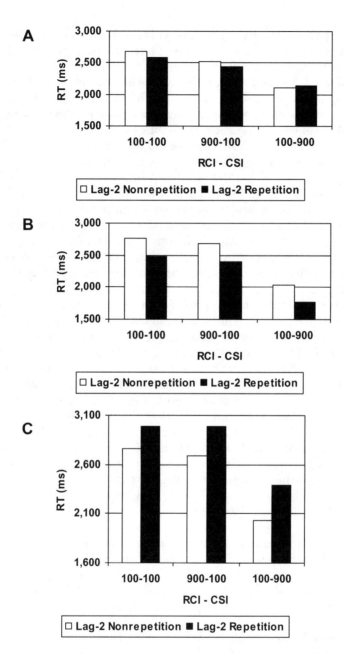

Figure 3.2. Repetition of perceptual dimension (A), response mapping (B), or both (C). RT = response time; RCI = response–cue interval; CSI = cue–stimulus interval.

zation turned out to be very wrong. The results were dramatically different from those of the first two experiments. For lag-2 repetitions of the perceptual dimension, but not the response mapping dimension, there was no evidence of backward inhibition. Significant facilitation occurred at RCI–CSI intervals of 100 and 900 milliseconds and 900 and 100 milliseconds, and nonsignificant inhibition occurred at the RCI–CSI intervals of 100 and 900 milliseconds. For lag-2 repetitions of the response mapping but not the perceptual dimension, significant facilitation occurred at all three RCI–CSI intervals. Thus, backward inhibition was not present when only one of the two relevant dimensions repeated across lag 2. Indeed, repeating one of the two relevant dimensions, but not both, appeared to speed performance rather than slowing it down. Significant differences in accuracy were not observed.

In contrast, when both the response mapping and perceptual dimensions were the same across the lag-2 repetition, significant backward inhibition was restored, appearing at each of the RCI–CSI intervals. Again, as in Mayr and Keele (2000), this backward inhibition did not appear to be targeted at specific display configurations per se—the observed inhibition was actually greater for nonspecific repetitions (e.g., the perceptual stimulus was the other deviant value) than for specific ones, although significant for both cases.

These particular results raise some questions about the representations that backward inhibition applies to, because they suggest that repetition of the complete specific task representation seems to be needed. We originally conceived of this experiment as a form of dual-task backward inhibition study, exposing the componentiality of task organization and investigating whether the backward inhibition process could inhibit two components simultaneously just as well as it could inhibit either when it was the only changing component in the experiment. However, the results suggest that rather than mapping each dimension, subjects were learning to perform nine different single tasks. Backward inhibition occurred only when the specific task set from this set of nine was reiterated across the lag-2 interval. When a different one of the nine tasks was reiterated, sharing a component with a previously switched-away-from task helped rather than hurt. Mayr (2002) observed a different pattern with repeated action rules, stimulus locations, and exact repetitions, and the reasons for these differences must be worked out.

Development of Backward Inhibition

Life-span changes in cognitive control processes remain relatively unexplored, especially in children. Although many deficits in cognitive control have been associated with cognitive aging, some work suggests that backward inhibition is at least as large in older adults as in younger adults (Mayr, 2001). However, we know of only one study that explored the early development of backward inhibition.

Duquette and Dagenbach (2003) looked at this issue in a study of first- ($n = 14$), third- ($n = 12$), and fifth- ($n = 15$) grade children using a variant of the three-location procedure described earlier in this chapter. In this study, stimuli varied in color (pink, red, purple), shape (rectangle, square, triangle), and location within the placeholder (top, center, bottom), with red, square, and center defined as the neutral values. A tape-recorded verbal cue was presented 500 milliseconds before the display onset to eliminate reading effects. Each participant completed 94 trials. As before, the critical comparison involved lag-2 repetition (backward inhibition) versus lag-2 nonrepetition (control) trials. The results are shown in Figure 3.3.

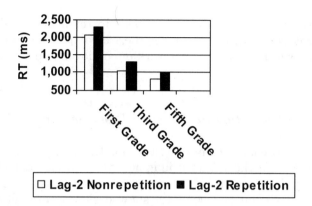

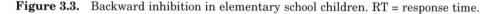

Figure 3.3. Backward inhibition in elementary school children. RT = response time.

Third and fifth graders both showed significant backward inhibition of response time. First graders were very slow overall, and slower on the backward inhibition than control trials, but the difference was not statistically significant. Accuracy ranged from 85% to 96%, suggesting that the children were reasonably able to perform the relatively demanding task. The overall pattern certainly indicates that backward inhibition is operational by third grade and perhaps even in first graders.

Issues in Center-Surround Selection

Center-surround selection is a potential inhibitory process that has been observed both in retrieval from semantic memory and in visual attention. When attention is directed toward retrieving a particular representation from memory, there is a "gradient of facilitation" around that representation defined on its semantic similarity and associative relatedness to other representations. This is the well-known phenomenon of semantic priming. However, when the focal representation is weakly activated or poorly learned and its retrieval is very slow and prone to error, the gradient of faster and more accurate processing turns to slower and less accurate processing. Representations that are closely related become temporarily more difficult to retrieve, evidenced by slower and less accurate processing than baseline performance. This reduction of speed and accuracy for material that is ordinarily easy to process is the phenomenon of center-surround selection in the domain of retrieval from memory.

When visual attention is directed toward a particular location in space, a gradient of facilitation is established such that stimuli at the focus are processed most rapidly and accurately. Stimuli spatially removed from the focus are processed less efficiently. However, under some conditions, a bigger drop in efficiency of processing occurs for stimuli a small distance away from the focus than for those further away—this is the phenomenon of center-surround selection that bears the signature of inhibition in the domain of visual attention. In this section we summarize work described elsewhere bearing on whether a center-surround mechanism might be used in retrieving weakly activated information from semantic memory when there is competition from other representations, and we then turn to new work on analogous phenomena observed in visual attention.

Center-Surround Selection in Retrieval From Semantic Memory

In studies of subthreshold priming effects for lexical decisions, participants who were trained to make semantic judgments (as opposed to more commonly used detection judgments) about masked primes during the threshold-setting phase of the experiment subsequently showed slower responding on lexical decision trials with semantically related masked primes compared with semantically unrelated masked primes (Dagenbach, Carr, & Wilhelmson, 1989). A working hypothesis was that these particular participants had learned to try to process weakly activated semantic information from masked primes and that one component of accessing such information might be a mechanism that inhibited related items to facilitate its retrieval.

In a more direct test of this idea, Carr and Dagenbach (1990) compared masked repetition and semantic priming of lexical decisions under normal detection threshold conditions and under semantic similarity judgment conditions. *Masked repetition priming* involves priming the target item with a masked version of itself, whereas *masked semantic priming* involves presentation of masked semantically related words. Significant facilitation was observed for both masked repetition primes and masked semantically related primes in the detection condition, but the semantic threshold setting procedure resulted in facilitation of lexical decisions for repetition primes but inhibition for semantically related primes. That is, lexical decision targets following semantically related primes were again less accessible than those following unrelated primes. These results were consistent with the pattern that would be produced by a center-surround retrieval mechanism, and they certainly met the reduced-accessibility test we described in the introduction to this chapter for attributing an effect to an inhibitory process.

Several subsequent studies yielded results consistent with the center-surround hypothesis. Another way to create weakly activated semantic information is to have subjects learn new vocabulary words. Dagenbach, Carr, and Barnhardt (1990) used newly learned vocabulary words as primes for a lexical decision task. Participants first studied new obscure words and their definitions briefly (e.g., *accipiter*—a hawk), and then those new words served as primes to familiar target words in the lexical decision phase. Afterwards, learning of the new words was assessed in terms of the ability both to intentionally recall the meaning of the word and to recognize its meaning. Those words whose meanings could be recalled produced the standard semantic priming effect of facilitation, but those whose meaning could not be recalled but could be recognized produced slower responding on semantically related trials.

Finally, a pattern similar to that seen for the vocabulary words has been observed in the learning of a classification task involving novel shapes—an attempt to build an artificial "semantic memory system" from scratch and watch its development (Carr et al., 1994). In this study, subjects were given novel shapes and were taught to classify them as "fleps" or "gleps." After extensive practice, a series of priming experiments tracked the integration of this new information into semantic memory using automatic semantic priming effects as an index. When these effects were obtained, new exemplars of fleps and gleps were introduced to subjects, and the speed of classification was used as an index of their learning. The critical result was that when used as primes, the items that were less well-learned, and hence harder to process, produced slowed responding to well-learned related items in the classification task compared with unrelated items. The items that were better learned, and hence easier to process, produced faster responding, as would be expected in a semantic priming task. These results again were consistent with a center-surround mechanism whose operation can be detected under conditions of weak target activation.

Center-Surround Selection in Visual Attention

Center-surround mechanisms also have been suggested by several studies of visual selective attention in which the selection of an item in an array of stimuli is accompanied by decreased sensitivity to other target items that are closer in space compared with farther away. For example, Bahcall and Kowler (1999) had subjects identify two red letters in a large, briefly presented array of green letters (or vice versa) and found that identification accuracy increased with target separation. Similarly, Cave and Zimmerman (1997) had subjects respond to an occasional probe that appeared after the display, but before the response, in a visual search task. Responses were fastest when the probe was in the same location as the target but slower for closer nontarget locations compared with locations farther away.

Such inhibitory surround patterns may be elicited by stimuli that capture attention. Caputo and Guerra (1998) reported an inhibitory surround of a target that was a feature singleton. In their experiment, a singleton form containing a line was the target, and one of six other forms was a singleton color distractor. The threshold for detecting a change in the length of the line increased when the singleton color distractor was closer to the target. They suggested that the distractor captured attention, and the result was an inhibition of the surround that in this case affected target processing.

Mounts (2000a, 2000b) also reported center-surround patterns in a series of experiments. In one study, subjects saw a briefly presented, masked array of block 8s. Select pieces of one 8 were missing to make it an upright or upside down A, and subjects were required to indicate its orientation. In addition, one of the block 8s was either a color singleton or an orientation singleton (slanted at a 22-degree angle). Target discrimination was poorest when the target was adjacent to the distractor singleton (Mounts, 2000b). In another study, attentional capture by color singleton distractors, with the resulting inhibitory surround, was shown to depend on subjects searching for singleton targets rather than targets based on feature conjunctions. However, abrupt-onset distractors captured attention and slowed responding to near targets compared with more distant ones, regardless of search mode (Mounts, 2000a).

Some neuroimaging data also provide support for the operation of a center-surround mechanism mediated by attention. Slotnik, Hopfinger, Klein, and Sutter (2002) used cortical source localization of event-related potential data stemming from 60 task-irrelevant stimuli in visual displays. Visual processing was enhanced at spatially attended locations and in a surrounding region but inhibited in a further surround. Using functional magnetic resonance imaging, Muller and Kleinschmidt (2004) presented subjects with an array of four rectangular placeholders in the upper hemifield. A central cue at fixation directed them to focus their attention on a particular one, and they had to indicate whether it contained a blue circle when small colored objects appeared in each placeholder. Activity in visual areas V1, V2, VP, and V4 was measured following the cue and compared with activity generated by passive viewing of the four placeholders. Enhanced activity for the attended region was found in retinotopic subregions of areas V1 through V4. Deactivation of the surrounding retinotopic areas was found in V1 for both areas occupied by the unattended placeholders and other unoccupied regions.

Although these studies suggest a center-surround pattern to the attentional spotlight, studies using other paradigms have yielded different stories and thus create an interesting paradox. In particular, studies using the Eriksen flanker task typically have found greater flanker compatibility effects for near versus distant stimuli (Eriksen & St. James, 1986). What underlies this seemingly contradictory set of a findings?

In a series of flanker paradigm experiments, we tried to identify the key differences between the flanker paradigm and those experiments that yielded evidence consistent with a center-surround mechanism (McCartney, 2001). Initial consideration suggested a host of possible factors. In the Eriksen task, target location is typically known in advance, whereas in many of the experiments yielding evidence for a center-surround pattern, the target must first be searched for. In many, although not all, experiments yielding a center-surround pattern, the "center" results from some form of attentional capture attributable to a unique property or onset of the stimulus. Most experiments yielding the center-surround pattern use more stimuli than the prototypical Eriksen task with a target and two flanker letters, and it may be that stimuli near the focus of attention will be automatically processed when just a few are present (see, e.g., Lavie, 2000) but not necessarily when there are more. Finally, most, although not all, of the experiments yielding a center-surround effect do so after a nontarget item has been selected or has competed for attention, resulting in slower processing of nearby targets.

An initial experiment tested whether the center-surround pattern would occur after selecting a sought-for item, as is typically the case in a flanker task, rather than having attention grabbed by an irrelevant distractor, as was the case in most, though not all, of the studies that found the center-surround pattern. In other words, is the center-surround pattern in part a function of conflict between the goals of endogenous and exogenous attentional orienting? In this experiment, subjects ($N = 14$) had to decide whether two Hs were present in a circular array of six block 8s and two letters that remained present until response. The other letter was an S when not an H. One letter was green, and all other stimuli were red. Given that one of the letters was a color singleton

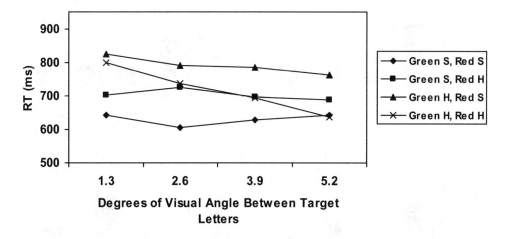

Figure 3.4. Effects of distance between target letters: Center-surround inhibition after target selection. RT = response time.

and also the object of an intentional search process, this might be thought of as a combination of exogenous and endogenous selection processes with both having the same goal. The distance between the two letters varied across trials, ranging from 1.3 to 5.2 degrees of visual angle.

On trials when the green stimulus was an H, there were significant systematic distance effects (see Figure 3.4). Responses were slowest when the other letter was one position away and became faster the farther away it was, consistent with a center-surround pattern. However, on trials when the green stimulus was an S, no distance effects were observed. Presumably, subjects were able to base their response on the first item sampled and did not need to ascertain the other letter on these trials.

Given that the center-surround mechanism seems to operate with intentional as well as unintentional selection, in a further series of experiments we attempted to elicit a center-surround pattern in variations of the prototypical flanker task. Because the center-surround pattern occurred after combined exogenous and endogenous orienting in the preceding experiment, we adapted the flanker paradigm to try to combine these features by having the target abruptly appear between two distractors whose identity became apparent through offsets, thus providing an exogenous boost to already deployed endogenous attention. The initial display consisted of a blank central space flanked by two block 8 figures that were 1.3, 2.6, 3.9, or 5.2 degrees of visual angle from the target location. The target appeared abruptly as parts of the block 8s offset to form the flanker letters. Subjects ($N = 12$) classified the target letter as belonging to one of two categories (the letters *H* or *C* vs. *S* or *E*). Flankers were either compatible or incompatible, and effects were measured in terms of the difference between these two conditions. The results are shown in Figure 3.5A. Significant flanker compatibility effects were observed in the first two positions, whereas flanker effects from further positions were reduced and not significant. The pattern was clearly not consistent with a center-surround mechanism.

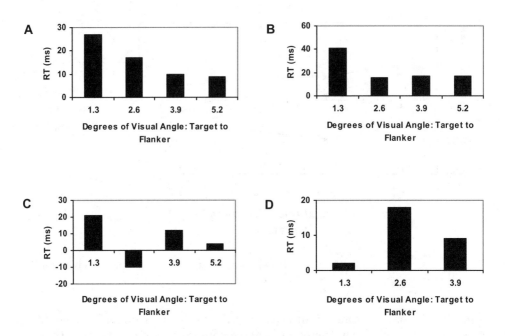

Figure 3.5. Flanker compatibility effects with abrupt-onset target, two flankers, location certainty (A); flanker–target display, two flankers, location uncertainty (B); eight flankers, abrupt-onset target, location certainty (C); and two flankers, five distractors, location uncertainty (D). RT = response time.

Another difference between the classic flanker experiment and most studies that find center-surround patterns is knowledge of the target's spatial location. In the typical flanker experiment, the target's location is known in advance, whereas in the typical experiment yielding the center-surround pattern, the target must be searched for. Indeed, in our first experiment that yielded a center-surround pattern, target selection may have reflected a combination of exogenous orienting and an intentional search. To assess whether having attention endogenously focused on the target location before the target's onset was a factor in eliminating the center-surround pattern in flanker experiments, we conducted an experiment in which a red target letter and two adjacent white flankers appeared abruptly at one of eight different locations arranged around the fixation point. Target–flanker distances varied as before. In this case, significant flanker compatibility effects were observed at each distance, although the effect was strongest at 1.3 degrees of visual angle (see Figure 3.5B). Hence, having to locate the target does not seem sufficient to trigger the center-surround mechanism. However, it also should be noted that the locational uncertainty in this experiment was a bit different than in the typical search experiment in that the location of the target within the target and flanker array was known in advance, but where that array would appear was not known in advance.

Another experiment tested whether the number of stimuli had something to do with when center-surround effects would be observed. Most experiments yielding that pattern have used displays with between 8 and 24 stimuli, whereas the flanker paradigm typically has just 3. In this experiment, the target appeared in a blank space at the center of a rectangular array of eight block 8s. The target appeared in a different color while parts of the block 8s offset to form the flanker letters, and participants categorized the center target letter as before. In this case, significant flanker effects were observed only at the closest distance (see Figure 3.5C), with distance measured between the target and the four closest flankers—those appearing directly above, below, or to the left or right rather than at the diagonals. There was a suggestion of elimination of the flanker compatibility effect at 2.6 degrees of visual angle, but it remained strong and significant at 1.3 degrees. This pattern could be seen as consistent with the event-related potential data of Slotnick et al. (2002), which suggested a region of facilitation around the attended area followed further out in space by a region of inhibition.

A further experiment suggested that the center-surround pattern may be in part contingent on an endogenous search for the target's location. In this final experiment, we observed elimination of flanker compatibility effects at 1.3 degrees of visual angle. In this experiment, participants classified the red target letter in a circular array of eight block letters. Two flankers were presented 1.3, 2.6, or 3.9 degrees of visual angle from the target in a single different color. Each of the remaining distractors was a neutral letter presented in a unique color, and thus there was nothing about the target that should have attracted exogenous attention. There was a main effect of flanker compatibility, as well as a flanker compatibility by distance interaction, that reflected significant compatibility effects when flankers were 2.6 degrees away from the target but no effects when they were 1.3 degrees away (see Figure 3.5D).

The preceding experiments offer a brief glimpse of the operations of a center-surround mechanism that includes inhibition of nearby information after target selection. Our data suggest that this mechanism is manifested after a search process with more than just a few stimuli present following an endogenous search. However, there are many additional details to work out regarding the mechanism: What are the exact conditions that lead to its use, and what is the relation between the inhibitory surround and facilitatory center (e.g., the consequences for the surround of changes in the size of the area selected)?

Finally, we return to an issue with which we started this discussion of why center-surround selection in visual attention might be more readily observable in some experimental paradigms than in others. This is the issue of the difficulty of encoding the visual stimuli and discriminating them from one another. Many of the successful demonstrations of center-surround inhibition in visual attention have involved brief, hard-to-encode displays using accuracy of target identification as the dependent variable. Our first experiment reported in this section showed that a brief display is not a crucial condition: Center-surround inhibition was obtained in reaction times with above-threshold displays that remained visible until response. But this finding does not eliminate all forms of processing difficulty as potential triggers for center-surround selection. The last two experiments described in this section suggest that the total number of stimuli, or perhaps their density, appears to be important. The greater the overall stimulus load imposed by the visual environment, the more likely a center-surround pattern was to be observed in selecting one stimulus for further processing.

Conclusion

We have briefly described research on several different manifestations of processes that leave an inhibitory signature of reduced access following some form of difficult selection process. One intriguing issue in the inhibition literature remains the extent to which various inhibitory phenomena are related, and therefore it is tempting to consider the relations among the phenomena that we have described. Other empirical research on this question in general has tended to find a lack of association between putative inhibitory processes (Grant & Dagenbach, 2000; Kramer, Humphrey, Larish, Logan, & Strayer, 1994). In the phenomena that we have examined in this chapter, the extent to which the center surround seems to be implemented in visual cortex (Muller & Kleinschmidt, 2004) also seems to suggest that a different mechanism produces that effect than the one that produces the center-surround pattern in retrieval from memory. The safer assumption at present would be that inhibition is a useful solution for a particular range of cognitive processing dilemmas and one that has been used by a variety of processing mechanisms to solve them.

References

Bahcall, D. O., & Kowler, E. (1999). Attentional interference at small spatial separations. *Vision Research, 39,* 71–86.

Caputo, G., & Guerra, S. (1998). Attentional selection by distractor suppression. *Vision Research, 38,* 669–689.

Carr, T. H., & Dagenbach, D. (1990). Semantic priming and repetition priming from masked words: Evidence for a center-surround attentional mechanism in perceptual recognition. *Journal of Experimental Psychology: Learning, Memory, and Cognition, 16,* 341–350.

Carr, T. H., Dagenbach, D., VanWieren, D., Carlson-Radvansky, L. A., Alejano, A. R., & Brown, J. S. (1994). Acquiring general knowledge from specific episodes of experience. In C. Umiltà & M. Moscovitch (Eds.), *Attention and performance* (Vol. 15, pp. 697–724). Hillsdale, NJ: Erlbaum.

Cave, K. R., & Zimmerman, J. M. (1997). Flexibility in spatial attention before and after practice. *Psychological Science, 8,* 399–403.

Dagenbach, D., Carr, T. H., & Barnhardt, T. M. (1990). Inhibitory semantic priming of lexical decisions due to failure to retrieve weakly activated codes. *Journal of Experimental Psychology: Learning, Memory, and Cognition, 16,* 328–340.

Dagenbach, D., Carr, T. H., & Wilhelmson, A. (1989). Task-induced strategies and near-threshold priming: Conscious influences on unconscious perception. *Journal of Memory and Language, 28,* 412–443.

Duquette, P. J., & Dagenbach, D. (2003, February). *The development of backward inhibition in elementary school children.* Paper presented at the annual meeting of the North Carolina Cognition Group, Duke University, Durham, NC.

Eriksen, C. W., & St. James, J. D. (1986). Visual attention within and around the field of focal attention: A zoom lens model. *Perception & Psychophysics, 40,* 225–240.

Grant, J. D., & Dagenbach, D. (2000). Further considerations regarding inhibitory processes, working memory, and cognitive aging. *American Journal of Psychology, 113,* 69–94.

Kramer, A. F., Humphrey, D. G., Larish, J. F., Logan, G. D., & Strayer, D. L. (1994). Aging and inhibition: Beyond a unitary view of inhibitory processing in attention. *Psychology and Aging, 9,* 491–512.

Lavie, N. (2000). Selective attention and cognitive control: Dissociating attentional functions through different types of load. In S. Monsell & J. Driver (Eds.), *Attention and performance* (Vol. 18, pp. 175–194). Cambridge, MA: MIT Press.

Mayr, U. (2001). Age differences in the selection of mental sets: The role of inhibition, stimulus ambiguity, and response-set overlap. *Psychology and Aging, 16,* 96–109.

Mayr, U. (2002). Inhibition of action rules. *Psychonomic Bulletin and Review, 9,* 93–99.

Mayr, U., & Keele, S. W. (2000). Changing internal constraints on action: The role of backward inhibition. *Journal of Experimental Psychology: General, 129,* 4–26.

McCartney, H. J. (2001). *Exploring conditions under which center-surround effects emerge in flanker tasks.* Unpublished honors thesis, Wake Forest University, Winston-Salem, NC.

Menzer, D., & Dagenbach, D. (2002, November). *Effects of variations in response mappings on backward inhibition.* Paper presented at the annual meeting of Object Perception and Memory, Kansas City, KS.

Mounts, J. R. W. (2000a). Attentional capture by abrupt onsets and feature singletons produces inhibitory surrounds. *Perception & Psychophysics, 62,* 1485–1493.

Mounts, J. R. W. (2000b). Evidence for suppressive mechanisms in attentional selection: Feature singletons produce inhibitory surrounds. *Perception & Psychophysics, 62,* 969–983.

Muller, N. G., & Kleinschmidt, A. (2004). The spotlight's penumbra: Evidence for a center-surround organization of spatial attention in visual cortex. *Neuroreport, 15,* 977–980.

Pillsbury, W. B. (1908). *Attention.* New York: MacMillan.

Slotnick, S. D., Hopfinger, J. B., Klein, S. A., & Suttern, E. E. (2002). Darkness beyond the light: Attentional inhibition surrounding the classic spotlight. *Neuroreport, 13,* 773–778.

Townsend, J. T. (1990). Serial vs. parallel processing: Sometimes they look like Tweedledum and Tweedledee but they can (and should) be distinguished. *Psychological Science, 1,* 46–54.

4

Mechanisms of Transfer-Inappropriate Processing

W. Trammell Neill

The appearance of an object or event sometimes facilitates responding to a subsequent similar stimulus, an effect often called *priming*. However, under some circumstances, responding to a similar stimulus may be slower or less accurate than to an unrelated stimulus, referred to as *negative priming*. The cause of negative priming has been a contentious issue in cognitive psychology. Early demonstrations of negative priming (e.g., Dalrymple-Alford & Budayr, 1966; Neill, 1977; Tipper, 1985) attributed the effect to direct inhibition of some aspect of stimulus processing. However, later theories (e.g., Milliken, Joordens, Merikle, & Seiffert, 1998; Neill & Mathis, 1998; Neill, Valdes, Terry, & Gorfein, 1992) offered alternative accounts that do not invoke inhibitory processes. This chapter reevaluates some of the evidence for and against inhibition as a cause of negative priming and considers the possibility that more than one mechanism may be required to fully account for negative priming.

The first published demonstration of negative priming was by Dalrymple-Alford and Budayr (1966), in a version of the Stroop (1935) color–word task. In this task, subjects must name the color in which words are written, ignoring the word meaning, which corresponds to a different color. Dalrymple-Alford and Budayr found that the time to name all of the colors in a list was especially slow if each distractor word named the next color in the list (e.g., *green* written in red ink, followed by *yellow* written in green ink). They reasoned that naming each color required suppressing the response to the distractor word. If the suppressed response was required for the next stimulus, naming was further slowed. Neill (1977) found a similar effect on reaction times to individual Stroop words, randomly intermixed. Tipper (1985; Tipper & Cranston, 1985) extended these results to ignored pictures in a picture-naming task and ignored letters in a letter-naming task. Negative priming has since been shown in a wide variety of tasks and stimulus materials (see review by Neill, Valdes, & Terry, 1995).

It is tempting to think of (positive) priming and negative priming as opposing effects on a mental representation, analogous to the opposing effects of excitation and inhibition on the activation level of a neuron. However, it has become abundantly clear that negative priming is not simply the persisting deactivation of an activated concept. Lowe (1979) found that negative priming in the Stroop task depended on whether the color in the next trial was embedded in a conflict or nonconflict stimulus. A distractor word on a "prime" trial actually caused positive priming for a subsequent "probe" trial consisting of colored dots, even though such trials were randomly intermixed with conflict-word probe trials, which yielded negative priming. Tipper and Cranston (1985) similarly found positive priming rather than negative priming in their letter-naming task if the probe letter was not also accompanied by a distractor. They concluded that the representation of the prime-trial distractor must remain activated across trials, and so the mechanism of negative priming must operate at a later stage of processing.

Transfer-Inappropriate Processing

My colleagues and I (Neill & Valdes, 1992; Neill, Valdes, Terry, & Gorfein, 1992) proposed that negative priming is caused not by inhibition per se but rather by the retrieval of a memory trace of how the current target stimulus had been processed on a recent trial. Following ideas developed by Logan (1988, 1990), we supposed that task performance can be mediated by either retrieval of past instances of the current stimulus or by application of rule-guided algorithmic processing. These two processes are assumed to proceed in parallel. If a processing episode that contains useful response information (e.g., "press key #1") is retrieved prior to the completion of algorithmic processing, responding is facilitated (i.e., positive priming). However, if the retrieved episode indicates that the current stimulus was recently ignored, responding is impaired (i.e., negative priming).

Because negative priming had been demonstrated primarily in selective attention paradigms in which a distracting stimulus had to be ignored, most researchers initially assumed that deliberately ignoring a stimulus was necessary for negative priming. However, more recent studies have shown negative priming even for attended stimuli. For example, MacDonald, Joordens, and Seergobin (1999) required subjects to judge which of two word referents was larger (e.g., *camel* or *mouse*). A very large negative priming effect was found if the word referring to the smaller animal then appeared as the target on the next trial (e.g., *mouse* or *flea*). Any such comparison task obviously requires attention to both stimuli, although one might argue that the word selected against is subsequently inhibited. However, such an argument cannot be made for the results of Wood and Milliken (1998), in which counting the corners of nonsense shapes impaired subsequent same–different judgments for those shapes relative to shapes that had not been previously seen.

Neither inhibitory theories nor the original episodic-retrieval theory account well for negative priming caused by attended stimuli. Such results led Neill and Mathis (1998) to modify the episodic-retrieval theory such that negative priming results from the retrieval of "transfer-inappropriate" processes. As proposed by Kolers (1976; Kolers & Ostry, 1974), Neill and Mathis assumed that a stimulus tends to reinstate processing operations similar to those applied to the same (or a similar) stimulus in the past. Reinstated processes may be

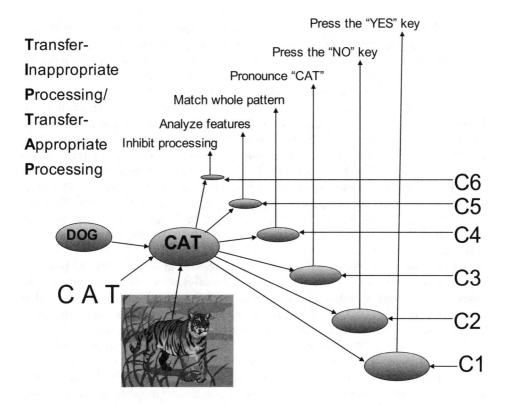

Figure 4.1.   A schematic of TIPTAP theory. C1 through C6 indicate different contexts in which various processing operations have been carried out.

either transfer appropriate or transfer inappropriate, depending on whether they are consistent with the current goal of processing.

The gist of the TIPTAP (transfer-inappropriate processing/transfer-appropriate processing) theory is displayed in Figure 4.1. In this theory, cognitive representations (i.e., "type nodes") are activated both by pattern recognition processes and by associations to related concepts. For example, the conceptual representation of "cat" might be activated by seeing a cat, by reading the word *cat*, or indirectly by its association with the activated concept "dog." Processing episodes are instantiated by tokens jointly associated to the type node, contextual information, and processes that were carried out in the particular instances. For example, in one context (C3 in Figure 4.1), subjects may have been required to pronounce the word *cat*. The "processing episode" represents the joint occurrence of the activation of the concept "cat," the specific context in which the activation occurred, and the various processes (including overt pronunciation) that were applied in that context.

As universally assumed in psychological theories, contexts vary in similarity. Accordingly, TIPTAP theory assumes that the degree to which past processing operations will be reinstated is a joint function of the activation of the type node and the similarity of the past context to the present one. For example, if the word *cat* is presented in a context similar to a previous encounter in which pronunciation was required (C3 in Figure 4.1), processing will be biased toward repeating the same operations. If those operations are appropriate to the current task requirements, positive priming will occur. However, if those operations are inappropriate to the current task requirements, they will interfere with the appropriate operations, and negative priming may occur.

The latter prediction is qualified by the assumption that even an ignored stimulus will activate its cognitive representation (type node), and positive priming can also be caused by such activation. (For arguments that positive priming can be caused by either activation of type nodes or retrieval of instances, see the review by Tenpenny, 1995.) An ignored stimulus, or one otherwise processed in a transfer-inappropriate fashion, is therefore expected to facilitate some aspects of processing while interfering with others. The net effect on responding to such a stimulus therefore depends on the relative strength of the positive and negative priming effects (Neill & Joordens, 2002; Neill & Kahan, 1999).

As suggested in Figure 4.1, reinstated processes may be construed broadly, including not only modes of processing (e.g., analytic vs. wholistic) but specific responses that were made in the presence of the stimulus. In the so-called negative priming paradigm, some response is usually made on the prime trial that is appropriate to the target but not the distractor. Rothermund, Wentura, and De Houwer (2005) provided direct evidence that the response made to a prime-trial target also becomes associated to the accompanying distractor. On prime trials, subjects were required to identify the color in which a word was written (yellow or green) by pressing one of two keys. On probe trials, subjects classified words as noun or adjective using the same two keys. On critical probe trials, the word was the same as presented on the prime trial. Relative to a new word requiring the same response, the repeated word resulted in positive priming if it required the same key press as the prime trial but negative priming if it required the opposite response.

Also as suggested by Figure 4.1, processing of a distractor might have been inhibited on a previous trial, and this inhibition might subsequently be reinstated. This possibility appears to be at the heart of Tipper's (2001) attempt to reconcile the inhibitory and episodic-retrieval views of negative priming:

> Inhibitory accounts of negative priming do not necessitate abstract logogen-like representations. Our current conceptions of inhibition are that these processes are flexibly applied to the relevant characteristics of the event or object that is selected against. It is the retrieval of this processing that is the source of negative priming, and such processing can apply equally well to any form of representation. (p. 335)

However, how does one know that negative priming in any particular experimental context is due to retrieval of inhibition rather than interference due to retrieval of some other task-incompatible operation? For example, in the comparison task of MacDonald et al. (1999), is the choice of *mouse* as larger than *flea* impaired because *mouse* was selected against on the prime trial or because it was just judged as smaller? Given that interference between processes and/or responses is well established (as evidenced by the Stroop task itself), interference effects on the probe trial seem sufficient to account for negative priming. As such, the assumption of an inhibitory process acting on the distractor during the prime trial seems gratuitous.

As noted earlier in this chapter, negative priming is often found to depend on whether a probe target is accompanied by a distractor (e.g., Lowe, 1979; Milliken et al., 1998; Neill & Kahan, 1999; Tipper & Cranston, 1985). TIPTAP theory accounts for this effect in two ways: First, retaining Logan's (1988, 1990) assumption that instance retrieval and algorithmic processing proceed in parallel, priming effects due to instance retrieval depend on the probability that such retrieval occurs prior to the completion of algorithmic processing. Consequently, faster algorithmic processing (as when no distractor accompanies the probe target) must reduce both positive and negative priming. Second, the absence of a distractor on the probe trial may reduce the contextual similarity to the prime trial (in which a distractor appeared). The reduction of contextual similarity should reduce the probability that the probe target cues the retrieval of the prime distractor.

Neill (1997) demonstrated that both negative priming and positive priming are affected by contextual similarity between prime and probe trials. Subjects were required to identify letter targets flanked by distractor letters (e.g., ABA). The contextual manipulation was whether the distractors appeared simultaneously with the target (early onset) or were delayed by 400 milliseconds (late onset). In Experiment 1, probe targets either matched the prime-trial distractor or were unrelated; in Experiment 2, probe targets either matched the prime-trial target or were unrelated. Negative priming in Experiment 1 was significant only when prime and probe trials had similar distractor onsets (see Figure 4.2). Repetition priming in Experiment 2 was also affected by contextual similarity, although significant priming remained even when contexts were mismatched. The latter effect is presumably due to persisting activation of the type node. Other studies have reported similar effects of contextual similarity on negative priming (e.g., Fox & De Fockert, 1998; Neill & Valdes, 1996).

Some researchers have attempted to manipulate contextual similarity but failed to find an effect on negative priming, leading them to conclude that negative priming was caused by inhibition instead of episodic retrieval. Such null results are unconvincing if there is no converging evidence that the manipulation of contextual similarity was sufficiently strong to measurably influence retrieval. However, Wong (2000) provided just such convergent evidence, yet still found negative priming independent of contextual similarity. Like Neill (1997), Wong required subjects to identify target letters flanked by distractor letters. In his Experiment 1, Wong manipulated context by presenting a pair of plus signs to the left and right of the triplet (e.g., +ABA+) or above and below it. In his Experiments 2 and 3, some triplets had exclamation points inserted between the letters (e.g., A!B!C), and others did not. In all three experiments, contextual similarity between prime and probe trials influenced positive priming but had no effect on negative priming.

Wong's (2000) results are problematic for TIPTAP theory as a complete account of negative priming. His results for positive repetition priming confirm that his contextual manipulation was strong enough to affect episodic retrieval. It is unclear why Wong's contextual manipulation affected positive priming

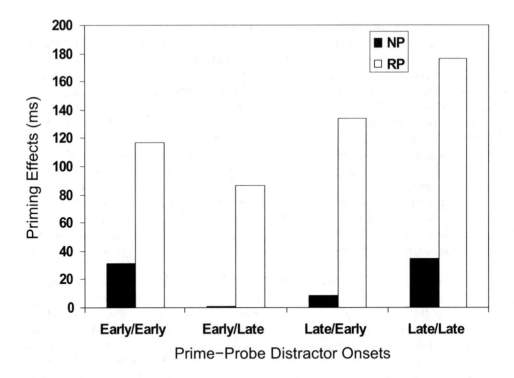

Figure 4.2. Negative priming (NP) and repetition priming (RP) as a function of prime and probe distractor onsets (Neill, 1997).

but not negative priming, whereas the manipulations by Neill (1997) and Fox and De Fockert (1998) did affect negative priming. Given that other evidence also supports a contribution of episodic retrieval (see review by Neill & Mathis, 1998, as well as Rothermund et al., 2005), one must entertain the possibility that there are at least two sources of negative priming, one context dependent and the other context independent. I speculate that the latter is response suppression, whereas the former operates at a perceptual and/or conceptual level for reasons I explain later in this chapter.

Levels of Processing in Negative Priming

In the Stroop task, there is no physical similarity between the letters of the word and any particular color. That ignoring a distractor word retards the response to its referent color on the next trial (Dalrymple-Alford & Budayr, 1966; Lowe, 1979; Neill, 1977) implies that the effect must occur postperceptually—that is, at a common abstract level of representation or possibly the naming response. Similarly, Tipper and Driver (1988) found negative priming between words and pictures, excluding a purely perceptual locus. Other studies seemed to rule out response suppression as the cause of negative priming: Tipper, MacQueen, and Brehaut (1988) found as much negative priming in a letter identification task when prime and probe trials required opposite response modalities (vocal or manual) as when they required the same modality. Neill, Lissner, and Beck (1990) investigated negative priming in a same–different matching task in which subjects had to match the second and fourth letters of a five-letter string (e.g., ABACA). Negative priming did not depend on whether the probe trial required the same response as the prime trial or the opposite response.

Given that some studies appear to exclude a perceptual locus of negative priming and some to exclude a response locus, a natural "default" conclusion has been that negative priming occurs at a "central" cognitive level of representation, postperceptual but preresponse (cf. Neill et al., 1990; Tipper et al., 1988). However, this logic is faulty. It is possible that negative priming can occur both for perceptual patterns and for responses. Indeed, response suppression remains a plausible explanation for negative priming in most experiments that have excluded perceptual effects, and perceptual effects may account for negative priming in most experiments that have controlled for response effects.

In the majority of experiments on negative priming, there is a one-to-one-to-one correspondence of perceptual pattern, conceptual representation, and response. For example, in a letter identification task, negative priming by an ignored letter A might be specific to the perceptual pattern (distinct from a), or it might occur for a more abstract orthographic representation (shared with a), or it might cause suppression of an overt naming response or corresponding key press. There are, however, a few studies that do indicate specifically perceptual effects of negative priming and a few others that indicate effects directly on responses.

Negative Priming as a Perceptual Effect

Although many experiments have investigated negative priming related to the form (shape or identity) of an ignored stimulus, some have investigated effects of the location of an ignored stimulus. Tipper, Brehaut, and Driver (1990) required subjects to press a key corresponding to the location of a target, @, ignoring a distractor, +, in one of three other locations. If a probe-trial target appeared in the same location as the prime-trial distractor, localization time was slowed relative to a target in a new location. The locations of the targets and distractors were confounded with the responses made to them in most experiments on location negative priming. However, Neill, Valdes, and Terry (1992; summarized in Neill et al., 1995) reported an experiment in which subjects pressed one key for a target in either of the two leftmost locations and another key for a target in either of the two rightmost locations. If a probe target appeared in the same location as the prime-trial distractor, reaction time was slower than if the target appeared in the other location requiring the same response. Hence, negative priming in the localization task must have a location-specific component independent of response.

I reported an experiment (Neill, 1991) using a same–different matching task similar to that of Neill et al. (1990) but with letter strings varying in case. Negative priming occurred for same-case sequences (e.g., ABABA–DADAD or ababa–dadad) but not for opposite-case sequences (e.g., ABABA–dadad). Hence, at least in a task that could be performed by matching the physical patterns, negative priming did not generalize to the more abstract orthographic representation. DeSchepper and Treisman (1996) also found negative priming in a same–different matching task with unfamiliar nonsense shapes. De-Schepper and Treisman argued that because there could be no preexisting cognitive representation to inhibit, the effect had to be due to a persisting trace of the perceptual encounter together with information that it had been ignored rather than attended—in other words, a processing episode.

An experiment by Treisman and DeSchepper (1996, Experiment 4) is particularly important for demonstrating that negative priming depends on retrieval of specific instances. They investigated the effect of presenting a nonsense shape twice as a prime—first as a to-be-ignored distractor and again as a to-be-matched target. Subjects were then tested on old and new patterns after a delay of 1 day, 1 week, or 1 month. At the 1-day delay, the old patterns produced positive priming relative to the new patterns, indicating that the most recent experience of attending to the pattern enhanced processing. However, for the 1-week and 1-month delays, priming reversed to negative, and negative priming at the longest delay was equivalent to patterns that had been previously ignored but not previously attended. Hence, the two priming exposures must have been retained as separate episodes, with the more recent episode dominating performance at the shortest delay but the initial episode dominating performance at longer delays. This was exactly the pattern found for proactive and retroactive interference in paired-associate learning (Koppenaal, 1963; Postman, Stark, & Fraser, 1968; Underwood, 1948).

These studies show that negative priming can be specific to perceptual patterns. An experiment by Neill and Terry (1995) demonstrated that negative priming can also have consequences for the conscious perception of a probe target. Whereas most studies of negative priming have used reaction time measures, this study used unspeeded identification accuracy. Subjects were required on each trial to identify a target letter flanked by distractor letters (e.g., ABA). On prime trials, the letter triplets were presented for 100 or 300 milliseconds, followed by a pattern mask. On probe trials, triplets were shown for 0, 33, 100, or 300 milliseconds, again followed by a pattern mask. For the nonzero exposure durations, identification accuracy was significantly reduced for probe-trial targets that matched the ignored prime-trial distractors. However, for the zero-duration trials (i.e., "catch trials"), subjects showed no bias against guessing the letter that had appeared as the prime-trial distractor.

Neill and Terry's (1995) results strongly indicate that some mechanism of negative priming—whether it is persisting inhibition or episodic retrieval—operates prior to the conscious awareness of the probe target. The effect appears to be wholly perceptual: Because speeded responses were not required, it seems implausible that subjects could become aware of the perceptual features yet have difficulty selecting or executing an appropriate response sometime thereafter. (Suppression of a response would also have been manifested on the catch trials.) By the same reasoning, the effect is not likely to be on a more abstract orthographic representation. Because only four letters were used (A, B, C,

and D), perception of the physical features should have been completely sufficient to identify the letter and to select a response.

An experiment by Buchner and Steffens (2001, Experiment 2) may have
implications similar to those of Neill and Terry (1995). Subjects were required
to make temporal-order judgments between two musical sounds, responding
according to which ear received the earlier sound. If the sound that was correctly
selected against on a prime trial appeared simultaneously with a new sound
on the probe trial, subjects were more likely to select the new sound as earlier.
Unfortunately, it is unclear whether the results are genuinely perceptual,
because they might instead be simply attributable to a decision bias resulting
from having just categorized the sound as later rather than earlier. Buchner
and Steffens also argued that their result favors an inhibitory theory of negative
priming over an episodic-retrieval theory. However, TIPTAP theory does not
make any assumptions about whether retrieval occurs before or after conscious
awareness of the probe target. It is possible that the processing operations
that are reinstated for a repeated stimulus affect the time at which the stimulus
is consciously perceived as well as the likelihood that it is perceived at all.

Negative Priming as a Response Effect

As discussed in the previous section, negative priming in some experiments is
specific to the perceptual pattern and cannot be explained as any form of
suppression of a response. Some experiments, such as that of Rothermund et al.
(2005), suggested that negative priming can occur as a result of associating an
inappropriate response to an ignored distractor. However, negative priming in
the Rothermund et al. study still depended on the identity of the ignored prime-
trial distractor and related probe target. For probe trials that did not repeat
the prime-trial word, there was no difference in reaction time between response
repetitions and response alternations. Thus, there was no evidence for a suppression of any response independent of the stimulus identity.

Conversely, there are at least a couple of studies in which the negative
priming effects do appear to be due to suppression of a specific response.
Buckolz, Goldfarb, and Khan (2004) used a localization task in which five
possible target locations were mapped to four possible responses. For the middle
location (L3), subjects could freely choose between the responses required for
the second or fourth locations (L2 or L4). On critical prime–probe sequences,
a distractor appeared at L3, followed by a target at L2 or L4. Reaction time
was slowed relative to when the prime distractor had occurred at an unrelated
position. Because L3 is related to L2 or L4 only by virtue of sharing a common
response, the negative priming effect must be due to response suppression.
Surprisingly, the effect was as great as when the prime-trial distractor and
probe-trial target actually appeared at the same location. Thus, contrary to
the result of Neill, Valdes, and Terry (1992) in a similar design, there was no
evidence for a location-specific component.

An experiment by Shiu and Kornblum (1996) demonstrated a response
suppression effect in a task requiring stimulus identification. Subjects were

taught new, incompatible naming responses to four pictures. For example, one group of subjects had to respond "boat" to a bicycle, "plane" to a boat, "bike" to a car, and "car" to an airplane. On critical prime–probe sequences, the required response to the probe picture was the same as that naturally evoked by the prime picture—for example, a bicycle (requiring the response "boat") following a boat (to which subjects responded "plane"). Reaction time was slowed relative to a probe target unrelated to the prime—for example, a bicycle (requiring the response "boat") following an airplane (to which subjects responded "car"). Shiu and Kornblum concluded that generating the new, incompatible response to a picture required suppressing the naturally compatible response, making that response less available for the next trial. (The logic in this experiment was essentially the same as in the independent cue technique devised by Anderson & Spellman, 1995, to probe retrieval-induced forgetting; see chap. 5, this volume.)

The negative priming results of Buckholz et al. (2004) and Shiu and Kornblum (1996) are awkward for TIPTAP theory to explain. In both studies, the only relation between the prime and probe is the response that must be withheld on the prime trial but executed on the probe trial. As Shiu and Kornblum acknowledged, it is conceivable that the response selected on the probe trial cues a memory that the same response was inappropriate in the previous trial. However, as they correctly observed, "This is a significant departure from the original theory" (p. 512). TIPTAP theory, like the earlier episodic-retrieval theory, assumes that episodic retrieval is part of the processing that ultimately leads to response selection, not the other way around. It seems more parsimonious to simply assume that conflicting responses can be inhibited and that this inhibition persists over time.

Negative Priming as a Conceptual Effect

Given that negative priming can occur at a perceptual level or at a response level, is there any evidence for an effect between those levels? That is, can it occur at a central level of representation, more abstract than the perceptual pattern but prior to the actual response? The evidence is surprisingly sparser than researchers have typically assumed. Tipper (1985) demonstrated what has often been interpreted as "semantic generalization" of negative priming, finding that an ignored prime-trial picture slowed the naming of a categorically related picture on the probe trial. For example, ignoring a picture of a cat slowed the subsequent naming of a pictured dog. However, as Tipper and Driver (1988) acknowledged, the semantically related pictures in the earlier study were also perceptually similar. Therefore, it is possible that negative priming simply occurred for the perceptual pattern and extended to other structurally similar patterns.

Tipper and Driver (1988) demonstrated negative priming between words and pictures not only for the same type of object (e.g., picture of a dog and the word *dog*) but also between words and pictures for different members of the same category (e.g., picture of a cat and the word *dog*). Because words are not perceptually similar to their referents, the effect had to be postperceptual.

However, the task used in this study was to name the superordinate category of the object to which the word or picture referred (e.g., *animal*). Because the categorically related objects required the same response, it is possible that generalized negative priming was due to suppression of the response per se rather than a shared semantic representation.

Although Tipper and Driver (1988) found negative priming between semantically related words and pictures, they did not find significant negative priming between two semantically related words. Chiappe and MacLeod (1995) investigated negative priming by ignored words in both naming and categorization tasks. In some conditions, subjects actually switched tasks between the prime and probe trials. If a prime-trial distractor word appeared as the probe-trial target, negative priming occurred regardless of whether the same task was repeated. Therefore, negative priming was not due to response suppression. However, Chiappe and MacLeod also failed to find any negative priming for a categorically related probe word, regardless of whether the same task was repeated. MacLeod, Chiappe, and Fox (2002) similarly failed to find negative priming between categorically related or associatively related words in a naming task.

Studies investigating negative priming effects in naming or categorization tasks typically use a small set of stimuli, repeated over the experiment, and often familiarize subjects with the stimuli beforehand to minimize ambiguity regarding the correct response. Although smaller, frequently repeated stimulus sets typically yield greater negative priming (Malley & Strayer, 1995; Strayer & Grison, 1999; see also discussion by Neill & Joordens, 2002), such familiarization may also diminish reliance on semantic processing, and so generalization of negative priming to related words may be more difficult to obtain. Lexical decision (word–nonword judgment) tasks, which accommodate larger stimulus sets, have yielded somewhat better success at obtaining semantic and/or associative generalization of negative priming between words (Fox, 1994, 1996; Fuentes & Tudela, 1992; Mari-Beffa, Fuentes, Catena, & Houghton, 2000; Ortells, Abad, Noguera, & Lupianez, 2001; Ortells & Tudela, 1996; Yee, 1991). Response suppression is ruled out as an explanation for negative priming in the lexical decision task, because the same response is required on both related and unrelated probe trials (i.e., *word*).

Hutchison (2002) shed some light on factors that may be necessary to obtain negative priming between different words by using asymmetrically associated word pairs (e.g., *stork* and *baby*). Subjects were required on each trial to make a word–nonword judgment for a letter string displayed in red, ignoring an overlapping distractor word in green. For prime–probe pairs in which the prime-trial distractor was related to the probe target, the words could be associated in the forward direction (*stork–baby*) or in the backward direction (*baby–stork*). Negative priming occurred only in the forward direction.

As discussed by Hutchison (2002), negative priming in the forward direction is predicted by inhibitory theories of negative priming. That is, a distractor *stork* on a prime trial would activate the concept "baby," which would then be inhibited and so slow responding to a probe word *baby*. In contrast, a distractor *baby* would not activate "stork," and so there would be no effect on responding to a probe word *stork*. The predictions of episodic retrieval are more ambiguous in this case: One possibility is that the probe word *stork* might activate "baby," which in turn would cue the retrieval of the prime-trial episode including *baby,* producing negative priming in the backward direction. However, it is also likely that *stork* on the prime trial would activate "baby," which would also be encoded in the processing episode. *Baby* on the probe trial would then cue the retrieval of that episode, causing negative priming in the forward direction. Thus, the implication of Hutchison's result for TIPTAP theory is that word associations are encoded in processing episodes but may not serve as effective retrieval cues.

As Hutchison (2002) noted, semantic (or associative) negative priming has been fragile in previous studies, often vanishing with relatively minor changes in conditions. However, it should also be noted that negative priming between associated words constitutes an especially stringent test for negative priming of conceptual representations, because it requires not only a conceptual representation of the ignored distractor word but, in addition, the generalization of negative priming to other associated conceptual representations. Thus, although negative priming between associated words implies a conceptual-level effect, the lack of such an effect does not imply the absence of negative priming for conceptual representations per se.

A more direct test of conceptual-level negative priming requires prime distractors and probe targets that (a) are perceptually dissimilar, (b) correspond to the same concept, and (c) share the same response with a control condition in which the prime and probe do not correspond to the same concept. To the best of my knowledge, only one published study has used this design: Buchner, Zabal, and Mayr (2003) required subjects to categorize either auditory or visual targets as *animal* or *musical instrument* by key press. Four animal sounds (bird, chicken, frog, lamb) and four musical sounds (English horn, guitar, piano, drum) corresponded to line drawings of the same animals and instruments. On an auditory trial, a click on the left or right ear cued which of two subsequent sounds was the target; on a visual trial, a red or blue dot cued which of two overlapping drawings was the target. Two groups of subjects received all trials in the same modality; two other groups received prime and probe trials in opposite modalities. The crucial result was that negative priming was obtained cross modally. For example, ignoring the sound of a frog on the prime trial resulted in slower classification of the picture of a frog as *animal* relative to having ignored the bleating of a lamb (which would require the same response as a frog). Because the ignored prime and related target were perceptually dissimilar, but required the same overt response as the control condition, negative priming must have resulted from their conceptual similarity.

Conclusion

In the debate over whether the construct of inhibition has explanatory power in the study of cognition and behavior, it is important to distinguish between inhibition as a cause and inhibition as an effect. In a broad sense, turning left inhibits turning right just because the one action precludes the other. In the same sense, driving north on a highway inhibits driving south, and choosing a career as a cognitive psychologist inhibits becoming a famous rock 'n' roll star. But inhibition by itself does not really explain why one is not turning right, not driving south, or not a famous rock 'n' roll star. Certain behaviors, and by extension certain cognitive processes, interfere with certain outcomes. It is for exactly this reason that the classic literature on learning paired associations shifted from the terminology of proactive and retroactive *inhibition* to proactive and retroactive *interference* to describe the effects of A–B/A–C learning paradigms. TIPTAP theory asserts that negative priming is simply proactive interference between what was learned on a prime trial and what must be retrieved or computed on a probe trial.

Although a number of studies implicate an episodic retrieval process underlying negative priming (e.g., DeSchepper & Treisman, 1996; Neill, 1997; Neill, Valdes, Terry, & Gorfein, 1992; Rothermund et al., 2005; Treisman & DeSchepper, 1996), a context-independent inhibitory process may account better for the results of some other studies (Buckolz et al., 2004; Shiu & Kornblum, 1996; Wong, 2000). It seems reasonable to conclude, therefore, that there are at least two distinctly different mechanisms that can cause negative priming.

The corpus of research on negative priming indicates that it can occur at least at three qualitatively different levels of representation: perceptual pattern, abstract concept, and response. There is no reason to assume that the same underlying mechanism applies to all three levels. In many experiments, it is difficult to pinpoint the locus of the negative priming effect because there is a one-to-one-to-one correspondence among the perceptual pattern, concept, and response (e.g., Neill, 1997; Wong, 2000). However, episodic retrieval is implicated in some studies that excluded response suppression as the cause of negative priming (DeSchepper & Treisman, 1996; Rothermund et al., 2005; Treisman & DeSchepper, 1996; Wood & Milliken, 1998). TIPTAP theory (Neill & Mathis, 1998) accounts for negative priming of perceptual and conceptual representations. However, of the three studies that pose difficulties for TIPTAP theory, two (Buckolz et al., 2004; Shiu & Kornblum, 1996) clearly implicated response suppression as a cause of negative priming, and the third (Wong, 2000) was ambiguous as to the locus of the effect. I speculate, then, that negative priming of perceptual and conceptual representations is caused by episodic retrieval, whereas negative priming of responses is truly caused by inhibition.

The proposal that negative priming can be caused by multiple mechanisms is not novel; similar proposals have been made by May and colleagues (Kane, May, Hasher, & Rahhal, 1997; May, Kane, & Hasher, 1995); Fox (1995); and Tipper and Milliken (1996). In opposition, my colleagues and I (Neill, 1997; Neill & Joordens, 2002; Neill & Mathis, 1998) have argued that episodic retrieval accounts equally well for the evidence cited by those authors (and others) in favor of inhibition. Given that recent data more strongly compel the conclusion of multiple mechanisms, the crucial question is how to distinguish between these mechanisms in a particular experimental setting. May et al. (1995) suggested that negative priming is more likely to reflect inhibition if (a) stimulus durations are long, (b) the task does not encourage postlexical processing, and (c) target repetitions are excluded. However, as I have discussed in an earlier work (Neill, 1997), all of the experiments that provided the strongest evidence for episodic retrieval satisfied these constraints perfectly.

In addition to its implications for theories of cognitive processing, negative priming has garnered much interest as a possible index of individual differences in inhibitory functioning. For example, some studies have found diminished negative priming in elderly subjects (e.g., Hasher, Stoltzfus, Zacks, & Rypma, 1991; McDowd & Oseas-Kreger, 1991; Tipper, 1991), leading to speculation that cognitive deficits in older adults are a consequence of impaired inhibition of distracting information. Of course, if negative priming is caused by episodic retrieval instead of inhibition, diminished negative priming would as plausibly result from impaired retrieval processes. The present analysis of the causes of negative priming suggests that it would be of benefit to use tasks that map multiple stimuli to the same response in order to determine whether individual differences in negative priming reflect perceptual, conceptual, or response processes.

References

Anderson, M. C., & Spellman, B. A. (1995). On the status of inhibitory mechanisms in cognition: Memory retrieval as a model case. *Psychological Review, 102,* 68–100.

Buchner, A., & Steffens, M. C. (2001). Auditory negative priming in speeded reactions and temporal order judgements. *Quarterly Journal of Experimental Psychology, 54A,* 1125–1143.

Buchner, A., Zabal, A., & Mayr, S. (2003). Auditory, visual, and cross-modal negative priming. *Psychonomic Bulletin & Review, 10,* 917–923.

Buckolz, E., Goldfarb, A., & Khan, M. (2004). The use of a distractor-assigned response slows later responding in a location negative priming task. *Perception & Psychophysics, 66,* 837–845.

Chiappe, D. L., & MacLeod, C. M. (1995). Negative priming is not task bound: A consistent pattern across naming and categorization tasks. *Psychonomic Bulletin & Review, 2,* 364–369.

Dalrymple-Alford, E. C., & Budayr, D. (1966). Examination of some aspects of the Stroop color–word test. *Perceptual & Motor Skills, 23,* 1211–1214.

DeSchepper, B., & Treisman, A. M. (1996). Visual memory for novel shapes: Implicit coding without attention. *Journal of Experimental Psychology: Learning, Memory, and Cognition, 22,* 27–47.

Fox, E. (1994). Attentional bias in anxiety: A defective inhibition hypothesis. *Cognition & Emotion, 8,* 165–195.

Fox, E. (1995). Negative priming from ignored distractors in visual selection: A review. *Psychonomic Bulletin & Review, 2,* 145–173.

Fox, E. (1996). Cross-language priming from ignored words: Evidence for a common representational system. *Journal of Memory and Language, 35,* 353–370.

Fox, E., & de Fockert, J. W. (1998). Negative priming depends on prime–probe similarity: Evidence for episodic retrieval. *Psychonomic Bulletin & Review, 2,* 107–113.

Fuentes, L. J., & Tudela, P. (1992). Semantic processing of foveally and parafoveally presented words in a lexical decision task. *Quarterly Journal of Experimental Psychology, 45A,* 299–322.

Hasher, L., Stoltzfus, E. R., Zacks, R. T., & Rypma, B. (1991). Age and inhibition. *Journal of Experimental Psychology: Learning, Memory, and Cognition, 17,* 163–169.

Hutchison, K. A. (2002). The effect of asymmetrical association on positive and negative semantic priming. *Memory & Cognition, 30,* 1263–1276.

Kane, M. J., May, C. P., Hasher, L., & Rahhal, T. (1997). Dual mechanisms of negative priming. *Journal of Experimental Psychology: Human Perception and Performance, 23,* 632–650.

Kolers, P. A. (1976). Reading a year later. *Journal of Experimental Psychology: Human Perception and Performance, 2,* 554–565.

Kolers, P. A., & Ostry, D. J. (1974). Time course of loss of information regarding pattern analyzing operations. *Journal of Verbal Learning and Verbal Behavior, 13,* 599–612.

Koppenaal, R. J. (1963). Time changes in the strengths of A–B, A–C lists: Spontaneous recovery? *Journal of Verbal Learning and Verbal Behavior, 2,* 310–319.

Logan, G. D. (1988). Toward an instance theory of automatization. *Psychological Review, 95,* 492–527.

Logan, G. D. (1990). Repetition priming and automaticity: Common underlying mechanisms? *Cognitive Psychology, 22,* 1–35.

Lowe, D. G. (1979). Strategies, context, and the mechanism of response inhibition. *Memory & Cognition, 7,* 382–389.

MacDonald, P. A., Joordens, S., & Seergobin, K. N. (1999). Negative priming effects that are bigger than a breadbox: Attention to distractors does not eliminate negative priming, it enhances it. *Memory & Cognition, 27,* 197–207.

MacLeod, C. M., Chiappe, D. L., & Fox, E. (2002). The crucial roles of stimulus matching and stimulus identity in negative priming. *Psychonomic Bulletin & Review, 9,* 521–528.

Malley, G. B., & Strayer, D. L. (1995). Effects of stimulus repetition on positive and negative identity priming. *Perception & Psychophysics, 57,* 657–667.

Mari-Beffa, P., Fuentes, L. J., Catena, A., & Houghton, G. (2000). Semantic priming in the prime task effect: Evidence of automatic semantic processing of distractors. *Memory & Cognition, 28,* 635–648.

May, C. P., Kane, M. J., & Hasher, L. (1995). Determinants of negative priming. *Psychological Bulletin, 118,* 35–54.

McDowd, J. M., & Oseas-Kreger, D. M. (1991). Aging, inhibitory processes, and negative priming. *Journal of Gerontology: Psychology Sciences, 46,* 340–345.

Milliken, B., Joordens, S., Merikle, P., & Seiffert, A. (1998). Selective attention: A re-evaluation of the implications of negative priming. *Psychological Review, 105,* 203–229.

Neill, W. T. (1977). Inhibitory and facilitatory processes in selective attention. *Journal of Experimental Psychology: Human Perception and Performance, 3,* 444–450.

Neill, W. T. (1991, August). *Consciousness and the inhibitory control of cognition.* Paper presented at the 99th Annual Convention of the American Psychological Association, San Francisco.

Neill, W. T. (1997). Episodic retrieval in negative priming and repetition priming. *Journal of Experimental Psychology: Learning, Memory, and Cognition, 23,* 1291–1305.

Neill, W. T., & Joordens, S. (2002). Negative priming and stimulus repetition: A reply to Grison and Strayer (2001). *Perception & Psychophysics, 64,* 855–860.

Neill, W. T., & Kahan, T. A. (1999). Response conflict reverses priming: A replication. *Psychonomic Bulletin & Review, 6,* 304–308.

Neill, W. T., Lissner, L. S., & Beck, J. L. (1990). Negative priming in same–different matching: Further evidence for a central locus of inhibition. *Perception & Psychophysics, 48,* 398–400.

Neill, W. T., & Mathis, K. M. (1998). Transfer-inappropriate processing: Negative priming and related phenomena. In D. L. Medin (Ed.), *The psychology of learning and motivation: Advances in research and theory* (Vol. 38, pp. 1–44). San Diego, CA: Academic Press.

Neill, W. T., & Terry, K. M. (1995). Negative priming without reaction time: Effects on identification of masked letters. *Psychonomic Bulletin & Review, 2,* 121–123.

Neill, W. T., & Valdes, L. A. (1992). The persistence of negative priming: Steady state or decay? *Journal of Experimental Psychology: Learning, Memory, and Cognition, 18,* 565–576.

Neill, W. T., & Valdes, L. A. (1996). Facilitatory and inhibitory aspects of attention. In A. F. Kramer, M. G. H. Coles, & G. D. Logan (Eds.), *Converging operations in the study of visual selective attention* (pp. 77–106). Washington, DC: American Psychological Association.

Neill, W. T., Valdes, L. A., & Terry, K. M. (1992, November). *Negative priming in target localization.* Paper presented at the meeting of the Psychonomic Society, St. Louis, MO.

Neill, W. T., Valdes, L. A., & Terry, K. M. (1995). Selective attention and the inhibitory control of attention. In F. N. Dempster & C. J. Brainerd (Eds.), *Interference and inhibition in cognition* (pp. 207–261). San Diego, CA: Academic Press.

Neill, W. T., Valdes, L. A., Terry, K. M., & Gorfein, D. S. (1992). The persistence of negative priming: II. Evidence for episodic trace retrieval. *Journal of Experimental Psychology: Learning, Memory, and Cognition, 18,* 993–1000.

Ortells, J. J., Abad, M. J. F., Noguera, C., & Lupianez, J. (2001). Influence of prime–probe stimulus onset asynchrony and prime precuing manipulations on semantic priming effects with words in a lexical decision task. *Journal of Experimental Psychology: Human Perception & Performance, 27,* 75–91.

Ortells, J. J., & Tudela, P. (1996). Positive and negative priming of attended and unattended parafoveal words in a lexical decision task. *Acta Psychologica, 94,* 209–226.

Postman, L., Stark, K., & Fraser, J. (1968). Temporal changes in interference. *Journal of Verbal Learning and Verbal Behavior, 7,* 672–694.

Rothermund, K., Wentura, D., & De Houwer, J. (2005). Retrieval of incidental stimulus–response associations as a source of negative priming. *Journal of Experimental Psychology: Learning, Memory, and Cognition, 31,* 482–495.

Shiu, L.-P., & Kornblum, S. (1996). Negative priming and stimulus–response compatibility. *Psychonomic Bulletin & Review, 3,* 510–514.

Strayer, D. L., & Grison, S. (1999). Negative identity priming is contingent on stimulus repetition. *Journal of Experimental Psychology: Human Perception and Performance, 25,* 24–38.

Stroop, J. R. (1935). Studies of interference in serial verbal reactions. *Journal of Experimental Psychology, 18,* 643–662.

Tenpenny, P. L. (1995). Abstractionist versus episodic theories of repetition priming and word identification. *Psychological Bulletin & Review, 2,* 339–363.

Tipper, S. P. (1985). The negative priming effect: Inhibitory priming by ignored objects. *Quarterly Journal of Experimental Psychology, 37A,* 571–590.

Tipper, S. P. (1991). Less attentional selectivity as a result of declining inhibition in older adults. *Bulletin of the Psychonomic Society, 29,* 45–47.

Tipper, S. P. (2001). Does negative priming reflect inhibitory mechanisms? A review and integration of conflicting views. *Quarterly Journal of Experimental Psychology, 54A,* 321–343.

Tipper, S. P., Brehaut, J. C., & Driver, J. (1990). Selection of moving and static objects for the control of spatially directed action. *Journal of Experimental Psychology: Human Perception and Performance, 16,* 492–504.

Tipper, S. P., & Cranston, M. (1985). Selective attention and priming: Inhibitory and facilitatory effects of ignored primes. *Quarterly Journal of Experimental Psychology, 37A,* 591–611.

Tipper, S. P., & Driver, J. (1988). Negative priming between pictures and words in a selective attention task: Evidence for semantic processing of ignored stimuli. *Memory & Cognition, 16,* 64–70.

Tipper, S. P., MacQueen, G. M., & Brehaut, J. C. (1988). Negative priming between response modalities: Evidence for the central locus of inhibition in selective attention. *Perception & Psychophysics, 43,* 45–52.

Tipper, S. P., & Milliken, B. (1996). Distinguishing between inhibition-based and episodic-retrieval-based accounts of negative priming. In A. F. Kramer, M. G. H. Coles, & G. D. Logan (Eds.), *Converging operations in the study of visual selective attention* (pp. 337–364). Washington, DC: American Psychological Association.

Treisman, A. M., & DeSchepper, B. (1996). Object tokens, attention, and visual memory. In T. Inui & J. L. McClelland (Eds.), *Attention and performance* (Vol. 16, pp. 15–46). Cambridge, MA: MIT Press.

Underwood, B. J. (1948). Retroactive and proactive inhibition after five and forty-eight hours. *Journal of Experimental Psychology, 38,* 29–38.

Wong, K. F. E. (2000). Dissociative prime–probe contextual similarity effects on negative priming and repetition priming: A challenge to episodic retrieval as a unified account of negative priming. *Journal of Experimental Psychology: Learning, Memory, and Cognition, 26,* 1411–1422.

Wood, T. J., & Milliken, B. (1998). Negative priming without ignoring. *Psychonomic Bulletin & Review, 5,* 470–475.

Yee, P. L. (1991). Semantic inhibition of ignored words during a figure classification task. *Quarterly Journal of Experimental Psychology, 43A,* 127–153.

Part III

Memory and Language

5

Theoretical Issues in Inhibition: Insights From Research on Human Memory

Michael C. Anderson and Benjamin J. Levy

Several years ago, Benjamin J. Levy married the woman he had been dating for several years. On numerous occasions after the wedding, he mistakenly referred to his new wife as his "girlfriend." During the years of courtship, he had become so accustomed to referring to her in this manner that the word just popped to mind when thinking of her. The recent marriage made that label problematic, however. His frequent references to his "girlfriend" left others to assume he had taken a mistress and was simply very candid about the fact. Although amusing at first, the humor of these mistakes was quickly lost on his wife. With effort and attention, however, he was able to override this well-practiced response and refer to her as his "wife." This example illustrates a simple point: Often people are victims of an overly effective retrieval system.

Although this example is amusing, people often encounter reminders of things that they are much more motivated to avoid thinking about, such as a painful breakup, a particularly odious task, or a loved one who has passed away. In these circumstances, they may exert effort to prevent these memories from occupying their thoughts. How can one prevent intrusive, unwanted memories from coming to mind? Research from our laboratory suggests that people recruit executive control to override the retrieval of unwanted memories and that this cognitive act induces a lasting suppression of the unwanted memories, making them more difficult to recall later even when they want to return to them (for a review, see M. C. Anderson, 2003).

A core theme of this research is that people's ability to control unwanted memories is directly analogous to their ability to control their overt behavior, a topic broadly studied in cognitive psychology and in cognitive neuroscience. In fact, avoiding unwanted memories resembles a classic situation that requires executive control, often referred to as *response override*. One must stop a prepotent response to a stimulus, either because that response must be withheld or because an alternative more weakly learned response to that stimulus is desired. The ability to stop prepotent responses is critical to the flexible control of behavior, whether the response is that of a baseball player stopping the swing of the bat when the pitch is a ball, a husband avoiding embarrassment, or a person preventing an unpleasant memory from coming to mind. Without this ability, people would be slaves to their habits and reflexes.

Our suggestion, one in keeping with other research on executive control, is that people accomplish this control through inhibition of the prepotent response. When people are presented with reminders of unwanted memories, activation spreads from the cue to the traces stored in memory. If the dominant trace is not currently desired, either because the rememberer wishes to avoid thinking about it or because a more weakly associated trace is sought, then inhibition can be engaged to weaken the dominant memory, enabling him or her to stop retrieval or to have selective control over what is retrieved. We argue that these inhibitory mechanisms also have a lasting effect, leading to memory impairments for the avoided memories even later when people want to retrieve them.

In this chapter, we discuss evidence that uniquely supports this inhibitory control perspective in two response override situations in memory: the desire to stop retrieval and the need to selectively retrieve a memory. Then we describe a theoretical problem in the measurement of inhibition that is typically ignored in studies of inhibition. This issue, the correlated costs and benefits (CCB) problem, has extremely important consequences for the ability to adequately test theoretical models of inhibition and particularly for the ability to test inhibitory deficit theories concerning different populations of subjects. We argue that to make a strong claim in any study about the presence or absence of inhibition or about variations in the magnitude of inhibition as a function of condition or population, it is necessary to include an independent probe of the impaired items' accessibility. Without the independent probe, measurements of inhibition will suffer the CCB problem, precluding principled predictions about how behavioral effects should vary according to inhibitory theories. This problem is not at all unique to memory research, and we provide examples from other research domains discussed in this volume. By drawing attention to this issue, we hope to steer the field toward experiments that isolate the involvement of inhibitory mechanisms and that prevent unnecessary confusion and theoretical controversy in the literature on inhibitory processes.

Selective Retrieval

When recalling a memory, the desired trace is rarely the only memory related to the cues guiding retrieval. In fact, often the nontarget memories are more strongly associated with the cue than is the currently desired trace. In such situations, the associated traces compete for access to conscious awareness, necessitating some process to enable selective retrieval. In our framework, selective retrieval represents a paradigmatic case of response override, where one must select a weaker memory in the face of interference from one or more prepotent competitors. If stopping prepotent responses engages inhibition, the same mechanisms might also be engaged to stop prepotent memories from coming to mind, promoting selective retrieval. If so, perhaps inhibition will

Practiced Category   **Unpracticed Category**

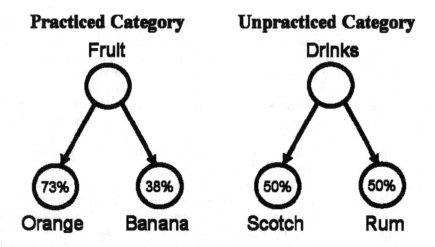

Figure 5.1. A standard categorical retrieval-induced forgetting (RIF) study. Illustrated are two items from each of two categories that subjects have studied. Subjects perform retrieval practice on *fruit–orange* but not on *fruit–banana* (unpracticed competitor) or on any members of the *drinks* category (unpracticed baseline category). The numbers show the percentage of items correctly recalled on the final cued-recall test. Practice facilitates recall of the practiced items relative to performance in baseline categories. RIF is reflected in the reduced recall of unpracticed members of the practiced category (banana) relative to performance in baseline categories (Scotch and rum).

induce long-lasting memory impairment for the competitors. Thus, the very act of remembering should cause forgetting of related memories.

This prediction has been tested in a procedure that we refer to as the "retrieval practice paradigm." Subjects study lists of category–exemplar word pairs (e.g., *fruits–orange, fruits–banana, drinks–Scotch*) and then practice retrieving half of the studied items from half of the categories (*fruits–or____*), each of which is practiced three times. After a delay, subjects are asked to recall all of the previously studied exemplars. Not surprisingly, practiced items (*orange*) are facilitated relative to items from nonpracticed categories (*Scotch*), which serve as a baseline for how well items are recalled with no practice. More interesting, nonpracticed items from practiced categories (*banana*) are recalled less often than baseline items (see Figure 5.1). Thus, retrieving some items during retrieval practice leads to worse memory for related items on the final test. According to the inhibitory control hypothesis, these items are inappropriately activated during the retrieval practice phase and then are inhibited to promote successful retrieval of the desired response (*orange*). This phenomenon, known as retrieval-induced forgetting (RIF), has been replicated many times using a broad array of stimuli (for reviews, see M. C. Anderson, 2003; Levy & Anderson, 2002).

A brief survey of recent demonstrations of RIF illustrates the striking breadth of this phenomenon. When bilingual persons retrieve the nonnative word for a concept, the native language phonology of that word is inhibited (Levy, McVeigh, Marful, & Anderson, 2007). Retrieving multiplication facts about a particular number (e.g., $7 \times 7 = 49$) impairs the ability to report unpracticed multiplications with that number (e.g., that $7 \times 8 = 56$; Phenix & Campbell, 2004). And retrieving individuating characteristics of a person from a stereotyped group causes inhibition of the target's stereotypic traits (Dunn & Spellman, 2003). Furthermore, recent research demonstrates that whereas most RIF studies induce competition by episodic exposure to the competitors, semantically related items can be inhibited even when not studied (Johnson & Anderson, 2004; Starns & Hicks, 2004). Thus, a wealth of experimental results suggest that RIF is a general phenomenon that results in impairment whenever unwanted items intrude during retrieval.

One of the goals of this volume, however, is to consider whether inhibition is actually involved in "inhibitory" effects such as RIF. The basic finding of RIF described in the preceding paragraphs is compatible with several noninhibitory mechanisms and by itself is not compelling evidence that inhibition is involved. For example, the practiced items may be so strengthened by retrieval practice that they interfere during the final test, effectively blocking the subject from coming up with the correct response. This type of retrieval competition has a long history in formal models of memory retrieval (e.g., J. R. Anderson, 1983; Raaijmakers & Shiffrin, 1981), where the probability of recalling an item is predicted by the relative strength of the association between the cue and the target compared with the strength of the association between the cue and all the competitors. Other noninhibitory mechanisms can explain RIF as well. For example, subjects may simply unlearn the connection between *fruits* and *banana*, or practicing some exemplars may bias the representation of that category toward the practiced items (retrieving *orange* might bias the cue *fruits* toward *citrus fruits*). According to all of these noninhibitory explanations, one need not claim that any change is occurring to the item itself (for a review of these noninhibitory sources of impairment, see M. C. Anderson & Bjork, 1994). However, this is a core claim of the inhibitory control perspective: The actual unwanted item itself is being made less accessible.

Several properties of RIF uniquely support the involvement of inhibition. First, the inhibitory control perspective (M. C. Anderson, 2003) makes the unique claim that RIF should be observed regardless of which cue is used to test the memory. In other words, forgetting should be cue independent and should generalize to novel cues in the test phase rather than being specific to those used to perform retrieval practice (M. C. Anderson & Spellman, 1995). For example, recall of *banana* should be impaired not only when it is tested with the studied category (*fruits*) but also when it is tested with a novel, independent retrieval cue (*monkey—b*). Such cue-independent forgetting is difficult for noninhibitory mechanisms to explain, because they predict that impairment should be specific to the cues used during retrieval practice. For example, associative blocking cannot explain this type of impairment because the new independent cue (*monkey*) is unrelated to the strengthened exemplars (e.g., *orange*); thus, there is no reason why they should block retrieval of *banana*.

Cue-independent forgetting has been observed many times (e.g., M. C. Anderson & Bell, 2001; M. C. Anderson, Green, & McCulloch, 2000; M. C. Anderson & Spellman, 1995; Camp, Pecher, & Schmidt, 2005; MacLeod & Saunders, 2005; Radvansky, 1999), suggesting that the competing item itself is inhibited. Other researchers have expanded on the notion of cue independence by arguing that if competitors are truly inhibited, then memory impairments should also occur on memory tests other than recall. RIF has now been found both on recognition tests (Hicks & Starns, 2004; Starns & Hicks, 2004) and on an implicit lexical decision test (Veling & van Knippenberg, 2004). The use of independent probes is the best tool available at present for distinguishing between interference and inhibition as mechanisms in long-term memory. Yet many researchers design studies of inhibition in memory without using independent probes. The problem is that one cannot isolate the role of inhibition in producing the memory impairment without a way of excluding contributions of noninhibitory factors. Lack of attention to this fact has led, we argue, to misleading conclusions about the nature of RIF and how it varies in different populations. We will return to this concept in greater detail later in this chapter.

Second, a hallmark of associative interference accounts of forgetting is that memory impairment should occur whenever competitors are strengthened. Several findings, however, have shown that strengthening practiced items does not always lead to impaired recall of competitors. For example, repeated study exposures to practiced items result in strengthening comparable to that produced by retrieval practice, yet this type of strengthening produces no forgetting of competing items provided that output interference at testing is controlled (M. C. Anderson, Bjork, & Bjork, 2000; Bäuml, 1996, 1997, 2002; Ciranni & Shimamura, 1999). If strengthening can occur without producing impairment of the related items, it suggests that retrieval practice, not strengthening, is what causes the impairment. Thus, RIF appears to be both recall specific and strength independent.

Finally, the amount of impairment depends on the extent to which the competitors interfere, a property referred to as *interference dependence*. For example, M. C. Anderson, Bjork, and Bjork (1994) observed more RIF when the competitors were high-frequency (e.g., *orange*) than lower frequency (e.g., *kiwi*) category members. Similarly, practicing retrieval of the meanings of asymmetric homographs results in significant impairment for the dominant meaning but not for the subordinate meaning (Shivde & Anderson, 2001). According to the associative blocking account, there is no reason to expect that the relative frequency of the unpracticed item should influence the degree to which the practiced item blocks retrieval during the final test. Each of these properties of RIF strongly implicates inhibition and provides serious challenges for any noninhibitory explanation. Taken together, these results support the inhibitory control perspective that selective retrieval is a special case of response override that results in lasting inhibition of the avoided memories.

Stopping Retrieval

The need to control behavior is not limited to selecting a nondominant response; it also sometimes is necessary to stop a behavior from occurring. A baseball player who makes the last-minute decision not to swing at a ball outside the strike zone is choosing to override a prepared response to swing. Sometimes a rememberer's goal is to do something remarkably similar: He or she is not

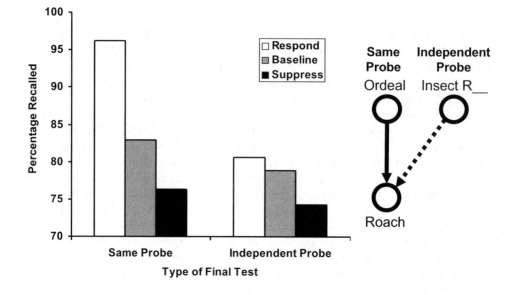

Figure 5.2. Final recall performance in the think/no-think (TNT) procedure. The graph shows the percentage of items correctly recalled on the final test as a function of whether subjects tried to recall the item (Respond), suppressed the item (Suppress), or had no reminders to the item (Baseline) during the TNT phase. The left side shows recall to the originally trained retrieval cue (i.e., the same probe); the right side shows recall to a novel, extralist category cue (i.e., the independent probe). The numbers are from a meta-analysis of 687 subjects run in the TNT paradigm in our lab.

trying to select a competing memory so much as trying simply to stop retrieval itself. When presented with a reminder of something upsetting (e.g., a photograph of a loved one who has recently died), one might desire to put those thoughts out of mind. Other times, one may simply want to stop a thought from popping into mind because one is trying to stay focused on a different thought. In fact, this type of control of internal thought is crucial for preventing one's mind from wandering. Can inhibitory mechanisms be engaged to serve these goals?

Evidence for the ability to stop memory retrieval comes from the think/no think (TNT) paradigm developed by M. C. Anderson and Green (2001). Subjects learned cue–target pairs (e.g., *ordeal–roach*). They then were presented with the cue (e.g., *ordeal*) and asked either to think of the associated target word (e.g., *roach*) or to prevent that associated memory from coming to mind. After seeing each type of either cue as many as 16 times, subjects were asked to recall all of the previously studied target memories. When provided with the same cue (*ordeal*) and asked to recall the correct target memory (*roach*), subjects had more difficulty if they had previously avoided thinking about that memory than if they had encountered no reminders of it during the TNT phase (see Figure 5.2). This finding is counterintuitive, because one would expect that repeated reminders to an item should make it more accessible, not less.

As was the case with RIF, the basic TNT suppression effect is compatible with noninhibitory accounts. For example, subjects might generate alternative thoughts during the TNT phase for each of the cues that require suppression (e.g., some ordeal they experienced personally). Then, on the final test, these diversionary thoughts might come to mind, blocking retrieval of the target item. M. C. Anderson and Green (2001) ruled out this possibility by demonstrating memory impairment for the avoided items using novel, extralist retrieval cues (e.g., *insect–r*_____ for *roach*) as independent probes. Associative interference from diversionary thoughts cannot explain independent-probe impairment, because the diversionary thoughts were generated unrelated to the originally studied cue. In their final experiment, M. C. Anderson and Green showed that simply asking subjects to avoid saying the response word does not result in the suppression effect, indicating that the attempt to prevent the unwanted memory from coming to mind is critical to producing the impairment. Taken together, these results indicate that the memory impairment arises from an inhibitory control mechanism that prevents the unwanted memory from entering awareness.

TNT suppression has now been replicated several times (M. C. Anderson et al., 2004; M. C. Anderson & Kuhl, 2007; M. C. Anderson, Reinholz, Kuhl, & Mayr, 2007; Bell & Anderson, 2007; Depue, Banich, & Curran, 2006; Hertel & Calcaterra, 2005 [aided condition]; Hertel & Gerstle, 2003 [nondysphoric subjects on positive word pairs]; Hotta & Kawaguchi, 2006; Joorman, Hertel, Brozovich, & Gotlib, 2005; Kawaguchi & Hotta, 2006; Wessel, Wetzels, Jelicic, & Merckelbach, 2005; but for failure to find below-baseline impairment, see Bulevich, Roediger, Balota, & Butler, in press). Although M. C. Anderson and Green (2001) used neutral word pairs, several recent studies have investigated whether the valence of the unwanted thought influences suppression success. Three of these studies have found that suppression of negative stimuli leads to comparable (nonsignificantly increased) inhibition relative to either neutral stimuli (M. C. Anderson et al., 2007; Depue et al., 2006) or positive stimuli (Joorman et al., 2005). However, Hertel and Gerstle (2003) found that nondepressed subjects were unable to suppress negative adjective–noun pairs. It is unclear what produced the different pattern in Hertel and Gerstle's study, but taken together these results suggest that the valence of the unwanted memory itself is not the primary determinant of success at suppression.

The memory impairment in TNT studies suggests that inhibitory control mechanisms may be recruited to prevent unwanted memories from coming to mind. This finding has obvious implications for when people wish to avoid persistent, intrusive thoughts. One approach might be simply to avoid reminders of those memories, but this strategy is often not practical. The foregoing results suggest that when presented with inescapable retrieval cues in more naturalistic settings, repeatedly avoiding memories may cause long-lasting impairments in recalling those memories. Thus, the TNT paradigm may be a useful laboratory model of the voluntary form of repression (suppression) proposed by Freud (1915/1963). If so, the TNT paradigm can be used as a tool for exploring clinical issues related to motivated forgetting.

Neural Substrates of Stopping Retrieval

Earlier in this chapter we outlined how stopping retrieval is analogous to stopping a motor response. A key difference between these two situations is that motor suppression is observable with the naked eye (e.g., one can see when a baseball player checks a swing), but there is no outwardly observable sign when someone chooses to stop a declarative memory. Despite the similarities between stopping actions and stopping thoughts outlined earlier, they could be accomplished in entirely different ways. One way of testing our idea about a fundamental similarity between these situations is by investigating whether these processes are produced by the same neural mechanisms. If stopping retrieval is really related to stopping a motor response, then a common underlying neural network should be involved in accomplishing both types of stopping.

Studies of motor response override have shown that a network of control-related regions, including the lateral prefrontal cortex, anterior cingulate cortex, lateral premotor cortex, and intraparietal sulcus, are recruited to stop motor responses (e.g., Garavan, Ross, Murphy, Roche, & Stein, 2002; Menon, Adleman, White, Glover, & Reiss, 2001). Thus, we predict that suppressing unwanted memories should also engage these regions. There should also be regions unique to memory control: those that are the target of suppression. Given the role of the hippocampus in conscious recollection of declarative memories (e.g., Eldridge, Knowlton, Furmanski, Bookheimer, & Engel, 2000; Squire, 1992) and the goal of suppressing conscious recollection in the TNT task, the hippocampus seems a likely region to target. M. C. Anderson et al. (2004) hypothesized that control-related regions (particularly lateral prefrontal regions) should be involved in disengaging hippocampal processes to prevent conscious recollection of the unwanted memories.

M. C. Anderson et al. (2004) used functional magnetic resonance imaging to identify the brain regions that support intentional memory suppression. Subjects were scanned while they participated in the TNT task. Again, subjects recalled significantly fewer suppression words than baseline words. M. C. Anderson et al. observed significantly more activation in control-related regions during the suppression trials than during the respond trials. Therefore, stopping retrieval is not simply a failure to engage retrieval processes: Instead, the heightened activation of these control regions during suppression trials suggests that subjects actively engage processes to prevent the unwanted memories from coming to mind. As predicted, the observed regions of increased activity overlapped highly with control-related regions involved in stopping motor responses: Common brain regions control stopping both unwanted memories and unwanted actions.

In addition to these control regions, M. C. Anderson et al. (2004) observed reduced hippocampal activity bilaterally on no-think relative to think trials. This difference could be attributed to increased activity during the think condition. However, the degree of hippocampal activity was correlated with behavioral memory inhibition, which is inconsistent with the difference on think and no-think trials being caused simply by heightened recollection in the think condition. Instead, it suggests that subjects can strategically down-regulate the hippocampus to prevent conscious recollection.

These neuroimaging results suggest that subjects can prevent unwanted memories from coming to mind by the same neural mechanisms that are recruited to stop motor actions. Instead of targeting a motor response, these regions are recruited to suppress declarative memory representations. So despite the difficulty involved with observing the stopping of memory retrieval, there now is both behavioral and neuroanatomical evidence to support the idea that people can prevent unwanted memories from coming to mind. The findings thus help to specify a model of how motivated forgetting might occur.

The Correlated Costs and Benefits Problem

In addition to isolating the role of inhibition in memory retrieval, the foregoing studies also revealed key theoretical issues about how inhibition should be measured. In the second half of this chapter, we discuss an important issue that has wide implications for investigators interested in inhibition: the CCB problem. We argue that failure to attend to this issue has contributed to significant confusion in the literature, especially in work on individual differences in inhibitory function. Such confusion has hindered theoretical development and generated doubt about inhibition phenomena—doubt that may underlie some of the skepticism evinced by opponents of inhibitory theories. We offer a solution that has proved useful in research on memory inhibition and that could be adapted for other cognitive domains.

All investigators would agree that whatever cognitive mechanisms are proposed to explain a phenomenon ought to operate consistently: If a mechanism is engaged under one set of circumstances, it ought to be engaged in future situations that have similar circumstances. Surprisingly, this seemingly uncontroversial premise is routinely ignored in studies of inhibition. Studies that induce inhibition at Time T and then later measure the behavioral aftereffects of that inhibition at Time T + 1 frequently fail to consider the involvement of inhibition at the time of the measurement (T + 1), even though inhibition should contribute to performance during the measurement process itself. The *CCB problem* refers to the theoretically predicted difficulty in quantifying the amount of inhibition that has taken place at Time T by measuring inhibition using an assessment at Time T + 1 that itself requires the same inhibitory process.

The retrieval task depicted in Figure 5.3A illustrates this problem. In both situations, a cue is associated with two items in memory, and the task is to retrieve either Item A in Situation A or Item B in Situation B. According to the inhibitory control perspective, in Situation A if the cue activates both traces A and B, they should compete for access to awareness; thus, if Item B interferes with the retrieval of Item A, inhibition should suppress Item B, facilitating the retrieval of Item A. The lingering effects of inhibition on Item B should make it harder to recall on later occasions. The analogous pattern should hold

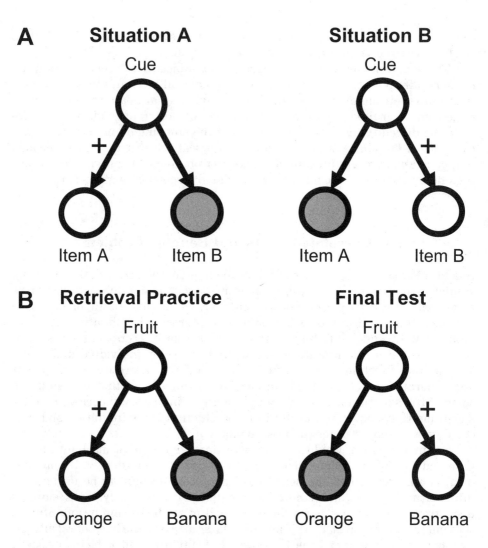

Figure 5.3. Illustration of the correlated costs and benefits problem. Panel A: In Situation A, a cue is associated with two responses. The inhibitory perspective predicts that practicing Item A in response to the cue should result in inhibition of Item B (provided that it interferes). Furthermore, in Situation B, practicing Item B should inhibit Item A, as Situations A and B are essentially equivalent. Panel B: These diagrams illustrate how Situations A and B apply to the retrieval practice paradigm. Practicing *orange* during the retrieval practice phase should inhibit *banana*. However, consistent application of the concept of inhibitory control at retrieval predicts that inhibition will also aid subjects in recalling *banana* at the time of test by inhibiting *orange*.

for Situation B. Inhibitory control should be involved in both of these equivalent retrieval situations.

Although this reasoning seems obvious, it has not been obvious to investigators studying the role of inhibition in memory retrieval. To illustrate this point, Figure 5.3B shows the different phases of the retrieval practice paradigm.

In the retrieval practice phase, subjects practice retrieving *orange,* suppressing the competitor *banana* and making it less accessible. The same items are on the final test, only now the goal is to retrieve the former competitor, which is now the target (e.g., *banana*). Clearly, consistency demands that the same inhibitory control mechanisms used to suppress *banana* in the retrieval practice phase ought to now be engaged to suppress *orange,* which has become the competitor. Indeed, inhibitory control should be more necessary during the test both because *banana* is inhibited (and harder to retrieve) and because *orange* is stronger from retrieval practice. Thus, the same inhibitory mechanisms that impaired *banana* during retrieval practice (Time T) should aid in the retrieval of *banana* by overcoming interference from the previously practiced item (*orange*) during the final test (Time T + 1). Importantly, the magnitude of both the cost and the benefit should be correlated, because they arise from the same underlying inhibition mechanism.

To see the impact of the CCB problem, RIF can serve as a model case. Suppose that researchers know, for each subject, how much of the RIF effect is produced by suppression during retrieval practice and how much is attributable to blocking on the final test. What would the predicted relation between these components and inhibitory control ability look like? How would they sum together to produce the aggregate RIF effect? Figure 5.4 plots the amount of RIF attributable to suppression, blocking, and both factors combined as a function of inhibitory control ability. Clearly, the suppression component should increase with inhibitory ability. So a patient with damage to the prefrontal cortex might be on the left side of this figure, unable to suppress competing items during retrieval practice, whereas a high-functioning young adult might be closer to the right side. If RIF were attributable solely to suppression induced during retrieval practice, then it clearly should increase with increasing inhibitory control ability.

Unfortunately, the CCB problem implies that the same inhibitory control ability that suppresses the competitor during retrieval practice (Time T) ought to assist in suppressing the practiced item during the final test (Time T + 1), reducing the blocking contribution to RIF. So as inhibitory control ability increases from left to right, the component of RIF attributable to blocking should diminish. Thus, on the left side of the figure, a hypothetical frontal patient, even one with absolutely no ability to suppress the competitor during retrieval practice, would be completely unable to suppress interference from the practiced items on the final test. To the extent that practiced items are strengthened, the frontal patient should experience exaggerated blocking from those strengthened items. Ignoring this fact would be quite curious given that perseverative behavior in memory tasks is largely what motivated the original inhibitory deficit hypothesis of frontal lobe dysfunction. By contrast, on the right side of the figure, the hypothetical young adult who effectively suppressed the competitor during practice would suffer little associative blocking on the final test. When the joint contributions of the costs (persisting suppression) and benefits (reduced blocking at T + 1) are summed, one can see that inhibitory control theory does not predict a clear relation between inhibitory control ability and the size of the RIF effect when subjects are tested with the same cue used to perform retrieval practice. Essentially, the costs and benefits should trade off, yielding

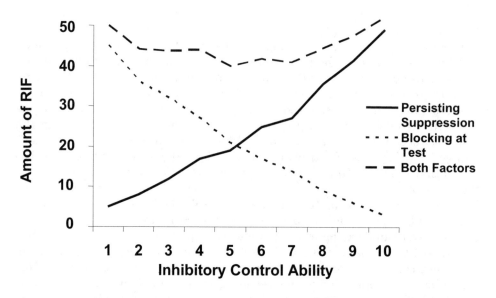

Figure 5.4. The correlated costs and benefits problem leads to unclear predictions on shared probe tests. Shown is the amount of retrieval-induced forgetting (RIF; numbers shown on the *y*-axis are arbitrary units and not amounts of specific data) observed on the final test that can be attributed to various causes as a function of inhibitory control ability. The solid black line shows the amount of RIF attributable to persisting suppression that was induced during retrieval practice, whereas the dotted line shows the amount attributable to blocking by practiced competitors on the final test. Subjects with more inhibitory control should suffer more persisting suppression, whereas subjects with less inhibitory control should experience more blocking. The dashed line represents the total effect, considering the combined influences of these factors. This total changes little with inhibitory control ability, illustrating how same-probe data may not clearly show differences between individuals with differing levels of inhibitory control ability.

effects that appear the same behaviorally but that are generated by different underlying chains of events.

Although this analysis may seem straightforward, several RIF studies testing inhibitory deficit hypotheses have not considered the role of suppression on the final test. For example, studies by Moulin et al. (2002) and Conway and Fthenaki (2003) both measured RIF with the standard category cued recall test (Figure 5.5). Both studies contrasted a patient population thought to have a deficit in inhibitory control (either Alzheimer's patients or frontal-lobe-damaged patients) against a control population. In both studies, RIF was observed in the deficit and control populations. If RIF is a pure measure of inhibition, then either these populations do not have deficits in inhibitory control or the inhibition measured by RIF is different from that supported by the prefrontal cortex.

These and other authors have used evidence such as this to argue that RIF reflects an automatic form of inhibition not mediated by the prefrontal cortex and not related to attentional control (Zellner & Bäuml, 2005). Yet if one invokes the inhibition process consistently when it is required, there should

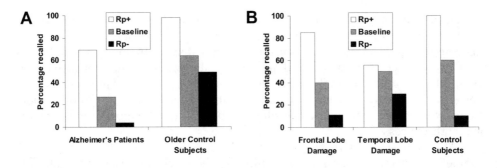

Figure 5.5. Examples of potentially misleading conclusions regarding retrieval-induced forgetting (RIF) on the basis of only same-probe data. Panel A: Moulin et al. (2002) found that both Alzheimer's patients and age-matched control subjects showed large RIF effects (recall of unpracticed items from practiced categories [Rp items] was lower than recall of baseline items [NRp items]). Panel B: Conway and Fthenaki (2003) also found large RIF effects that did not differ across patients with frontal lobe damage, patients with temporal lobe damage, and control subjects. Both studies suggested that RIF may reflect a more automatic form of inhibition, distinct from inhibitory control. However, these groups should show same-probe impairment if they were unable to prevent blocking from practiced competitors on the test.

be no clear relation between RIF and the deficit status of these populations as measured by the same-probe test. Put simply, the Alzheimer's disease and frontal-lobe-damaged patients, even if they were completely lacking in inhibitory control, would be expected to show significant forgetting by virtue of their compromised ability to resolve interference at the time of the final test. This finding would make their RIF effect appear similar to control subjects with intact inhibitory function despite entirely different underlying causes.

Failing to consider the CCB problem can lead to theoretically significant conclusions about the nature of RIF or, alternatively, about the populations being studied—conclusions that, based on a more thorough consideration of CCB analysis, are not warranted and potentially very misleading. Evidence of this potential to mislead is provided in the next section, along with a solution to the problem.

A Solution With Examples

The key to solving the CCB problem is to redesign the final assessment of inhibition to eliminate or reduce the benefits of inhibition. Although illustrated with memory inhibition, the principle applies generally to all paradigms in which inhibition is measured. This approach requires devising a final T + 1 assessment that minimizes heightened interference from practiced items, allowing the test to better reflect suppression that took place in the retrieval practice phase (Time T). Fortunately, this test already exists: the independent-probe method. Testing the inhibited item with a novel cue circumvents associative interference that might otherwise arise from the stronger practiced items, permitting a measure of inhibition at Time T + 1 not contaminated by blocking. If this test truly minimizes blocking, then there should be less need to engage inhibitory control on the final test, reducing the benefits of that process. Thus, with the independent-probe method, the measured RIF should better reflect inhibition caused by retrieval practice (Time T), making performance on this test more sensitive to individual differences in inhibition capacity than performance on the same-probe test, in which costs and benefits are both expressed.

Although subjects in the TNT paradigm do not explicitly strengthen a competitor during the TNT phase (unlike in the retrieval practice paradigm), they may generate diversionary thoughts that become associated with the cue word, introducing a blocking component to the same-probe effect (see Hertel & Calcaterra, 2005). If so, independent-probe impairment should better track individual differences in inhibitory function. This predicted finding was obtained in three series of TNT experiments that examined the size of the forgetting effect as a function of working memory capacity (Bell & Anderson, 2007), age (M. C. Anderson et al., 2007), and trauma history (M. C. Anderson & Kuhl, 2007), all factors that might moderate how well someone can suppress distracting memories. In each series, inhibition was assessed both with the same test cue initially used to induce inhibition (same-probe condition) and with a novel cue (independent-probe condition), permitting greater isolation of the persisting inhibition component.

Figure 5.6 presents the results from the same-probe and the independent-probe tests. The data have been simplified by collapsing the individual experiments in each series, though the pattern was replicated in each individual study. These graphs reveal a pattern highly consistent with the CCB problem. In each case, the amount of impairment on the same-probe test is, at best, weakly consistent with an inhibitory deficit. However, in all cases, the impairment does not vary reliably with subject group. In contrast, in all three series, the independent-probe test revealed significant differences in inhibition as a function of subject group. In fact, the differences in inhibition are quite striking on the independent-probe measure, and the three-way interaction of inhibition, subject group, and test type is significant in each case. Thus, whether an inhibitory deficit was observed varied reliably as a function of test type in each series, exactly as predicted by the CCB analysis.

These findings illustrate the dangers of the CCB problem. If we had based our conclusions about the relative inhibitory abilities of these different populations on performance on the same-probe test, as did Moulin et al. (2002) and Conway and Fthenaki (2003), we might have concluded that these groups did not differ in inhibitory function and that inhibition is unrelated to working memory capacity or executive control. Yet we know from our neuroimaging work (M. C. Anderson et al., 2004) that the TNT task engages frontal cortical regions known to be involved in executive function. The independent-probe measure, by reducing the potential benefits of inhibition at testing, provided much more striking evidence for variation in inhibition, in line with prior theoretical expectations. Thus, this method provides a solution to the CCB problem that can prevent theoretical confusion.

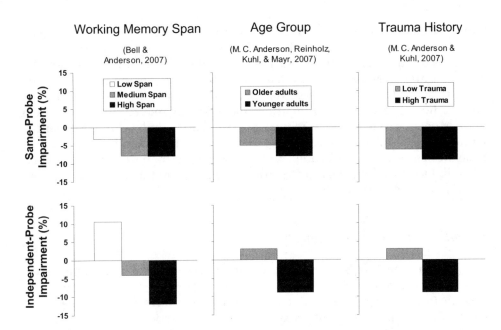

Figure 5.6. The utility of the independent-probe method. Each graph plots difference scores (baseline–suppression recall) to indicate the amount of memory impairment. The columns show data from studies investigating the relation between inhibition and working memory, age, and trauma. We predicted greater inhibition with greater working memory capacity, younger age, and higher level of experience with trauma. All three studies showed the predicted pattern numerically in the same-probe condition, but the differences in inhibition across groups were far from reliable. In contrast, the independent-probe data clearly and significantly showed the predicted differences between the groups, and the three-way interaction of group by inhibition by test type was significant in each series of studies.

Generality of the Problem

Although we have used RIF and the TNT paradigm to illustrate the CCB problem, this problem applies broadly to a variety of paradigms in memory, attention, and language. In this section, we provide several examples of the problem in these settings so that investigators in those areas can better recognize how this problem applies to their research.

Episodic and Semantic Memory Paradigms

Like RIF, several memory paradigms have the characteristic that strengthening some associates of a cue impairs later recall of other associates of the cue, such as retroactive and proactive interference in the A-B, A-C design; output interference for items associated with a common experimental or contextual cue; and part-set cuing impairment. The standard practice of measuring impairment by a shared cue at testing reflects the joint costs and benefits of inhibition. Semantic fluency tasks, in which subjects must produce as many exemplars of a category as they can within 1 minute, also suffer from this problem: As one generates new exemplars, other, yet-to-be-listed exemplars in semantic memory ought to be suppressed, yielding a cost to total fluency performance; on the other hand, that same inhibition process should reduce interference from already-generated exemplars, reducing perseveration and yielding a benefit to performance. Ironically, total fluency performance has often been taken as a measure of executive control ability, and in particular inhibitory control ability, when in fact no straightforward relation between total fluency and inhibitory function is predicted by inhibitory control theories.

Executive Control Paradigms

In the phenomenon of backward inhibition in task-set switching, subjects are presented with a stimulus on which they must perform a task as rapidly as possible (e.g., adding a pair of visually presented numbers). Other trials might cue subjects to perform a different task (e.g., subtraction) on the same class of stimuli. People generally are slower to perform the target task if they had just performed a different task, reflecting the time that it takes to switch task sets. It has been proposed that on switch trials, subjects engage inhibitory mechanisms to suppress the preceding task set (e.g., subtraction) so that a new set may be selected. For instance, Mayr and Keele (2000) found that if subjects performed Task A (e.g., subtraction) for one block of trials (Block 1) and then switched to Task B (e.g., addition) in the next block (Block 2), switching back to the switched-out-of task (e.g., addition) in the next block (Block 3) took significantly longer than switching to a new Task C (e.g., multiplication). Thus, there was some additional cost associated with having to switch back to a previously rejected set relative to a new set. Mayr and Keele interpreted this as evidence for inhibition in task-set switching and termed the phenomenon *backward inhibition*.

Backward inhibition has been used to study individual differences in inhibitory function in older adults (Mayr, 2001) and in frontal-lobe-damaged patients (Mayr, Diedrichsen, Ivry, & Keele, 2006) on the assumption that it provides a clean measure of the effects of inhibition. However, backward inhibition is subject to the CCB problem. On the one hand, the better subjects' inhibitory control, the slower they should be to respond to the recently inhibited task set, because the effects of prior inhibition at Time T should persist to T + 1. On the other hand, when inhibition is measured on Block 3 (T + 1), subjects must also suppress interference from the recently engaged task set from Block 2 and retrieve the suppressed task set (evoked in part by the common stimulus— numbers). Thus, inhibitory control benefits the subject, helping to combat interference from the most recent set. Although it might seem that the experimental (Tasks A, B, and A) and control (Tasks A, B, and C) conditions are matched for the need to suppress Task B during the final test, this is not the case. In the experimental condition, the strength of Task B relative to the inhibited Task Set A should be greater than the strength of Task B relative to the new

Task Set C in the control condition, making inhibitory control more beneficial in the experimental condition. Thus, inhibition induces both costs and benefits that, when taken together, make it quite difficult to predict a clear relation between inhibitory function and the backward inhibition effect.

Visual Selective Attention Paradigms

Very similar arguments can be made about the negative priming phenomenon (for reviews, see Milliken, Joordens, Merikle, & Seiffert, 1998; Neill & Valdes, 1996; Tipper, 2001). In negative priming, the inhibition of a target on a preceding trial (Time T) is typically measured on a probe trial (Time T + 1) that itself requires subjects to resolve competition. As in backward inhibition, this design provides the opportunity for inhibition to yield a greater measurement-epoch benefit in the experimental condition, in which the competition is between the suppressed target and a nonsuppressed distractor, compared with the control condition, in which the competition is between a nonsuppressed target and a nonsuppressed distractor. Again, the putative costs of inhibitory control are mixed with their benefits, yielding no clear predictions about how negative priming should vary as a function of inhibitory ability.

Language Processing Paradigms

The CCB problem also arises in language tasks that have been used to assess inhibition. One example is the role of inhibition in lexical ambiguity resolution (see Gorfein, 2001, for a collection of reviews). During sentence processing, interpreting a word that has multiple meanings requires that its contextually appropriate sense be accessed. It is generally thought that competition between the word's multiple meanings must be resolved, and this function has been attributed to inhibition by some investigators (Gernsbacher & Faust, 1991; Simpson & Kang, 1994). In these studies, subjects viewed trials composed of a briefly presented prime word followed by a probe letter string requiring a lexical decision. When the prime is a homograph (e.g., *bank*), reaction time to a related probe (e.g., *river*) is speeded. More interesting, when the following trial represents the same prime (*bank*) followed by a probe related to the previously rejected sense (e.g., *money*), probe lexical decision times are slower than if the first prime–probe trial had presented an entirely unrelated homograph (e.g., *arm shoulder*). The slowed response to the previously rejected sense has been taken as evidence that the meaning (*money*) was inhibited during the first prime–probe trial.

The assessment of inhibition in this paradigm again mixes the lingering effects of inhibition on the prime trial (Time T) with the need to overcome interference on the probe trial (Time T + 1). When the probe trial re-presents the homograph cue word, the recently selected meaning grows very active in response, creating a situation analogous to associative blocking in RIF. Thus, processing of the probe on the second trial requires subjects not only to overcome the inhibition of the previously rejected sense but also to combat the heightened interference from the competing sense. Similar problems arise in numerous other language processing tasks thought to involve inhibition, including ana-phoric reference (Gernsbacher, 1989) and metaphor comprehension (Gerns-bacher, Keysar, Robertson, & Werner, 2001). Thus, if one's goal is to use such behavioral effects to examine individual differences in inhibition or to study the theoretical conditions under which inhibition occurs, one needs a measure that does not conflate these sources of impairment (for examples of the indepen-dent-probe method in language processing, see Johnson & Anderson, 2004; Shivde & Anderson, 2001).

Conclusion

To the extent that inhibitory control has been assessed using measures that suffer from the CCB problem, the literature should be plagued with inconsisten-cies in the support of inhibitory deficit theories, generating reasonable doubt about the utility of these theories. We argue that such variability is not neces-sarily a sign of weakness of the theories but rather a sign of the poorly consid-ered measures that have been used to assess inhibition. As a solution, we argue for the importance of developing testing methods for measuring inhibition that minimize the potential benefit of inhibition during the test epoch itself. By minimizing the benefits of inhibition, variation in inhibitory function can be measured more cleanly. On the basis of results from several studies, we argue that the independent-probe method provides one such example that has proved to be sensitive as a means of testing individual differences in this function. We believe that the logic underlying this method can be adapted to any domain in which inhibition might be studied.

The purpose of this volume is to review perspectives on the role of inhibition in cognition. On the one hand, many investigators have presupposed inhibition as part of a broader theory of cognition. The existence of inhibition seems both plausible and necessary: plausible, because many behavioral effects appear to arise from inhibition, and necessary, because some process for limiting the influence of distracting representations seems essential—a proposal supported by the widespread involvement of inhibition in the nervous system and by computational analyses indicating that inhibition is necessary for stability in neural networks (e.g., Easton & Gordon, 1984). On the other hand, skeptics of inhibition correctly emphasize that the mere presence of performance decre-ments does not by itself require such processes. Indeed, many behavioral phe-nomena labeled "inhibition" may be adequately explained without proposing an additional inhibition process. If so, parsimony dictates that the simpler theory be preferred, though it remains a point of debate whether such alterna-tive noninhibitory theories are always simpler.

Our approach has been to develop clear standards to judge whether a behavioral deficit constitutes inhibition. In this chapter, we reviewed this work, which establishes functional properties of memory inhibition that uniquely favor the role of inhibitory mechanisms in memory retrieval. Collectively, these properties strongly support the view that inhibition overrides prepotent re-sponses in memory. Thus, one of the key imperatives advocated by reasonable skeptics of inhibition—to go beyond the mere equating of a performance decrement with inhibition—has been programmatically addressed in the context of memory retrieval over the past decade. We do not imply that some noninhibitory mechanisms do not also contribute to apparent inhibitory effects in memory, only that inhibition clearly contributes to producing such effects.

In fact, the contributions of noninhibitory sources of impairment to apparent inhibitory phenomena motivated our discussion of the CCB problem. Put simply, measuring the behavioral consequences of an earlier act of inhibition on some target representation ought itself to engage the very same inhibitory processes to successfully process that inhibited representation. If so, the putative cost of inhibition ought to be mitigated by its putative benefit at the time of testing. When inhibitory functioning is impaired (because of either an inhibitory deficit or experimental manipulations), the costs should be reduced, but so too should the benefits, opening the door for noninhibitory components to contribute to an effect. Thus, to effectively measure inhibition, a test should minimize the benefits of inhibition. We have argued that the independent-probe method provides such a test and that its logic can be applied in any domain in which inhibition is studied. This proposal has been validated in three TNT studies that consistently showed that the independent-probe method provides a significantly more reliable index of inhibitory control deficits than do tests that suffer from the CCB problem.

We strongly emphasize that the CCB problem is not limited to memory retrieval: It applies broadly in domains such as executive control, visual attention, and language processing. We hope that recognition of this problem will encourage investigators to develop theoretically targeted methods of testing inhibition theories, enabling the field to advance beyond an indefinite cycle of assertion and skepticism that plagues the study of such processes. We believe that sufficient evidence exists for inhibitory processes in memory retrieval and that such processes are likely to contribute broadly to cognitive function, but reasonable doubt will remain as long as the field neglects the issue of measurement. Thus, our challenge to investigators of executive control, visual attention, and language processing is to develop solutions to the CCB problem to determine whether the properties of inhibition, identified in memory, also apply in other cognitive domains.

References

Anderson, J. R. (1983). *The architecture of cognition.* Cambridge, MA: Harvard University Press.

Anderson, M. C. (2003). Rethinking interference theory: Executive control and the mechanisms of forgetting. *Journal of Memory and Language, 49,* 415–445.

Anderson, M. C., & Bell, T. A. (2001). Forgetting our facts: The role of inhibitory processes in the loss of propositional knowledge. *Journal of Experimental Psychology: General, 130,* 544–570.

Anderson, M. C., Bjork, E. L., & Bjork, R. A. (2000). Retrieval-induced forgetting: Evidence for a recall-specific mechanism. *Psychonomic Bulletin & Review, 7,* 522–530.

Anderson, M. C., & Bjork, R. A. (1994). Mechanisms of inhibition in long-term memory: A new taxonomy. In D. Dagenbach & T. H. Carr (Eds.), *Inhibitory processes in attention, memory and language* (pp. 265–326). San Diego, CA: Academic Press.

Anderson, M. C., Bjork, R. A., & Bjork, E. L. (1994). Remembering can cause forgetting: Retrieval dynamics in long-term memory. *Journal of Experimental Psychology: Learning, Memory, and Cognition, 20,* 1063–1087.

Anderson, M. C., & Green, C. (2001, March 15). Suppressing unwanted memories by executive control. *Nature, 410,* 366–369.

Anderson, M. C., Green, C., & McCulloch, K. C. (2000). Similarity and inhibition in long-term memory: Evidence for a two-factor theory. *Journal of Experimental Psychology: Learning, Memory, & Cognition, 26,* 1141–1159.

Anderson, M. C., & Kuhl, B. A. (2007). *Psychological trauma and its enduring effects on memory suppression: Evidence for the plasticity of memory control.* Manuscript in preparation.

Anderson, M. C., Ochsner, K., Kuhl, B., Cooper, J., Robertson, E., Gabrieli, S. W., et al. (2004, January 9). Neural systems underlying the suppression of unwanted memories. *Science, 303,* 232–235.

Anderson, M. C., Reinholz, J., Kuhl, B. A., & Mayr, U. (2007). *Inhibition in aging and long-term memory: A cognitive aging study using the think/no-think paradigm.* Manuscript in preparation.

Anderson, M. C., & Spellman, B. A. (1995). On the status of inhibitory mechanisms in cognition: Memory retrieval as a model case. *Psychological Review, 102,* 68–100.

Bäuml, K. (1996). Revisiting an old issue: Retroactive interference as a function of the degree of original and interpolated learning. *Psychonomic Bulletin & Review, 3,* 380–384.

Bäuml, K. (1997). The list-strength effect: Strength-dependent competition or suppression. *Psychonomic Bulletin & Review, 4,* 260–264.

Bäuml, K. (2002). Semantic recall can cause episodic forgetting. *Psychological Science, 13,* 356–360.

Bell, T. A., & Anderson, M. C. (2007). *Keeping things in and out of mind: Individual differences in working memory capacity predict successful memory suppression.* Manuscript in preparation.

Bulevich, J. B., Roediger, H. L., Balota, D. A., & Butler, A. C. (in press). Failures to find suppression of episodic memories in the think/no-think paradigm. *Memory & Cognition.*

Camp, G., Pecher, D., & Schmidt, H. G. (2005). Retrieval-induced forgetting in implicit memory tests: The role of test awareness. *Psychonomic Bulletin & Review, 12,* 490–494.

Ciranni, M. A., & Shimamura, A. P. (1999). Retrieval-induced forgetting in episodic memory. *Journal of Experimental Psychology: Learning, Memory, and Cognition, 25,* 1403–1414.

Conway, M. A., & Fthenaki, A. (2003). Disruption of inhibitory control of memory following lesions to the frontal and temporal lobes. *Cortex, 39,* 667–686.

Depue, B. E., Banich, M. T., & Curran, T. (2006). Suppression of emotional and nonemotional content in memory: Effects of repetition on cognitive control. *Psychological Science, 17,* 441–447.

Dunn, E. W., & Spellman, B. A. (2003). Forgetting by remembering: Stereotype inhibition through rehearsal of alternative aspects of identity. *Journal of Experimental Social Psychology, 39,* 420–433.

Easton, P., & Gordon, P. E. (1984). Stabilization of Hebbian neural nets by inhibitory learning. *Biological Cybernetics, 51,* 1–9.

Eldridge, L. L., Knowlton, B. J., Furmanski, C. S., Bookheimer, S. Y., & Engel, S. A. (2000). Remembering episodes: A selective role for the hippocampus during retrieval. *Nature Neuroscience, 3,* 1149–1152.

Freud, S. (1915/1963). Repression (C. M. Baines & J. Strachey, Trans.). In J. Strachey (Ed.), *The standard edition of the complete psychological works of Sigmund Freud* (Vol. 14, pp. 146–158). London: Hogarth Press. (Original work published 1915)

Garavan, H., Ross, T. J., Murphy, K., Roche, R. A. P., & Stein, E. A. (2002). Dissociable executive functions in the dynamic control of behavior: Inhibition, error detection, and correction. *NeuroImage, 17,* 1820–1830.

Gernsbacher, M. A. (1989). Mechanisms that improve referential access. *Cognition, 32,* 99–156.

Gernsbacher, M. A., & Faust, M. E. (1991). The mechanism of suppression: A component of general comprehension skill. *Journal of Experimental Psychology: Learning, Memory & Cognition, 17,* 245–262.

Gernsbacher, M. A., Keysar, B., Robertson, R. R. W., & Werner, N. K. (2001). The role of suppression and enhancement in understanding metaphors. *Journal of Memory and Language, 45,* 433–450.

Gorfein, D. (Ed.). (2001). *On the consequences of meaning selection: Perspectives on resolving lexical ambiguity.* Washington, DC: American Psychological Association.

Hertel, P. T., & Calcaterra, G. (2005). Intentional forgetting benefits from thought substitution. *Psychonomic Bulletin & Review, 12,* 484–489.

Hertel, P. T., & Gerstle, M. (2003). Depressive deficits in forgetting. *Psychological Science, 14,* 573–578.

Hicks, J. L., & Starns, J. J. (2004). Retrieval-induced forgetting occurs in tests of item recognition. *Psychonomic Bulletin & Review, 11,* 125–130.

Hotta, C., & Kawaguchi, J. (2006, January). *The effect of test delay on memory for suppressed items in the think/no-think paradigm.* Poster presented at the International Symposium on Inhibitory Processes in the Mind, Kyoto, Japan.

Johnson, S. K., & Anderson, M. C. (2004). The role of inhibitory control in forgetting semantic knowledge. *Psychological Science, 15,* 448–453.

Joorman, J., Hertel, P. T., Brozovich, F., & Gotlib, I. H. (2005). Remembering the good, forgetting the bad: Intentional forgetting of emotional material in depression. *Journal of Abnormal Psychology, 114,* 640–648.

Kawaguchi, J., & Hotta, C. (2006, January). *Intention to forget, but not distraction, is critical to forget: The effect of distraction task on memory retrieval in a five minute delay test.* Poster presented at the International Symposium on Inhibitory Processes in the Mind, Kyoto, Japan.

Levy, B. J., & Anderson, M. C. (2002). Inhibitory processes and the control of memory retrieval. *Trends in Cognitive Sciences, 6,* 299–305.

Levy, B. J., McVeigh, N. D., Marful, A., & Anderson, M. C. (2007). Inhibiting your native language: The role of retrieval-induced forgetting during second language acquisition. *Psychological Science, 18,* 29–34.

MacLeod, M. D., & Saunders, J. (2005). The role of inhibitory control in the production of misinformation effects. *Journal of Experimental Psychology: Learning, Memory & Cognition, 31,* 964–979.

Mayr, U. (2001). Age differences in the selection of mental sets: The role of inhibition, stimulus ambiguity, and response-set overlap. *Psychology and Aging, 16,* 96–109.

Mayr, U., Diedrichsen, J., Ivry, R., & Keele, S. W. (2006). Dissociating task-set selection from task-set inhibition in the prefrontal cortex. *Journal of Cognitive Neuroscience, 18,* 14–21.

Mayr, U., & Keele, S. W. (2000). Changing internal constraints on action: The role of backward inhibition. *Journal of Experimental Psychology: General, 129,* 4–26.

Menon, V., Adleman, N. E., White, C. D., Glover, G. H., & Reiss, A. L. (2001). Error-related brain activation during a go/nogo response inhibition task. *Human Brain Mapping, 12,* 131–143.

Milliken, B., Joordens, S., Merikle, P. M., & Seiffert, A. E. (1998). Selective attention: A reevaluation of the implications of negative priming. *Psychological Review, 105,* 203–229.

Moulin, C. J. A., Perfect, T. J., Conway, M. A., North, A. S., Jones, R. W., & James, N. (2002). Retrieval-induced forgetting in Alzheimer's disease. *Neuropsychologia, 40,* 862–867.

Neill, W. T., & Valdes, L. A. (1996). Facilitatory and inhibitory aspects of attention. In A. F. Kramer, M. G. H. Coles, & G. D. Logan (Eds.), *Converging operations in the study of visual selective attention* (pp. 45–76). Washington, DC: American Psychological Association.

Phenix, T. L., & Campbell, J. I. D. (2004). Effects of multiplication practice on product verification: Integrated structures model or retrieval-induced forgetting? *Memory & Cognition, 32,* 324–335.

Raaijmakers, J. W., & Shiffrin, R. M. (1981). Search of associative memory. *Psychological Review, 88,* 93–134.

Radvansky, G. A. (1999). Memory retrieval and suppression: The inhibition of situation models. *Journal of Experimental Psychology: General, 128,* 563–579.

Shivde, G., & Anderson, M. C. (2001). The role of inhibition in meaning selection: Insights from retrieval-induced forgetting. In D. Gorfein (Ed.), *On the consequences of meaning selection: Perspectives on resolving lexical ambiguity* (pp. 175–190). Washington, DC: American Psychological Association.

Simpson, G. B., & Kang, H. (1994). Inhibitory processes in the recognition of homograph meanings. In D. Dagenbach & T. H. Carr (Eds.), *Inhibitory processes in attention, memory, and language* (pp. 359–381). San Diego, CA: Academic Press.

Squire, L. R. (1992). Memory and the hippocampus: A synthesis from findings with rats, monkeys, and humans. *Psychological Review, 99,* 195–231.

Starns, J. J., & Hicks, J. L. (2004). Episodic generation can cause semantic forgetting: Retrieval-induced forgetting of false memories. *Memory & Cognition, 32,* 602–609.

Tipper, S. P. (2001). Does negative priming reflect inhibitory mechanisms? A review and integration of conflicting views. *Quarterly Journal of Experimental Psychology, 54A,* 321–343.

Veling, H., & van Knippenberg, A. (2004). Remembering can cause inhibition: Retrieval-induced inhibition as a cue independent process. *Journal of Experimental Psychology: Learning, Memory, and Cognition, 30,* 315–318.

Wessel, I., Wetzels, S., Jelicic, M., & Merckelbach, H. (2005). Dissociation and memory suppression: A comparison of high and low dissociative individuals' performance on the think-no think task. *Personality and Individual Differences, 39,* 1461–1470.

Zellner, M., & Bäuml, K. (2005). Intact retrieval inhibition in children's episodic recall. *Memory & Cognition, 33,* 396–404.

6

Saying No to Inhibition: The Encoding and Use of Words

David S. Gorfein and Vincent R. Brown

Modelers of cognitive processes have been identified as belonging to one or the other of two camps: inhibitophiles or inhibitophobes (see chap. 15, this volume). Therefore, it seems reasonable to make clear our points of view on the issue that underlies this volume, namely, what is the proper role of the construct of inhibition in cognitive theory? David S. Gorfein falls into the inhibitophobic camp, whereas Vincent R. Brown admits to inhibitophilic tendencies but with several caveats. Brown suggests that honest inhibitophiles

1. see if they can account for your results without inhibition;
2. then make sure they haven't implicitly snuck inhibition into their model; and
3. to the extent that their model uses inhibition, ask whether it really is cognitive inhibition.

As a subscriber to the principle of least effort, Gorfein is struck by the extraordinary difficulty of inhibiting anything once it has been activated. Anecdotally, he remembers a day in the mid-1960s when he was lecturing on classical conditioning and in particular on the work of Razran (1935) with respect to salivary conditioning in human participants. He had just made the point that in an effort to avoid satiation from the mints commonly used as unconditional stimuli in salivary conditioning, Razran had experimented with saying "saliva" as the unconditional stimulus to his participants. This assertion aroused furious hand waving by one of the students, who rose to say that the whole idea was ridiculous and that no one need salivate to the word *saliva*—at least, that was her intent, but she found herself spitting instead of talking because she had a mouth full of saliva she could not control. In short, the activation of a single word resulted in a bodily response that was outside the control of any potential inhibitory mechanism.

Investigators of a wide variety of cognitive tasks have identified the process of determining meaning for the single word as a basic unit for studying everything from list and paired-associate learning and memory (e.g., Melton & Martin, 1972) to the highly complex processes associated with human communication (e.g., Gernsbacher, 1990). Although these studies have provided substantial insight into human cognition, only a few models have offered a mechanism that might serve to integrate the individual areas (e.g., the spreading-activation theory of Collins & Loftus, 1975, as well as the ACT model of J. R. Anderson, 1983). A purpose of this chapter is to examine the evolution and applications of the activation-selection model (ASM) of meaning selection (Gorfein, 2001a; Gorfein, Brown, & DeBiasi, in press; Gorfein & Bubka, 1989). This model aims to account for a variety of meaning selection data without explicitly postulating inhibition between alternative meaning representations.

Although we credit the origins of ASM to Gorfein and Bubka's (1989) chapter, the impetus of the work can be traced to earlier work on what is called *proactive interference* or *proactive inhibition* (PI) in the short-term memory distractor task (J. A. Brown, 1958; Peterson & Peterson, 1959). Gorfein and Viviani (1981) made use of nonhomophonic homographs such as *minute* ('mi-nət, a unit of time, or mī-'nüt, extremely small) and showed that meaning selection influenced proactive interference by producing release from PI when the meaning context was changed on the trial following the presentation of the homograph (for a description of that work, see Gorfein, 1987, pp. 162–165).

In this chapter, we begin with a review of a portion of the literature on the process of meaning selection for ambiguous words and in particular the effect of such selection on subsequent encounters with the same ambiguous word. Ambiguity resolution is a useful place to study meaning selection, in that unlike tapping into the nuances of words, the results of such processing are relatively easy to see. We then describe ASM and review data from our own laboratory on ambiguity processing. Finally, we complete the circle by offering a little evidence and some speculation as to how ASM can be related to episodic memory processes.

On Proposals for a Role for Inhibition in the Processing of Lexical Ambiguity

A major impetus to the idea that the selection of an appropriate meaning of a homograph leads to the suppression of the inappropriate meaning came from the cross-modal priming studies of Onifer and Swinney (1981). Earlier work using the lexical decision task had indicated that a homograph presented in the absence of a biasing context could serve as a prime for words related to either meaning. Two things were special about the cross-modal study: (a) Even a highly constraining context related to the dominant meaning of a highly polarized homograph resulted in the immediate priming of words related to both the dominant and the secondary meaning of the homograph in a lexical decision task, and (b) words related to the dominant meaning were still primed 1.5 seconds after the presentation of the homograph, but words related to the secondary meaning were not. This mechanism leading to the eventual selection of a single meaning was labeled *suppression* by Swinney (1981), and Gernsbacher (1990) developed it into a theory of ambiguity processing as part of her structure-building theory.

Gernsbacher and Faust (1991a, 1991b, 1995) reported that skilled readers showed the pattern of initial activation of both meanings of an ambiguous word followed by decreased activation of the context-inappropriate meaning, whereas unskilled readers showed activation for both meanings across the interval following an ambiguous word, typically 1,300 to 1,400 milliseconds in their studies. This result has been used as the basis for the claim that poor readers are less able to suppress the inappropriate meaning. Alternatively, Perfetti and Hart (2001) showed that poor comprehenders initiated the activation of word meaning later than good comprehenders, so this delay in onset could account for the observed difference in persistence of activation for the less-skilled comprehenders—they simply start later.

Simpson and Kellas (1989) reported that once a homograph had been used as a prime for a word related to one of its less common meanings (e.g., *bank* as a prime for *river*), even after a lag of 12 intervening trials, a target word related to the dominant meaning of the homograph (e.g., *bank* followed by *money*) showed a prolonged naming time relative to a neutral baseline. Simpson and Kang (1994) extended the idea of temporary suppression of the nonselected meaning of an ambiguous word to an inhibitory process that endured over a period of time. In similar fashion, Gorfein and Walters (1989) reported that for nonhomographic homophones (e.g., *sun* and *son*), when a participant had filled in the blank in a sentence designed to bias the secondary (less frequent) meaning of the homophone (*Like father, like s____*), an increased probability of the response *son* was observed on a spelling test administered 24 hours later.

Gernsbacher, Robertson, and Werner (2001) reported that for sentence sensibility judgments, there is a large cost of changing the meaning of a homograph on consecutive sentence trials. Participants were slower and less accurate in deciding that "She blew out the match" made sense on Trial $n + 1$ after deciding on Trial n that "She won the match" was a sensible sentence. In contrast to the cost found in the naming task used by Simpson and Kang (1994) over 12 intervening trials, Gernsbacher et al. found that after four intervening sentences, there was no cost associated with the meaning change, but there was a benefit when meaning was maintained (e.g., when the target sentence on Trial $n + 5$, "She blew out the match," was preceded on Trial n by the sentence, "She lit the match").

There is considerable agreement by a number of investigators that the amount of suppression or inhibition that will result from the selection of a homograph meaning will depend on the amount of competition between the two meanings (i.e., with balanced homographs eliciting greater competition). Both Simpson (Simpson & Adamopolous, 2001) and M. C. Anderson (Shivde & Anderson, 2001) endorsed such a hypothesis, and it is implicit in recent attempts to model M. C. Anderson's retrieval-induced inhibition view (Norman, Newman, Detre, & Polyn, 2006). However, direct tests of this hypothesis are lacking.

In summary, these studies support the view that although contextual support for one meaning is present at the initial processing of an ambiguous word, the context-inappropriate meaning is available as well, as shown by the priming of words related to the context-inappropriate meaning or meanings (Onifer & Swinney, 1981). Activation of the context-inappropriate meaning falls quickly to baseline, whereas activation of the context-appropriate meaning persists (Gernsbacher & Faust, 1995; Perfetti & Hart, 2001). Once a meaning is selected, however, the long-term effects of such selection are a matter of dispute. Simpson and his colleagues (Simpson & Adamopolous, 2001; Simpson & Kang, 1994; Simpson & Kellas, 1989) showed a cost with respect to the context-inappropriate meaning and a lack of benefit for the context-appropriate meaning at long intervals. In contrast, Gernsbacher et al. (2001) showed benefits of maintaining the same meaning over long intervals but no cost when meanings were altered. Explanation of these apparently conflicting outcomes is crucial to distinguishing between transient suppression and longer lasting inhibition. Finally, Simpson and Adamopolous (2001) made, but did not directly test, the theoretical prediction that the magnitude of the effect of processing depends on the degree of conflict that exists at the time of processing; that is, contextual constraints may either reduce or enhance the conflict, depending on the degree of dominance of the homograph meaning as well as the strength of the contextual constraints.

Theory

A number of theories or frameworks have been offered to explain the process of meaning selection, but few have provided the detail necessary to make precise predictions of the outcomes of a wide variety of experiments. We briefly describe some of these with respect to the focus of this volume—the place of inhibition in cognition:

- *Structure-building framework* (Gernsbacher, 1990). Gernsbacher proposed two processes; one is activation of memory that enhances the activity of words that fit the activated meaning, and the second is active suppression of meanings that do not fit the context. Suppression is a transient process decaying in a matter of seconds.
- *Negative priming* (Simpson & Adamopolous, 2001; Simpson & Kang, 1994). To the extent that competing meanings occur when an ambiguous word is processed, the requirement to ignore the competing meaning results in relatively long-lasting negative priming through the inhibition of the competing meaning.
- *Independent-activation model* (Twilley & Dixon, 2000). Twilley and Dixon (2000) explicitly acknowledged that their independent-activation model, which also postulates a suppressive meaning-selection mechanism, can fit the effects of local contextual constraint (priming) but cannot produce the results of studies like those of Simpson and Kang (1994) that show decrements due to meaning change over the lag of several intervening trials. They suggested a change in the resting levels in their model as a possible modification but have not explored the viability of this solution.
- *Interactive activation and competition (IAC) model* (Erickson & Allred, 2001). Erickson and Allred (2001) believed that their IAC model shows promise in explaining priming costs and benefits over short intervals,

although the model does not yield effects beyond one or two intervening trials.

- *Retrieval-induced forgetting model* (M. C. Anderson & Spellman, 1995). The extension of this memory model suggests that the active retrieval of one meaning of an ambiguous word (e.g., by using memory retrieval cues related to that meaning) will tend to inhibit the alternative meanings of that word (see Shivde & Anderson, 2001).

- *Reordered-access model* (Duffy, Kambe, & Rayner, 2001; Duffy, Morris, & Rayner, 1988). Each meaning of a given word has two primary sources of support: the relative frequency of each meaning determined by prior experience and information provided by the current context. Like ASM, this model does not explicitly include an inhibitory mechanism. A main goal of this model is to show that although context does have an influence on performance, it cannot completely override a strong frequency-based bias toward one meaning. A formal implementation of this model based on the constraint satisfaction architecture of Spivey and Tanenhaus (1998) provided a specific mechanism for predicting decision times as a function of weights representing the contextual support for both the meanings of an ambiguous word and the baseline frequency of occurrence of each meaning. As currently specified, this model does not have an explicit mechanism for accounting for long-term effects of meaning selection over many intervening trials or long time intervals. However, modifying the constraint satisfaction implementation of the model so that the weights representing the frequency of each meaning retain their altered values following meaning selection may give it the flexibility to account for some of the observed long-term effects.

- *Activation-selection model* (Gorfein et al., in press). Presenting a word for processing activates attributes associated with its meanings. The meaning of a word is a consequence of those attributes of a word that are active. Selecting a meaning for any word results in a reweighting of the attributes of the word toward the meaning selected. The processing of ambiguous words is a fertile field for the testing of this model.

The Activation-Selection Model

ASM was developed with the intent of explaining long-term effects of meaning selection. Typically, experiments in our laboratory show the effects of meaning selection over periods from 1 to 20 minutes and, on one occasion, over 24 hours. Further, we have demonstrated transfer of meaning selection across a variety of tasks. The effects of meaning selection persist even when the nature of the task is altered from initial meaning selection to testing. The following are six principles of the activation-selection model:

1. Words are represented by a weighted set of attributes (e.g., Bower, 1967). An attribute is a hypothetical construct for representing the various (semantic, contextual, graphemic, acoustic, etc.) features associated with a word.

2. The initial processing of a word activates a small number of attributes; the number is determined by task constraints and the processing time available.

3. Attributes are activated in proportion to their current weight.

4. The *set principle* is as follows: Processing a word in the context of an active attribute results in selection of that attribute whenever the current word possesses the active attribute as one of its features, and this selection results in an increment to the activation of the selected attribute, resulting in greater activation than for an attribute activated under Principle 2.

5. Activation of an attribute decays exponentially to a resting level as a function of the initial strength of activation.

6. When a meaning is selected, the weights of active attributes associated with that meaning are increased. Incrementing the weight of an attribute has the effect of increasing the likelihood that that attribute will be activated on subsequent encounters with the word. With respect to ambiguity processing, the reweighting of the selected attributes is the primary means by which one can account for the long-term effects of meaning selection, which produces results such as those for homophone word association cited in the previous section (Gorfein & Walters, 1989).

Principles 1 to 4 explain normal priming. A prime stimulus (sentence, word, or picture) activates a number of attributes associated with the meaning of the prime. If an ambiguous stimulus is presented in the presence of these active attributes, its interpretation will be biased to the extent that the active attributes overlap with the attributes associated with one of the alternative meanings of the stimulus. In addition, Principle 6 leads to the prediction that accessing the meaning of an ambiguous word in the context of a word related to one of its meanings will, as the result of changes in the attribute weights, bias multiple subsequent encounters with the word toward that meaning (see the discussion later in this chapter of V. R. Brown, Gorfein, & Amster, 2005).

Testing the Consequences of the Activation-Selection Model

In reviewing the differences between studies that showed long-term costs associated with homograph disambiguation (for reviews, see Bubka & Gorfein, 1989; Gorfein, 2001b; Simpson & Kang, 1994) and the sentence study in which costs were obtained only on an immediate trial (Gernsbacher et al., 2001), we were immediately struck by the fact that on the test trials in the sentence study, the homograph was always preceded by the disambiguating context (the homographs had been placed last in the sentence, as in other studies that used postsentence, related words to measure meaning priming). According to ASM, local context will tend to dominate under these constraints, because it activates attributes associated with a particular meaning (i.e., the set principle). The reordered-access model would seem to make similar predictions, because the early portion of the sentence creates a contextual bias toward a specific meaning. This is exactly the condition that should be most effective in overcoming the effects of previous priming. Other models would in all likelihood make similar predictions, but the need to distinguish between transient suppression and a more enduring inhibition mechanism suggested that we test the hypothesis directly.

To test the hypothesis that the effect of the meaning change in the sentence data had been hidden by the contextual constraint, we rewrote the second-occurrence sentences[1] to place the ambiguous word before the disambiguating context. In a between-groups design, we tested the original sentences and the rewritten sentences with four items separating the prime and test sentences. For the original sentence order (homograph at the end of the sentence), no effect of meaning change was obtained. In contrast, when the homograph preceded the disambiguating context, large costs were observed when the meaning of the sentence changed between the two trials (Gorfein, 2002). These findings are similar to the effects that Simpson and his colleagues (Simpson & Adamopolous, 2001; Simpson & Kang, 1994; Simpson & Kellas, 1989) reported and are consistent with the view that there are long-term costs associated with changing the context-appropriate meaning.

Gorfein and Amster (1998) studied homograph repetition with same or altered meaning in the relatedness decision task, a task in which the participant is required to decide whether a pair of words presented successively are related (e.g., *roof* and *beam*). When the homograph occurred first in the second-occurrence (target) pair (e.g., *beam* and *laser*), the effect of meaning change was almost double that of the condition in which the related word preceded the homograph in the target pair (e.g., *laser* and *beam*). (This study is discussed again in greater detail later in this chapter.)

ASM makes the claim that the effect of meaning change results from a readjustment of the weights of a word's semantic attributes. Although we have not yet found a direct way to test this claim, we have consistently found that meaning selection effects persist across tasks as well as temporal intervals. As early as 1962, Segal demonstrated transfer from analogy processing to word association. When a homograph was presented as part of an analogy, the meaning engendered by the analogy affected the choice of meaning for the homograph in a subsequent association test. In a recognition memory test, Light and Carter-Sobell (1970) showed that when an adjective biased one meaning of an ambiguous noun at study (e.g., *traffic* paired with *jam*) but a different meaning at testing (e.g., *grape* and *jam*), there was a significant decrease in recognizing the noun (*jam*).

Balota (1983) reported a related experiment involving transfer from a lexical decision task to a recognition memory task. Priming in the lexical decision task was essentially equal for threshold and suprathreshold presentations of the prime. With respect to recognition memory, however, repetition of the prime produced a benefit in the suprathreshold group but not in the threshold group. Balota interpreted his results to mean that lexical activation in the absence of being able to read the masked prime was insufficient for directing

---

[1] We thank Morton Gernsbacher for making these sentences available to us.

the attentional resources required to encode the prime. Later in this chapter, when we discuss how the activation-selection model applies to *episodic memory* (memory for specific past experiences), we offer our own explanation of these results and propose a test of that explanation.

In our laboratory, we have reported transfer from generating homophones using a word-fragment completion task (sometimes called a *cloze* procedure) to spelling and word association to that homophone (Gorfein & Walters, 1989) and from a picture location task to the spelling of, and word associations to, homophones (Gorfein et al., in press). In a single study, transfer was obtained from picture-location memory of homographs to sentence-sensibility judgment, word association, relatedness decision, short-term memory, and free recall (Gorfein, Black, & Edwards, 2005). Transfer from sentence-sensibility judgment to relatedness decision was also found in an independent study (Gorfein, 2002). Because environmental context varies across tasks in these studies, it is our belief that these findings argue against an episodic-retrieval explanation of transfer, because theories such as Logan's (1988) episodic-retrieval view are dependent on contextual consistency. In a similar fashion, the reduction of contextual retrieval cues resulting from response changes make Neill and Valdes's (1995) episodic-retrieval explanation of negative priming inapplicable to the transfer effects obtained in these studies.

Testing the alternative models of homograph processing was the goal of two studies conducted in our laboratory, one using homographs (Gorfein, Berger, & Bubka, 2000) and the other using homophones (Gorfein et al., in press). Both studies demonstrated that even after participants had responded in the direction of the dominant meaning in a context designed to elicit the dominant meaning, they reverted to an earlier primed secondary meaning on a subsequent test of the ambiguous word in an unbiased context. In the study of homophone processing (Gorfein et al., in press), we made use of two dependent measures to ensure generality of the conclusions: homophone spelling and word association to homophones. Because the two measures yielded highly similar results, we describe only the results for the combined measures.

For a normative baseline, a voice tape was prepared containing 42 homophones and 23 nonhomophones in random order. This tape was then presented to participants, half of whom were told to write the first word to come to mind to the auditory word and half of whom were to spell the word they heard. Performance on the two tasks was highly correlated, and the combined mean proportion of dominant responses was .74. This value was used as a baseline for two other studies.

In the first study, we compared the efficacy of pictures representing the homophone versus the printed word as cues for the disambiguation of the auditory presentation of the homophone. The homophones were presented four to a page with one homophone—presented either as a picture or as a word—in each quadrant of the page, making a booklet of 11 pages (Figure 6.1 shows a sample page). Participants were told that they were being tested on their memory for the location (quadrant) on the page and for whether the word was presented as a picture or as a word. The experimenter read aloud the four words on each page as the participant looked at the booklet. A memory test followed in which the experimenter read the 44 homophones in random order

Figure 6.1. A sample booklet page with the auditory description being *sun*, *hair*, *none*, and *tail* for Quadrants 1 to 4, respectively.

and the participants endeavored to recall location and form of presentation (word or picture). The tape recording used in the normative study was then introduced. Half of the participants were told to write the first word to come to mind for each word presented, and half were told to write what they heard ("spell the word"). Priming of the secondary meaning was greater for pictures (mean proportion of dominant responses = .52) than for words (mean proportion of dominant responses = .61), and both were significantly below the mean dominance of .74 in the normative group.

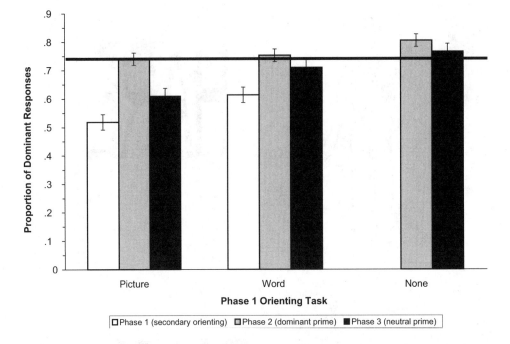

Figure 6.2. Proportion of dominant responses to homophones as a function of form of presentation in the Phase 1 orienting task. The data are averages of the word association and spelling responses. The horizontal line represents baseline performance. Error bars indicate 1 standard error of the mean.

From the viewpoint of the experimenter, the second and critical experiment had three parts. Phase 1 was a picture–word orienting phase similar to that described in the preceding paragraph. It was followed by Phase 2, an auditory word-association or spelling task in which the critical homophone was preceded by a prime related to the dominant meaning of the homophone (e.g., Item n is *star* and Item $n + 1$ is *sun*). In this portion of a continuous list, three homophone conditions were randomly presented: those shown in Phase 1 as pictures, those shown in Phase 1 as words, and those not shown in Phase 1. Without a break, this tape was completed with Phase 3: The same 69-item voice tape used in the normative and baseline studies presented the homophones in a nonbiasing context.

Figure 6.2 shows the combined results for the location memory study and the final two phases of the current experiment—Phase 2, with homophones in a dominant biasing context, and Phase 3, with the same items presented in the absence of a biasing context among the last 63 items of the list. As can be seen, items came out of the orienting phase much less likely to be responded to in the dominant direction than was the case in the normative control. However, in the dominant biasing context of Phase 2, the items were basically back at baseline except for the control condition, which showed priming in the direction of the dominant meaning as expected. The data from Phase 2 can be viewed as consistent with suppression–inhibition theories in that performance

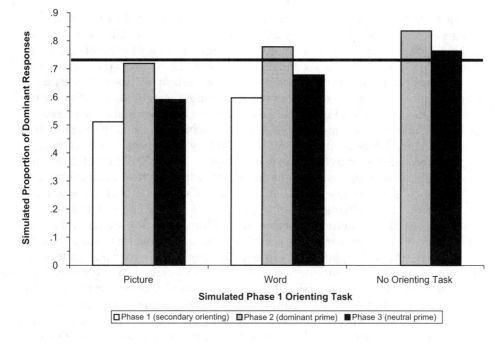

Figure 6.3. Results of the simulation of the activation-selection model.

in the picture and word conditions was below the control condition, indicating that the initial secondary priming in the orienting phase served to reduce the effect of the Phase 2 dominant prime. According to suppression–inhibition theories, it is necessary to inhibit or suppress the Phase 1 tendency to respond toward the secondary meaning resulting from the Phase 1 experience. In Phase 3, performance moved back toward the secondary meaning (below baseline), especially in the case of those items presented as pictures in the orienting phase. Such a recovery and movement away from the normative baseline is in our view incompatible with inhibition models as a class: Long-term inhibition of the secondary meaning carried over from Phase 2 would seem to lead to a smaller proportion of secondary responses in Phase 3, and short-term suppression that does not carry over would seem to predict a return to baseline performance in Phase 3. However, most suppression–inhibition models have not been specified in sufficient detail to attempt a direct fit to these data.

We have simulated the data shown in Figure 6.2 using an algorithm based on the principles of ASM outlined earlier in this chapter. Figure 6.3 presents the results of our simulation, which are clearly consistent with the Figure 6.2 data. To the extent that the simulation fits the data, the question remains whether we have somehow "snuck" cognitive inhibition into the model. That question is addressed in chapter 14 in this volume.

It is the increase in the weights of attributes associated with the selected meaning of an ambiguous word (Principle 6) that provides the basis for the ASM's explanation of the data presented in Figure 6.2. In Phase 1, the picture stimuli are seen to be more effective primes for the secondary meaning of the homographs than are the words. In ASM, this is represented as the activation of a greater number of secondary attributes in response to the pictures than to the words that visually accompany the auditory presentation of the homophones. The weights of the secondary attributes activated by the picture and word primes in Phase 1 are increased as the participant uses the prime to disambiguate the homophone. These more strongly weighted secondary attributes are in turn more likely to be selected when the homophone is presented again in Phase 2, this time following a word priming its dominant meaning. This procedure leads to slightly more secondary responses (fewer dominant responses) compared with the control condition in Phase 2. Although the dominant Phase 2 prime and subsequent dominant responses lead to an increase in the weights of the activated dominant attributes, the weights of the secondary attributes remain unchanged from their Phase 1 level. (The weights of a few secondary attributes actually increased in Phase 2 to the extent that they contributed to the proportion of secondary responses observed in Phase 2). Thus, when the homophone was presented again in a neutral context in Phase 3, the balance of attribute weights was still tipped in the direction of the secondary meaning primed in Phase 1 relative to a control condition that was not subject to secondary priming. This process leads to the observed increase in the number of secondary responses in the neutral Phase 3. This shift is particularly apparent for the homophones primed by pictures in Phase 1, because the more effective picture prime caused the weights of more secondary attributes to be increased. The long-term effect of prior meaning selection observed in Figure 6.2 is explained by ASM apparently without assuming that the representations of the competing primary and secondary meanings of the homographs inhibit each other in any way.

Because the reordered-access model also does not postulate direct inhibition between meaning representations, it should be considered whether that model could account for the long-term effects depicted in Figure 6.2. A modified version of the constraint-satisfaction implementation of the model, which allows the weights representing meaning frequency to remain altered following meaning selection, may be able—in a manner similar to the ASM—to account for the return of responses in neutral Phase 3 toward the initially selected secondary meaning. That is, if the revised frequency weights following secondary meaning selection in Phase 1 are sufficiently altered and the reweighting is not largely reversed by the dominant decision in Phase 2, then the frequency weights may be sufficient to return the Phase 3 responses back in the direction of the secondary meaning. The exact behavior of the modified model would depend, among other things, on the way in which the proportion of responses is determined by the model (which is currently designed as a model of processing time).

As we noted earlier in this chapter, a prediction of suppression–inhibition models is that the greater the conflict between meanings at the point of disambiguation, the greater the need should be to suppress the context-inappropriate meaning. For homographs where the two meanings are balanced (i.e., the frequency of each meaning is close to 50% in word association norms), eye-tracking studies indicate that there is maximal conflict (as measured by gaze duration) when the homograph occurs prior to its disambiguating context in a sentence (Duffy et al., 1988). Therefore, for suppression–inhibition theories, this finding suggests that were the balanced homograph to occur prior to a related word in a relatedness decision task and subsequently to be disambiguated by the related word, the inhibitory effect of meaning selection on a later encounter with the same homograph would be maximized. When the related word precedes the homograph on the initial encounter, little competition should exist, and therefore there should be little need to suppress or inhibit the alternative meaning.

The opposite prediction is made by ASM. The attributes of a related word that overlap with that meaning of the following homograph will be activated (the set principle), and to the extent that more attributes of the appropriate meaning are activated, the impact of their reweighting will be greater on future occurrences of the homograph. Thus, ASM predicts that related word–homograph pairs should produce both greater benefits and greater costs than homograph–related word pairs (although, again, suppression–inhibition models predict that first-occurrence homograph–related word pairs should produce greater costs of a homograph than related word–homograph pairs at the second presentation).

We tested that hypothesis in a relatedness decision experiment. In a within-subject design, the first occurrence of a homograph was in one of two orders: related word–homograph or homograph–related word (V. R. Brown et al., 2005). Figure 6.4 reports the order of the outcomes for reaction time, and Figure 6.5 shows the results for accuracy. The effects of order of the priming pair are consistent with the predictions of ASM. When the related word precedes the homograph, the related word acts as a prime that preactivates attributes related to that particular meaning of the homograph. This process leads to an increase in the number of attributes reweighted when that meaning is selected, which in turn increases the likelihood of the same meaning being selected on a later presentation of the homograph. Thus, benefits are obtained when the subsequent presentation is of the same meaning, whereas costs are obtained when the subsequent presentation is in a different meaning context.

Priming and the Activation-Selection Model

In a more formal analysis of our model, we examined how the probability of the dominant meaning being selected affected the number of attributes of the secondary meaning initially activated. We based our analysis on the parameters used in the Gorfein et al. (in press) study, where to select a meaning, a simple majority of sampled 19 attributes was needed (i.e., 10 or more attributes). The result of calculations based on the binomial distribution shown in Figure 6.6 indicates that as the probability of a dominant response increases from 0.5 to 1.0, there is very little diminution in the mean number of secondary attributes selected, with a mean of six secondary attributes still obtained at p(dominant) = .95 and falling below four only when p(dominant) > .99. Inasmuch as ASM assumes that forward priming is a consequence of active attributes, this suggests little diminution of secondary priming as dominance increases. Such a finding is consistent with the lexical decision priming of secondary meanings across a wide expanse of homograph balance (e.g., Simpson & Burgess, 1985).

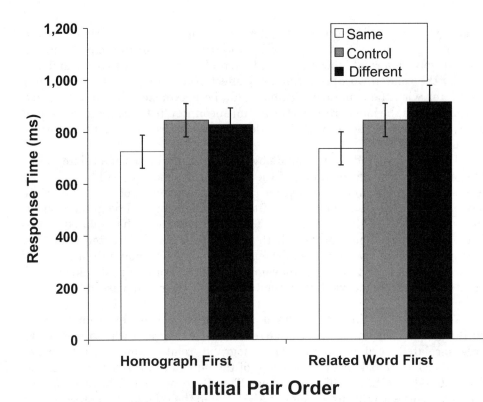

Figure 6.4. Decision latency in the relatedness decision task as a function of the order of first-occurrence prime and the relation of the pair meaning to the first-occurrence meaning. Error bars indicate 1 standard error of the mean.

Application of the Activation-Selection Model to Episodic Memory

As indicated in the introduction to this chapter, in this section we complete the circle from episodic memory, especially short-term memory (Gorfein, 1987), to ambiguity processing and back to some data and speculations about how ASM can contribute to an understanding of episodic memory. To apply ASM to episodic tasks in general and short-term memory in particular, we add three principles to the model:

7. The amount of activation given attributes is partly a controlled process.
8. Context (stimulus sample; Estes, 1950) is attached to active attributes at the time of encoding. Active attributes at encoding are marked with a sample of the contextual features present at encoding.
9. The context at retrieval is used to evaluate items presented for recognition or to aid in recall.

Muter (1980) used a task that paralleled in structure the standard Brown–Peterson short-term memory task (Brown, 1958; Peterson & Peterson, 1959;

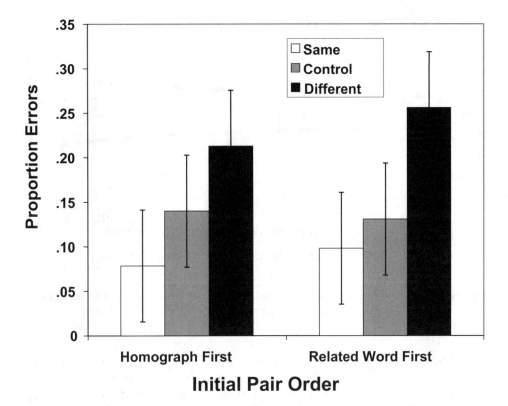

Figure 6.5. Probability of an error in the relatedness decision task as a function of the order of first-occurrence prime and the relation of the pair meaning to the first-occurrence meaning. Error bars indicate 1 standard error of the mean.

i.e., ready signal, brief presentation of subspan materials to be remembered, filled retention interval and test). Participants who processed the materials without memory instructions showed a complete loss of those materials on an unexpected memory test at a 2-second retention interval, in contrast to participants under memory instructions, who showed a decline in performance to about 20 seconds, at which point the function reached a nonzero asymptote. Muter interpreted his results as indicating that participants engaged in surreptitious rehearsals when alerted that later recall was expected (see Crowder & Greene, 1987, for a discussion of the import of this finding). However, there is an alternative view to the meaning of these results based on Principle 7, and we believe that the alternative has much greater predictive power.

It is clear that the rehearsal hypothesis would predict that in well-practiced participants, one of the following outcomes would be observed in the Muter (1980) study: Either there would be no retention interval effect because rehearsal-proficient participants would overcome the effects of retention interval, or (more likely) the effect of retention interval on performance would be that typically observed in distractor tasks—that is, performance would decline as a function of retention interval, because it would be easier to rehearse for

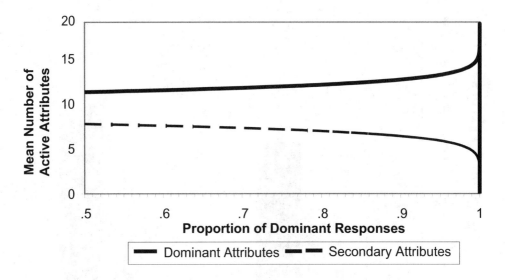

Figure 6.6.   Number of active attributes of the dominant meaning of an ambiguous word required to produce a dominant response, with probability varying from 0.5 to 1.0.

shorter than for prolonged intervals. Alternatively, under Principle 7 of ASM, it might be possible for a participant to adjust activation so as to minimize PI. The question then arises as to what the ideal adjustment might be. According to ASM, the model performance depends on being able to use the context at the time of recall both to help in retrieving the item from memory and in evaluating the retrieved item as to whether it was the one most recently presented. To the degree that the item is still active in memory, the retrieval step might be bypassed. However, evaluation depends on the similarity of the contextual features initially encoded with the item and the contextual features present at the time of retrieval. To the degree that more than one item shares these features, successful retrieval becomes more problematic. Thus, if an item's attributes are still active when the next item is presented for study, the set principle suggests that the active attributes of the earlier item will select those attributes that the two items have in common, thereby creating potential difficulties (competition) at a subsequent retrieval attempt. Further, consistent with Principle 4 of ASM, the activation that is the consequence of the set principle will be incremented, making it more difficult for the participant to control activation, and thereby will tend to ensure that the item on the next trial will be similarly encoded.

Before fully discussing the consequences of this view, we describe an experiment that supports these claims. Gorfein and Viviani (1980) used a procedure similar to that of Loess (1968): Word triads drawn from taxonomic categories such as animals or clothing were used as memory items. The experiment consisted of 18 blocks of 4 trials each, arranged so that within a block all items came from the same category, and categorical blocks were arranged so as to maximize the judged semantic dissimilarity between adjacent blocks. We reasoned that when retention intervals vary at random across trials, as is

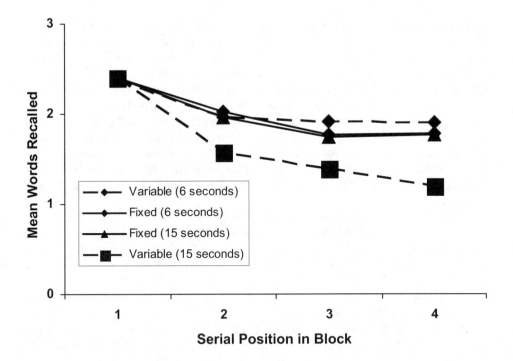

Figure 6.7.   Number of words correct out of three as a function of trial position in a block and whether the retention interval was fixed or variable (from Gorfein & Viviani, 1980).

typical in short-term memory studies, the participant can do little to adjust activation to maximize performance. If the retention interval is fixed in duration, however, the participant can work to maximize performance. We therefore created three conditions: a typical manipulation in which the retention interval was either 6 seconds or 15 seconds, varied at random, and two fixed interval conditions, a pure 6-second and a pure 15-second condition. Counter to the rehearsal prediction—that performance would decline with increasing length of retention interval—we expected performance on the fixed 6-second interval to be the same as that of the fixed 15-second interval. When the retention interval was randomly arranged, we reasoned that the best the participant could do would be to adjust activation to an intermediate level, which would result in better performance at 6 seconds and poorer performance at 15 seconds. As shown in Figure 6.7, those results are exactly what we obtained.

In the context of episodic-memory experiments, we sought to determine how the principles of ASM would apply to the finding of Balota (1983) that recognition memory was influenced only when a prime word at study was suprathreshold. In applying Principle 9 to the question, we suggest the possibility that the participant may on some trials compare the contextual markings of the prime and the homograph to help decide whether the homograph was previously presented. Two possibilities come to mind. First, in the absence of awareness of the priming word in the lexical decision task (i.e., the threshold condition), the participant may fail to undertake this comparison in the recognition task. Or, second, under the threshold activation of the prime word, the participant may fail to attach a contextual sample to the activated attributes of the prime. A way to test these possibilities may exist. If participants perform both a threshold and a suprathreshold lexical decision task followed by the recognition task for the combined set of items, we might expect participants to use the contextual comparison task for the combined set. To the extent that the threshold primes were contextually encoded, we would expect a similar advantage for same-meaning primes. If the threshold primes were not contextually marked, then the results would be similar to those of Balota (1983)— that is, a differential effect of threshold and suprathreshold primes but under circumstances in which we could be confident that the comparison was undertaken.

In the past several years, we have begun to try to connect ASM to the memory literature (V. R. Brown & Gorfein, 2004, 2005) and in particular to ideas that suggest a memory process based on two types of memory traces: verbatim and gist traces (Brainerd, Payne, Wright, & Reyna, 2003; Brainerd, Reyna, & Mojardin, 1999; see also chap. 10, this volume).

It is our belief that the two trace types represent the effect of encoding mechanisms similar to those proposed for ASM. The verbatim trace dominates when a significant majority of contextually encoded attributes of an item are unique to the item in the memory context. This happens when there is little overlap between the item's attributes and the attributes of other items presented within the memory context. On Trial 1 in the Brown–Peterson task, performance is at ceiling regardless of the duration of the retention interval, because there are no other items to share the current contextual encoding. In similar fashion, when care is taken to maximize the dissimilarity of adjacent category blocks in this task, the first trial of a block will show no effect of retention interval (compare performance between the 6-second and 15-second retention intervals on Trial 1 in Figure 6.5).

From our viewpoint, the gist trace dominates whenever there is significant overlap between the attributes activated for closely spaced items (close spacing maximizes contextual similarity) and the overlap in attributes diminishes the effectiveness of the verbatim trace. When attributes of successive items are selected under the set principle (i.e., the active attributes of a prior item select the current item's attributes), they ensure a commonality of contextual marking. Although it is highly probable that when *lion* and *tiger* are presented on successive trials, *animal* will be part of the current activated sense of each word, and it is only under the following circumstances that a gist trace will result. Common attribute marking has three potential sources: (a) Context does not fluctuate greatly between the independent occurrences of the common attribute, resulting in highly similar encoding; (b) the active attribute *animal* from the word *tiger* presented on an earlier trial is still active when *lion* is presented on a later trial, resulting in both attributes being marked with the context of the later trial; or (c) the presentation of the word *lion* on a later trial brings *tiger* back to mind and thereby leads to common encoding. In this regard, Rundus (1971) showed that it was not uncommon for a later word in a free-recall list to bring back into the active rehearsal set an item presented earlier in the list that had dropped out of the rehearsal set.

To the extent that a participant in a Brown–Peterson task could control the activation of the current memory item, performance would be enhanced if the activation ended at the time of retrieval or recognition. Activity to that point would guarantee the presence of the memory trace of the current item and therefore make retrieval relatively easy. However, to the extent that activation persists until the next item, the set principle becomes operative as described above (i.e., overlapping attributes tend to remain active from item to item). When common attributes remain active, it becomes difficult to constrain the activation of the current item, because under Principle 4 of ASM, an increment in activation is automatically applied to a selected attribute or attributes. We are currently investigating the circumstances that allow the control of activation. One line of our investigation is considering the possibility that the reason high-memory-span individuals show less PI is that these individuals are more able to control activation. (For a fuller discussion of memory span, see chap. 7, this volume.)

Conclusion

We believe that the ASM outlined in this chapter can account for the process of selecting the meaning of an ambiguous word without requiring the suppression or inhibition of the unselected meaning. In ASM, a word is assumed to be represented as a collection of abstract attributes. Each attribute of an ambiguous word is assumed to be associated with one of the alternative meanings. The meaning associated with the majority of active attributes is the meaning selected for a given occurrence of the word. The relative balance of the alternative meanings is assumed to be dynamic: Each time a meaning is selected, the attributes associated with that meaning are increased in weight. Because the probability of an attribute being activated is proportional to its weight, this change in an attribute's weight has the effect of biasing future occurrences of the ambiguous word in the direction of the recently selected meaning. The strength of a word's representation does not return to some baseline level after each experience. This finding accounts for long-term effects such as the primacy effect shown in the location memory task and in prior work with the continuous word association task (Gorfein et al., 2000).

Despite an intervening dominant prime, participants in the location memory task who were initially primed with the secondary meaning of a homograph made a greater proportion of secondary responses to the homograph in a neutral context many minutes later compared with control participants not initially exposed to a secondary prime. Suppression–inhibition models would seem to have difficulty explaining how the activation of the secondary meaning can continue beyond the subsequent dominant prime, which by definition would lead to the inhibition or suppression of the secondary meaning. Lingering inhibition would cause the proportion of secondary responses to remain below the control condition during a subsequent encounter with the homograph in a neutral context, whereas transient suppression might allow the proportion of secondary responses to return to the level of the control condition. In neither case, however, should the proportion of secondary responses increase above the control condition in the subsequent neutral context, as the data indicate and as ASM predicts. (As discussed in this chapter, it is possible that a modified version of the reordered-access model, which also does not postulate inhibition or suppression of the nonselected meaning, could account for these data, but that remains unclear at this point.)

In addition, the ASM view has implications for the processing of words in situations ranging in scope from semantic memory tasks such as sentence-sensibility instructions to episodic-memory tasks like the Brown–Peterson paradigm. Furthermore, the addition of contextual stimulus sampling at encoding connects ASM to two-process memory models such as fuzzy-trace theory. Thus, in the future we hope to show that ASM is part of a broader theory of cognitive processing that does not assume that selecting among conflicting representations necessarily requires a mechanism that suppresses the unselected alternative.

References

Anderson, J. R. (1983). *The architecture of cognition.* Cambridge, MA: Harvard University Press.

Anderson, M. C., & Spellman, B. A. (1995). On the status of inhibitory mechanisms in cognition: Memory retrieval as a model case. *Psychological Review, 102,* 68–100.

Balota, D. A. (1983). Automatic semantic activation and episodic memory encoding. *Journal of Verbal Learning and Verbal Behavior, 22,* 88–104.

Bower, G. (1967). A multicomponent theory of the memory trace. In K. W. Spence & J. T. Spence (Eds.), *The psychology of learning and motivation* (Vol. 1, pp. 229–325). New York: Academic Press.

Brainerd, C. J., Payne, D. G., Wright, R., & Reyna, V. F. (2003). Phantom recall. *Journal of Memory and Language, 48,* 445–467.

Brainerd, C. J., Reyna, V. F., & Mojardin, A. H. (1999). Conjoint recognition. *Psychological Review, 106,* 160–179.

Brown, J. A. (1958). Some tests of the decay theory of immediate memory. *Quarterly Journal of Experimental Psychology, 10,* 12–21.

Brown, V. R., & Gorfein, D. S. (2004). A new look at recognition in the Brown–Peterson distractor paradigm: Towards the application of new methodology to unsolved problems of recognition memory. *Memory & Cognition, 32,* 674–685.

Brown, V. R., & Gorfein, D. S. (2005, November). *Another look at recognition in the distractor paradigm: PI build-up and release mediated by operation span.* Poster presented at the annual meeting of the Psychonomic Society, Minneapolis, MN.

Brown, V. R., Gorfein, D. S., & Amster, H. (2005, May). *Order effects in the semantic priming of homographs: An application of the activation–selection model.* Paper presented at the 77th annual meeting of the Midwestern Psychological Association, Chicago.

Bubka, A., & Gorfein, D. S. (1989). Resolving semantic ambiguity: An introduction. In D. S. Gorfein (Ed.), *Resolving semantic ambiguity* (pp. 1–12). New York: Springer-Verlag.

Collins, A. M., & Loftus, E. F. (1975). A spreading-activation theory of semantic processing. *Psychological Review, 82,* 407–428.

Crowder, R. G., & Greene, R. L. (1987). The context of remembering: Comments on the chapters by Glenberg, Gorfein, and Wickens. In D. S. Gorfein & R. R. Hoffman (Eds.), *Memory and learning: The Ebbinghaus centennial conference* (pp. 191–199). Hillsdale, NJ: Erlbaum.

Duffy, S. A., Kambe, G., & Rayner, K. (2001). The effect of prior disambiguating context on the comprehension of ambiguous words: Evidence from eye movements. In D. S. Gorfein (Ed.), *On the consequences of meaning selection: Perspectives on resolving lexical ambiguity* (pp. 27–43). Washington, DC: American Psychological Association.

Duffy, S. A., Morris, R. K., & Rayner, K. (1988). Lexical ambiguity and fixation times in reading. *Journal of Memory and Language, 27,* 429–446.

Erickson, J. R., & Allred, S. (2001). A model of repetition priming for lexical decisions. In D. S. Gorfein (Ed.), *On the consequences of meaning selection: Perspectives on resolving lexical ambiguity* (pp. 191–214). Washington, DC: American Psychological Association.

Estes, W. K. (1950). Towards a statistical theory of learning. *Psychological Review, 11,* 145–154.

Gernsbacher, M. A. (1990). *Language comprehension as structure building.* Hillsdale, NJ: Erlbaum.

Gernsbacher, M. A., & Faust, M. E. (1991a). The mechanism of suppression: A component of general comprehension skill. *Journal of Experimental Psychology: Learning, Memory, and Cognition, 17,* 245–262.

Gernsbacher, M. A., & Faust, M. (1991b). The role of suppression in sentence comprehension. In G. B. Simpson (Ed.), *Understanding word and sentence* (pp. 97–128). Amsterdam: North Holland.

Gernsbacher, M. A., & Faust, M. (1995). Skilled suppression. In F. N. Dempster & C. N. Brainerd (Eds.), *Interference and inhibition in cognition* (pp. 295–327). San Diego, CA: Academic Press.

Gernsbacher, M. A., Robertson, R. R. W., & Werner, N. K. (2001). The costs and benefits of meaning. In D. S. Gorfein (Ed.), *On the consequences of meaning selection: Perspectives on resolving lexical ambiguity* (pp. 119–137). Washington, DC: American Psychological Association.

Gorfein, D. S. (1987). Explaining context effects on short-term memory. In D. S. Gorfein & R. R. Hoffman (Eds.), *Memory and learning: The Ebbinghaus centennial conference* (pp. 153–172). Hillsdale, NJ: Erlbaum.

Gorfein, D. S. (2001a). An activation-selection view of homograph disambiguation: A matter of emphasis? In D. S. Gorfein (Ed.), *On the consequences of meaning selection: Perspectives on resolving lexical ambiguity* (pp. 157–173). Washington, DC: American Psychological Association.

Gorfein, D. S. (2001b). On the consequences of meaning selection: An overview. In D. S. Gorfein (Ed.), *On the consequences of meaning selection: Perspectives on resolving lexical ambiguity* (pp. 3–8). Washington, DC: American Psychological Association.

Gorfein, D. S. (2002, May). *Resolving lexical ambiguity: Sentence order influences effects on homograph reprocessing.* Paper presented at the 74th annual meeting of the Midwestern Psychological Association, Chicago.

Gorfein, D. S., & Amster, H. (1998, November). *Some consequences of homograph disambiguation.* Paper presented at the annual meeting of the Psychonomic Society, Dallas, TX.

Gorfein, D. S., Berger, S. A., & Bubka, A. (2000). The selection of homograph meaning: Word association when context changes. *Memory & Cognition, 28,* 766–773.

Gorfein, D. S., Black, L. S., & Edwards, E. A. (2005, November). *Transfer of meaning selection.* Paper presented at the annual meeting of the Psychonomic Society, Toronto, Ontario, Canada.

Gorfein, D. S., Brown, V. R., & DeBiasi, C. (in press). A simulation of the activation–selection model of meaning: The sun comes out after the son. *Memory & Cognition.*

Gorfein, D. S., & Bubka, A. (1989). A context-sensitive frequency-based theory of meaning achievement. In D. S. Gorfein (Ed.), *Resolving semantic ambiguity* (pp. 84–106). New York: Springer-Verlag.

Gorfein, D. S., & Viviani, J. M. (1980, November). *There are no effects of retention interval.* Paper presented at the annual meeting of the Psychonomic Society, St. Louis, MO.

Gorfein, D. S., & Viviani, J. M. (1981, November). *What is PI release the release of?* Paper presented at the annual meeting of the Psychonomic Society, Philadelphia.

Gorfein, D. S., & Walters, M. F. (1989). When does "soar" become "sore"? Some comments on the chapter of Simpson and Kellas. In D. S. Gorfein (Ed.), *Resolving semantic ambiguity* (pp. 57–62). New York: Springer-Verlag.

Light, L. L., & Carter-Sobell, L. (1970). Effects of changed semantic contest on recognition memory. *Journal of Verbal Learning and Verbal Behavior, 9,* 1–11.

Loess, H. (1968). Short-term memory and item similarity. *Journal of Verbal Learning and Verbal Behavior, 7,* 87–92.

Logan, G. D. (1988). Toward an instance theory of automatization. *Psychological Review, 95,* 492–527.

Melton, A. W., & Martin, E. (Eds.). (1972). *Encoding processes in human memory.* Washington, DC: V. H. Winston & Sons.

Muter, P. (1980). Very rapid forgetting. *Memory & Cognition, 8,* 174–179.

Neill, W. T., & Valdes, L. A. (1995). Faciliatory and inhibitory aspects of selective attention. In A. F. Kramer, M. G. H. Coles, & G. D. Logan (Eds.), *Converging operations in the study of visual selective attention* (pp. 77–106). Washington, DC: American Psychological Association.

Norman, K., Newman, E. L., Detre, G. J., & Polyn, S. M. (2006). How inhibitory oscillations can train neural networks and punish competitors. *Neural Computation, 18,* 1577–1610.

Onifer, W., & Swinney, D. A. (1981). Accessing lexical ambiguity during sentence comprehension: Effects of frequency of meaning and contextual bias. *Memory & Cognition, 9,* 225–236.

Perfetti, C. A., & Hart, L. (2001). The lexical basis of comprehension skill. In D. S. Gorfein (Ed.), *On the consequences of meaning selection: Perspectives on resolving lexical ambiguity* (pp. 67–86). Washington, DC: American Psychological Association.

Peterson, L. R., & Peterson, M. J. (1959). Short-term retention of individual items. *Journal of Experimental Psychology, 58,* 193–198.

Razran, G. H. S. (1935). Salivating and thinking in different languages. *Journal of Psychology: Interdisciplinary and Applied, 1,* 145–151.

Rundus, D. (1971). Analysis of rehearsal processes in free recall. *Journal of Experimental Psychology, 89,* 63–77.

Segal, S. J. (1962). *The effect of different contextual conditions on the priming of free and continued word association.* Unpublished doctoral dissertation, New York University, New York.

Shivde, G., & Anderson, M. C. (2001). The role of inhibition in meaning selection: Insight from retrieval-induced forgetting. In D. S. Gorfein (Ed.), *On the consequences of meaning selection: Perspectives on resolving lexical ambiguity* (pp. 175–190). Washington, DC: American Psychological Association.

Simpson, G. B., & Adamopoulos, A. C. (2001). Repeated homographs on word and sentence contexts: Multiple processing of multiple meanings. In D. S. Gorfein (Ed.), *On the consequences of meaning selection: Perspectives on resolving lexical ambiguity* (pp. 157–173). Washington, DC: American Psychological Association.

Simpson, G. B., & Burgess, C. (1985). Activation and selection processes in the recognition of ambiguous words. *Journal of Experimental Psychology: Human Perception and Performance, 11,* 28–39.

Simpson, G. B., & Kang, H. (1994). Inhibitory processes in the recognition of homograph meanings. In D. Dagenbach & T. H. Carr (Eds.), *Inhibitory processes in attention, memory, and language* (pp. 359–381). New York: Academic Press.

Simpson, G. B., & Kellas, G. (1989). Dynamic contextual processes and lexical access. In D. S. Gorfein (Ed.), *Resolving semantic ambiguity* (pp. 40–56). New York: Springer-Verlag.

Spivey, M. J., & Tannenhaus, M. K. (1998). Syntactic ambiguity resolution in discourse: Modeling the effects of referential context and lexical frequency. *Journal of Experimental Psychology: Learning, Memory, and Cognition, 24,* 1521–1543.

Swinney, D. (1981). Lexical processing during sentence comprehension: Effects of higher order constraints and implications for representation. In T. Myers, J. Laver, & J. M. Anderson (Eds.), *The cognitive representation of speech* (pp. 201–210). Amsterdam: North Holland.

Twilley, L. C., & Dixon, P. (2000). Meaning resolution processes for words: A parallel independent model. *Psychonomic Bulletin & Review, 7,* 49–82.

7

Working Memory Capacity and Inhibition: Cognitive and Social Consequences

Thomas S. Redick, Richard P. Heitz, and Randall W. Engle

The construct of inhibition plays a prominent role within cognitive psychology (Dagenbach & Carr, 1994; Dempster & Brainerd, 1995) despite ongoing controversy surrounding its utility as a concept (MacLeod, Dodd, Sheard, Wilson, & Bibi, 2003). For researchers who agree on the existence of inhibition, there are additional debates as to whether inhibition is the cause (Hasher & Zacks, 1988; May, Hasher, & Kane, 1999) or a consequence (Kane, Bleckley, Conway, & Engle, 2001) of individual differences in working memory capacity (WMC). This chapter provides a brief introduction to our executive-attention theory of WMC and how exactly WMC relates to inhibition, and then we review research from the cognitive and social domains that connects WMC and inhibition.

Individual Differences in Working Memory Capacity and Executive Attention

Individual differences in WMC are related to a number of important abilities and behaviors, including fluid intelligence, reading comprehension, and acquisition of various skills (for recent reviews, see Conway et al., 2005; Engle & Kane, 2004; Heitz, Unsworth, & Engle, 2004; Kane, Conway, Hambrick, & Engle, 2007; Unsworth, Heitz, & Engle, 2005). These relations have been discovered mainly in the context of relating criterion measures to individual differences in performance on complex span tasks such as operation span (OSPAN; Turner & Engle, 1989), reading span (Daneman & Carpenter, 1980), and counting span (Case, Kurland, & Goldberg, 1982). These complex span tasks were developed originally as a way to measure the multifaceted nature of cognition based on the Baddeley and Hitch (1974) model of working memory. Complex span tasks such as OSPAN combine the elements of a serial recall task (e.g., list of words) interleaved with a simple decision task (e.g., solving basic mathematic operations). For example, participants taking OSPAN would see a series of items such as the following: IS $(2 \times 1) + 3 = 6$? DOG. After two to seven items are presented, the participant would then be signaled to recall the words in serial order. Thus, complex span tasks have also been labeled "processing-and-storage tasks," in contrast to "storage-only tasks" such as digit span, which are commonly included in psychological test batteries.

From this perspective, individual differences in WMC, as measured by the various complex span tasks, represent the ability to maintain item and order information while dividing attention with the processing component of the task. Across trials, the opportunity for interference arises, and WMC is important for selecting only the currently relevant memory representations. Our framework for explaining the relations between measures of WMC and higher order cognition is that *executive attention*, or the ability to control attention in a goal-directed manner, is critical for accurate and efficient cognition. More specifically, WMC is most important when goal-related information must be actively maintained to guide response selection, especially if viable but contextually inappropriate response alternatives are also available (Engle & Kane, 2004). The label *executive attention* was explicitly chosen to emphasize our contention that individual differences in WMC represent mainly the domain-free, limited-capacity functioning of the central executive in the Baddeley and Hitch (1974) working memory model (Kane, Poole, Tuholski, & Engle, 2006).

Although we use the term *working memory capacity*, we view individual differences in WMC as representing an ability to control attention, which leads to differences in the number of items one can store in memory. Therefore, another way to view individual differences in WMC is to think of them as differences in the ability to allocate attention resources. Norman and Bobrow (1975) outlined two kinds of capacity limitations on information processing: (a) data limitations and (b) resource limitations. Critically, performance in a given situation is determined by a combination of the two types of process, but data limitations (e.g., stimulus degradation) occur independent of the amount of attention resources an individual allocates to the task. We argue that individual differences in WMC are akin to resource limitations on processing, and people high in WMC can more flexibly allocate attention resources to achieve some goal (for a related view on the flexibility of attention allocation, see Cowan, 2004).

To study the importance of individual differences in WMC, our research has taken two main forms (Engle & Kane, 2004). Our macroanalytic research with young adults has used the full range of individual differences in several abilities, including WMC, short-term memory, processing speed, and fluid and crystallized intelligence, and has attempted to account for the nature of the relations between these constructs at the latent level using confirmatory factor analysis and structural equation modeling (Conway, Cowan, Bunting, Therriault, & Minkoff, 2002; Engle, Tuholski, Laughlin, & Conway, 1999; Kane et al., 2004). Our microanalytic research, which is the focus of this chapter, has measured young adults on complex span tasks such as OSPAN and has had individuals who score in the upper and lower quartiles (called *high-span* and *low-span participants*, respectively) perform various cognitive psychology experiments, primarily in the memory and attention domains.

A Resource Account of Inhibition

Several researchers (Friedman & Miyake, 2004; Kipp Harnishfeger, 1995; Mac-Leod et al., 2003; Nigg, 2000) have recently acknowledged the prevalence of inhibition as an explanatory mechanism in different psychological domains. However, as those authors also noted, the exact meaning of inhibition hypothesized in various studies is often poorly defined. Our view is that inhibition is a controlled and resource-demanding process that influences performance in situations where task success is aided by inhibiting not only task-specific information but also irrelevant thoughts and distracting events (Conway & Engle, 1994; Engle, 1996). Therefore, our use of *inhibition* is equivalent to the active, goal-directed process that Bjork (1989) referred to as *suppression*; our focus is on inhibition as suppression and not inhibition as *blocking*, which Bjork described as "a by-product of the activation of other items in memory . . . [that] may not be adaptive" (Bjork, 1989, p. 325).

Engle, Conway, Tuholski, and Shisler (1995) presented an account of inhibition as an effortful, resource-dependent process that would be impaired if one did not have sufficient attention resources. Engle et al. (1995) tested the inhibition-resource hypothesis by administering a negative priming task under varying conditions of concurrent memory load. Specifically, participants saw a pair of letters on each trial and were instructed to name the red letter while ignoring the green letter. Trials were divided into primes and probes, with one third of the probe trials representing the interference condition, because the probe target had just been presented as the distractor on the prime trial. The other two thirds of the probe trials were control trials, with completely different red and green letters on both the prime and probe trial pair. The critical manipulation involved the presentation of a word to be remembered for later recall after certain probe trials. No word was presented after the probe trial for the initial prime–probe pair in a set of five trials (Load 0); however, a different word for recall was presented after each of the subsequent probe trials in the set (Loads 1, 2, 3, and 4). After completing five trials, participants were instructed to recall the four words in serial order. The negative priming effect (the difference between control and inhibition trials) was compared for each memory load (0–4) and also to a separate experiment in which participants completed the negative priming task without the concurrent memory task.

If inhibition is a resource-dependent process, then the negative-priming effect reflecting inhibition should vary with the increasing attention resources being devoted to the concurrent memory task. That is, as the resources demanded by the memory task increase with the number of items held in memory, there should be fewer resources available to devote to the letter identification task and to suppression of the distractor, as reflected in a decrease in the amount of slowing seen on interference trials compared with control trials. Participants in the control experiment showed the typical negative-priming effect; however, as predicted, this relation changed with increasing load for participants who also performed the memory task. Although interference trials were slower than control trials for the Load 0 condition, the Load 3 and 4 conditions showed that interference trials were actually faster than control trials. The so-called interference trials showed a positive-priming effect, which is what would be expected if the representation of the distractor from the previous trial was not adequately suppressed. The modification of the negative-priming effect by adding a memory load demonstrates that inhibitory processes are indeed resource dependent.

Conway, Tuholski, Shisler, and Engle (1999) proposed that individual differences in WMC also affect inhibitory efficiency by comparing high- and low-span participants on a version of the negative-priming task used in Engle et al. (1995). Replicating their earlier work, negative priming was seen only on trials with a memory load of 0, supporting the argument that inhibition is a resource-dependent process. The critical finding involving WMC was that although high-span participants showed a significant negative-priming effect at Load 0, low-span participants did not produce a reliable negative-priming effect in any memory load condition. These results suggest that even in the easiest version of the task, low-span participants did not suppress the distractor item. Going back to the earlier discussion of the factors involved in determining the resources available for inhibitory processes, these results show that individual differences in WMC influence the effectiveness of inhibition.

Working Memory Capacity and Cognitive Inhibition

As mentioned earlier in this chapter, there are differing views regarding the primary cause of individual differences in WMC. As will become clear, we are confident that WMC is in fact related to inhibition. However, our position is that individual differences in WMC represent a differential ability to control attention, which causes (among other things) individual differences in inhibitory ability. Admittedly, this account makes many predictions similar to those of an alternative view that individual differences in inhibitory processes lead to differences in WMC (Hasher & Zacks, 1988). Although presented originally as a theory to explain the cognitive deficits often seen in older adults, this view can often account for the differences in performance seen within individuals of the same age group, resulting in what has been described as the "chicken–egg" dilemma (Kane et al., 2001; May et al., 1999). However, research conducted in our lab from the time of our last review of WMC and inhibition (Engle, 1996) has provided additional evidence that WMC is the causal factor, and not the consequence, of inhibition.

Especially relevant to our discussion of competing theories of WMC, Hasher, Zacks, and May (1999) put forth a taxonomy of inhibition that distinguishes among the access, deletion, and restraint functions in their discussion of inhibitory failures in older adults. Borrowing from a similar point made by Friedman and Miyake (2004), these separate inhibitory functions can be considered in terms of the three different stages of information processing at which each occurs: (a) Access occurs at the perceptual stage, (b) deletion happens at an intermediate stage after representations enter the focus of attention (Cowan, 1995), and (c) restraint arises at the output level of processing. These separate types of inhibition provide the framework for reviewing our research in the cognitive domain relating WMC to inhibition.

Access

Hasher et al. (1999) defined the *access* function of inhibition as "preventing any activated but goal-irrelevant information (triggered automatically by familiar stimuli in the physical or mental environment) from entering working memory" (p. 654). The physical stimuli correspond to external information, whereas the mental stimuli are analogous to internal thoughts. The research described in this section focuses mainly on the "physical" environment, whereas the research described later in the WMC and Social Inhibition section centers more on the "mental" environment.

DICHOTIC LISTENING. Although primarily used as a means to study early-versus late-filter attention theories, dichotic listening also provides a powerful demonstration that WMC is related to one's ability to select what enters memory. Conway, Cowan, and Bunting (2001) used dichotic listening to study the relation between WMC and the ability to inhibit a highly salient distractor—namely, one's own name, as in the cocktail party phenomenon (Moray, 1959). High- and low-span participants were presented with different auditory streams in two channels and told to shadow one input while ignoring the other. As in the original study, the shadowing task was used as a guise to examine whether individuals reported hearing their name, which had been presented in the irrelevant auditory channel.

The authors argued that two opposing hypotheses regarding WMC were possible: (a) High-span participants could have been able to both successfully shadow the relevant channel while also monitoring the irrelevant channel, resulting in more reports of hearing their own name, or (b) high-span participants could have been better at focusing on the relevant channel and actively suppressing the irrelevant channel, resulting in fewer reports of hearing their own name. The latter prediction is exactly what they found; low-span participants were much more likely to report hearing their names than high-span participants (65% vs. 20%, respectively), and they made more shadowing errors than high-span participants at the time their name was presented. The results suggest two very important conclusions: (a) Individual differences in WMC represent differences in ability versus the amount of stored information as a property of an individual, and (b) WMC is determined by an ability to control attention in the service of achieving task goals.

FLANKER TASK. Another experimental situation where distractor information can interfere with the task goal is the flanker task (Eriksen & Eriksen, 1974). This paradigm demonstrates the importance of being able to selectively focus on a specific aspect of a stimulus, even when it is surrounded by distractors competing for attention. In one version of the task, participants are instructed to respond to a central target letter flanked either by the same letters (e.g., *HHHHH;* compatible) or letters mapped to the competing response (e.g., *HHSHH;* incompatible). Performance on incompatible trials is slower and more error prone when compared with compatible trials because the influence of the distractors interferes with processing of the target letter. Gratton, Coles, Sirevaag, Eriksen, and Donchin (1988) analyzed the response time (RT) distributions for compatible and incompatible flanker trials and measured accuracy as a function of RT. They found that incompatible-trial performance was at chance on the fastest trials, but performance on slightly slower trials was actually less than chance, consistent with the idea that the distractors were not being filtered and in fact were biasing participants toward the competing, incorrect response. In contrast, the slowest incompatible trials were performed without error, suggesting that the flankers were no longer affecting responses.

Heitz and Engle (in press) extended the Gratton et al. (1988) findings by testing high- and low-span participants on the flanker task on the basis of the notion that high-span participants are faster at constraining their attention to the target and less likely to be affected by the distracting information on incompatible trials. High- and low-span participants did not differ in accuracy during either the fastest or slowest incompatible trials. Replicating Gratton et al., on the fastest trials, all participants were performing at chance, suggesting that they were merely guessing; on the slowest trials, all participants were near ceiling. However, high-span participants were significantly more accurate on trials in the middle of the RT distribution, indicating that they were faster in their ability to selectively attend to the target letter and remove the influence of the distractors.

Redick and Engle (2006) also examined individual differences in WMC on a version of the flanker test embedded within the attention network test (Fan, McCandliss, Sommer, Raz, & Posner, 2002). Instead of using letters, the attention network test displays left- and right-pointing arrows as the targets and distractors. Despite the differences in the overall task structure, we corroborated the findings of Heitz and Engle (in press) showing that the presence of incompatible flankers was more detrimental for low-span compared with high-span participants. Overall, these results suggest that individuals high in WMC are more effective at preventing interfering information from affecting further cognition.

Deletion

As part of the memory retrieval process, one must identify and select the appropriate item from among other activated representations within memory. This search through memory is aided if one can inhibit "the activation of any marginally relevant or irrelevant information, along with the activation of any information that becomes irrelevant" (Hasher et al., 1999, p. 654). The *deletion* function is similar both to what Nigg (2000) called *cognitive inhibition* and to the effortful suppression form of retrieval inhibition that Bjork (1989) distinguished from blocking. As stated earlier, the key distinction between *suppression* and *blocking* is that suppression is actively used to achieve some goal, whereas blocking is more of a consequence of retrieving a nontarget item that subsequently impairs access to the target. In addition to the proactive interference (PI) studies that follow, the interested reader is referred to Engle (1996) for a discussion of previous research with WMC and inhibition during memory retrieval.

PAIRED-ASSOCIATES TASK. Rosen and Engle (1998) examined the role of WMC in a modified paired-associates task. High- and low-span participants were presented with lists of cue–target pairs to learn and then tested for target recall after each list presentation for a total of three separate lists. Although all participants received semantically related cues on each list, the exact list composition was determined by two between-subjects conditions. Participants in the control condition received cues from a new category for each list, and target words were never repeated. In contrast, participants in the interference condition received the same 12 cues for each list and received the same target words on the first and third lists. Thus, we labeled the design for the control condition *EF–CD–AB* and the interference condition *AB–AC–AB* to represent that List 3 items were the same for both conditions. Comparing the span groups in the interference condition allowed us to make the following predictions: (a) If high-span participants are better at suppressing, then List 2 performance should be worse for low-span participants because the List 1 cue–target associations should interfere, and (b) low-span participants should actually be faster than high-span participants on List 3 relearning because they did not inhibit these associations as effectively as high-span participants did.

The results showed that low-span participants were more likely to intrude List 1 targets at recall of List 2 items, and they also took more trials to correctly recall all 12 target items. This finding is consistent with the idea that low-span persons have more difficulty suppressing previously learned information, but one could also argue that low-span persons are slower at learning associations, and thus their deficit is not inhibitory in nature. To test the second prediction, RT on List 3 relearning was compared for both span groups across experimental conditions. On List 3, high-span participants in the interference condition, despite having previously encountered the same cue–target relationships in List 1, were slower to recall the target compared with high-span participants in the control condition. Low-span participants showed the opposite pattern in that they were faster in the interference condition than the control condition at List 3, presumably because they had not suppressed the List 1 associations when learning the List 2 items. Even stronger evidence for the relation between WMC and suppression is taken from the within-subject comparison of participants in the interference condition: High-span participants were slower to recall the target on List 3 compared with List 1 by a much greater degree than low-span participants (157 milliseconds vs. 53 milliseconds, respectively). The demonstration of a cost of suppression for high-span participants, who normally outperform low-span participants in a variety of complex situations, provides strong evidence for the relation between WMC and inhibition.

BROWN–PETERSON TASK. An obvious choice to examine differences in the way high- and low-span persons inhibit irrelevant items during retrieval is to measure their susceptibility to PI in the classic Brown–Peterson task (Brown, 1958; Peterson & Peterson, 1959). Kane and Engle (2000) studied the effects of load in a design similar to a version of the PI buildup task used by Craik and Birtwistle (1971). Across two experiments, high- and low-span groups received three lists of words from the same semantic category (e.g., animals) and were then presented with a fourth list of words from a different semantic category (e.g., occupations). To study the effects of divided attention, participants also concurrently performed variations of a sequential finger-tapping task corresponding to control (no tapping), simple (compatibly mapped tapping), and complex (incompatibly mapped tapping) conditions.

The experimental design allowed the examination of the combined effects of interference, WMC, and divided attention on retrieval. Lists 2 and 3 correspond to buildup of PI, where interference is highest because of the previous lists from the same category. In contrast, List 4 represents release from PI, and interference is lower because the to-be-recalled words are from a different category. Whereas high-span participants should show less PI buildup than low-span participants because of their superior ability to devote attention to suppressing previous-list items, the span groups should achieve similar levels of PI release given that the number of activated items competing for retrieval should be low. In addition, if individual differences in WMC reflect differential ability to allocate attention, then adding an attention-demanding task such as complex tapping should actually impair high-span participants' inhibitory processes. The logic is that high-span persons are allocating attention resources across several processes in the memory and tapping tasks requiring controlled attention, whereas low-span persons are unlikely to change the allocation of resources they are devoting to performing either type of task.

Although both groups showed effects of PI buildup, only high-span participants were affected by the tapping condition. High-span participants were less affected by PI buildup than low-span participants in the control and simple conditions, supporting the view that WMC is related to inhibitory processes during retrieval in high-interference situations. However, high- and low-span participants showed similar PI buildup in the complex tapping condition; as high-span individuals devoted more attention to the difficult secondary task, their ability to sufficiently allocate resources to suppression in the memory task decreased, and their performance fell to the level of the low-span individuals. As predicted, both span groups showed similar levels of PI release across the tapping conditions, demonstrating that WMC is specifically important when dealing with interfering representations. The load manipulation provides further support for our view that individual differences in WMC drive inhibitory abilities. High-span participants' inhibitory efficiency is determined by their ability to allocate attention to various controlled processes, including suppression. Low-span participants are unaffected by secondary tasks (see also Rosen & Engle, 1997) because they lack flexibility in allocating their attention, and thus any processes requiring attention may be impaired. If WMC was determined by inhibitory ability, it is unclear how dividing attention would affect only high-span participants.

Restraint

The final function of inhibition described by Hasher et al. (1999) is the *restraint* function, which aids cognition by "preventing prepotent candidates for response from immediately seizing control . . . so that other, less probable response candidates can be considered" (p. 654). This type of inhibition can be thought of as a kind of last resort for the system, thwarting an automatic, momentarily inappropriate response in favor of an alternative option. Engle and Kane (2004) argued that one of the main determinants of cognitive control is the ability to resolve response competition, especially when an alternative choice is a habitual response in conflict with the current task goals. The following studies are also important in supporting the executive-attention view of WMC, as the surface properties of these low-level attention tasks have little in common with complex span tasks such as OSPAN.

STROOP TASK. Kane and Engle (2003) conducted a series of experiments using the well-known Stroop (1935) task. In the color–word Stroop task, individuals are instructed to name the color of the ink (or font) of the word that is presented. The *Stroop interference effect* refers to the common finding that individuals are slower and make more incorrect responses on trials in which the word and color conflict (e.g., the word *green* written in red; incongruent) compared with trials in which the word and color information correspond (e.g., the word *red* written in red; congruent) or the word and color are unrelated to each other (e.g., *book* written in red; neutral). Similar to Friedman and Miyake (2004), we view the color–word Stroop task as predominantly reflecting response inhibition and not perceptual filtering, because reading the word is such a strong competing response for literate individuals. The Stroop task provides a good way to test specific hypotheses regarding the importance of WMC to maintain goal information and resolve response conflict (Engle & Kane, 2004).

For example, Logan and Zbrodoff (1979) demonstrated that the number of incongruent trials relative to all other trials affects the magnitude of the Stroop effect. They found that as the proportion of incongruent trials increases, the magnitude of the Stroop effect decreases. A Stroop task with all incongruent trials reduces the burden on the participant to actively maintain the task goal of saying the color and not reading the word, and therefore each incongruent trial serves as a reminder of the goal to name the ink color. In contrast, a Stroop task with relatively few incongruent trials produces a larger Stroop effect, especially for individuals who have not actively maintained the color-naming goal and instead rely on the prepotent response of reading the word (a strategy that works well for the majority of congruent trials). Across several experiments in Kane and Engle (2003; see also Long & Prat, 2002), low-span participants showed a greater Stroop interference effect in terms of RT and/or error rate in blocks with infrequent incongruent trials. Interestingly, low-span participants also showed a larger facilitation effect than high-span participants, indicating that they were actually faster to respond to congruent compared with neutral trials. In this case, a larger facilitation effect provides additional evidence that low-span participants are responding by word reading on most trials, showing that because they were not maintaining the task goal, they were also less likely to suppress the prepotent response.

ANTISACCADE TASK. The antisaccade task (Hallett, 1978) is particularly well suited for studying goal-oriented responding in the presence of an incorrect prepotent response. In most versions of this task, participants move their eyes from a central fixation point when a peripheral stimulus is presented either to the left or right of fixation. The direction of the eye movement depends on the instructions for that trial; correct prosaccade trials are made by moving toward the stimulus, whereas successful antisaccade trials are performed by moving the gaze in the direction opposite of the stimulus. As Roberts, Hager, and Heron (1994) noted, moving one's eyes toward a presented stimulus is an automatic, highly prepotent reaction, and thus preventing such a response in favor of moving in the opposite direction is difficult. Roberts et al. pointed out another advantage of this task in that most normal individuals likely do not differ on the ability or speed at which they can move their eyes; other tasks have the potential problem that individuals have differentially learned the stimulus–response mapping to be used in the experiment (for further discussion of this issue, see Wilhelm & Oberauer, 2006).

Kane et al. (2001) administered the prosaccade and antisaccade conditions to high- and low-span participants. Participants fixated centrally before a peripheral cue flashed on the left or right side of the screen. After this cue, a letter briefly appeared before being masked, and participants were asked to identify the letter. In the prosaccade condition, the letter appeared in the same position as the cue that had just previously disappeared, and in the antisaccade condition, the letter appeared on the opposite side of the screen. Because correct responses in the prosaccade condition were based primarily on making reflexive saccades, high- and low-span participants were not predicted to differ. However, because the ability to control attention via maintenance of the task goals and suppression of inappropriate, habitual responses is important for success in the antisaccade condition, low-span participants were predicted to make more errors and take longer to respond on antisaccade trials. The results confirmed the importance of WMC in dealing with prepotent responses: The span groups did not differ in errors or RT on prosaccade trials, but low-span participants were slower to respond and made more errors on antisaccade trials than high-span participants.

One problem that could limit the interpretation of these results is the nature of the letter identification task. Specifically, previous research (Roberts et al., 1994) has shown that secondary tasks performed concurrently with antisaccade tasks impair performance. It is possible that the letter identification task was more difficult for low-span participants, and thus the differences in the dependent measures in Kane et al. (2001) were due not to the control of eye movements but instead to the letter identification process. Unsworth, Schrock, and Engle (2004) alleviated this concern by replicating Kane et al., with the exception that there was no letter identification. Instead, high- and low-span participants moved their eyes toward (prosaccade) or away from (antisaccade) a flashing cue, and response latency was measured by analyzing eye movement data. Corroborating the findings of Kane et al., high- and low-span participants did not differ in the time to move their gaze in the prosaccade condition, but low-span participants were slower on antisaccade trials. In addition, low-span participants made more errors only on antisaccade trials.

The final experiment in Unsworth et al. (2004) provided strong evidence for solving the chicken–egg dilemma—namely, trying to differentiate between executive-attention and inhibition theories of WMC. They noted the following distinction between the processes necessary for prosaccade and antisaccade trials:

> Prosaccade trials simply require looking toward the flashing cue, and this response is thought to rely on exogenous, automatic attentional capture and should not require the recruitment of executive control. Antisaccade trials, however, require not only the inhibition of a prepotent response (i.e., *don't look at the flashing box*) but also require the planning and execution of a voluntary saccade in the opposite direction. (p. 1303)

The implication is that although suppression of the prepotent response is important for accurate performance on antisaccade trials, the ability to plan and execute a controlled eye movement also determines trial success. Therefore, if high- and low-span participants differ only in the ability to inhibit, they should not differ in the voluntary saccade aspect of the trial. However, if the critical determinant of WMC is actually controlled attention, then individual differences in WMC should be important for both response inhibition and saccade generation on antisaccade trials.

In Experiment 3, Unsworth et al. (2004) presented high- and low-span participants with the previous exogenous versions of the prosaccade and anti-saccade tasks, in which a flashing box at the periphery determined the direction in which the participant was to make a saccade. However, participants also performed endogenous prosaccade and antisaccade trials in which the cue informing participants which way to move their eyes was a centrally presented left- or right-pointing arrow. By making the cue endogenous, the prosaccade condition now required a planned saccade based on interpreting the cue rather than reliance on a reflexive saccade to a flashing peripheral cue. Thus, the important comparison for distinguishing the executive-attention and inhibition theories of WMC is the exogenous and endogenous prosaccade conditions. The results showed that low-span participants were now slower than high-span participants on the endogenous prosaccade trials, suggesting that controlled processes in addition to suppression of the prepotent response were partly responsible for the differences between the span groups on antisaccade trials. This result is difficult to explain using a theory of WMC based solely on inhibitory functions, because inhibition does not seem important for making an eye movement based on the direction of a central arrow.

Working Memory Capacity and Social Inhibition

We now shift our focus to applications of the executive-attention theory of WMC to social phenomena related to the ability to suppress irrelevant thoughts. Thought suppression is an important component of an influential theory of mental control (Wegner, 1994) that has been extended to several neuropsychological conditions. Recently, WMC has been hypothesized as an important factor related to mental control in social cognition (Feldman Barrett, Tugade, & Engle, 2004). The studies discussed next have one common theme: examining the role of individual differences in WMC related to the suppression of irrelevant thoughts in many different domains.

Posttraumatic Stress Disorder

Posttraumatic stress disorder (PTSD) has received increased media attention in the United States following the events of September 11, 2001, and the ongoing military campaigns in Iraq and Afghanistan. The syndrome is characterized by frequent thoughts of traumatic experiences in the form of flashbacks that can severely debilitate an individual's ability to achieve a normal life (Brewin, 2001). Brewin and colleagues (Brewin & Beaton, 2002; Brewin & Smart, 2005) proposed that this condition could temporarily reduce WMC, which would impair an affected individual's ability to suppress disturbing thoughts. Brewin and Beaton (2002) used the white bear paradigm (Wegner, Schneider, Carter, & White, 1987) to study intrusions. The procedure for this task was to compare a condition in which students were told to *not* think of a white bear (suppression) with a condition in which they were told to think of a white bear (expression). Any instances of white bear thoughts were obtained by verbal report and/or by a bell the participants were instructed to ring if they thought of a white bear. OSPAN was significantly correlated with the number of white bear occurrences only in the suppression condition ($r = -.51$).

Brewin and Smart (2005) extended these findings by modifying the white bear task so that the material to suppress was personally relevant. Instead of thinking about white bears, students identified their most frequent intrusive thought before the experiment and then were instructed to either suppress or express that thought internally. In spite of the difficulties in verifying that participants were actually following the task instructions, Brewin and Smart found that OSPAN was again significantly correlated to the number of reported intrusive thought failures in the suppression condition ($r = -.23$). Both of these studies were conducted with nonpatient students; the following section deals with the relation between WMC and intrusive-thought suppression in clinical patients.

Depression

Another clinical condition believed to be related in part to impaired thought suppression is depression (Arnett et al., 1999). Depressed patients may focus on negative thoughts to a greater degree than healthy individuals, and similar to those with PTSD, people with depression may resemble low-span individuals by having a reduced ability to allocate attention resources to processes such as inhibition. Arnett et al. (1999) argued that depression may act as a cognitive load that affects performance on tasks requiring WMC. More explicitly, having to allocate attention resources to suppress frequently occurring negative thoughts is similar to devoting resources to a secondary task in the studies discussed earlier (Conway et al., 1999; Kane & Engle, 2000; see also Rosen & Engle, 1997). Arnett et al. studied the relation between WMC and depression in multiple sclerosis (MS) patients and found that compared with a nondepressed MS group and a nondepressed non-MS group, MS patients with depression showed worse performance on reading span. The authors argued for clinical evaluations of MS patients to rule out depression as the cause of the impaired central executive functioning observed in MS patients.

Life Stress

Similar to frequent traumatic flashbacks in PTSD and constant negative thoughts in depression, individuals dealing with a high amount of life stress may have performance decrements on tasks that tap WMC (Klein & Boals, 2001). Individuals who are devoting resources to attempting to suppress unwanted, task-irrelevant thoughts have less attention to devote to task performance. Klein and Boals (2001) argued that unlike other task-irrelevant thoughts, "unwanted thoughts about adverse life events continue to require effort to inhibit" (p. 566). In two experiments, they found a significant correlation between the self-reported number of negative life stress events recently encountered and OSPAN performance ($rs = -.46$ and $-.36$); that is, lower WMC was associated with more adverse stress. However, positive life stress was not correlated with OSPAN. In a third study, participants identified two major life events and then were given a scale measuring the amount of intrusive (e.g., "I thought about it when I didn't mean to") and avoidant (e.g., "I tried to remove it from memory") thinking they engaged in related to each event. Klein and Boals found that individuals with lower OSPAN scores engaged in more intrusive–avoidant thinking ($r = -.22$). Similar to Wegner's (1994) theory of thought suppression, although thoughts about positive events are task irrelevant, they are not unwanted thoughts like negative stress-related concerns are, and thus they can easily be discounted. Thoughts about negative life events are more difficult to suppress and consume attention resources that could otherwise be devoted to the primary task (in this case, OSPAN).

Stereotype Threat

WMC has recently been explored as a mediating factor in susceptibility to stereotype threat. Following the work of Steele and Aronson (1995), *stereotype threat* refers to the impaired test performance that individuals show after a stereotype about their in-group has been made salient (Schmader & Johns, 2003). Examples of how stereotypes have been activated experimentally include framing the test as an intelligence measure, having participants identify their race and ethnicity, or informing participants that their scores would be compared with those of another racial or ethnic group. The interpretation of test decrements associated with stereotype threat is that test takers have to contend with the added pressure and concern of confirming the negative stereotype with their performance. Similar to the previous research on life stress, the negative stereotype information works as a type of stressor.

Schmader and Johns (2003) hypothesized that stereotype threat reduces WMC because test takers must devote resources to suppressing these extratask thoughts and anxiety. In their first experiment, women and men were assigned to either a stereotype-threat or a control group. All participants performed the OSPAN task, but those in the stereotype-threat group were first informed about previous research showing that women score lower on tests of "quantitative capacity" compared with men. They found that women and men in the control group and men in the stereotype-threat group had equivalent OSPAN scores, but the women in the stereotype-threat group scored significantly lower, representing reduced WMC. In Experiment 2, the participants were instead Latino and non-Hispanic White, and the stereotype-threat instructions were that the OSPAN task was a test highly correlated with intelligence and that their scores would be used to establish ethnic norms. A similar result to Experiment 1 was obtained; Latino participants in the stereotype-threat group had much lower OSPAN scores than the other groups, which were all equivalent to each other. Stereotype threat is yet another form of task-irrelevant, intrusive thought that competes with the attention resources one has to allocate to task performance. The situational reductions in WMC reviewed in this section need to be studied further, given the importance of WMC in higher order cognition and performance on various ability tests used as selection criteria in educational and occupational settings.

Conclusion

In this chapter, we have presented evidence showing that WMC is related to inhibition in many different areas of psychology. We have argued that WMC reflects the ability to control attention and that this is an important construct for higher order cognition, including inhibitory processes. On the basis of our research with divided-attention tasks (Conway et al., 1999; Kane & Engle, 2000; Rosen & Engle, 1997) and the endogenous prosaccade condition of the antisaccade task (Unsworth et al., 2004), we maintain that WMC determines inhibitory ability and not vice versa (cf. May et al., 1999). However, the possibility remains that individual differences among young adults and group differences between young and old adults do not have the same causal mechanism and that older adults may have an additional general inhibitory deficit that impairs their cognition.

By using the terminology of Hasher et al. (1999), we have attempted to be explicit regarding the function of inhibition implied by using the term as an explanatory agent. However, future research with WMC should focus on whether the interference seen in tasks such as the flanker (Heitz & Engle, in press) and Stroop (Kane & Engle, 2003) tasks occurs only at the input and output levels of processing, respectively, as has been presented in this chapter. For example, with the flanker task, it is possible that high- and low-span participants differ in the ability both to suppress distractors during encoding and to stop an incorrectly activated response if the perceptual filtering fails.

Determining more precisely the processing stage at which interference occurs may be aided by studies from the cognitive neuroscience domain. Although we have previously asserted that WMC is related to prefrontal cortex functioning (Kane & Engle, 2002), research published since that review has provided direct evidence of prefrontal cortex involvement.[1] For example, similar to our microanalytic design, a few studies have measured WMC before completing the experiment of interest to examine the role of the prefrontal cortex in both individual differences in WMC and situations involving interference control (Burgess, Gray, Conway, & Braver, 2005; Heitz, Corballis, Parks, & Engle, 2005; Mecklinger, Weber, Gunter, & Engle, 2003). Additional work (Kondo, Osaka, & Osaka, 2004; Osaka et al., 2003) has separated high- and low-span participants on the basis of one complex span task and then measured activation levels during performance of a variant of another complex span task. These results suggest that high- and low-span individuals show a different pattern of frontal activation via an interaction between the dorsolateral prefrontal cortex and anterior cingulate cortex areas. As neuroimaging methodologies improve, cognitive neuroscience should provide additional evidence elucidating the shared relation between WMC and higher order cognition.

In addition, more research should address the alternative explanations (MacLeod et al., 2003) of the many inhibitory effects described here (for an account of WMC focusing on interference caused by inefficient use of retrieval cues, see Unsworth and Engle, in press). Although we have asserted that individual differences in WMC do not represent exclusively inhibitory processes, perhaps an explanation based solely on differences in allocating attention could account for some of the results we presented. Nonetheless, establishing the exact relation between WMC and inhibition is becoming an increasingly important goal for researchers in many areas of psychology.

References

Arnett, P. A., Higginson, C. I., Voss, W. D., Bender, W. I., Wurst, J. M., & Tippin, J. M. (1999). Depression in multiple sclerosis: Relationship to working memory capacity. *Neuropsychology, 13,* 546–556.

Baddeley, A. D., & Hitch, G. (1974). Working memory. In G. A. Bower (Vol. Ed.), *The psychology of learning and motivation* (Vol. 8, pp. 47–89). New York: Academic Press.

Bjork, R. A. (1989). Retrieval inhibition as an adaptive mechanism in human memory. In H. L. Roediger III & F. I. M. Craik (Eds.), *Varieties of memory and consciousness* (pp. 309–330). Hillsdale, NJ: Erlbaum.

Brewin, C. R. (2001). A cognitive neuroscience account of posttraumatic stress disorder and its treatment. *Behaviour Research and Therapy, 39,* 373–393.

Brewin, C. R., & Beaton, A. (2002). Thought suppression, intelligence, and working memory capacity. *Behaviour Research and Therapy, 40,* 923–930.

Brewin, C. R., & Smart, L. (2005). Working memory capacity and suppression of intrusive thoughts. *Journal of Behavior Therapy and Experimental Psychiatry, 36,* 61–68.

Brown, J. A. (1958). Some tests of the decay theory of immediate memory. *Quarterly Journal of Experimental Psychology, 10,* 12–21.

---

[1] Bunge, Klingberg, Jacobsen, and Gabrieli (2000) and Smith et al. (2001) administered modified versions of complex span tasks to participants in functional magnetic resonance imaging and positron-emission tomography, respectively, but the differences between typical complex span tasks and the tasks they used, mainly the recall period, make it difficult to make firm comparisons between the existing behavioral literature and their work.

Bunge, S. A., Klingberg, T., Jacobsen, R. B., & Gabrieli, J. D. E. (2000). A resource model of the neural basis of executive working memory. *Proceedings of the National Academy of Sciences, USA, 97,* 3573–3578.

Burgess, G. C., Gray, J. G., Conway, A. R. A., & Braver, T. S. (2005, April). *Relationships among fluid intelligence, working memory span, and brain activity during high-interference trials.* Poster presented at the Annual Meeting of the Cognitive Neuroscience Society, New York.

Case, R., Kurland, D. M., & Goldberg, J. (1982). Operational efficiency and the growth of short-term memory span. *Journal of Experimental Child Psychology, 33,* 386–404.

Conway, A. R. A., Cowan, N., & Bunting, M. F. (2001). The cocktail party phenomenon revisited: The importance of working memory capacity. *Psychonomic Bulletin & Review, 8,* 331–335.

Conway, A. R. A., Cowan, N., Bunting, M. F., Therriault, D. J., & Minkoff, S. R. B. (2002). A latent variable analysis of working memory capacity, short-term memory capacity, processing speed, and general fluid intelligence. *Intelligence, 30,* 163–183.

Conway, A. R. A., & Engle, R. W. (1994). Working memory and retrieval: A resource-dependent inhibition model. *Journal of Experimental Psychology: General, 123,* 354–373.

Conway, A. R. A., Kane, M. J., Bunting, M. F., Hambrick, D. Z., Wilhelm, O., & Engle, R. W. (2005). Working memory span tasks: A methodological review and user's guide. *Psychonomic Bulletin & Review, 12,* 769–786.

Conway, A. R. A., Tuholski, S. W., Shisler, R. J., & Engle, R. W. (1999). The effect of memory load on negative priming: An individual differences investigation. *Memory & Cognition, 27,* 1042–1050.

Cowan, N. (1995). *Attention and memory: An integrated framework.* Oxford, England: Oxford University Press.

Cowan, N. (2004). Understanding intelligence: A summary and an adjustable-attention hypothesis. In O. Wilhelm & R. W. Engle (Eds.), *Handbook of understanding and measuring intelligence* (pp. 469–488). Thousand Oaks, CA: Sage.

Craik, F. I. M., & Birtwistle, J. (1971). Proactive inhibition in free recall. *Journal of Experimental Psychology, 91,* 120–123.

Dagenbach, D., & Carr, T. H. (1994). *Inhibitory processes in attention, memory, and language.* San Diego, CA: Academic Press.

Daneman, M., & Carpenter, P. A. (1980). Individual differences in working memory and reading. *Journal of Verbal Learning and Verbal Behavior, 19,* 450–466.

Dempster, F. N., & Brainerd, C. J. (1995). *Interference and inhibition in cognition.* San Diego, CA: Academic Press.

Engle, R. W. (1996). Working memory and retrieval: An inhibition-resource approach. In J. T. E. Richardson, R. W. Engle, L. Hasher, R. H. Logie, E. R. Stoltzfus, & R. T. Zacks (Eds.), *Working memory and human cognition* (pp. 89–119). London: Oxford University Press.

Engle, R. W., Conway, A. R. A., Tuholski, S. W., & Shisler, R. J. (1995). A resource account of inhibition. *Psychological Science, 6,* 122–125.

Engle, R. W., & Kane, M. J. (2004). Executive attention, working memory capacity, and a two-factor theory of cognitive control. In B. Ross (Vol. Ed.), *The psychology of learning and motivation* (Vol. 44, pp. 145–199). New York: Elsevier.

Engle, R. W., Tuholski, S. W., Laughlin, J. E., & Conway, A. R. A. (1999). Working memory, short-term memory and general fluid intelligence: A latent-variable approach. *Journal of Experimental Psychology: General, 128,* 309–331.

Eriksen, B. A., & Eriksen, C. W. (1974). Effects of noise letters upon the identification of a target letter in a nonsearch task. *Perception and Psychophysics, 16,* 143–149.

Fan, J., McCandliss, B. D., Sommer, T., Raz, A., & Posner, M. I. (2002). Testing the efficiency and independence of attentional networks. *Journal of Cognitive Neuroscience, 14,* 340–347.

Feldman Barrett, L., Tugade, M. M., & Engle, R. W. (2004). Individual differences in working memory capacity and dual-process theories of mind. *Psychological Bulletin, 130,* 553–573.

Friedman, N. P., & Miyake, A. (2004). The relations among inhibition and interference control functions: A latent-variable analysis. *Journal of Experimental Psychology: General, 133,* 101–135.

Gratton, G., Coles, M. G. H., Sirevaag, E. J., Eriksen, C. W., & Donchin, E. (1988). Pre- and post-stimulus activation of response channels: A psychophysiological analysis. *Journal of Experimental Psychology: Human Perception and Performance, 14,* 331–344.

Hallett, P. E. (1978). Primary and secondary saccades to goals defined by instructions. *Vision Research, 18,* 1279–1296.

Hasher, L., & Zacks, R. T. (1988). Working memory, comprehension, and aging: A review and a new view. In G. H. Bower (Vol. Ed.), *The psychology of learning and motivation* (Vol. 22, pp. 193–225). New York: Academic Press.

Hasher, L., Zacks, R. T., & May, C. P. (1999). Inhibitory control, circadian arousal, and age. In D. Gopher & A. Koriat (Vol. Eds.), *Attention and performance: XVII. Cognitive regulation of performance: Interaction of theory and application* (pp. 653–675). Cambridge, MA: MIT Press.

Heitz, R. P., Corballis, P. M., Parks, N. A., & Engle, R. W. (2005, April). *Working memory capacity and attentional control: An electrophysiological analysis.* Poster session presented at the annual meeting of the Cognitive Neuroscience Society, New York.

Heitz, R. P., & Engle, R. W. (in press). Focusing the spotlight: Individual differences in visual attention control. *Journal of Experimental Psychology: General.*

Heitz, R. P., Unsworth, N., & Engle, R. W. (2004). Working memory capacity, attention control, and fluid intelligence. In O. Wilhelm & R. W. Engle (Eds.), *Handbook of understanding and measuring intelligence* (pp. 61–77). Thousand Oaks, CA: Sage.

Kane, M. J., Bleckley, M. K., Conway, A. R. A., & Engle, R. W. (2001). A controlled-attention view of working-memory capacity. *Journal of Experimental Psychology: General, 130,* 169–183.

Kane, M. J., Conway, A. R. A., Hambrick, D. Z., & Engle, R. W. (2007). Variation in working-memory capacity as variation in executive attention and control. In A. R. A. Conway, C. Jarrold, M. J. Kane, A. Miyake, & J. N. Towse (Eds.), *Variation in working memory* (pp. 21–48). New York: Oxford University Press.

Kane, M. J., & Engle, R. W. (2000). Working-memory capacity, proactive interference, and divided attention: Limits on long-term memory retrieval. *Journal of Experimental Psychology: Learning, Memory, and Cognition, 26,* 336–358.

Kane, M. J., & Engle, R. W. (2002). The role of prefrontal cortex in working-memory capacity, executive attention, and general fluid intelligence: An individual-differences perspective. *Psychonomic Bulletin & Review, 9,* 637–671.

Kane, M. J., & Engle, R. W. (2003). Working-memory capacity and the control of attention: The contributions of goal neglect, response competition, and task set to Stroop interference. *Journal of Experimental Psychology: General, 132,* 47–70.

Kane, M. J., Hambrick, D. Z., Tuholski, S. W., Wilhelm, O., Payne, T. W., & Engle, R. W. (2004). The generality of working memory capacity: A latent-variable approach to verbal and visuospatial memory span and reasoning. *Journal of Experimental Psychology: General, 133,* 189–217.

Kane, M. J., Poole, B. J., Tuholski, S. W., & Engle, R. W. (2006). Working memory capacity and the top-down control of visual search: Exploring the boundaries of "executive attention." *Journal of Experimental Psychology: Learning, Memory, and Cognition, 32,* 749–777.

Kipp Harnishfeger, K. (1995). The development of cognitive inhibition: Theories, definitions, and research evidence. In F. N. Dempster & C. J. Brainerd (Eds.), *Interference and inhibition in cognition* (pp. 175–204). San Diego, CA: Academic Press.

Klein, K., & Boals, A. (2001). The relationship of life event stress and working memory capacity. *Applied Cognitive Psychology, 15,* 565–579.

Kondo, H., Osaka, N., & Osaka, M. (2004). Cooperation of the anterior cingulate cortex and dorsolateral prefrontal cortex for attention shifting. *NeuroImage, 23,* 670–679.

Logan, G. D., & Zbrodoff, N. J. (1979). When it helps to be misled: Facilitative effects of increasing the frequency of conflicting stimuli in a Stroop-like task. *Memory & Cognition, 7,* 166–174.

Long, D. L., & Prat, C. S. (2002). Working memory and Stroop interference: An individual differences investigation. *Memory & Cognition, 30,* 294–301.

MacLeod, C. M., Dodd, M. D., Sheard, E. D., Wilson, D. E., & Bibi, U. (2003). In opposition to inhibition. In B. Ross (Ed.), *The psychology of learning and motivation* (Vol. 43, pp. 163–214). New York: Elsevier.

May, C. P., Hasher, L., & Kane, M. J. (1999). The role of interference in memory span. *Memory & Cognition, 27,* 759–767.

Mecklinger, A., Weber, K., Gunter, T. C., & Engle, R. W. (2003). Dissociable brain mechanisms for inhibitory control: Effects of interference content and working memory capacity. *Cognitive Brain Research, 18,* 26–38.

Moray, N. (1959). Attention in dichotic listening: Affective cues and the influence of instructions. *Quarterly Journal of Experimental Psychology, 11,* 56–60.

Nigg, J. T. (2000). On inhibition/disinhibition in developmental psychopathology: Views from cognitive and personality psychology and a working inhibition taxonomy. *Psychological Bulletin, 126,* 220–246.

Norman, D. A., & Bobrow, D. G. (1975). On data-limited and resource-limited processes. *Cognitive Psychology, 7,* 44–64.

Osaka, M., Osaka, N., Kondo, H., Morishita, M., Fukuyama, H., Aso, T., & Shibasaki, H. (2003). The neural basis of individual differences in working memory capacity: An fMRI study. *Neuro-Image, 18,* 789–797.

Peterson, L. R., & Peterson, M. J. (1959). Short-term retention of individual verbal items. *Journal of Experimental Psychology, 58,* 193–198.

Redick, T. S., & Engle, R. W. (2006). Working memory capacity and attention network test performance. *Applied Cognitive Psychology, 20,* 713–721.

Roberts, R. J., Hager, L. D., & Heron, C. (1994). Prefrontal cognitive processes: Working memory and inhibition in the antisaccade task. *Journal of Experimental Psychology: General, 123,* 374–393.

Rosen, V. M., & Engle, R. W. (1997). The role of working memory capacity in retrieval. *Journal of Experimental Psychology: General, 126,* 211–227.

Rosen, V. M., & Engle, R. W. (1998). Working memory capacity and suppression. *Journal of Memory and Language, 39,* 418–436.

Schmader, T., & Johns, M. (2003). Converging evidence that stereotype threat reduces working memory capacity. *Journal of Personality and Social Psychology, 85,* 440–452.

Smith, E. E., Geva, A., Jonides, J., Miller, A., Reuter-Lorenz, P., & Koeppe, R. A. (2001). The neural basis of task-switching in working memory: Effects of performance and aging. *Proceedings of the National Academy of Sciences, USA, 98,* 2095–2100.

Steele, C. M., & Aronson, J. (1995). Stereotype threat and the intellectual test performance of African Americans. *Journal of Personality and Social Psychology, 69,* 797–811.

Stroop, J. R. (1935). Studies of interference in serial verbal reactions. *Journal of Experimental Psychology, 18,* 643–662.

Turner, M. L., & Engle, R. W. (1989). Is working memory capacity task dependent? *Journal of Memory and Language, 28,* 127–154.

Unsworth, N., & Engle, R. W. (in press). The nature of individual differences in working memory capacity: Active maintenance in primary memory and controlled search from secondary memory. *Psychological Review.*

Unsworth, N., Heitz, R. P., & Engle, R. W. (2005). Working memory capacity in hot and cold cognition. In R. W. Engle, G. Sedek, U. Hecker, & D. N. McIntosh (Eds.), *Cognitive limitations in aging and psychopathology* (pp. 19–43). New York: Oxford University Press.

Unsworth, N., Schrock, J. C., & Engle, R. W. (2004). Working memory capacity and the antisaccade task: Individual differences in voluntary saccade control. *Journal of Experimental Psychology: Learning, Memory, and Cognition, 30,* 1302–1321.

Wegner, D. M. (1994). Ironic processes of mental control. *Psychological Review, 101,* 34–52.

Wegner, D. M., Schneider, D. J., Carter, S. R., III, & White, T. L. (1987). Paradoxical effects of thought suppression. *Journal of Personality and Social Psychology, 53,* 5–13.

Wilhelm, O., & Oberauer, K. (2006). Why are reasoning ability and working memory capacity related to mental speed? An investigation of stimulus–response compatibility in choice reaction time tasks. *European Journal of Cognitive Psychology, 18,* 18–50.

Part IV _____

Development and Aging

8

Inhibitory Deficit Theory: Recent Developments in a "New View"

Cindy Lustig, Lynn Hasher, and Rose T. Zacks

A major view in cognitive psychology presumes the existence of limits on mental capacity, limits that vary with circumstances and task demands and that largely determine the performance of individuals (see, e.g., Kahneman, 1973). The Daneman and Carpenter (1980) measure of working memory (and its many variants; see, e.g., Engle, Cantor, & Carulo, 1992; Friedman & Miyake, 2004) is thought to give a snapshot of capacity by assessing an individual's ability to actively maintain important information while also engaging in some form of ongoing processing. From a capacity viewpoint, the bigger the mental desk space, the better performance should be on a wide range of tasks, including reading comprehension and reasoning. On the assumption that older adults have reduced working memory capacity, age differences might be explained.

However, a study on reading comprehension and memory had findings that were uninterpretable from this perspective (Hamm & Hasher, 1992). Older adults showed comprehension of stories that equaled that of young adults but did so by keeping more, not less, information in mind as they read. These capacity-challenging findings were critical to the development of an alternative view of cognition and of age (and individual) differences in cognition (Hasher & Zacks, 1988). Two simple hypotheses were advanced: (a) that activation in response to familiar cues and thoughts is largely automatic, as is its spread through a network, and (b) that activation requires down-regulation for goals to be accomplished. Activation was presumed to be equivalent across people and circumstances. Down-regulation was presumed to require inhibition and also to differ among individuals and across groups and circumstances to account for performance in a wide range of tasks.

Thanks go to Amanda K. Govenar and David Bissig for their help in organizing the material for this chapter. Support for this project came from National Institute on Aging Grant R37 AG04306.

The Functions of Inhibition

The inhibitory framework suggests that an efficient (i.e., fast and accurate) mental life requires the ability to limit activation to information most relevant to one's goals. Various behavioral and neurological data also suggest that inhibitory deficiency is decreased in older adults; in very young children; and for people operating under conditions of fatigue, reduced motivation, or emotional stress or at a nonoptimal point in their circadian arousal cycle (Hasher, Zacks, & May, 1999). Three functions of inhibition were proposed: (a) controlling access to attention's focus, (b) deleting irrelevant information from attention and working memory, and (c) suppressing or restraining strong but inappropriate responses. In this section, we review and provide some evidence on each of the proposed functions of inhibition.

Access

Early in the processing stream, inhibition functions to prevent irrelevant information from gaining access to the focus of attention. Deficits in access control enable distraction to influence the processing of target stimuli, sometimes by disrupting and at other times by facilitating performance, depending on the relation between the distractors and the targets. For example, relative to appropriate control baselines, older adults are differentially slowed in reading aloud when distraction is inserted in unpredictable locations in text (e.g., Carlson, Hasher, Connelly, & Zacks, 1995). The reduced ability to ignore distraction may also partially account for widely reported age differences in speed of processing. Several of the tests commonly used to assess speed (e.g., letter comparison) present a cluttered display with many items on each page. If older adults have difficulties preventing irrelevant information from gaining access to the focus of attention, this cluttered, distracting display might slow them down. Consistent with this hypothesis, reducing the clutter (by presenting the items one at a time) speeded older adults' performance by over 15% on computerized versions of several such tests (Lustig, Hasher, & Tonev, 2006; see Figure 8.1) but had no impact on the performance of younger adults.

Deficits in control over access can also improve performance. For example, May (1999) presented young and older adults with a problem-solving task in which target words were presented either alone or in the presence of distraction. When the distraction led toward a solution, older adults showed greater benefits than younger adults. More recent evidence suggests that older adults' greater tacit knowledge of distraction can actually improve their performance on subsequent tasks. For example, older adults showed priming for irrelevant words that were superimposed on pictures in the context of a picture identification task, whereas younger adults showed no priming for those same words (Rowe, Valderrama, Hasher, & Lenartowicz, 2006; see also Kim, Hasher, & Zacks, in press).

A frequent concern about inhibitory explanations is the degree to which the results reflect a deficit in inhibition of distraction as opposed to a failure to increase activation of relevant information. A number of findings suggest

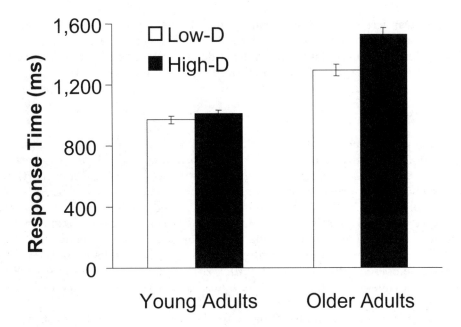

Figure 8.1. Effects of distraction on digit symbol performance. Data are from a computerized version of the Digit Symbol substitution test, part of the Wechsler battery (Wechsler, 1981) and a common measure of fluid intelligence. Young adults showed little or no effect of the distraction manipulation, whereas older adults were much faster in the reduced distraction (Low-D) condition. Error bars indicate standard error of the mean. Adapted from "Distraction as a Determinant of Processing Speed," by C. Lustig, L. Hasher, and S. T. Tonev, 2006, *Psychonomic Bulletin & Review, 13,* p. 621. Copyright 2006 by the Psychonomic Society.

that activation processes are largely preserved, at least with age. For example, older and younger adults do not differ on a variety of tasks entailing activation but little or no inhibition (e.g., categorization decisions, most repetition and semantic priming tasks; see Hasher et al., 1999).

Recent neuroimaging results using functional magnetic resonance imaging also support the idea of preserved activation and specific deficits in inhibition for older adults. Gazzaley, Cooney, Rissman, and D'Esposito (2005) asked participants to view alternating photographs of scenes and faces under conditions in which they were instructed to either (a) remember one category (e.g., scenes) and ignore the other (e.g., faces) and vice versa or (b) passively view faces and scenes. Under instruction to remember scenes, both younger and older adults showed at least equivalent activation, relative to the passive-viewing baseline, in the area selective for scene processing (the left parahippocampal/lingual gyrus). In contrast, although young adults showed substantially less activation during the ignore condition than during the passive-viewing condition, older adults showed equivalent activation across the ignore and passive conditions. The groups were equally able to increase activation to the scene information when it was relevant, but older adults showed a specific deficit in preventing the irrelevant scene information from gaining access to this stage of processing when it was irrelevant. Furthermore, only the degree of reduced activation under the ignore instruction predicted memory for scenes; heightened activation under the attend instruction did not do so, providing further evidence of the importance of age and individual differences in down-regulation.

Deletion

Inhibition also functions to delete irrelevant information from the focus of attention. Irrelevant information may be information that eluded the access function but was subsequently recognized as irrelevant, or information that was relevant in a previous situation but is not relevant in the current one. Both explicit and implicit directed forgetting procedures require participants to forget some information, sometimes in the service of better memory for relevant, to-be-remembered information. Older adults often produce more of the irrelevant information, especially relative to their production of relevant, to-be-remembered information (e.g., May, Zacks, Hasher, & Multhaup, 1999; Zacks, Radvansky, & Hasher, 1996), suggesting a reduced ability to down-regulate no-longer-relevant information.

The deletion function also appears to play an important role in estimates of working memory capacity. Such tasks typically present lists in an increasing order of length from shortest to longest (e.g., Daneman & Carpenter, 1980) or in a random order (e.g., Engle et al., 1992), setting the stage for recall of the longest lists to be vulnerable to disruption from any nonsuppressed material from earlier lists. When the longest sets are given first to younger and older adults, age differences in span are reduced and can even be eliminated (see Lustig, May, & Hasher, 2001; May, Hasher, & Kane, 1999; Rowe, Hasher, & Turcotte, 2006). The typical age differences seen on working memory span tasks thus seem to be the product of a reduced ability to delete or suppress no longer relevant materials rather than of age differences in mental work space per se (see also Bunting, 2006; Friedman & Miyake, 2004; Hedden & Park, 2003). In other words, the similarity of young and older adults' working memory scores under conditions that reduce the need to suppress the information from prior trials suggests that working memory space is relatively age invariant but that under conditions of high interference, more of that space is taken up with irrelevant information for older than younger adults. Indeed, a recent study suggested that all of the age-related variance in standard working memory scores was accounted for by measures of the ability to regulate distraction (Hambrick, Helder, Hasher, Zacks, & Swensen, 2005). Another important finding from this research is that scores derived from the reversed sequence procedure do not predict performance on a standard outcome measure (prose recall in Lustig et al., 2001).

Restraint

Perhaps the most studied function of inhibition is to suppress or restrain strong responses that are inappropriate for the current situation. Go/no-go and stop-signal tasks are often used to study this function across different populations (e.g., children, young adults, older adults, people with brain damage or mental disorders) and are also popular in neuroimaging research. These tasks typically require participants to respond rapidly to all stimuli except a specific (no-go) stimulus, to which they are to withhold responding, or to respond rapidly to stimuli unless a signal (e.g., a tone) is presented that indicates no response should be made (Logan, 1994). These tasks seem to be strongly dependent on the dorsolateral prefrontal cortex regions that show pronounced changes with age (e.g., Raz, 2005). Parallel to the development of these structures, performance on stop-signal and go/no-go tasks improves from childhood through early adulthood and then declines (e.g., Bedard et al., 2002; Kramer, Humphrey, Larish, Logan, & Strayer, 1994). Age differences in the inhibitory component of these tasks appear to have a different developmental trajectory than do differences in overall response speed (Bedard et al., 2002).

Likewise, age differences in the ability to inhibit a strong but incorrect response are separable from the ability to activate and produce the appropriate response. May and Hasher (1998) asked participants to perform a category verification task (e.g., *furniture–chair*, with the correct response of yes; *furniture–hamburger*, with the correct response of no) as quickly as possible but to withhold responding on trials in which a tone was sounded after the category–item pair was presented. Although older adults were generally slower, their accuracy in making the category judgments was the same as that of the young adults. In contrast, older adults' ability to withhold a response on stop trials was significantly impaired. Furthermore, for older adults, deficits in restraint on the stop-signal task were correlated with deficits in restraint on two standard neuropsychological tasks (Stroop [Stroop, 1935] and Trails [Reitan & Wolfson, 1995]).

Age differences in restraint are evident on both low-level and high-level tasks. For example, the antisaccade task requires participants to look away from a cue that automatically attracts attention. Butler, Zacks, and Henderson (1999) found that older adults were more likely than younger adults to make errors by looking toward the attention-attracting stimulus rather than away from it. Restraint may also play a role in language processing if the context leads toward a strong but incorrect inference (see Yoon, May, & Hasher, 2000).

Inhibitory Failures: Not Just for Older Adults

Inhibitory deficit theory provides a theoretical framework for understanding which aspects of cognitive functioning change with age and which remain relatively stable. The theory is a general one, intended to cover a broad array of phenomena and people. Breakdowns due to aging or other disorders were proposed as extreme cases that would provide insights into inhibition's role in normal cognition, just as the performance of patients with amnesia provides important insights into memory.

Individual and group differences in inhibitory function may underlie many individual and group differences in cognition. Patient populations with inhibitory deficits provide even more extreme cases than do healthy older adults (see chaps. 11, 12, and 13, this volume). Normal variation in academic achievement and intelligence scores is influenced by inhibitory abilities. This variation includes differences between individuals and between different developmental stages, as well as between those with specific reading and language difficulties (e.g., Chiappe, Hasher, & Siegel, 2000; Dempster & Corkill, 1999; Gernsbacher, 1997; Kail, 2002). To the degree that inhibitory abilities play a role in working memory span measures (see the preceding discussion), much of the work on high-span versus low-span college students can also be understood from the perspective of group differences in inhibitory function.

Circadian Influences

Inhibitory function may differ not only among individuals, but also within the same individual over different mental or physiological states. In particular, the circadian cycle is a significant source of intraindividual variation in inhibitory function. A wide variety of biological functions show regular circadian cycles, including those that are likely to affect the brain. These include the actions of cholinergic and catecholamine neurotransmitters that are likely to be especially related to attention and inhibitory function (Arnsten, 1988; Aston-Jones, Chen, Zhu, & Oshinsky, 2001). The functions of these systems also vary with age (Sarter & Bruno, 2004; Volkow et al., 1998). Further, there are age differences in the circadian function of these neurotransmitters, with older individuals frequently showing shorter, flatter, and often more irregular cycles (Edgar, 1994; Monk & Kupfer, 2000).

Circadian fluctuations in biological processes correlate well with responses on the Horne and Ostberg (1976) Morningness–Eveningness Questionnaire. This questionnaire classifies individuals on a continuum from *definitely evening* to *definitely morning* types. Membership in these categories appears to have a genetic basis and is associated with fluctuations in many physiological processes (e.g., Hur, Bouchard, & Lykken, 1998). In keeping with age differences in the circadian fluctuations of many physiological measures, distributions of scores change across adulthood: Most young adults identify as evening or neutral types, whereas the vast majority of older adults identify as morning types (e.g., Yoon et al., 2000).

Age–circadian interactions have been reported for all three functions of inhibition that we described earlier in this chapter (Hasher et al., 1999). With respect to the access function, there is evidence that both the costs and benefits of distraction are greater at off-peak than at peak times of day (May, 1999; Rowe, Hasher, & Turcotte, 2006).

The deletion function also varies across the day, with greater effectiveness at peak than at off-peak times. For example, both young and older adults showed large effects of testing time in a sentence-based version of a directed forgetting task (May & Hasher, 1998). Participants first generated the likely ending to a sentence (e.g., "Before you go to bed, remember to turn out the _____"; with the correct response of *lights*) and were then told to remember a new, experimenter-provided ending instead (e.g., *stove*). During a subsequent implicit test, participants completed sentences that had a medium-range probability of being completed by either the self-generated, no-longer-relevant ending (e.g., "The baby was fascinated by the bright ____; correct response *lights*) or the experimenter-generated, to-be-remembered ending (e.g., "She remodeled her kitchen and replaced the old ____"; correct response *stove*).

Performance on the critical test varied with testing time and age. For participants tested in the afternoon (young adults' optimal time, older adults' nonoptimal time), young adults produced even fewer of the no-longer-relevant items than would be predicted by normative completion probabilities, whereas older adults produced a relatively large proportion of such items. For participants tested in the morning (young adults' nonoptimal time, older adults' optimal time), there were no age differences in the production of to-be-deleted items. Both groups produced more no-longer-relevant items at their nonoptimal time of day, indicating that this inhibitory function varies across the day.

The restraint function also shows strong circadian influences. Strong motor responses are less controllable at nonoptimal times, with more slips of action than at other times (e.g., Manly, Lewis, Robertson, Watson, & Datta, 2002). In the stop-signal task (May & Hasher, 1998), the usual age differences in stopping probability and efficiency were found for participants tested in the afternoon. However, there were no age differences for participants tested in the morning. These findings reflected a crossover interaction: Young adults showed their worst performance in the morning and best performance at the later testing time. In contrast, older adults showed their best performance in the morning and their worst performance in the late afternoon. Again, these patterns were limited to the aspects of the task that depended on inhibitory restraint. For the go trials, which did not make inhibitory demands, older adults were slower overall, but neither response time nor accuracy varied with time of day or interacted with age. Roughly comparable findings have been reported for old rats at the end of their activity cycle (Winocur & Hasher, 2004).

Time of day may also have a strong influence on social judgments and decision making. At nonoptimal times of day, people are more likely to be distracted by the peripheral aspects of a persuasive text, such as the status of the source or heuristics such as "the majority is always right," as opposed to processing the central meaning (Martin & Marrington, 2005). The tendency to judge people on the basis of stereotypes is also stronger at nonoptimal times (Bodenhausen, 1990). These effects might respectively be seen as reflecting failures in the access and restraint functions of inhibition.

Time of day effects seem to be strongest for inhibitory functions. Tasks that simply require activation do not show much variation with circadian phase. For example, completing sentences with high-probability endings did not change over the course of the day for either young or older adults, nor did response time in go trials of the go/no-go task (May & Hasher, 1998). Many other relatively simple speeded tasks also do not show circadian variation per se, although they do vary with related factors such as sleepiness (e.g., Graw, Krauchi, Knoblauch, Wirz-Justice, & Cajochen, 2004; Song & Stough, 2000). Even challenging tasks that require only activation, not inhibition (e.g., a difficult vocabulary test), do not vary over the day (e.g., May & Hasher, 1998). There is some suggestion that expertise in a domain (e.g., reading) may spare performance even when inhibition is required (Li, Hasher, Jonas, Rahhal, & May, 1998). These patterns fit well with a theoretical framework suggesting that inhibition, not activation, is a major source of variation in cognitive performance (Hasher et al., 1999).

Questions and New Directions

Inhibitory deficit theory provides a powerful framework for understanding variation in performance in healthy young adults as well as more extreme examples due to developmental changes or disease. However, the development of this theory has not been without challenges. The following sections describe how the theory has evolved in response to critiques and new data while remaining true to its central tenets: Inhibitory processes are the major source of performance differences, whereas automatic activation processes are largely constant across individuals, groups, and situations. Inhibition serves goals by reducing the activation of one or more competitors for thought or action, enabling the selection of those consistent with objectives.

Defining Inhibition

Questions have been asked about what type of theory inhibition theory is (e.g., Burke, 1997). Zacks and Hasher (1997) borrowed the term *pragmatic* from Baddeley (1992) to describe their approach to theory building. This approach emphasizes general principles, nonreductionist reasoning, and verbal theory statements. The alternative, a formal computational modeling approach, has significant strengths, especially its precision in assumptions and predictions (see chaps. 5 and 9, this volume). The strength of the more informal, verbally based approach stems from its applicability across a wide variety of tasks that are sometimes seen as issues in themselves.

The term *inhibition* (like many other terms) is used differently across literatures and investigators, and this variation can result in misunderstandings and misattributions. Many researchers do not include the access and deletion functions of inhibition, reserving the term *inhibition* for the restraint-related functions involved in tasks such as the stop-signal procedure (e.g., Friedman & Miyake, 2004). Others collapse across the three processes we suggest, although the interdependence (or not) of these processes remains to be empirically determined. Ideas about potentially separable processes of inhibition are a relatively new research focus and are likely to undergo further development as more evidence (including that from neuroimaging and circadian dissociations) becomes available. At its core, inhibitory deficit theory is largely concerned with inhibition as an active, goal-directed process that acts in conjunction with automatic activation processes to control the contents of consciousness (Hasher & Zacks, 1988; Hasher et al., 1999; Zacks & Hasher, 1997).

Measuring Inhibition: Are Its Functions Related?

Concerns have also been raised over the attempt to find agreed-on, stable measures of inhibitory function (e.g., McDowd, 1997). For a time, negative-priming tasks were seen as promising candidates to measure inhibition, but they were quickly found to be quite complex, vulnerable to several influences (e.g., May, Kane, & Hasher, 1995; see also chap. 4, this volume), and not consistently reliable as an index of inhibition. A lack of stable, canonical measures has been especially troublesome for large-scale, individual-differences studies that attempted to statistically derive factors on the basis of shared variance among multiple tests that putatively converge onto a hypothesized construct (e.g., Salthouse, Atkinson, & Berish, 2003).

At least three factors may contribute to the difficulty of finding inhibitory measures with good psychometric properties (for a similar list, see Friedman & Miyake, 2004). First, inhibitory deficits by their nature lead to performance that changes across trials. Furthermore, the degree of change varies according to the severity of an individual's inhibitory deficit. Such cross-trial variation may be an especially important factor for the deletion function. Failures to delete irrelevant information from prior trials lead to greater and greater buildup of proactive interference across trials, with a steeper slope of decline for individuals who are poor at deletion. Furthermore, failures in deletion can also lead to cross-task contamination (Lustig & Hasher, 2002), especially if the tasks use similar materials. The opposite problem may also come into play, especially for the other functions of inhibition: As participants become practiced at the task, they may become more skilled in exercising inhibition, or they may find alternative, idiosyncratic strategies to solve the task without using inhibition (Davidson, Zacks, & Williams, 2003).

Second, tasks are not process pure (Jacoby, 1991), and individuals may differ in which functions they emphasize or at which stages of processing. For example, in the Stroop task, the word information is irrelevant and is to be inhibited, whereas the ink color information is relevant. Participants may try both to prevent the word information from gaining access to consciousness and, to the degree that access control fails, to restrain themselves from responding on the basis of word information as opposed to ink color.

Third, until recently, many studies did not recognize the different functions of inhibition, reducing the chances of finding shared variance. One task that loads highly on deletion and one that emphasizes restraint might well be expected to share less variance than two tasks that both make high demands on the restraint function. In earlier studies, all of these tasks would be considered to measure a single construct, inhibition, although many authors have proposed multiple mechanisms (e.g., Dempster, 1993; Nigg, 2000; see also chap. 13, this volume).

More recently, there have been attempts to assess the different components of inhibition (e.g., Friedman & Miyake, 2004) using multiple measures of each component process to create latent variables, followed by structural equation modeling. The Friedman and Miyake components do not entirely agree with the Hasher and Zacks functions discussed in this chapter. For example, resistance to proactive interference was used as a measure of inhibition, but from the present framework, it is an outcome (of reduced control over access and deletion). The latent variable approach is extremely valuable for assessing the existence of separate inhibitory functions, their interrelations across adulthood, and their impact on various outcomes.

The idea of related, but separable, inhibitory functions is an important theoretical and methodological development. However, it is also relatively recent, and many questions remain. How many functions of inhibition are there? Are they related, and if so, how? Do the functions of inhibition map directly onto specific mechanisms? What are the biological bases of the shared and distinct aspects of inhibitory function?

Preliminary answers to these questions may be emerging. For example, there is evidence that populations with deficits in one inhibitory function also tend to have deficits in others, although the degree to which different functions are impaired may vary (e.g., Barkley, 1997; Chiappe et al., 2000; Faust & Balota, 1997; Spieler, Balota, & Faust, 1996; Stuss et al., 1999). Studies of healthy college students indicate related but separable constructs (e.g., Friedman & Miyake, 2004), as do studies of circadian variations in both young and older adults (Hasher et al., 1999; West, Murphy, Armilio, Craik, & Stuss, 2002). Data from recent neuroimaging studies also support the idea of a small number of inhibitory functions that are related but distinct.

A growing body of evidence suggests that different inhibitory functions tap a common network that includes anterior cingulate cortex, dorsolateral prefrontal cortex, inferior frontal gyrus, posterior parietal cortex, and anterior insula (Nee, Wager, & Jonides, 2005; Nelson, Reuter-Lorenz, Sylvester, Jonides, & Smith, 2003; Sylvester et al., 2003; Wager et al., 2005).[1] These regions are found in common both in single studies that test the same participants on multiple tasks (Sylvester et al., 2003; Wager et al., 2005) and in meta-analyses that compare across experiments (Nee et al., 2005).

Different functions of inhibition also show distinct regions of activation. For example, Sylvester et al. (2003) compared task-switching activations (possibly requiring the deletion of one task set to focus on another) with activations associated with response inhibition or restraint (responding in the opposite direction of a given cue). In addition to the common network, the deletion task also activated the left prefrontal and left parietal cortex; the restraint-related task showed preferential activation for more medial, subcortical regions and the frontal polar cortex (for similar results using different tasks, see Nelson et al., 2003).

In summary, a common network of regions is shared across tasks that differentially emphasize the different functions of inhibition. There is at least heuristic similarity across experiments in the distinct regions activated for different functions of inhibition, with some variation that may be due to specific task demands, materials, and baseline conditions. A meta-analysis that included restraint-related tasks such as go/no-go, Stroop, and response-compatibility tasks reached similar conclusions, with medial regions largely in common and some variation in lateral regions across different types of

---

[1]These authors used the theoretically neutral term *interference resolution* in describing their data. Our use of terms related to different inhibitory functions (*access*, *deletion*, *suppression*) is a reinterpretation of the data in light of the current discussion of inhibitory deficit theory. However, it is interesting that these studies often subtract out activation from conditions that presumably require intentional, goal-oriented processing but do not make strong demands on inhibition (e.g., positive trials in Nelson et al., 2003).

task (Nee et al., 2005). Attempts to understand the shared and independent aspects of different inhibitory functions hold a great deal of promise for future research.

Activation, Goals, and Compensation

Critiques of the inhibitory view often question the degree to which performance differences can be ascribed to inhibition as opposed to a failure to activate relevant information. Hasher et al. (1999) pointed out that failures to activate information are unlikely to be the sole cause of age differences in performance: Across several different tasks (directed forgetting, repetition priming, garden path sentences, garden path paragraphs), older adults showed, if anything, greater activation of information than did young adults (Hamm & Hasher, 1992; May, Zacks, et al., 1999; Zacks et al., 1996). The neuroimaging data of Gazzaley et al. (2005) are also consistent with this view. When told to remember scenes, older adults showed activity at least as strong as that of young adults in brain regions involved with scene processing. However, although young adults reduced activation in these regions when told to ignore scenes, suggesting that they were suppressing the processing of scene information, older adults did not. Further, as expected from inhibition theory, individual differences in suppression, not activation, predicted memory performance.

By now, greater or more distributed activation by older than by younger adults is a common neuroimaging finding in both frontal and posterior regions (for a recent review, see Reuter-Lorenz & Lustig, 2005). Additional activations are often interpreted as reflecting compensation, but there are several examples of greater activation being associated with poorer performance, either between young and older adults or within a sample of older adults (e.g., Madden et al., 1999). Whether greater activation reflects compensation or inappropriate processing likely differs by task and region (for a review of these interactions, see Rajah & D'Esposito, 2005).

New data on task-related deactivations and "default-mode" processing also suggest a specific inhibitory deficit in older adults. A network of regions, including the posterior cingulate and medial frontal cortex, are more active during unconstrained, no-task conditions than during cognitive tasks (Shulman et al., 1997). These regions show below-baseline activation (deactivation) during active, cognitively demanding tasks and are inversely correlated with positive activations in prefrontal regions involved in task performance (Fox et al., 2005). The deactivation of these regions during active tasks is thought to reflect a switch from unconstrained, largely self-directed thinking (e.g., thinking about one's day, monitoring one's comfort and internal state) to a focus on the task (Raichle et al., 2001). Young adults deactivate these regions more as tasks become more difficult, and greater deactivation has been associated with better performance (Daselaar, Prince, & Cabeza, 2004; McKiernan, Kaufman, Kucera-Thompson, & Binder, 2003).

Older adults show impaired deactivation of these regions, even in situations in which they show frontal activations as great as or greater than those of young adults (Lustig et al., 2003; Persson, Lustig, & Reuter-Lorenz, 2005).

Age differences in deactivation are apparent even by middle age and increase across the life span (Grady, Springer, Hongwanishul, McIntosh, & Winocur, 2006). For example, Lustig et al. (2003) found that older adults activated the left frontal cortex to an even greater degree than did young adults during a semantic decision task. However, in regions that show deactivation in young adults, older adults showed little or no modulation. Time courses of activation (see Figure 8.2) showed that young adults quickly suppressed activation in these regions, whereas in older adults, activation was roughly constant during both task and baseline (fixation) conditions. Persson et al. (2005) found that failures to deactivate correlated with interference effects on a verb-generation task. Although other interpretations are possible (baseline differences, compensation), these data are consistent with the idea that older adults have difficulty inhibiting default-mode processing—despite an apparently spared ability to activate regions associated with task performance.

Questions have been raised about the degree to which performance on different tasks reflects inhibition as opposed to other processes, such as goal maintenance (e.g., Braver et al., 2001; see chaps. 1 and 7, this volume). Older adults can fail to deactivate task-irrelevant regions, even when regions related to the task are robustly activated (Lustig et al., 2003, Persson et al., 2005). This pattern seems inconsistent with the idea that older adults are not able to successfully activate and maintain goal-directed behavior. Likewise, older adults may maintain task-irrelevant information even when they show task-relevant performance (requiring goal maintenance) similar to that of young adults (e.g., Hamm & Hasher, 1992). Furthermore, individual differences analyses from the Gazzaley et al. face–scene suppression task indicate that suppression, not activation, is related to measures of working memory capacity for both young and older adults (Gazzaley, Cooney, McEvoy, Knight, & D'Esposito, 2005; Gazzaley, Cooney, Rissman, et al., 2005).

It has been suggested that working memory capacity is intrinsically linked to goal maintenance and that goal maintenance in turn is the determining factor in inhibitory performance (see chap. 7, this volume). However, Hester, Murphy, and Garavan (2004) identified several brain regions that were sensitive to both working memory load and inhibition demands, but they also identified regions uniquely associated with inhibition. Data from the think/no-think procedure (see chap. 5, this volume) also seem incongruent with the idea that inhibition is isomorphic with goal maintenance. In this procedure, participants first learn arbitrary paired associates (e.g., *ordeal–roach*). During each test trial, they are presented with a cue word and asked either to retrieve its paired associate from memory or to avoid thinking of the associate during the trial. Presumably, both of these conditions require effortful processing and attention to the goal. Indeed, on an a priori basis, one might predict that the retrieval (think) condition should be the one more dependent on effortful, goal-directed processing. However, Anderson et al. (2004) identified several prefrontal and hippocampal regions that were more active during the no-think condition, which required inhibition of the associate. Furthermore, activation in these regions was correlated with subsequent forgetting, as revealed on a later memory test. These patterns support the idea of active, effortful inhibition over and above the goal maintenance required in the think condition.

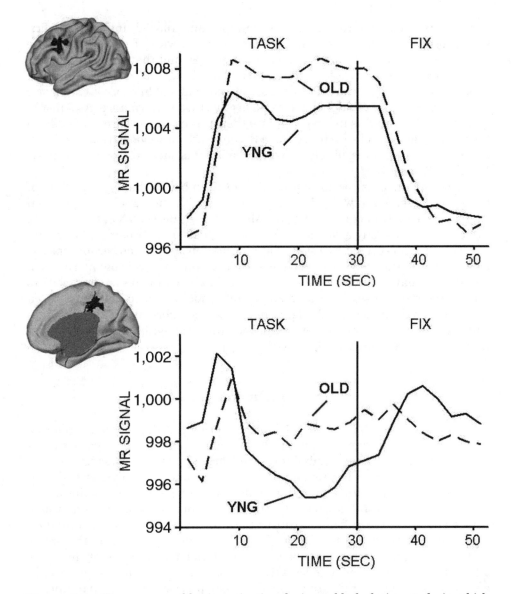

Figure 8.2. Time course of brain activation during a block design study in which people alternated between an active task (semantic decision) and staring at a fixation. Older adults showed successful frontal activation that was, if anything, greater than that of young adults (top panel). Young adults showed the typical pattern of deactivation (suppression during the task as compared with the baseline [fixation] condition) in a posterior cingulate region (bottom panel). Deactivation magnitude was reduced in older adults. MR = magnetic resonance; OLD = older adults; YNG = young adults; SEC = seconds. Adapted from "Functional Deactivations: Change With Age and Dementia of the Alzheimer Type," by C. Lustig, A. Z. Snyder, M. Bhakta, K. C. O'Brien, M. McAvoy, M. E. Raichle, et al., 2003, *Proceedings of the National Academy of Sciences, USA, 100,* p. 14506. Copyright 2003 by the National Academy of Sciences, USA.

This is not to say that goals are unimportant. Indeed, inhibitory deficit theory proposed that inhibition operates in the service of goals, that these goals might differ between individuals and groups, and that these differences might have consequences for behavior (Hasher et al., 1999; Hasher & Zacks, 1988). Hasher and Zacks (1988) proposed that older adults may emphasize personal values and relationships over objective task performance. As a result, they may integrate this information into their processing or perform better on tasks that make use of such processing. Recent work on socioemotional selectivity theories of aging is highly congruent with this idea (e.g., Carstensen & Mikels, 2005).

Older adults often perform as well as or even better than young adults if tasks are presented in ways that are consistent with their goals and personal experience (e.g., Kim & Hasher, 2005; May, Rahhal, Berry, & Leighton, 2005). Inhibitory deficits may also lead to changes in goals and strategies. For example, if retrieval of specific, task-relevant information is impaired because the cue for that information is also associated with irrelevant, interfering information, individuals may increasingly rely on immediate cues in the environment to control their response. Such a strategy shift should lead to more gist-based processing and intrusions of related but incorrect information—performance patterns that are typical of older adults and others thought to have poor inhibitory function (Hasher & Zacks, 1988).

Conclusion

Hasher and Zacks (1988) made a simple, if controversial, proposal: Inhibition of information irrelevant to one's goals is a major contributor to performance and to differences among individuals and groups. As our overview in this chapter suggests, there is strong evidence for this view from a variety of behavioral tasks as well as from emerging evidence in the neuroimaging literature. New applications of statistical methods and neuroimaging techniques may help to resolve some of the difficulties caused by different uses of the term *inhibition* across investigators and the fact that tasks are not process pure. Of course, such issues are not exclusive to the idea of inhibition but rather apply to nearly all putative mechanisms, particularly those that are general or high level in nature. Challenges for the future include a more precise definition of inhibitory functions and their relations and further integration with neuroimaging findings and research on goals. Our reading of the current evidence, including evidence offered in this book by us and other authors, is that inhibition—from the Hasher and Zacks perspective as it has developed over the years—is alive and well and extremely useful.

References

Anderson, M. C., Ochsner, K. N., Kuhl, B., Cooper, J., Robertson, E., Gabrieli, S. W., et al. (2004, January 9). Neural systems underlying the suppression of unwanted memories. *Science, 303,* 232–235.

Arnsten, A. F. T. (1998). Catecholamine modulation of prefrontal cortical cognitive function. *Trends in Cognitive Sciences, 2*, 436–447.

Aston-Jones, G., Chen, S., Zhu, Y., & Oshinsky, M. L. (2001). A neural circuit for circadian regulation of arousal. *Nature Neuroscience, 4*, 732–738.

Baddeley, A. (1992). Is working memory working? The fifteenth Bartlett lecture. *Quarterly Journal of Experimental Psychology, 44A*, 1–31.

Barkley, R. A. (1997). Behavioral inhibition, sustained attention, and executive functions: Constructing a unifying theory of ADHD. *Psychological Bulletin, 121*, 65–94.

Bedard, A. C., Nichols, S., Barbosa, J. A., Schachar, R., Logan, G. D., & Tannock, R. (2002). The development of selective inhibitory control across the life span. *Developmental Neuropsychology, 21*, 93–111.

Bodenhausen, G. V. (1990). Stereotypes as judgmental heuristics—Evidence of circadian variations in discrimination. *Psychological Science, 1*, 319–322.

Braver, T. S., Barch, D. M., Keys, B. A., Carter, C. S., Cohen, J. D., Kaye, J. A., et al. (2001). Context processing in older adults: Evidence for a theory relating cognitive control to neurobiology in healthy aging. *Journal of Experimental Psychology: General, 130*, 746–763.

Bunting, M. F. (2006). *Why working memory measures "work": Proactive interference in tests of immediate memory.* Unpublished doctoral dissertation, University of Illinois, Chicago.

Burke, D. M. (1997). Language, aging, and inhibitory deficits: Evaluation of a theory. *Journals of Gerontology Series B—Psychological Sciences and Social Sciences, 52*, P254–P264.

Butler, K. M., Zacks, R. T., & Henderson, J. M. (1999). Suppression of reflexive saccades in younger and older adults: Age comparisons on an antisaccade task. *Memory & Cognition, 27*, 584–591.

Carlson, M. C., Hasher, L., Connelly, S. L., & Zacks, R. T. (1995). Aging, distraction, and the benefits of predictable location. *Psychology and Aging, 10*, 427–436.

Carstensen, L. L., & Mikels, J. A. (2005). At the intersection of emotion and cognition—Aging and the positivity effect. *Current Directions in Psychological Science, 14*, 117–121.

Chiappe, P., Hasher, L., & Siegel, L. S. (2000). Working memory, inhibitory control, and reading disability. *Memory & Cognition, 28*, 8–17.

Daneman, M., & Carpenter, P. A. (1980). Individual-differences in working memory and reading. *Journal of Verbal Learning and Verbal Behavior, 19*, 450–466.

Daselaar, S. M., Prince, S. E., & Cabeza, R. (2004). When less means more: Deactivations during encoding that predict subsequent memory. *NeuroImage, 23*, 921–927.

Davidson, D. J., Zacks, R. T., & Williams, C. C. (2003). Stroop interference, practice, and aging. *Aging Neuropsychology and Cognition, 10*, 85–98.

Dempster, F. N. (1993). Resistance to interference: Developmental changes in a basic processing dimension. In M. L. Howe & R. Pasnak (Eds.), *Emerging themes in cognitive development: Vol. 1. Foundations* (pp. 3–27). New York: Springer-Verlag.

Dempster, F. N., & Corkill, A. J. (1999). Interference and inhibition in cognition and behavior: Unifying themes for educational psychology. *Educational Psychology Review, 11*, 1–88.

Edgar, D. M. (1994). Sleep–wake circadian cycles and aging: Potential etiologies and relevance to age-related changes in integrated physiological systems. *Neurobiology of Aging, 15*, 499–501.

Engle, R. W., Cantor, J., & Carullo, J. J. (1992). Individual differences in working memory and comprehension: A test of 4 hypotheses. *Journal of Experimental Psychology: Learning, Memory, and Cognition, 18*, 972–992.

Faust, M. E., & Balota, D. A. (1997). Inhibition of return and visuospatial attention in healthy older adults and individuals with dementia of the Alzheimer type. *Neuropsychology, 11*, 13–29.

Fox, M. D., Snyder, A. Z., Vincent, J. L., Corbetta, M., Van Essen, D. C., & Raichle, M. E. (2005). The human brain is intrinsically organized into dynamic, anticorrelated functional networks. *Proceedings of the National Academy of Sciences, USA, 102*, 9673–9678.

Friedman, N. P., & Miyake, A. (2004). The relations among inhibition and interference control functions: A latent-variable analysis. *Journal of Experimental Psychology: General, 133*, 101–135.

Gazzaley, A., Cooney, J. W., McEvoy, K., Knight, R. T., & D'Esposito, M. (2005). Top-down enhancement and suppression of the magnitude and speed of neural activity. *Journal of Cognitive Neuroscience, 17*, 507–517.

Gazzaley, A., Cooney, J. W., Rissman, J., & D'Esposito, M. (2005). Top-down suppression deficit underlies working memory impairment in normal aging. *Nature Neuroscience, 8*, 1298–1300.

Gernsbacher, M. A. (1997). Group differences in suppression skill. *Aging, Neuropsychology and Cognition, 4,* 175–184.

Grady, C. L., Springer, M. V., Hongwanishul, D., McIntosh, A. R., & Winocur, G. (2006). Age-related changes in brain activity across the adult lifespan. *Journal of Cognitive Neuroscience, 18,* 227–241.

Graw, P., Krauchi, K., Knoblauch, V., Wirz-Justice, A., & Cajochen, C. (2004). Circadian and wake-dependent modulation of fastest and slowest reaction times during the psychomotor vigilance task. *Physiology & Behavior, 80,* 695–701.

Hambrick, D. Z., Helder, E. A., Hasher, L., Zacks, R. T., & Swensen, E. (2005, November). *The relationship between inhibition and working memory: A latent-variable approach.* Paper presented at the annual meeting of the Psychonomic Society, Toronto, Ontario, Canada.

Hamm, V. P., & Hasher, L. (1992). Age and the availability of inferences. *Psychology and Aging, 7,* 56–64.

Hasher, L., & Zacks, R. T. (1988). Working memory, comprehension, and aging: A review and new view. In G. H. Bower (Ed.), *The psychology of learning and motivation: Advances in research and theory* (Vol. 22, pp. 193–225). New York: Academic Press.

Hasher, L., Zacks, R. T., & May, C. P. (1999). Inhibitory control, circadian arousal, and age. In D. Gopher & A. Koriat (Eds.), *Attention and performance: XVII. Cognition regulation and performance: Interaction of theory and application* (pp. 653–675). Cambridge, MA: MIT Press.

Hedden, T., & Park, D. C. (2003). Contributions of source and inhibitory mechanisms to age-related retroactive interference in verbal working memory. *Journal of Experimental Psychology: General, 132,* 93–112.

Hester, R., Murphy, K., & Garavan, H. (2004). Beyond common resources: The cortical basis for resolving task interference. *NeuroImage, 23,* 202–212.

Horne, J. A., & Ostberg, O. (1976). A self-assessment questionnaire to determine morningness–eveningness in human circadian rhythms. *International Journal of Chronobiology, 4,* 97–110.

Hur, Y., Bouchard, T. J., & Lykken, D. T. (1998). Genetic and environmental influence on morningness–eveningness. *Personality and Individual Differences, 25,* 917–925.

Jacoby, L. L. (1991). A process dissociation framework: Separating automatic from intentional uses of memory. *Journal of Memory and Language, 30,* 513–541.

Kahneman, D. (1973). *Attention and effort.* Englewood Cliffs, NJ: Prentice-Hall.

Kail, R. S. (2002). Developmental change in proactive interference. *Child Development, 73,* 1703–1714.

Kim, S., & Hasher, L. (2005). The attraction effect in decision making: Superior performance by older adults. *Quarterly Journal of Experimental Psychology: Section A. Human Experimental Psychology, 58,* 120–133.

Kim, S., Hasher, L., & Zacks, R. T. (in press). Aging and a benefit of distractibility. *Psychonomic Bulletin & Review.*

Kramer, A. F., Humphrey, D. G., Larish, J. F., Logan, G. D., & Strayer, D. L. (1994). Aging and inhibition: Beyond a unitary view of inhibitory processing in attention. *Psychology and Aging, 9,* 491–512.

Li, K. Z. H., Hasher, L., Jonas, D., Rahhal, T. A., & May, C. P. (1998). Distractibility, circadian arousal, and aging: A boundary condition? *Psychology and Aging, 13,* 574–583.

Logan, G. D. (1994). On the ability to inhibit thought and action: A user's guide to the stop signal paradigm. In T. H. Dagenbach & D. Carr (Eds.), *Inhibitory processes in attention, memory, and language* (pp. 189–239). San Diego, CA: Academic Press.

Lustig, C., & Hasher, L. (2002). Working memory span: The effect of prior learning. *American Journal of Psychology, 115,* 89–101.

Lustig, C., Hasher, L., & Tonev, S. T. (2006). Distraction as a determinant of processing speed. *Psychonomic Bulletin & Review, 13,* 619–625.

Lustig, C., May, C. P., & Hasher, L. (2001). Working memory span and the role of proactive interference. *Journal of Experimental Psychology: General, 130,* 199–207.

Lustig, C., Snyder, A. Z., Bhakta, M., O'Brien, K. C., McAvoy, M., Raichle, M. E., et al. (2003). Functional deactivations: Change with age and dementia of the Alzheimer type. *Proceedings of the National Academy of Sciences, USA, 100,* 14504–14509.

Madden, D. J., Gottlob, L. R., Denny, L. L., Turkington, T. G., Provenzale, J. M., Hawk, T. C., & Coleman, R. E. (1999). Aging and recognition memory: Changes in regional cerebral blood flow associated with components of reaction time distributions. *Journal of Cognitive Neuroscience, 11,* 511–520.

Manly, T., Lewis, G. H., Robertson, I. H., Watson, P. C., & Datta, A. K. (2002). Coffee in the cornflakes: Time-of-day as a modulator of executive response control. *Neuropsychologia, 40,* 1–6.

Martin, P. Y., & Marrington, S. (2005). Morningness–eveningness orientation, optimal time-of-day and attitude change: Evidence for the systematic processing of a persuasive communication. *Personality and Individual Differences, 39,* 367–377.

May, C. P. (1999). Synchrony effects in cognition: The costs and a benefit. *Psychonomic Bulletin & Review, 6,* 142–147.

May, C. P., & Hasher, L. (1998). Synchrony effects in inhibitory control over thought and action. *Journal of Experimental Psychology: Human Perception and Performance, 24,* 363–379.

May, C. P., Hasher, L., & Kane, M. J. (1999). The role of interference in memory span. *Memory & Cognition, 27,* 759–767.

May, C. P., Kane, M. J., & Hasher, L. (1995). Determinants of negative priming. *Psychological Bulletin, 118,* 35–54.

May, C. P., Rahhal, T., Berry, E., & Leighton, E. (2005). Aging, source memory, and emotion. *Psychology and Aging, 20,* 571–578.

May, C. P., Zacks, R. T., Hasher, L., & Multhaup, K. S. (1999). Inhibition in the processing of garden-path sentences. *Psychology and Aging, 14,* 304–313.

McDowd, J. M. (1997). Inhibition in attention and aging. *Journals of Gerontology Series B—Psychological Sciences and Social Sciences, 52,* P265–P273.

McKiernan, K. A., Kaufman, J. N., Kucera-Thompson, J., & Binder, J. R. (2003). A parametric manipulation of factors affecting task-induced deactivation in functional neuroimaging. *Journal of Cognitive Neuroscience, 15,* 394–408.

Monk, T. H., & Kupfer, D. J. (2000). Circadian rhythms in healthy aging: Effects downstream from the pacemaker. *Chronobiology International, 17,* 355–368.

Nee, D. E., Wager, T. D., & Jonides, J. (2005). *Interference-resolution: Insights from a meta-analysis of neuroimaging tasks.* Manuscript submitted for publication.

Nelson, J. K., Reuter-Lorenz, P. A., Sylvester, C.-Y. C., Jonides, J., & Smith, E. E. (2003). Dissociable neural mechanisms underlying response-based and familiarity-based conflict in working memory. *Proceedings of the National Academy of Sciences, USA, 100,* 11171–11175.

Nigg, J. T. (2000). On inhibition/disinhibition in developmental psychopathology: Views from cognitive personality psychology and a working inhibition taxonomy. *Psychological Bulletin, 127,* 571–598.

Persson, D. J., Lustig, C., & Reuter-Lorenz, P. A. (2005, November). *Task-induced deactivations: Effects of age and selection demand.* Poster presented at the Society for Neuroscience Meeting, Washington, DC.

Raichle, M. E., MacLeod, A. M., Snyder, A. Z., Powers, W. J., Gusnard, D. A., & Shulman, G. L. (2001). A default mode of brain function. *Proceedings of the National Academy of Sciences, USA, 98,* 676–682.

Rajah, M. N., & D'Esposito, M. (2005). Region-specific changes in prefrontal function with age: A review of PET and fMRI studies on working and episodic memory. *Brain, 128,* 1964–1983.

Raz, N. (2005). The aging brain observed in vivo: Differential changes and their modifiers. In R. Cabeza, L. Nyberg, & D. C. Park (Eds.), *Cognitive neuroscience: Linking cognitive and cerebral aging* (pp. 17–55). New York: Oxford University Press.

Reitan, R. M., & Wolfson, D. (1995). Category Test and Trail Making Test as measures of frontal lobe functions. *Clinical Neuropsychologist, 9,* 50–56.

Reuter-Lorenz, P. A., & Lustig, C. (2005). Brain aging: Reorganizing discoveries about the aging mind. *Current Opinion in Neurobiology, 15,* 245–251.

Rowe, G., Hasher, L., & Turcotte, J. (2006). *Visuospatial working memory, aging and interference.* Manuscript in preparation.

Rowe, G., Valderrama, S., Hasher, L., & Lenartowicz, A. (2006). Attention disregulation: A long-term memory benefit. *Psychology and Aging, 21,* 826–830.

Salthouse, T. A., Atkinson, T. M., & Berish, D. E. (2003). Executive functioning as a potential mediator of age-related cognitive decline in normal adults. *Journal of Experimental Psychology: General, 132,* 566–594.

Sarter, M., & Bruno, J. P. (2004). Developmental origins of the age-related decline in cortical cholinergic function and associated cognitive abilities. *Neurobiology of Aging, 25,* 1127–1139.

Shulman, G. L., Fiez, J. A., Corbetta, M., Buckner, R. L., Miezin, F. M., Raichle, M. E., & Petersen, S. E. (1997). Common blood flow changes across visual tasks: 2. Decreases in cerebral cortex. *Journal of Cognitive Neuroscience, 9,* 648–663.

Song, J., & Stough, C. (2000). The relationship between morningness–eveningness, time-of-day, speed of information processing, and intelligence. *Personality and Individual Differences, 29,* 1179–1190.

Spieler, D. H., Balota, D. A., & Faust, M. E. (1996). Stroop performance in healthy younger and older adults and in individuals with dementia of the Alzheimer's type. *Journal of Experimental Psychology: Human Perception and Performance, 22,* 461–479.

Stroop, J. R. (1935). Studies of interference in serial verbal reactions. *Journal of Experimental Psychology, 18,* 643–662.

Stuss, D. T., Toth, J. P., Franchi, D., Alexander, M. P., Tipper, S., & Craik, F. I. M. (1999). Dissociation of attentional processes in patients with focal frontal and posterior lesions. *Neuropsychologia, 37,* 1005–1027.

Sylvester, C. Y. C., Wager, T. D., Lacey, S. C., Hernandez, L., Nichols, T. E., Smith, E. E., & Jonides, J. (2003). Switching attention and resolving interference: fMRI measures of executive functions. *Neuropsychologia, 41,* 357–370.

Volkow, N. D., Wang, G. J., Fowler, J. S., Ding, Y. S., Gur, R. C., Gatley, J., et al. (1998). Parallel loss of presynaptic and postsynaptic dopamine markers in normal aging. *Annals of Neurology, 44,* 143–147.

Wager, T. D., Sylvester, C.-Y. C., Lacey, S. C., Nee, D. E., Franklin, M., & Jonides, J. (2005). Common and unique components of response inhibition revealed by fMRI. *NeuroImage, 27,* 323–340.

Wechsler, D. (1981). *The Wechsler Adult Intelligence Scale—Revised.* New York: Psychological Corporation.

West, R., Murphy, K. J., Armilio, M. L., Craik, F. I. M., & Stuss, D. T. (2002). Effects of time of day on age differences in working memory. *Journals of Gerontology Series B—Psychological Sciences and Social Sciences, 57,* P3–P10.

Winocur, G., & Hasher, L. (2004). Age and time-of-day effects on learning and memory in a nonmatching-to-sample test. *Neurobiology of Aging, 25,* 1107–1115.

Yoon, C., May, C. P., & Hasher, L. (2000). Aging, circadian arousal patterns, and cognition. In D. C. Park & N. Schwarz (Eds.), *Cognitive aging: A primer* (pp. 151–171). Philadelphia: Psychology Press.

Zacks, R., & Hasher, L. (1997). Cognitive gerontology and attentional inhibition: A reply to Burke and McDowd. *Journals of Gerontology Series B—Psychological Sciences and Social Sciences, 52,* P274–P283.

Zacks, R. T., Radvansky, G., & Hasher, L. (1996). Studies of directed forgetting in older adults. *Journal of Experimental Psychology: Learning, Memory, and Cognition, 22,* 143–156.

9

Aging and Inhibition Deficits: Where Are the Effects?

Deborah M. Burke and Gabrielle Osborne

Aging has broad but not universal effects on cognitive performance. One popular explanation for why some, but not all, aspects of memory, language, and attention decline in old age (e.g., Burke & MacKay, 1997; McDowd & Shaw, 2000) is that inhibitory processes become less efficient with aging (e.g., Hasher, Zacks, & May, 1999; Zacks & Hasher, 1997). *Inhibition* is conceptualized as a process that regulates attention and the contents of working memory, thereby affecting cognitive performance broadly, including the ability to focus attention, comprehend and produce language, solve problems, and learn new information (West, 1996; Zacks & Hasher, 1994). Cognitive operations that do not involve inhibitory processes or that are automatic, operating with little cognitive control, are postulated to be well maintained in old age (e.g., Zacks & Hasher, 1997). This inhibition deficit (ID) model of aging has been applied to adult age differences in a broad range of cognitive performance from early perceptual processing of stimuli, including the inhibition of competing words activated during spoken word recognition (Sommers & Danielson, 1999), to higher level processing such as the regulation of topic in conversation (Arbuckle & Gold, 1993). Unfortunately, however, researchers rarely developed the ID model in light of their findings. Hasher and Zacks have been primarily responsible for advancing the model by specification and elaboration of the theory in response to recent findings (e.g., chap. 8, this volume).

The strongest support for a scientific theory comes when it withstands vigorous attempts to falsify it. Although scientists rarely seem to practice this Popperian principle with respect to their own theories, they do practice it in their efforts to disconfirm other people's theories (Higgins, 2004). The principle of falsifiability is an essential component of theory development, and it requires that a theory be testable; it is this aspect of the ID model that is the focus of this chapter. The ID model has been productive in generating predictions that have been tested in a valuable collection of cognitive aging studies. These studies provide information about how to measure inhibition and its

Preparation of this chapter was supported by National Institute of Aging Grant AG08835.

development during adulthood. Although the viability of inhibition as a cognitive process in general has been scrutinized (e.g., MacLeod, Dodd, Sheard, Wilson, & Bibi, 2003; Tipper, 2001), there has been less critical evaluation of theories of inhibition deficits in cognitive aging (but see Burke, 1997; McDowd, 1997). We evaluate in this chapter two aspects of the evidence from cognitive aging research testing the ID model.

The first issue we address is whether the ID model has been adequately revised in response to disconfirmatory data—that is, predicted results that have consistently failed to materialize. We consider findings on negative priming as an example. The second issue we address concerns research that produced confirmatory results but ignored the impact of more fundamental mental processes on performance. Relevant is the argument of MacLeod et al. (2003) that "in most cases where inhibitory mechanisms have been offered to explain cognitive performance, non-inhibitory mechanisms can accomplish the same goal" (p. 203). We focus on the role of fundamental noninhibitory mechanisms—namely, sensory and perceptual processes—that show universal declines with aging. We consider evidence that age-related declines in these processes are responsible for age differences in cognitive performance that have been consistently attributed to inhibition deficits.

The ID theory has become a popular explanation for empirical findings, and our goal in this chapter is not to widen further the scope of performance attributed to inhibition deficits. Rather, our goal is to motivate revision of the model in response to incompatible findings and to motivate more rigorous evaluation of the model that considers confounding factors in behavioral measures. This approach attempts to shed confirmatory biases and seems essential if researchers are to know what ID theory can contribute to an understanding of the fundamental mechanisms of cognitive aging.

In their development of the ID model, Hasher, Zacks, and their colleagues have emphasized the role of theoretical inhibition in controlling the content of selective attention and working memory (e.g., Hasher et al., 1999). They have argued that age-related declines in the efficiency of inhibition allow irrelevant information to clutter working memory, with negative consequences for attention, memory, and language processing. We focus primarily on the access function of inhibition, which controls the activated representations that are selected for attention (Hasher et al., 1999). In the ID model, inhibitory processes keep nonrelevant representations out of attention and working memory. Hasher and Zacks and their colleagues have viewed inhibition as a controlled attentional process that occurs after automatic activation processes during the access function. For example, spreading activation and inhibition postulated during lexical selection in some language-processing models are automatic and thus not relevant to ID (e.g., Zacks & Hasher, 1997).

When Predictions Fail: The Case of Negative Priming

One of the most vigorous evaluations of inhibition deficits in old age is the investigation of negative-priming effects in a selective attention task. In the negative-priming paradigm, the task is to identify a target stimulus (e.g., letter, word, or picture) as rapidly as possible and ignore a distractor stimulus usually distinguished from the target by color or location. Negative-priming effects occur when the distractor becomes the target on the succeeding trial and response latency to it is delayed compared with a control condition where the target is not the distractor from the previous trial. The initial and dominant interpretation of this delay in latency is that selection of a target includes inhibition of distractors as irrelevant information (e.g., Neill, 1977; Tipper, 1985; see also chap. 4, this volume). Under this theoretical approach, the distractor in the negative-priming paradigm is inhibited on the initial trial as part of the process of selecting the target, and the inhibition lingers to the next trial, when the distractor becomes a target. The residual inhibition slows processing of the target, delaying the response (Hasher, Stoltzfus, Zacks, & Rypma, 1991; McDowd, 1997; Tipper, 1985). Within this theoretical framework, negative priming is an empirical measure of the strength of the theoretical process of inhibition during selective attention. Indeed, some researchers have proposed negative priming as the best direct index of inhibitory functioning (Kane, May, Hasher, Rahhal, & Stoltzfus, 1997; May, Kane, & Hasher, 1995).

When the negative-priming paradigm was used to test the ID model of cognitive aging, the initial results showed reduced or no negative-priming effect for older adults, as predicted by the model. These findings were taken as evidence that older adults were less able than young adults to inhibit distractors (e.g., Hasher et al., 1991; McDowd & Oseas-Kreger, 1991; Tipper, 1991). It was concluded that older adults' inhibition deficits weakened or eliminated their negative-priming effects and that this was a general phenomenon that was independent of the nature of the target (May et al., 1995).

There were, however, wrinkles in the results from negative-priming studies, even in the early 1990s, in terms of support for a global ID aging model (for a review, see McDowd, 1997). First, some studies reported diminished negative-priming effects for older adults compared with young adults when the target had the same identity (name) as the distractor on the previous trial, but they found no age differences in the magnitude of negative-priming effects when the target appeared in the same location as the distractor on the previous trial (e.g., Connelly & Hasher, 1993). Proponents of the ID model of aging handled this dissociation of aging effects by proposing two separate inhibitory systems, one for location and one for identity, with only the latter vulnerable to aging (Connelly & Hasher, 1993).

A fundamental role of inhibition within an inhibition model is to reduce behavioral interference from irrelevant information by preventing its access to attention or working memory (Hasher et al., 1999). This theoretical principle predicts that as inhibition of distractors increases, interference from distractors decreases. Behaviorally, this principle predicts that the size of the negative-priming effect will be negatively correlated with the interference from the distractors. This interference can be measured as the difference in target identification time between conditions in which targets are presented without distractors and conditions in which targets are presented with distractors.

A second wrinkle is that the predicted negative correlation between negative priming and interference was obtained in some studies of young and older adults (Earles et al., 1997; Sullivan & Faust, 1993) but not others (Connelly

& Hasher, 1993; Kramer, Humphrey, Larish, Logan, & Strayer, 1994; Stoltzfus, Hasher, Zacks, Ulivi, & Goldstein, 1993). In response to this failure to find the predicted relation between inhibition and interference, it was proposed that inhibition is not involved in selection of the target but rather serves a postselection process: Inhibition of distractors develops after selection of the target is completed and functions to keep the distractors out of attentional focus (May et al., 1995; Stoltzfus et al., 1993). The ability to identify and respond to the relevant target rather than the irrelevant distractors during selection is accomplished by some noninhibitory but unspecified mechanism. This observation raises the unanswered question of why this unspecified mechanism rather than an additional inhibitory process is not also responsible for maintaining the postselection attentional focus.

These early wrinkles were perhaps a harbinger of the results of subsequent experiments that failed to find age differences in negative priming on the basis of either target identity or target location (e.g., Gamboz, Russo, & Fox, 2000; Grant & Dagenbach, 2000; Kieley & Hartley, 1997; Kramer et al., 1994; Schooler, Neumann, Caplan, & Roberts, 1997; Sullivan & Faust, 1993). An initial meta-analysis including experiments reported through 1996 showed significant negative-priming effects in both young and older adults but a slightly smaller effect size for older adults than young adults (Verhaeghen & De Meersman, 1998a). In a more recent meta-analysis, Gamboz, Russo, and Fox (2002) used 36 experiments published through 2000, including 16 experiments not available for the earlier meta-analysis; they found no age difference in the effect size for negative priming. Using a second approach, Gamboz et al. (2002) conducted a regression analysis testing the relation between response times (RTs) in the negative-priming and the control conditions for young and older adults. Figure 9.1 shows RT in the negative-priming condition as a function of RT in the control condition for both age groups as reported by Gamboz et al. (We added the zero-intercept function, slope = 1.0, for comparison.) Negative-priming effects are seen in the data points that lie slightly above the zero-intercept (slope = 1.0) function; there is no discernible age difference in these points. Gamboz et al. reported that the data were well described by a linear model (intercept = −20.3, slope = 1.06, R^2 = .992) and that the addition of age and the Age × Condition interaction term did not improve the fit. Thus, neither of two different meta-analytic approaches provided support for age differences in the magnitude of negative-priming effects (for similar conclusions, see Verhaeghen & Cerella, 2002).

In response to findings of age-invariant negative-priming effects, proponents of the ID model revisited the role of inhibition in negative priming. Neill and colleagues had previously proposed an alternative account of negative-priming effects—namely, that they are caused by episodic retrieval of the representation of previous experience with the target (Neill & Valdes, 1992; Neill, Valdes, Terry, & Gorfein, 1992). When that representation includes the target stimulus as a distractor that was ignored, this conflicts with a response to the stimulus as a target on the current trial, slowing RT. Kane et al. (1997) argued that this episodic-retrieval mechanism replaces the inhibition mechanism under certain experimental conditions, explaining the inconsistency in reports of age-related differences in negative priming: Older adults show re-

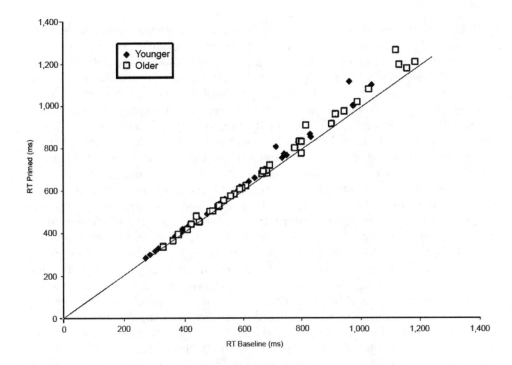

Figure 9.1.   Mean response times (RTs) in the negative-priming condition (RT primed) as a function of mean RT in the baseline condition for young and older adults. From "Age Differences and the Identity Negative Priming Effect: An Updated Meta-Analysis," by N. Gamboz, R. Russo, and E. Fox, 2002, *Psychology and Aging, 17,* p. 528. Copyright 2002 by the American Psychological Association.

duced negative-priming effects when inhibition is involved and show age-invariant negative-priming effects under specific experimental conditions that encourage episodic retrieval rather than inhibition (see also Zacks & Hasher, 1997). For example, increasing the percentage of successive trials using the same stimulus as the target would encourage an episodic-retrieval mechanism, because it would benefit processing under these conditions, according to Kane et al. They demonstrated that when 40% of trials had the same target on a successive trial—a condition favoring episodic retrieval—negative-priming effects were age invariant. In a prior experiment with the same stimuli but no repeated targets on successive trials, older adults showed no negative-priming effect.

An episodic-retrieval mechanism, however, seems inauspicious as an explanation of age constancy in negative priming. First, declines in episodic memory with aging are consistently observed and have been attributed to age-related declines in binding target information to its context (e.g., Burke & Light, 1981; MacKay & Burke, 1990; Naveh-Benjamin, 2000), even for very short term memory (Hartman & Warren, 2005). A mechanism depending on binding an item to its distractor status seems an unlikely candidate for providing age-invariant performance.

Second and more important, results do not support the proposal that age differences in negative priming are found under conditions favoring inhibition but not under conditions favoring episodic retrieval. As McDowd (1997) pointed out, age invariance in negative-priming effects has been found under conditions that according to Kane et al. (1997) favor an inhibitory mechanism rather than an episodic-memory mechanism—namely, no repetition of targets on successive trials (Buchner & Mayr, 2004; Kieley & Hartley, 1997; Schooler et al., 1997). Indeed, Grant and Dagenbach (2000) observed equivalent negative-priming effects for young and older adults under the same conditions used by Hasher et al. (1991), who reported negative-priming effects for young but not older adults and attributed the age difference to age-related declines in inhibition.

Buchner and Mayr (2004) recently reported age-invariant negative-priming effects for young and older adults in an auditory target identification task for which there was independent evidence that selection involved suppression of distractors. In a previous experiment (Buchner & Steffens, 2001), the identification task was alternated with a temporal order judgment task: Participants made a temporal order judgment for two tones on trials that alternated with the identification task in which they identified a target tone and ignored a distractor tone. In the temporal order judgment task, the probability of selecting a tone as coming first was reduced when it had been the distractor on the prior trial. This finding is consistent with distractor inhibition, which delays processing of the same tone when it is a target on the next trial (Buchner & Steffens, 2001). Thus, the observed age-invariant negative-priming effects in the auditory target identification task are inconsistent with age-related inhibition deficits.

Finally, if age differences in negative-priming effects occur under some experimental conditions and not others (Kane et al., 1997; Zacks & Hasher, 1997), there should be heterogeneity in the age effect sizes in different experiments, demonstrating the effects of a moderator variable. Heterogeneity of effect sizes, however, was found in neither the Gamboz et al. (2002) nor the Verhaegen and De Meersman (1998a) meta-analyses.

In summary, systematic and rigorous tests of the ID model's prediction of age differences in negative priming, identified as the best index of inhibition, have yielded conclusive results: No age differences in negative-priming effects were found across a range of experimental conditions. The theoretical mechanism underlying negative-priming effects has become controversial (e.g., Chao & Yeh, 2004), and there is disagreement about whether negative priming is caused by inhibition or by episodic retrieval (e.g., Neill & Joordens, 2002; Strayer, Drews, & Albert, 2002). Some investigators postulated dual mechanisms, with the involvement of either inhibition or episodic retrieval depending on experimental conditions (e.g., Kane et al., 1997; May et al., 1995). Other investigators argued for an integrated model in which inhibition and episodic retrieval affect different components of selective attention (e.g., Tipper, 2001). Both of these positions are incompatible with predictions of the ID model, because age invariance in negative priming has been found under conditions where dual or integrated mechanisms specify inhibition of distractors.

There are at least two important implications of the age invariance in negative priming. First, these results require revision of the ID model, because it proposes both that older adults suffer reduced inhibitory efficiency and that inhibition decreases activation of distracting, irrelevant information, preventing its access to focal attention (Hasher et al., 1999; Hasher, Lustig, & Zacks, in press). One or both of these principles is inconsistent with the age equivalence in selective attention in this paradigm. Even if inhibition is banished from any role in negative priming, a step that has not been taken in the context of ID theory, the ID model's account of how distracting information is processed must be revised. Although it has been suggested that inhibition does not aid selection but rather functions to prevent attention from returning to ignored distractors after selection (May et al., 1995), it is unclear how this suggestion is compatible with the access function of inhibition. Recent descriptions of the model have addressed neither this point nor the implications of the negative-priming results.

There is no clear experimental measure of inhibition to replace negative priming. The absence of an adequate measure of the process of inhibition was documented in studies that failed to find predicted correlations among different experimental measures of inhibition (e.g., Earles et al., 1997; Kramer et al., 1994). The Stroop task has been used in aging studies as an index of the efficiency of inhibitory functioning (e.g., Sommers & Danielson, 1999), but its validity as such an index is undermined by the absence of correlation among different versions of the Stroop task (Shilling, Chetwynd, & Rabbitt, 2002); the lack of independence of Stroop performance from other, noninhibition cognitive measures (Salthouse, Atkinson, & Berish, 2003); and controversy about the mechanisms contributing to Stroop interference (Kane & Engle, 2003). There is evidence that age-related increases in Stroop interference are attributable to general slowing with age (Salthouse & Meinz, 1995) or age differences in other cognitive processes (Basak & Verhaeghen, 2003); no age difference in Stroop interference was found in a meta-analysis when slowing was taken into account (Verhaeghen & De Meersman, 1998b; but see Spieler, Balota, & Faust, 1996).

When Mechanisms Compete:
Sensory Processes and Inhibition

To identify the specific processes that are responsible for aging-related changes in cognition, it is essential to disentangle and isolate the contributions of different processes that affect cognitive performance. Sensory processes are ubiquitous in cognitive tasks, and there is clear evidence that cognitive performance is affected by the integrity of sensory processes. The interdependence of sensory and cognitive operations complicates identification of mental processes causing cognitive change in old age, because visual and auditory sensory processes decline with aging during adulthood. Declines in sensory processes with aging reduce thresholds for identification of visual and auditory stimuli (e.g., Committee on Hearing and Bioacoustics and Biomechanics [CHABA], 1988; Fozard & Gordon-Salant, 2001). Moreover, even when thresholds are controlled across age, older adults have difficulty with vision and hearing because of deficits in sensory processes that cause, for example, auditory temporal asynchrony (e.g., Brown & Pichora-Fuller, 2000; Schneider, 1997) and blurred retinal image (Artal, Ferro, Miranda, & Navarro, 1993; for a review, see Schneider & Pichora-Fuller, 2000).

Sensory acuity not only correlates with level of cognitive performance in adults (e.g., Baltes & Lindenberger, 1997; Lindenberger & Baltes, 1994) but also is a causal influence in determining cognitive performance. Although some of the shared age-related variance between sensory acuity and cognitive performance may be attributable to a common cause such as neurophysiological functioning (Lindenberger & Baltes, 1994), there is also evidence for a direct causal link: A number of recent studies have shown that age-related sensory impairments disrupt perception of stimuli and thereby disrupt cognitive performance (e.g., Brown & Pichora-Fuller, 2000; Murphy, McDowd, & Wilcox, 1999; Schneider, Daneman, & Murphy, 2005; Schneider, Daneman, Murphy, & See, 2000).

Baltes and Lindenberger (1997) pointed out that there has been little consideration of sensory functioning in studies of aging effects on cognition. This oversight especially characterizes research on aging and inhibition deficits. In the following sections, we consider the contribution of age-related changes in sensory processes to findings interpreted as evidence for age-linked inhibition deficits.

Irrelevant Sensory Information: Visual Processing

Many studies have reported that older adults' performance is impaired more than that of young adults by irrelevant sensory information. One frequently cited finding involves the effect of visual distractors on reading. Older adults are slower to read text interspersed with irrelevant information that must be ignored (i.e., inhibited, within the ID model). To read correctly in these studies, the participant must discriminate between italicized and normal font, because the targets are written in one font and the distractors in the other (Carlson, Hasher, Zacks, & Connelly, 1995; Connelly, Hasher, & Zacks, 1991; Duchek, Balota, & Thessing, 1998; Dywan & Murphy, 1996; Earles et al., 1997; K. Z. H. Li, Hasher, Jonas, May, & Rahhal, 1998). Older adults' reading was slowed by distractors more than young adults' reading. These results were interpreted as showing that inhibition deficits in older adults allowed distractors to enter working memory, thereby undermining the process of attending only to targets.

Is older adults' greater distractor interference with reading an effect of inhibition deficits? There is a strong noninhibitory explanation that has not been addressed in these studies—namely, that age-related declines in visual acuity are responsible for age differences in the effect of distractors on reading. Because auditory and visual acuity are related to performance on higher level cognitive tasks (Anstey, Dain, Andrews, & Drobny, 2002; Baltes & Lindenberger, 1997; Schneider & Pichora-Fuller, 2000), a critical issue is how visual acuity is controlled across age in studies of reading with distraction. The reading-with-distraction studies cited in the preceding paragraph, however, did not report visual acuity for their participants.

Even if one assumes that these studies used the common practice of including only participants who reported corrected-to-normal vision, the results of

Table 9.1. Close-Range Acuity (Jaeger Test) for Young and Older Participants
With Self-Reported Normal Vision

Acuity score	Young adults (n = 29)	Older adults (n = 40)
20/20	23	8
20/25	6	14
20/30	0	4
20/40	0	5
20/50	0	6
20/70	0	3

MacKay, Taylor, and Marian (2006) indicate that this practice is inadequate for controlling acuity across age. MacKay et al. gave close-vision acuity tests to young and older adults who self-reported that their corrected vision was 20/20. They found that only 20% of older adults actually had 20/20 corrected vision according to their performance on the acuity test, whereas 79% of young adults had 20/20 vision according to test performance. Thirty-five percent of the older adults had vision of 20/40 or worse. Table 9.1 shows acuity scores based on performance for these participants by age. Could acuity levels in the range obtained for older adults affect reading? MacKay et al. found that participants with 20/20 vision were faster to read single words than participants with vision worse than 20/20. Moreover, older participants with vision worse than 20/20 were slower to read small-font words (24 point) than large-font words (30 point). Both fonts are larger than those typically used in reading-with-distraction studies. These results suggest multiple ways that acuity of less than 20/20 would affect reading with distraction. For example, it would slow differentiation of target from distractor text, producing greater slowing with distractors compared with no distractors for participants with lower acuity.

Schneider and Pichora-Fuller (2000) argued that aging produces "declines in visual processing abilities that occur in the absence of any observable pathology and persist even after correction for optical abnormalities" (p. 168). Even with corrected vision, older adults suffer impaired visual functions such as retinal blurring (Artal et al., 1993), reduced retinal illumination, and loss of contrast sensitivity (Haegerstrom-Portnoy, Schneck, & Brabyn, 1999) and reduced accuracy of voluntary saccadic eye movements (Scialfa, Hamaluk, Pratt, & Skaloud, 1999). These characteristics of older eyes would increase the difficulty of perceiving subtle visual variations required, for example, to differentiate italics and standard font to distinguish targets from distractors. If older adults are less able than young adults to see the difference between target and distractors, a prerequisite for selecting one and ignoring the other, they will appear to have inhibitory deficits. Indeed, when discrimination between italics and standard font was no longer required for identifying the targets because targets were also spatially distinct from the distractors, no age differences in distractor interference were observed (Carlson et al., 1995). Spatial separation would also reduce the impact of older adults' less accurate voluntary saccadic eye movement (Scialfa et al., 1999).

One of the findings emerging from studies of reading with distraction is that distractors that are semantically related to the target text show larger age-related increases in interference than unrelated distractors (Carlson et al., 1995; Connelly et al., 1991; K. Z. H. Li et al., 1998). This finding is consistent with the principle that the difficulty of inhibiting irrelevant information increases with its similarity to the target (Lustig & Hasher, 2001). However, the age interaction with target–distractor similarity is also compatible with age differences in sensory processing of the material, because older adults compensate for sensory losses under conditions of difficult reading by engaging in more top-down processing than young adults (e.g., Speranza, Daneman, & Schneider, 2000). Relying on top-down processes more than bottom-up sensory processes would increase the difficulty of differentiating targets and distractors when they are semantically related. Consistent with this interpretation, Duchek et al. (1998) did not obtain the typical finding of greater interference for older than young adults for related compared with unrelated distractors when the visual contrast between targets and distractors was increased by presenting targets in bold and upper case font. When the target is perceptually more distinct, older adults may rely more on bottom-up processes and less on top-down processes.

In summary, studies of reading with distraction have failed to include appropriate control of visual sensory processing across age. Age-related differences in acuity make differentiation of targets and distractors more difficult, influencing the effect of distraction, and this factor precludes interpretation of age differences in distraction effects as support for age-related deficits at a cognitive level—namely, in inhibition. Moreover, even when acuity is controlled across age, older adults' decline in other visual functions (e.g., contrast sensitivity, effective retinal illumination) impairs perception. Thus, controlling perceptibility of the stimuli across age is necessary to eliminate sensory processes as a cause of age differences in performance. Although reading-with-distraction experiments lack such controls, experiments using other visual attention paradigms have eliminated age differences in performance when visual acuity was tested and controlled across age. For example, response-compatible and response-incompatible distractors had the same effect on responses to targets by young and older adults matched on visual acuity (Kramer et al., 1994) except when brief exposure durations made perceptual processing more difficult (Madden & Langley, 2003).

Irrelevant Sensory Information: Auditory Processing

Age differences in the effect of distraction on perception of target speech are parallel to those found in visual distractor studies: Older adults are impaired more by distraction in the form of background noise (speech or white noise) than young adults (CHABA, 1988; Pichora-Fuller, Schneider, & Daneman, 1995). In the literature on auditory processing, however, the contribution of sensory deficits to age differences in distraction effects is widely acknowledged (CHABA, 1988; Humes, 1996; Wingfield, Tun, & McCoy, 2005). Results from a series of recent studies support the view that age differences in sensory-

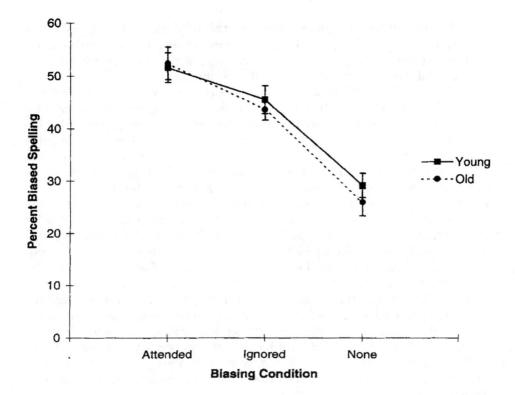

Figure 9.2. Mean percentage of homophones spelled in their less common way as a function of biasing condition. From "Inhibition and Aging: Similarities Between Younger and Older Adults as Revealed by the Processing of Unattended Auditory Information," by D. R. Murphy, J. M. McDowd, and K. A. Wilcox, 1999, *Psychology and Aging, 14,* p. 54. Copyright 1999 by the American Psychological Association.

level processes, rather than in cognitive-level processes such as inhibition, are responsible for the larger effects of auditory distraction in older adults (e.g., L. Li, Daneman, Qi, & Schneider, 2004; for a review, see Schneider, Daneman, & Pichora-Fuller, 2002).

Some of the most powerful evidence for the role of age-related sensory deficits comes from experiments that equate perceptibility of stimuli across age. Murphy et al. (1999) obtained speech reception thresholds for each of their young and older participants and presented stimuli at 40 to 45 decibels above each participant's individual threshold. In three experiments each using a different paradigm to measure the ability to process target stimuli and ignore distractors, there were no age differences in the distractor effect. Figure 9.2 shows the results for their homophone spelling task in which spoken homophones were preceded by a word biasing the less common spelling of the homophone, with the biasing word spoken in a target voice or an ignored voice. As can be seen in the figure, when the biasing word was in an ignored voice, its effect on homophone spelling was reduced compared with when it was attended, and there were no age differences in the reduction. Under an ID model, the participant inhibited the ignored voice, and this inhibition was responsible for the reduced effect of the ignored word. This model suggests that with stimuli that are equivalent in perceptibility across age, older adults should show no deficit in inhibiting distracting (ignored) information.

Schneider et al. (2000) tested comprehension of prose presented with or without background noise (babble). They adjusted the signal-to-noise ratio for each young and older adult based on the individual speech reception and babble thresholds. Immediately after listening to a passage, participants responded to detail and integrative questions. There were no age differences in correct answers to integrative questions in quiet and in two levels of noise and no age differences for detail questions in quiet or in a moderate level of noise, even when participants were required to perform a concurrent task. Only at the loudest noise level did younger adults tend to recall more detail than older adults. Schneider et al. also tested young and older adults under identical listening conditions, making no adjustment in signal-to-noise ratios to compensate for the poorer hearing of older adults. Under these conditions, older adults correctly answered fewer detail questions than younger adults, either in quiet or in noise; although there was no age difference for integrative questions, floor effects may have been a factor. Overall, the Schneider et al. results show that age differences in the effects of distraction can be erroneously attributed to age-related inhibition deficits rather than to basic sensory processes. Older adults' hearing deficits appear to negatively influence perception of specific words, which impairs performance on tests that require comprehension of these specific details.

Conclusions on Language Processing With Sensory Distraction

The role of age-related declines in visual sensory processes has typically been ignored in reading-with-distraction studies. Results from auditory distraction studies, however, present strong evidence that age-related declines in bottom-up sensory processing affect older adults' ability to differentiate targets from distractors. This is a noninhibitory mechanism that needs to be carefully considered in future distraction studies testing the ID model.

Under the ID model, inhibition prevents activated but irrelevant information from entering conscious awareness (Hasher et al., 1999). There are two sources of irrelevant information that become candidates for inhibition. We have evaluated age differences in processing external irrelevant information that is perceived through bottom-up processes triggered by sensory stimulation. Irrelevant information can also be internal, self-generated through spreading-activation processes such as top-down processes affecting stored representations that share conceptual properties with perceived information. A comparison of how young and older adults perform with irrelevant information from these two different sources is instructive. Inasmuch as older adults suffer inhibitory deficits, their performance should be more affected than that of young adults by both self-generated irrelevant information and sensory irrelevant information. Alternatively, if older adults' performance with distractors is impaired by declines in sensory processes, and not by inhibition deficits, then age-related declines in performance would be obtained for sensory irrelevant information but not for self-generated irrelevant information. Much of the evidence is consistent with the latter hypothesis.

Internally Generated Irrelevant Information

There is little evidence for age differences in dealing with irrelevant information activated through top-down processes (see Burke, 1997). If inhibition deficits allowed more irrelevant information from top-down processes to gain access to conscious awareness in older compared with young adults, one consequence would be greater variability in their responses in language production tasks. For example, in a word association task, irrelevant semantic information activated by the stimulus word would be more available for response in older adults compared with young adults. It has been suggested that older adults are less able to use inhibition to eliminate esoteric or personal autobiographical responses from conscious awareness (Arbuckle & Gold, 1993; Zacks & Hasher, 1994), and this hypothesis would predict more unique responses among older than young adults. However, no age differences were observed in three different measures of variability of word association responses: number of different words given as responses, number of unique responses, and proportion of responses that were the first or second most popular responses for that age group (Burke & Peters, 1986).

Zacks and Hasher (1997) argued that word associations are produced on the basis of automatic activation, with little need for inhibition of distractors because of the strength of a primary associate that is automatically activated. According to this argument, age equivalence in variability occurs because there is a dominant, highly associated response that is available and appropriate (Hasher et al., 1999). This was not the case, however, for the Burke and Peters (1986) word association results, because age equivalence was obtained even though there was considerable variability in responses. For example, 25% to 33% of the word association responses were unique responses given by a single participant and no one else; nonetheless, the percentage of unique responses was unaffected by age. More recently, Hirsh and Tree (2001) reported that older adults produced fewer unique word associations than young adults. All four of their measures of heterogeneity of word association responses yielded greater heterogeneity in young adults' responses.

A verb-generation task has been developed specifically to measure the effect of internally generated response alternatives on performance (e.g., Thompson-Schill, D'Esposito, Aguirre, & Farah, 1997). Participants produced verbs as quickly as possible to presented nouns that were classified either as low response competition, because each noun elicited a single dominant verb response from participants (e.g., *broom → sweep*), or as high response competition, because each noun elicited several verbs with no dominant verb response across participants (e.g., *pill → swallow, take*). Using functional magnetic resonance imaging, Thompson-Schill et al. (1997) found greater neural activation of the left inferior frontal cortex for generation of a verb for a high-response-competition noun compared with a low-response-competition noun. They argued that left inferior frontal regions are activated when word selection is difficult because of competing alternatives.

Under the ID model, suppression of competing alternative verbs is required for selection of a response to high-response-competition nouns, and thus age differences in performance should be greater for high- than for low-response-competition nouns. In studies investigating age effects, however, both young and older adults were faster to produce verbs for low- than for high-response-competition nouns, and there was no age difference in the magnitude of this effect (Baggette & Burke, 2006; Persson et al., 2004; Prull, Godard-Gross, & Karas, 2004). Both young and older adults also produced a smaller pool of verbs for low- than for high-response-competition nouns, and again the effect did not vary by age. The slower RT for verb production in the high-response-competition compared with the low-response-competition condition shows interference from internally generated, competing alternative responses, and under an ID model these alternatives should be inhibited more effectively by young than older adults. Neither the response variability results nor the response latency results are consistent with the ID model predictions for age differences.

Studies of word production failures yield another measure of the ability to inhibit irrelevant self-generated information so that it does not gain access to conscious awareness. One of the most dramatic word finding failures is the tip-of-the-tongue (TOT) state, when a person is certain that he or she knows a word but is unable to retrieve it at the moment. Alternate words related to the target often pop into mind persistently, even though the person knows these words are incorrect (Burke, MacKay, Worthley, & Wade, 1991). If older adults have more information cluttering working memory because of an impaired access function (Hasher et al., in press; Zacks & Hasher, 1994), they should report more alternate words than young adults. Table 9.2 presents

Table 9.2. Mean Number of Tip-of-the-Tongue Experiences During Everyday Life Over a 4-Week Interval and Percentage of Experiences That Occurred With a Persistent Alternate

Adult age	Burke et al. (1991)		Heine et al. (1999)	
	TOTs (mean no.)	% with alternates	TOTs (mean no.)	% with alternates
Young	3.92	67	5.21	83
Middle aged	5.40	58	6.62	66
Older	6.56	48	9.33	58

Note. TOTs = tip-of-the-tongue experiences. The data in column 1 are from "On the Tip of the Tongue: What Causes Word Finding Failures in Young and Older Adults?" by D. M. Burke, D. G. MacKay, J. S. Worthley, and E. Wade, 1991, *Journal of Memory and Language, 30,* pp. 554 and 558. Copyright 1991 by Elsevier. Reprinted with permission. The data in column 2 are from "Naturally Occurring and Experimentally Induced Tip-of-the-Tongue Experiences in Three Adult Age Groups," by M. K. Heine, B. A. Ober, and G. K. Shenaut, 1999, *Psychology and Aging, 14,* p. 454. Copyright 1999 by the American Psychological Association.

results from two studies reporting the probability of production of a persistent alternate word given the spontaneous occurrence of a TOT during everyday life. Older and young adults recorded information about the TOT experience in a structured diary (Burke et al., 1991; Heine, Ober, & Shenaut, 1999). Older adults reported more TOTs than young adults, but they reported persistent alternates for a smaller percentage of TOTs compared with young adults. The same age pattern has been reported in studies investigating lab-induced TOTs and the probability of persistent alternates (Burke et al., 1991; Maylor, 1990). Thus, when word production fails in a TOT, young adults are more likely than older adults to have an alternative but incorrect word come to mind. This finding has been explained in terms of weaker transmission of excitation in the lexicon for older than young adults (Burke et al., 1991; James & Burke, 2000). The finding is clearly incompatible with the ID model, which predicts that older adults will be less able to keep consciousness free of irrelevant information that can impede completion of a goal (Hasher et al., in press). Persistent alternate words, once they come to mind, impede completion of the goal, because they increase the time required for resolution of the TOT (Burke et al., 1991).

Slips of the tongue are another type of production failure; the speaker produces erroneously a sound in the intended word—for example, substituting an incorrect sound (*ripped* when intending *tipped*) or omitting a sound (*beach* when intending *breach*). Using a technique for inducing slips in the laboratory, MacKay and James (2004) compared the types of speech errors made by young and older adults. Older adults were more likely than young adults to omit sounds, whereas young adults were more likely than older adults to substitute a different sound. This result is the reverse of the predictions of age-related inhibition deficits. If older adults are less efficient in inhibiting irrelevant sounds or words during production, they should produce more of these sounds when they make errors. In contrast to this, young adults, not older adults, seemed to have activated multiple irrelevant sounds that were available for production.

There is, however, evidence from studies of phonological neighborhood density effects on auditory word recognition that older adults are less able to suppress irrelevant internally generated words. Two words are considered "neighbors" if they differ by the addition, subtraction, or substitution of exactly one phoneme. Words with dense neighborhoods have many phonological neighbors and are more difficult to perceive than words with sparse neighborhoods, an effect attributed to lexical competition for recognition among phonologically similar words (Luce & Pisoni, 1998). Sommers (1996; Sommers & Danielson, 1999) adjusted signal-to-noise ratios for young and older adults so that their accuracy in identifying sparse-neighborhood (easy) words was approximately the same across age. Identification accuracy declined from this level for dense-neighborhood (hard) words, and the decline was greater for older than young adults. Sommers argued that older adults show greater difficulty than young adults for high- compared with low-neighborhood density because they are inefficient in inhibiting competing alternative words during word recognition. Sommers and Danielson (1999) supported this interpretation by showing that an interference score, derived from performance on an auditory switching task and an auditory Stroop task believed to measure inhibition, was related to identification of dense-neighborhood words. Participants with high interference (poor inhibition) on the switching and Stroop tasks identified fewer hard words. Thus, Sommers's findings are consistent with the ID model prediction that older adults will be more influenced than young adults by competing internal candidates for word recognition.

Alternatively, the auditory phonetic processing required for target word identification is more difficult when the target has a dense rather than a sparse neighborhood, because dense-neighborhood words require more fine phonetic discrimination to differentiate them from competitors (Bradlow & Pisoni, 1999). Indeed, fine phonetic discrimination must precede inhibition processes, because it is the basis for identifying which activated words deviate from the target phonetic structure and thus should be inhibited. Consistent with this hypothesis, neighborhood density had a larger effect on groups of people who were less facile in perception of fine phonetic detail—for example, nonnative speakers compared with native speakers (Bradlow & Pisoni, 1999). However, Carter and Wilson (2001) reported no age difference in neighborhood effects in dichotic listening for older adults with mild hearing loss (although lexical frequency was confounded with neighborhood density in this study). Clearly, further research is needed to clarify the role of aging, sensory factors, and inhibition deficits in neighborhood density effects. Moreover, the theoretical basis for neighborhood effects must be reconciled with the ID model, because Hasher, Zacks, and colleagues have postulated that age-related deficits do not occur for automatic inhibition processes such as those involved in word recognition (e.g., chap. 8, this volume; Zacks & Hasher, 1997).

Conclusion

Testing inhibition theories has been hampered by the difficulty of finding a behavioral measure that reflects the theoretical cognitive process of inhibition (Burke, 1997; Dell & O'Seaghdha, 1994; MacLeod et al., 2003). Negative-priming effects were proposed as such a measure. Age differences in negative-priming effects, however, are absent in most studies and in meta-analyses. These disconfirming results eliminated negative priming as a measure of inhibition. They have not, however, stimulated revision of the ID model so that it is consistent with the apparent age constancy in selective attention mechanisms in the negative-priming paradigm. Rather, the response to the disconfirming results is based on circular reasoning: Older adults suffer inhibitory deficits, and if a measure does not produce age differences, it does not measure inhibition. This reasoning renders the ID model untestable. If researchers are to gain useful knowledge from the ID model, it must be revised to explain why older adults are unimpaired in some aspects of the regulatory function of inhibition, as revealed in performance in the negative-priming paradigm within an inhibition framework.

Our review of research on reading and listening with distraction demonstrates the difficulty of developing a behavioral measure of inhibition. Inhibition of distractors assumes a prior process of perceptual analysis that differentiates targets and distractors. We have argued that older adults are impaired in this prior process because of aging-related sensory deficits. The negative effect of difficult sensory processing on cognitive-level processes has long been known to cognitive psychologists (e.g., Rabbitt, 1968). It is widely acknowledged in research involving spoken language that age differences in the difficulty of sensory processing affect the cognitive performance of young and older adults (CHABA, 1988; Humes, 1996; Schneider & Pichora-Fuller, 2000; Wingfield et al., 2005). This insight is less visible in aging research on reading with distraction. The strong form of our argument is that older adults are impaired in reading with distraction relative to young adults because they are less able to differentiate distractors and targets, which slows reading time. A weaker form of the argument is that the sensory processing of targets and distractors is more difficult for older than young adults and that this difficulty interferes with cognitive processes such as inhibition. In neither case is the primary age-related deficit in inhibition. The ID model is testable only if a valid behavioral measure of theoretical inhibition can be identified.

References

Anstey, K. J., Dain, S., Andrews, S., & Drobny, J. (2002). Visual abilities in older adults explain age differences in Stroop and fluid intelligence but not face recognition: Implications for the vision–cognition connection. *Aging, Neuropsychology and Cognition, 9,* 253–265.

Arbuckle, T. Y., & Gold, D. P. (1993). Aging, inhibition, and verbosity. *Journal of Gerontology: Psychological Sciences, 48,* 225–232.

Artal, P., Ferro, M., Miranda, I., & Navarro, R. (1993). Effects of aging in retinal image quality. *Journal of the Optical Society of America A: Optics, Image & Science, 10,* 1656–1662.

Baggette, N., & Burke, D. M. (2006). *Competition effects in verb generation in young and older adults.* Unpublished manuscript.

Baltes, P. B., & Lindenberger, U. (1997). Emergence of a powerful connection between sensory and cognitive functions across the adult life span: A new window to the study of cognitive aging? *Psychology and Aging, 12,* 12–21.

Basak, C., & Verhaeghen, P. (2003). Subitizing speed, subitizing range, counting speed, the Stroop effect, and aging: Capacity differences and speed equivalence. *Psychology and Aging, 18,* 240–249.

Bradlow, A. R., & Pisoni, D. B. (1999). Recognition of spoken words by native and non-native listeners: Talker-, listener-, and item-related factors. *Journal of the Acoustical Society of America, 106,* 2074–2085.

Brown, S., & Pichora-Fuller, M. K. (2000). Temporal jitter mimics the effects of aging on word identification and word recall in noise. *Canadian Acoustics, 28,* 126–128.

Buchner, A., & Mayr, S. (2004). Auditory negative priming in younger and older adults. *Quarterly Journal of Experimental Psychology, 57,* 769–787.

Buchner, A., & Steffens, M. C. (2001). Auditory negative priming in speeded reactions and temporal order judgments. *Quarterly Journal of Experimental Psychology, 54A,* 1125–1142.

Burke, D. M. (1997). Language, aging and inhibitory deficits: Evaluation of a theory. *Journal of Gerontology: Psychological Sciences, 52,* 254–264.

Burke, D., & Light, L. (1981). Memory and aging: The role of retrieval processes. *Psychological Bulletin, 90,* 513–554.

Burke, D. M., & MacKay, D. G. (1997). Memory, language and ageing. *Philosophical Transactions of the Royal Society: Biological Sciences, 352,* 1845–1856.

Burke, D. M., MacKay, D. G., Worthley, J. S., & Wade, E. (1991). On the tip of the tongue: What causes word finding failures in younger and older adults? *Journal of Memory and Language, 30,* 542–579.

Burke, D. M., & Peters, L. (1986). Word associations in old age: Evidence for consistency in semantic encoding during adulthood. *Psychology and Aging, 1,* 283–291.

Carlson, M. C., Hasher, L., Zacks, R. T., & Connelly, S. L. (1995). Aging, distraction, and the benefits of predictable location. *Psychology and Aging, 10,* 427–436.

Carter, A. S., & Wilson, R. H. (2001). Lexical effects on dichotic word recognition in young and elderly listeners. *Journal of the American Academy of Audiology, 12,* 86–100.

Chao, H., & Yeh, Y. (2004). Distracters of low activation can produce negative priming. *Memory & Cognition, 32,* 979–989.

Committee on Hearing and Bioacoustics and Biomechanics. (1988). Speech understanding and aging. *Journal of the Acoustical Society of America, 83,* 859–895.

Connelly, S. L., & Hasher, L. (1993). Aging and inhibition of spatial location. *Journal of Experimental Psychology: Human Perception and Performance, 19,* 1238–1250.

Connelly, S. L., Hasher, L., & Zacks, R. T. (1991). Age and reading: The impact of distraction. *Psychology and Aging, 6,* 533–541.

Dell, G. S., & O'Seaghdha, P. G. (1994). Inhibition in interactive activation models of linguistic selection and sequencing. In D. Dagenbach & T. H. Carr (Eds.), *Inhibitory processes in attention, memory, and language* (pp. 409–453). San Diego, CA: Academic Press.

Duchek, J. M., Balota, D. A., & Thessing, V. C. (1998). Inhibition of visual and conceptual information during reading in healthy aging and Alzheimer's disease. *Aging, Neuropsychology, and Cognition, 5,* 169–181.

Dywan, J., & Murphy, W. E. (1996). Aging and inhibitory control in text comprehension. *Psychology and Aging, 11,* 199–206.

Earles, J. L., Connor, L. T., Frieske, D., Park, D. C., Smith, A. D., & Zwahr, M. (1997). Age differences in inhibition: Possible causes and consequences. *Aging, Neuropsychology, and Cognition, 4,* 45–57.

Fozard, J. L., & Gordon-Salant, S. (2001). Changes in vision and hearing with aging. In J. E. Birren & K. W. Schaie (Eds.), *Handbook of the psychology of aging* (5th ed., pp. 241–250). San Diego, CA: Academic Press.

Gamboz, N., Russo, R., & Fox, E. (2000). Target selection difficulty, negative priming, and aging. *Psychology and Aging, 15,* 542–550.

Gamboz, N., Russo, R., & Fox, E. (2002). Age differences and the identity negative priming effect: An updated meta-analysis. *Psychology and Aging, 17,* 525–531.

Grant, J. D., & Dagenbach, D. (2000). Further considerations regarding inhibitory processes, working memory, and cognitive aging. *American Journal of Psychology, 113,* 69–94.

Haegerstrom-Portnoy, G., Schneck, M. E., & Brabyn, J. A. (1999). Seeing into old age: Vision function beyond acuity. *Optometry and Vision Science, 76,* 141–158.

Hartman, M., & Warren, L. H. (2005). Explaining age differences in temporal working memory. *Psychology and Aging, 20,* 645–656.

Hasher, L., Lustig, C., & Zacks, R. (in press). Inhibitory mechanisms and the control of attention. In A. Conway, C. Jarrold, M. Kane, A. Miyake, & J. Towse (Eds.), *Variation in working memory.* New York: Oxford University Press.

Hasher, L., Stoltzfus, E. R., Zacks, R. T., & Rypma, B. (1991). Age and inhibition. *Journal of Experimental Psychology: Learning, Memory, and Cognition, 17,* 163–169.

Hasher, L., Zacks, R. T., & May, C. P. (1999). Inhibitory control, circadian arousal and age. In D. Gopher & A. Koriat (Eds.), *Attention and performance: XVII. Cognitive regulation and performance: Interaction of theory and application* (pp. 653–675). Cambridge, MA: MIT Press.

Heine, M. K., Ober, B. A., & Shenaut, G. K. (1999). Naturally occurring and experimentally induced tip-of-the-tongue experiences in three adult age groups. *Psychology and Aging, 14,* 445–457.

Higgins, E. T. (2004). Making a theory useful: Lessons handed down. *Personality and Social Psychology Review, 8,* 138–145.

Hirsh, K. W., & Tree, J. J. (2001). Word association norms for two cohorts of British adults. *Journal of Neurolinguistics, 14,* 1–44.

Humes, L. E. (1996). Speech understanding in the elderly. *Journal of the American Academy of Audiology, 7,* 161–167.

James, L. E., & Burke, D. M. (2000). Phonological priming effects on word retrieval and tip-of-the-tongue experiences in young and older adults. *Journal of Experimental Psychology: Learning, Memory, and Cognition, 26,* 1378–1391.

Kane, M. J., & Engle, R. W. (2003). Working memory capacity and the control of attention: The contributions of goal neglect, response competition, and task set to Stroop interference. *Journal of Experimental Psychology: General, 132,* 47–70.

Kane, M. J., May, C. P., Hasher, L., Rahhal, T., & Stoltzfus, E. R. (1997). Dual mechanisms of negative priming. *Journal of Experimental Psychology: Human Perception and Performance, 23,* 632–650.

Kieley, J. M., & Hartley, A. A. (1997). Age-related equivalence of identity suppression in the Stroop color–word task. *Psychology and Aging, 12,* 22–29.

Kramer, A. F., Humphrey, D. G., Larish, J. F., Logan, G. D., & Strayer, D. L. (1994). Aging and inhibition: Beyond a unitary view of inhibitory processing in attention. *Psychology and Aging, 9,* 491–512.

Li, K. Z. H., Hasher, L., Jonas, D., May, C. P., & Rahhal, T. A. (1998). Distractibility, circadian arousal, and aging: A boundary condition? *Psychology and Aging, 13,* 574–583.

Li, L., Daneman, M., Qi, J. G., & Schneider, B. A. (2004). Does the information content of an irrelevant source differentially affect spoken word recognition in younger and older adults? *Journal of Experimental Psychology: Human Perception and Performance, 30,* 1077–1091.

Lindenberger, U., & Baltes, P. (1994). Sensory functioning and intelligence in old age: A strong connection. *Psychology and Aging, 9,* 339–355.

Luce, P. A., & Pisoni, D. B. (1998). Recognizing spoken words: The neighborhood activation model. *Ear & Hearing, 19,* 1–36.

Lustig, C., & Hasher, L. (2001). Implicit memory is not immune to interference. *Psychological Bulletin, 127,* 618–628.

MacKay, D. G., & Burke, D. M. (1990). Cognition and aging: New learning and the use of old connections. In T. M. Hess (Ed.), *Aging and cognition: Knowledge, organization, and utilization* (pp. 213–263). Amsterdam: North Holland.

MacKay, D. G., & James, L. E. (2004). Sequencing, speech production, and selective effects of aging on phonological and morphological speech errors. *Psychology and Aging, 19,* 93–107.

MacKay, D. G., Taylor, J. K., & Marian, D. E. (2006). *Unsuspected age-linked acuity deficits and research on reading: Practical and empirical implications.* Unpublished manuscript.

MacLeod, C. M., Dodd, M. D., Sheard, E. D., Wilson, D. E., & Bibi, U. (2003). In opposition to inhibition. In B. H. Ross (Ed.), *The psychology of learning and motivation: Advances in research and theory* (Vol. 43, pp. 163–214). New York: Elsevier Science.

Madden, D. J., & Langley, L. K. (2003). Age-related changes in selective attention and perceptual load during visual search. *Psychology and Aging, 18,* 54–67.

May, C. P., Kane, M. J., & Hasher, L. (1995). Determinants of negative priming. *Psychological Bulletin, 11,* 35–54.

Maylor, E. A. (1990). Recognizing and naming faces: Aging, memory retrieval, and the tip of the tongue state. *Journals of Gerontology, 45,* 215–226.

McDowd, J. M. (1997). Inhibition in attention and aging. *Journal of Gerontology: Psychological Sciences, 52,* 265–273.

McDowd, J. M., & Oseas-Kreger, D. M. (1991). Aging, inhibitory processes, and negative priming. *Journal of Gerontology, 46,* 340–345.

McDowd, J. M., & Shaw, R. J. (2000). Aging and attention: A functional perspective. In F. I. M. Craik & T. A. Salthouse (Eds.), *The handbook of aging and cognition* (pp. 221–292). Mahwah, NJ: Erlbaum.

Murphy, D. R., McDowd, J. M., & Wilcox, K. A. (1999). Inhibition and aging: Similarities between younger and older adults as revealed by the processing of unattended auditory information. *Psychology and Aging, 14,* 44–59.

Naveh-Benjamin, M. (2000). Adult age differences in memory performance: Tests of an associative deficit hypothesis. *Psychology and Aging, 26,* 1170–1187.

Neill, W. T. (1977). Inhibitory and facilitatory processes in attention. *Journal of Experimental Psychology: Human Perception and Performance, 3,* 444–450.

Neill, W. T., & Joordens, S. (2002). Negative priming and multiple repetition: A reply to Grison and Strayer (2001). *Perception & Psychophysics, 64,* 855–860.

Neill, W. T., & Valdes, L. A. (1992). The persistence of negative priming: Steady-state or decay? *Journal of Experimental Psychology: Learning, Memory, and Cognition, 18,* 565–576.

Neill, W. T., Valdes, L. A., Terry, K. M., & Gorfein, D. S. (1992). The persistence of negative priming: II. Evidence for episodic trace retrieval. *Journal of Experimental Psychology: Learning, Memory, and Cognition, 18,* 993–1000.

Persson, J., Sylvester, C.-Y. C., Nelson, J. K., Welsh, K. M., Jonides, J., & Reuter-Lorenz, P. A. (2004). Selection requirements during verb generation: Differential recruitment in older and young adults. *NeuroImage, 23,* 1382–1390.

Pichora-Fuller, M. K., Schneider, B. A., & Daneman, M. (1995). How young and old adults listen to and remember speech in noise. *Journal of the Acoustical Society of America, 97,* 593–608.

Prull, M. W., Godard-Gross, C., & Karas, E. M. (2004, April). *How verb generation repetition priming in adulthood is influenced by age and response competition.* Poster presented at the Cognitive Aging Conference, Atlanta, GA.

Rabbitt, P. M. (1968). Channel-capacity, intelligibility and immediate memory. *Quarterly Journal of Experimental Psychology, 20,* 241–248.

Salthouse, T. A., Atkinson, T. M., & Berish, D. E. (2003). Executive functioning as a potential mediator of age-related cognitive decline in normal adults. *Journal of Experimental Psychology: General, 132,* 566–594.

Salthouse, T. A., & Meinz, E. J. (1995). Aging, inhibition, working memory, and speed. *Journal of Gerontology: Psychological Sciences, 50B,* P297–P306.

Schneider, B. (1997). Psychoacoustics and aging: Implications for everyday listening. *Journal of Speech–Language Pathology and Audiology, 21,* 111–124.

Schneider, B. A., Daneman, M., & Murphy, D. R. (2005). Speech comprehension difficulties in older adults: Cognitive slowing or age-related changes in hearing? *Psychology and Aging, 20,* 261–271.

Schneider, B. A., Daneman, M., Murphy, D. R., & See, S. K. (2000). Listening to discourse in distracting settings: The effects of aging. *Psychology and Aging, 15,* 110–125.

Schneider, B. A., Daneman, M., & Pichora-Fuller, M. K. (2002). Listening in aging adults: From discourse comprehension to psychoacoustics. *Canadian Journal of Experimental Psychology, 56,* 139–152.

Schneider, B. A., & Pichora-Fuller, M. K. (2000). Implications of perceptual deterioration for cognitive aging research. In F. I. M. Craik & T. A. Salthouse (Eds.), *The handbook of aging and cognition* (pp. 155–220). Mahwah, NJ: Erlbaum.

Schooler, C., Neumann, E., Caplan, L. J., & Roberts, B. R. (1997). Continued inhibitory capacity throughout adulthood: Conceptual negative priming in younger and older adults. *Psychology and Aging, 12,* 667–674.

Scialfa, C. T., Hamaluk, E., Pratt, J., & Skaloud, P. (1999). Age differences in saccadic averaging. *Psychology and Aging, 14,* 695–699.

Shilling, V. M., Chetwynd, A., & Rabbitt, P. M. A. (2002). Individual inconsistency across measures of inhibition: An investigation of the construct validity of inhibition in older adults. *Neuropsychologia, 40,* 605–619.

Sommers, M. S. (1996). The structural organization of the mental lexicon and its contribution to age-related declines in spoken-word recognition. *Psychology and Aging, 11,* 333–341.

Sommers, M. S., & Danielson, S. M. (1999). Inhibitory processes and spoken word recognition in young and older adults: The interaction of lexical competition and semantic context. *Psychology and Aging, 14,* 458–472.

Speranza, F., Daneman, M., & Schneider, B. A. (2000). How aging affects the reading of words in noisy backgrounds. *Psychology and Aging, 15,* 253–258.

Spieler, D. H., Balota, D. A., & Faust, M. E. (1996). Stroop performance in healthy younger and older adults and in individuals with dementia of the Alzheimer's type. *Journal of Experimental Psychology: Human Perception and Performance, 22,* 461–479.

Stoltzfus, E. R., Hasher, L., Zacks, R. T., Ulivi, M. S., & Goldstein, D. (1993). Investigations of inhibition and interference in younger and older adults. *Journal of Gerontology: Psychological Sciences, 48,* 179–188.

Strayer, D. L., Drews, F. A., & Albert, R. W. (2002). Negative priming and stimulus repetition: A reply to Neill and Joordens (2002). *Perception & Psychophysics, 64,* 861–865.

Sullivan, M. P., & Faust, M. E. (1993). Evidence for identity inhibition during selective attention in old adults. *Psychology and Aging, 8,* 589–598.

Thompson-Schill, S. L., D'Esposito, M., Aguirre, G. K., & Farah, M. J. (1997). Role of left inferior prefrontal cortex in retrieval of semantic knowledge: A reevaluation. *Proceedings of the National Academy of Sciences, USA, 94,* 14792–14797.

Tipper, S. P. (1985). The negative priming effect: Inhibitory priming by ignored objects. *Quarterly Journal of Experimental Psychology, 37,* 571–590.

Tipper, S. P. (1991). Less attentional selectivity as a result of declining inhibition in older adults. *Bulletin of the Psychonomic Society, 29,* 45–47.

Tipper, S. P. (2001). Does negative priming reflect inhibitory mechanisms? A review and integration of conflicting views. *Quarterly Journal of Experimental Psychology, 54A,* 321–343.

Verhaeghen, P., & Cerella, J. (2002). Aging, executive control, and attention: A review of meta-analyses. *Neuroscience & Biobehavioral Reviews, 26,* 849–857.

Verhaeghen, P., & De Meersman, L. (1998a). Aging and the negative priming effect: A meta-analysis. *Psychology and Aging, 13,* 435–444.

Verhaeghen, P., & De Meersman, L. (1998b). Aging and the Stroop effect: A meta-analysis. *Psychology and Aging, 13,* 120–126.

West, R. L. (1996). An application of prefrontal cortex function theory to cognitive aging. *Psychological Bulletin, 120,* 272–292.

Wingfield, A., Tun, P. A., & McCoy, S. L. (2005). Hearing loss in older adulthood: What it is and how it interacts with cognitive performance. *Current Directions in Psychological Science, 14,* 144–148.

Zacks, R. T., & Hasher, L. (1994). Directed ignoring: Inhibitory regulation of working memory. In D. Dagenbach & T. H. Carr (Eds.), *Inhibitory mechanisms in attention, memory and language* (pp. 241–264). San Diego, CA: Academic Press.

Zacks, R. T., & Hasher, L. (1997). Cognitive gerontology and attentional inhibition: A reply to Burke and McDowd. *Journal of Gerontology: Psychological Sciences, 52,* 274–283.

10

Interference Processes in Fuzzy-Trace Theory: Aging, Alzheimer's Disease, and Development

Valerie F. Reyna and Britain A. Mills

Contemporary memory theories have their roots in two divergent traditions, either schematic approaches (constructivism) or learning theories in which mechanisms of interference and inhibition have played a prominent role. Fuzzy-trace theory captures key elements of both traditions. It is an interference theory in that it emphasizes the susceptibility of verbatim memory to interference, especially output interference and interference between alternative memory representations of background facts in reasoning (Reyna, 1995; Reyna & Brainerd, 1995). But fuzzy-trace theory also subsumes the classic findings of schema theory, such as false recognition of meaning-consistent statements, by assuming that gist memory representations of information are encoded in parallel with verbatim representations (Brainerd & Reyna, 2002). These gist representations have been found to be the basis of false memories and suggestibility effects across a wide variety of stimuli from numbers to witnessed events (Reyna, Holliday, & Marche, 2002; Reyna & Lloyd, 1997).

In this chapter, we focus mainly on the range of interference and inhibition effects predicted by fuzzy-trace theory, illustrating them with data that characterize these mechanisms across the life span and in cognitively impaired populations. Tasks that we review include recall, recognition, and reasoning (e.g., unpacking and conjunction fallacy effects in probability judgment). An implication of this analysis is that the line between memory and reasoning tasks is an artificial one. Tasks in both domains boil down to the representation of information, whether of experienced events or of background facts in reasoning problems; retrieval of knowledge, values, or reasoning principles that operate on such representations; application of retrieved knowledge, values, or principles to those representations; and, finally, metacognitive judgments to withhold or to output responses derived from these processes. Interference and inhibition come into play at each stage: representation, retrieval, application, and output.

To briefly preview, *fuzzy-trace theory* holds that inhibitory control processes can be used to mitigate interference effects in memory and reasoning. For example, when a subject hears *dog* and claims to remember *animal* (but rejects *chair*), a gist representation of the meaning of the original word has interfered with its verbatim memory. However, such meaning-based false memories can be inhibited by careful instructions (Reyna & Kiernan, 1994); subjects exert conscious control over interfering gist memories, although some still slip through and are falsely reported. In recognition tasks, a subject's ability to exert control over responses is measured by estimating response bias; young children, for example, have difficulty inhibiting a yes response on a recognition test, especially to adult authority figures (Reyna & Brainerd, 1998; see the section "Developmental Differences in True and False Memory"). Response biases can also reflect strategic or other cognitive control processes (Brainerd, Reyna, & Mojardin, 1999). A nay-saying bias might reflect a strategy of rejecting all words that do not evoke a mental picture when all words in the study session were presented with pictures. In recall tasks, some responses are reconstructed on the basis of the gist rather than directly retrieved from verbatim memory (discussed in the section "Developmental Differences in True Recall"). We are able to estimate, using mathematical models, the probability that subjects will output a reconstructed response rather than self-censoring, another metacognitive control process.

In reasoning, as in false memory, multiple representations of a problem often compete. Inhibitory processes can be brought to bear by reasoners to improve their performance (see the section "Representational and Retrieval Interference"). When asked whether Moses brought two animals of each type on the ark, our knowledge of Noah interferes with answering the question quickly and correctly. Or asked the class-inclusion question whether there are more cows or more animals, a display of seven cows and three horses interferes with correct responding (children will say there are more cows than animals because there are more cows than horses). However, when children inhibit this interference by covering their eyes, their performance improves. Simply waiting for 15 seconds and withholding responses during that period also improves reasoning performance in this and other tasks (Reyna, 1991). Thus, memory and reasoning performance often reflects underlying opposing processes, processes of interference that are, at best, partially inhibited by cognitive control, including interference among alternative memory representations, competition among cues to stored knowledge, and confusion in applying retrieved knowledge to multiple memory representations (Brainerd & Reyna, 2005b; Reyna, 1995; see the section "Processing Interference"). Although we emphasize how parameters that measure representation, retrieval, and inhibition account for data, the assumptions of fuzzy-trace theory have been tested with respect to specific hypotheses about processing (e.g., how changing a single word in a class-inclusion question is predicted to change responses). Indeed, tests of fuzzy-trace theory go beyond describing data with parameters to evaluating how parameters (and behaviors) respond to theoretically motivated experimental manipulations (e.g., Brainerd et al., 1999; Reyna & Brainerd, 1995).

Background: Theoretical Assumptions

The assumptions of fuzzy-trace theory were arrived at through empirical tests and were developed to explain findings that contradicted initial hypotheses (Brainerd & Reyna, 1990a; Reyna & Brainerd, 1990, 1995, 1998). The theory originated, in part, from findings that challenged explanations of biases in judgment and choice that invoked notions of limited memory capacity (e.g., Simon, 1982), such as the cognitive economy and fast-and-frugal hypotheses (e.g., Nisbett & Ross, 1980). Subsequent data consistently showed independence of memory for background facts from reasoning performance based on those facts (Reyna & Brainerd, 1990, 1995). The three basic principles of fuzzy-trace theory are as follows:

1. Reasoners encode multiple representations of information in parallel and retrieve them independently.
2. These representations differ in degree of precision, from specific surface representations (called *verbatim*; e.g., the exact wording of a statement in a conversation, the exact quantities of numerical information in a gamble) to vague meaning-based representations (called *gist*; e.g., the essential meaning of a statement in a conversation, ordinal or categorical differences in numerical quantities).
3. People have a "fuzzy-processing preference," using gist representations to support judgments and choices unless features of the task demand otherwise. Gist representations encompass the meaning of targets (e.g., words, pictures, events) and other relational information (e.g., inferences), including relations among targets. Thus, most experiences yield memories that form hierarchies of gist, such as memory for the meanings of individual sentences plus memory for inferences that connect sentences or memory for the meanings of individual words plus memory for the theme of a semantically related set of words (e.g., Reyna & Kiernan, 1994; Reyna, Mills, Estrada, & Brainerd, in press; Roediger & McDermott, 1995).

Instructions in traditional memory tasks encourage heavy reliance on verbatim representations, whereas gist processing dominates in most reasoning scenarios. This differential representational support for responses in the two types of task thus explains findings of memory–reasoning independence (because memory tasks typically require verbatim memory, whereas reasoning tasks typically require gist memory). Evidence for parallel storage of verbatim and gist representations includes findings that semantic storage precedes complete processing of instantiating targets (Brainerd & Reyna, 1993). Retrieval mechanisms assumed for verbatim versus gist representations also differ. In recall, if verbatim memories are sufficiently intact to be accessible, they can be directly read out (Reyna & Titcomb, 1997). Gist memories are not directly read out, because they were not directly experienced and hence only approximate experience. Instead, gist memories can be reconstructed and then reported, provided that they pass a metacognitive review that reflects the degree of trust in the reconstruction. That review can be stringent (withholding most reconstructed responses) or lenient (outputting most reconstructed responses), reflecting an inhibitory mechanism that becomes more effective with development. In recognition, a probe is supplied for comparison to the contents of memory. Verbatim memories support an identity judgment (surface match). The probe either exactly matches the contents of memory or it does not, and the memory judgment is all or none, although the verbatim memory itself may represent only the disintegrated fragments of original experience. In contrast, because gist representations only approximate experience, they support a more graded similarity judgment.

Parameters representing these three basic processes—verbatim retrieval, gist-based reconstruction, and metacognitive review (an inhibitory process)— are estimated in the dual-recall model of fuzzy-trace theory. The procedure used to generate data to estimate parameters for the dual-recall model is simple. First, subjects study any set of meaningful targets (e.g., words, sentences, pictures). Then they recall the studied list multiple times, either with or without additional study opportunities. The fate of each item across recall attempts (to oversimplify, whether recall is stable across trials, indicating direct readout, or variable, indicating an imperfect reconstructive process) is used as input to mathematical models, which are evaluated statistically. In recognition models (e.g., Brainerd et al., 1999), analogous parameters are estimated: When verbatim representations are retrieved, I and N parameters reflect identity and nonidentity judgments to targets and distractors, respectively; the similarity judgment (S) parameter is the probability of retrieving a gist trace, and the bias (β) parameter reflects an inhibitory response–bias process. These assumptions about representation, retrieval, and metacognitive judgment are then subject to tests of goodness of fit to observed data (for mathematical details, see Brainerd, Wright, Reyna, & Payne, 2002). Moreover, the need for each parameter can be formally assessed by comparing simpler with more inclusive models and determining whether fit significantly increases with additional parameters. Although such results from modeling studies provide additional support, fuzzy-trace theory's perspective on interference effects is rooted in experimental results from reasoning and memory tasks collected during the theory's early development (Reyna, 1992, 1995). In addition to memory–reasoning independence, the theory has been used to predict specific circumstances under which facilitation and interference effects would be observed (i.e., positive and negative dependencies, respectively, between memory and reasoning performance; Brainerd & Reyna, 1993; Reyna & Kiernan, 1994, 1995). Six types of interference are acknowledged in fuzzy-trace theory, four of which we discuss in this chapter: representational interference, retrieval interference, processing interference, and response inhibition.

In representational interference, verbatim and gist representations are used that are inappropriate for the task. For example, rejecting a true statement in an inference task because the experimenter "didn't say that" constitutes verbatim interference (Brainerd & Reyna, 1993). Rejecting the conclusion "Socrates is mortal" given the premises "Socrates is a man" and "all men are mortal" because the conclusion was not directly stated is not appropriate in an inference task (although it is appropriate in a task testing memory for exact wording). Conversely, gist can interfere with verbatim representations in tasks testing memory for exact wording, such as false memory tasks (Robinson & Roediger, 1997), and inappropriate gists can interfere with correct gists, as when people confuse the relative numbers of cows and horses with the relative numbers of cows and animals, relative risk estimates with absolute risk estimates (Reyna & Hamilton, 2001), or the probability of A given B with the probability of B given A in conditional probability judgment tasks (see the section "Reasoning"; Reyna, 2004; Reyna, Lloyd, & Brainerd, 2003).

In addition to the appropriate representation of task information, most reasoning tasks also require retrieval of a reasoning principle that can be applied to that representation. The influence of interference is seen when contextual cues misdirect reasoning by prompting the retrieval of inappropriate reasoning principles. For example, in class-inclusion tasks, subjects must make comparisons of a superordinate category and one of its subsets: A series of cows and horses might be displayed followed by the question, "Are there more cows or animals?" Such questions can cue retrieval of a relative numerosity principle (the word *more* cues the principle pertaining to which class has a greater number of members) instead of the appropriate cardinal ordering principle (which class includes the others as subordinate classes), leading to high error rates in children and long response times in adults (Brainerd & Reyna, 1990b).

Having the appropriate representation and retrieval principle for a given reasoning problem is not sufficient, however. Accurate reasoning still requires that the principle be applied coherently to the representation to arrive at a correct response. Lack of coherence sometimes results in processing interference, seen most clearly in judgment or choice tasks when overlapping classes create confusion in reasoning. In syllogistic reasoning tasks, when presented with premises of the form "all As are Bs" and "some Bs are Cs," reasoners often lose track of the marginal members of the classes—the Bs that are not As—and erroneously conclude that some As are Cs.

Once previous representational, retrieval, and processing stages have run to completion, response inhibition governs the ability to withhold responses. Children, for example, have difficulty with response inhibition (i.e., they are more impulsive; Bjorklund, 1989; Reyna & Farley, 2006). Later in this chapter we present data illustrating an increasing developmental tendency to inhibit responses—in this instance, responses based on reconstructed gist representations.

Finally, there are input and output interference. In the former, attentional interference due to noise or distraction interferes with encoding; in the latter, there is nonspecific interference with processing attributable to the need to schedule and output responses. Susceptibility to input interference contributes to encoding differences in younger versus older learners (e.g., Reyna & Kiernan, 1994). Output interference has figured centrally in fuzzy-trace theory's account of "cognitive triage," so named because weaker items in memory are pushed to the front of recall queues, much as weaker patients are triaged to the front of the line in emergency rooms, to optimize recall accuracy (Reyna & Brainerd,

1995). Although input and output interference are important in fuzzy-trace theory, we focus in this chapter on the other four types of interference: representational, retrieval, and processing interference, as well as response inhibition.

In summary, fuzzy-trace theory is a dual-process theory in which verbatim and gist representations compete to support responses in memory and reasoning tasks, aided by strategic and metacognitive control processes that involve inhibition (for reviews, see Reyna, 1992, 2004). Many textbooks assert that memory is reconstructed rather than recorded, but extant data require dual memories—both reconstructed gist memories and directly accessed verbatim memories—to account for such effects as "recollection rejection" (i.e., verbatim recollection that prevents interference from gist-based false memories; Brainerd, Payne, et al., 2003; Brainerd, Reyna, Wright, & Mojardin, 2003; Gallo, 2004; Reyna & Kiernan, 1995). The theoretical assumptions that we use to explain interference include parallel encoding of representations that range from precise surface form to vague skeletal outlines of meaning, independent retrieval of those representations, and a preference for relying on the meaning representations in reasoning tasks.

Developmental Differences in True Recall

We now turn to discussion of interference effects that these assumptions predict in children, adults, older adults, and those with Alzheimer's disease.

Adulthood, Aging, and Alzheimer's Disease

Fuzzy-trace theory makes straightforward predictions about developmental differences in memory processes in childhood, which are mirrored in old age (Koutstaal & Schacter, 1997; Tun, Wingfield, Rosen, & Blanchard, 1998). That is, the ability to encode accurate verbatim memories, which depends on neurological development, increases in childhood and decreases in old age, as a function of maturation and degeneration, respectively. We call this the *neural integrity hypothesis*. Although gist extraction also depends on neurological development, gist representations are relatively more robust in memory: Because relational patterns are redundant, partial loss or degeneration does not result in complete inability to identify a gist trace. We call this the *neural redundancy hypothesis*. In addition, gist extraction depends on knowledge, education, and experience, all attributes that stabilize or increase in adulthood (Reyna & Adam, 2003). For example, the gist of words or sentences stabilizes in adulthood (although gist extraction in domains of expertise continues to grow; e.g., Reyna et al., 2003). Thus, gist memory for ordinary material, such as common words, ought to remain relatively stable from young adulthood to old age, with more profound disease processes of the brain required to depress gist memory.

To evaluate these hypotheses, Reyna and Brainerd (2004) had college-age adults (M = 20 years), older healthy adults (M = 68 years), and patients with mild Alzheimer's disease (M = 66 years) study 20 words and then do six free-

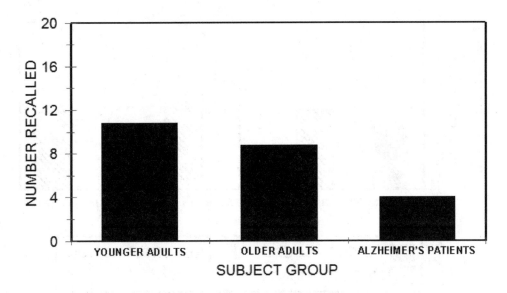

Figure 10.1. Overall decline in recall from young adults to healthy older adults to Alzheimer's patients (from Reyna & Brainerd, 2004).

recall tests. We then used the dual-recall model to estimate parameters for each age group that represented direct access of verbatim memory, reconstruction of gist, and metacognitive judgment probabilities. As shown in Figure 10.1, relative to the young adults, recall declined in old age and declined further for the Alzheimer's patients. The model unpacks this overall performance into an instructive pattern of underlying processes in Figure 10.2. In this and other figures, memory process level corresponds to parameter estimates of the corresponding processes: that is, to the probability that the corresponding process was engaged. Although direct access of verbatim memory declined from young adulthood to old age (as expected), reconstructive processes increased and compensated for the loss of verbatim recall. The decline in recall in old age would have been significantly worse had the tendency to engage in gist-based reconstructive processes not increased. The tendency to output a reconstructed item did not differ across age groups or for the Alzheimer's group. Alzheimer's patients exhibited a similar amount of verbatim memory decline to that of older adults but showed a further decline in gist-based reconstructive processes. Thus, Alzheimer's patients could not compensate for a loss of verbatim memory by reconstructing presented items from gist, resulting in a considerable drop in recall performance.

Childhood

Relative to the high point of young adulthood, memory in middle childhood is less accurate and in young childhood is less accurate still (Figure 10.3). According to the best-fitting model, the probability of accurate verbatim recall (direct access) correspondingly increases from early to middle childhood and again

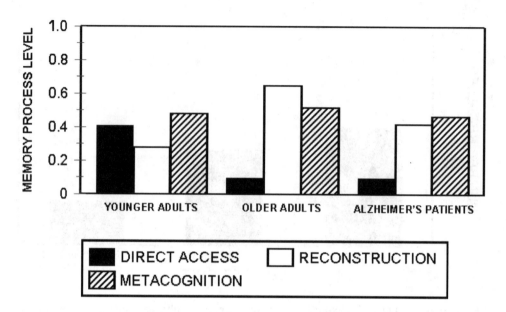

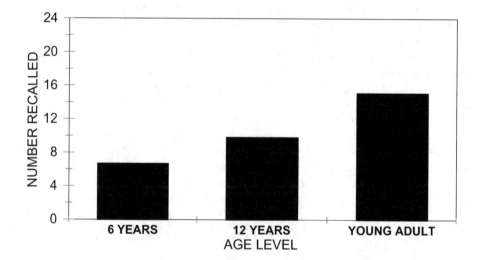

Figure 10.2. Effect of age and Alzheimer's disease in adults on the three memory processes in adult recall: direct access, reconstruction, and metacognition (from Reyna & Brainerd, 2004).

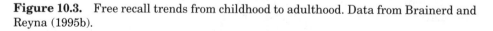

Figure 10.3. Free recall trends from childhood to adulthood. Data from Brainerd and Reyna (1995b).

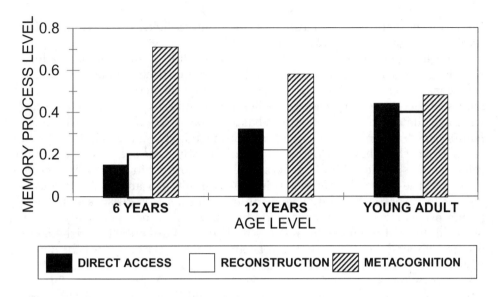

Figure 10.4. Developmental effects on the three memory processes in recall: direct access, reconstruction, and metacognition. Data from Brainerd and Reyna (1995b).

between middle childhood and adulthood (Figure 10.4). Gist-based reconstruction, however, does not change across the younger groups but rather increases between childhood and adulthood. Interestingly, and consistent with other observations about childhood (e.g., Bjorklund, 1989), the tendency to respond impulsively—to report whatever is reconstructed—declines in childhood. Thus, 12-year-olds were more likely than 6-year-olds to inhibit reconstructed responses, in the sense that 12-year-olds had a lower probability of reporting an item given that it was successfully reconstructed.

Summary of Developmental Differences in True Recall

In summary, obtained values for the three parameters of the dual-recall model provide distinct characterizations of each group of subjects. Corroborating earlier research, verbatim memory improved substantially in childhood. Younger children also exhibited a lower threshold for emitting a reconstructed response, suggesting a lack of response inhibition in early childhood. Younger children's proclivity to act impulsively has been well documented (e.g., younger children's reasoning performance resembles older children's if they are explicitly instructed to inhibit responding for 15 seconds; Bjorklund, 1989). Given the assumptions of the model, subjects resort to reconstructing gist only if verbatim responses are not accessible. Thus, reconstruction does not involve a competing response; there is no interference in the sense of retrieving reconstructions that actively compete with alternative verbatim memories. The metacognitive parameter, however, expresses the probability that subjects inhibit reconstructed responses. Because the probability of outputting a reconstructed response is conditional on successful reconstruction, any probability greater than 0 for the metacognitive parameter can be interpreted as actively inhibiting a response, which is increased in childhood.

The deficit in verbatim memory among older adults relative to young adults resembles the deficit among young children, but this decline in older adults is compensated for by an increase in gist-based reconstruction. Hence, in older adults, observed memory accuracy belies a drop in verbatim memory accuracy with age that is masked using gist-based reconstruction. Apparently, older adults can draw on their experience with meaningful materials to infer or reconstruct what they can no longer recall directly. *Gist-based compensation* refers to the specific ability to generate items accurately in recall using reconstruction, the probability of which increases in old age and partially offsets deficits in verbatim readout. The spontaneous use of this gist-based strategy to improve memory performance might be expanded on therapeutically to help older adults and others with memory difficulties. Patients with Alzheimer's disease exhibit deficits in verbatim readout but also apparently lack the ability to compensate as successfully for this loss by using gist-based reconstruction. The ravages of Alzheimer's disease weaken even the more robust form of memory, gist representations, although it should be noted that neither form of memory is entirely absent, and gist-based reconstruction remains more probable than verbatim readout. This conclusion parallels the findings of Balota et al. (1999), who showed that, controlling for levels of true recognition, Alzheimer's patients demonstrated a higher degree of false recognition to semantic associates—that is, they relied more heavily on gist representations than did healthy adults.

Developmental Differences in True and False Memory

In this section we discuss developmental differences in true memory (recognition) and false memory (including false recognition and false recall).

True Memory: Recognition

On standard recognition tests, studied items reappear along with unstudied distractors. According to fuzzy-trace theory, verbatim support should attenuate developmental differences in verbatim memory, because test items can then act as retrieval cues for stored memories. Providing gist-consistent (or semantically related) items on the recognition test should support gist-based false recognition (to the degree that subjects cannot reject the gist-consistent item by using verbatim memory for what was actually presented). By comparing acceptance rates of related items to those of unrelated items, gist-based responding can be estimated. However, this difference is not process pure, because it also reflects the opposing process of verbatim-based rejection of related items (Brainerd & Reyna, 2005b; Reyna & Kiernan, 1994). These underlying processes can be disentangled by varying instructions to subjects and then deriving mathematical models to estimate verbatim, gist, and response bias parameters,

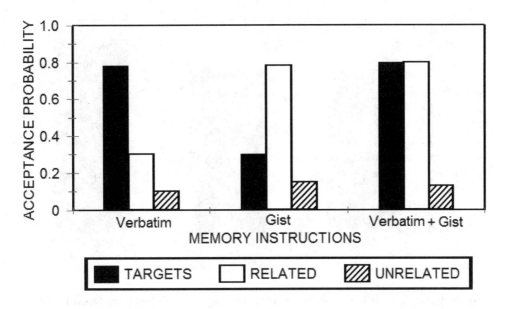

Figure 10.5. How conjoint recognition works: Influence of test instructions on use of the instructions in recall.

roughly analogous to the three recall parameters discussed earlier (see Brainerd et al., 1999; Brainerd, Wright, Reyna, & Mojardin, 2001). This conjoint recognition paradigm involves studying a set of meaningful targets and performing a recognition test under one of three instructions: verbatim (accept only presented targets); gist (accept only meaning-sharing distractors); or verbatim plus gist (accept both verbatim and gist-consistent items; see Figure 10.5). This process permits estimation of the probability that judgments were based on verbatim identity, gist similarity, and response bias for all age levels.

Brainerd, Holliday, and Reyna (2004), for example, presented young children (age 7 years), older children (age 12 years), and young adults (age 20 years) with nine lists of semantically related words that shared an associate (Roediger & McDermott, 1995). Participants studied three Deese–Roediger–McDermott (DRM) lists followed by a recognition test for three cycles (i.e., a total of nine lists was studied). As is typical, recognition produced a shallower developmental trend than recall across a similar age range, consistent with the assumption of verbatim support (Figure 10.6). Similar to recall, the ability to summon verbatim memory increases considerably in childhood, whereas gist-based recognition changes little over the same age range (Figure 10.7). Response bias—the tendency to acquiesce to whatever is presented, including unrelated items—decreased significantly with age (e.g., Reyna & Brainerd, 1998). Thus, children respond impulsively before taking adequate time to retrieve verbatim details, which takes longer than retrieving gist (Rotello, Macmillan, & Van Tassel, 2000).

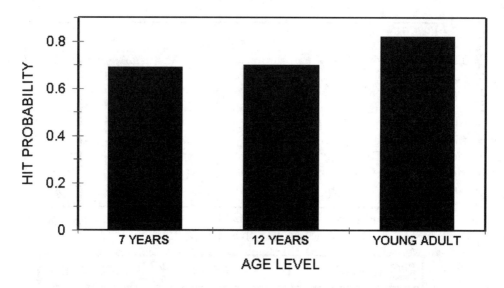

Figure 10.6. Trends in true memory (recognition) from childhood to adulthood. From "Behavioral Measurement of Remembering Phenomenologies: So Simple a Child Can Do It," by C. J. Brainerd, R. E. Holliday, and V. F. Reyna, 2004, *Child Development, 75,* p. 508. Copyright 2004 by Blackwell Publishing. Adapted with permission.

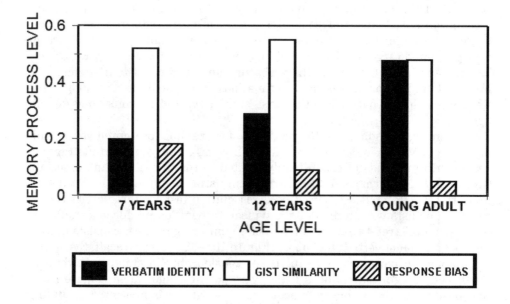

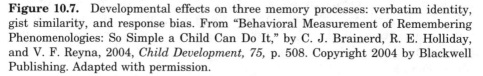

Figure 10.7. Developmental effects on three memory processes: verbatim identity, gist similarity, and response bias. From "Behavioral Measurement of Remembering Phenomenologies: So Simple a Child Can Do It," by C. J. Brainerd, R. E. Holliday, and V. F. Reyna, 2004, *Child Development, 75,* p. 508. Copyright 2004 by Blackwell Publishing. Adapted with permission.

False Recognition and False Recall

One might conclude from recognition performance for targets that gist-based processing does not develop appreciably throughout childhood. Although that conclusion is true at the level of individual words, the tendency to spontaneously connect meanings across words develops significantly during this period. Until around age 11 or 12, for instance, children do not cluster semantically related words in free recall, despite their easy familiarity with the meaning of each word (Bjorklund, 1987; Bjorklund & Hock, 1982). In contrast, adults routinely link meaningfully related items, which is reflected in semantic clustering in free recall and other aspects of their memory performance (Reyna & Brainerd, 1990; Reyna & Kiernan, 1994). Indeed, a hallmark of the DRM false memory paradigm is that adults spontaneously recognize the semantic connection among the related words on a list and falsely remember never-presented words that express the semantic theme of the list (e.g., Brainerd & Reyna, 1998). False alarms to critical lures that capture the gist of the related study words occur at almost the same frequency as hits to actual list words, and false recall of these semantic theme words is also high. If the tendency to connect meanings increases in childhood, then paradoxically, false memories ought to increase during the same period as the accuracy of true memories is increasing.

As Figures 10.8 and 10.9 show, this surprising prediction has been borne out both for recognition (false alarms; Brainerd et al., 2004) and for recall (intrusion; Brainerd, Reyna, & Forrest, 2002) using the DRM paradigm (for a

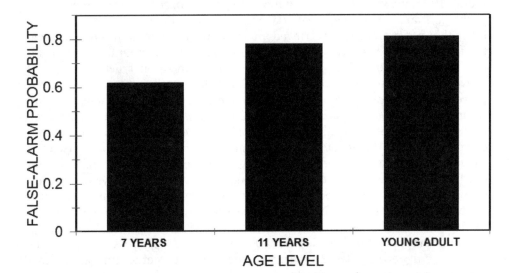

Figure 10.8. Development of Deese–Roediger–McDermott false memory from childhood to adulthood in recognition (false alarms). From "Behavioral Measurement of Remembering Phenomenologies: So Simple a Child Can Do It," by C. J. Brainerd, R. E. Holliday, and V. F. Reyna, 2004, *Child Development, 75,* p. 508. Copyright 2004 by Blackwell Publishing. Adapted with permission.

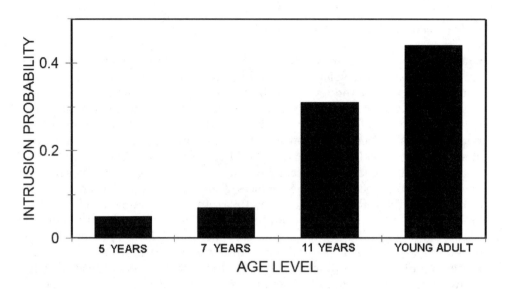

Figure 10.9. Development of Deese–Roediger–McDermott false memory from childhood to adulthood for recall (intrusion). Data from Brainerd, Reyna, and Forrest (2002).

review of the developmental literature on the DRM paradigm, see Reyna et al., in press). False memories increase with age in childhood, and the increase is sharper around 11 or 12, consistent with the clustering data in free recall. Figure 10.10 shows developmental increases in gist-based phantom recollection in recognition, as well as in recollection rejection (*similarity* refers to the probability that a gist trace was retrieved and a similarity judgment made between the trace and the test probe). Figure 10.11 shows developmental increases in two gist-based processes, phantom recollection and reconstruction, in recall, as well as decreases in metacognition. (The difference between the gist-based processes is that phantom recollection has a more vivid phenomenology than reconstruction.) As the discussion of true memory illustrated, however, overt performance can obscure underlying opposing processes. To uncover these processes, Brainerd, Payne, et al. (2003) applied the dual-recall model discussed earlier in this chapter, as well as a conjoint-recall model with three instructional conditions, to data from the DRM paradigm. Six-year-olds, 12-year-olds, and college-age adults exhibited the now-familiar trend of increasing verbatim memory with age. But gist-based processes that supported false memories also increased with age: Reconstruction of gist increased for each age group, as well as phantom recollection (see Reyna, 2000; see Figure 10.11). As in other studies, the probability of outputting a reconstructed response (metacognition) declined between early and middle childhood. That is, response inhibition increased in childhood. False recognition also showed a pattern similar to that obtained in earlier studies: Both gist-based phantom recollection and verbatim-based recollection rejection increased with age in recognition, although gist-based similarity judgment remained roughly constant (Figure 10.10). These under-

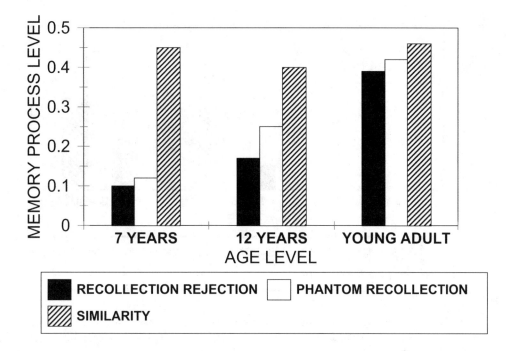

Figure 10.10. Developmental effects on three memory processes involved in false recognition: recollection rejection, phantom recollection, and similarity. (*Similarity* refers to the probability that a gist trace was retrieved and a similarity judgment made between the trace and the test probe.) From "Behavioral Measurement of Remembering Phenomenologies: So Simple a Child Can Do It," by C. J. Brainerd, R. E. Holliday, and V. F. Reyna, 2004, *Child Development, 75,* p. 508. Copyright 2004 by Blackwell Publishing. Adapted with permission.

lying opposing processes account for false memory findings in a variety of tasks (for comparisons with alternative accounts, see Brainerd et al., 1999; Reyna et al., in press; Reyna & Lloyd, 1997).

Summary of Developmental Differences in True and False Memory

False memories occur as a result of the ordinary meaning building that humans engage in as they experience events (Reyna & Brainerd, 1998). This kind of spontaneous false memory—as opposed to that induced by misinformation (Titcomb & Renya, 1995)—is an example of representational interference. In the DRM paradigm, but also in everyday life, we encode the semantic gist of experience and then recall that gist instead of verbatim memories. The traditional view has been that when task instructions or context requires verbatim responses, gist is recalled because verbatim memories are no longer accessible. However, we now know that this view is misleading, because verbatim and gist memories are encoded, retrieved, and stored independently (Reyna & Kiernan,

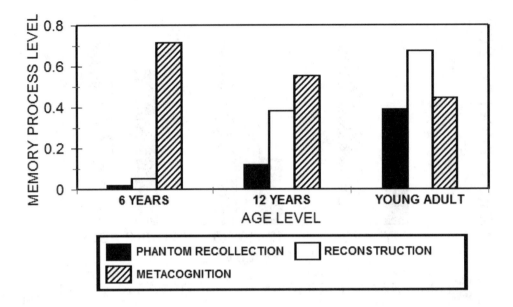

Figure 10.11. Developmental effects on three memory processes involved in false recall: phantom recollection, reconstruction, and metacognition. Data from Brainerd and Reyna (2005b).

1994, 1995). Rather, memory for the gist of presented information, such as studied words, usurps the role of verbatim memory in tasks that clearly stipulate verbatim responses, which is a product of factors such as age, delay, materials, repetition, and retrieval cues (Reyna, 1996; Reyna & Brainerd, 1995). Data suggest that this usurpation is unconscious, one reason that false memories can be dangerous in important applied contexts such as in legal proceedings (Reyna et al., in press).

Verbatim memories can also interfere with gist memories, exemplified when children reject inferences because the experimenter "didn't say that." During childhood, verbatim memories become increasingly accessible and thus are increasingly used to combat gist-based false memories (i.e., recollection rejection, see Figure 10.10). According to the data presented earlier, older adults and Alzheimer's patients should be less able to engage in recollection rejection, a prediction that aligns with published observations. For example, Budson, Daffner, Desikan, and Schacter (2000) demonstrated that list repetition in the DRM paradigm decreases false recognition for young adults but increases it for Alzheimer's patients. Verbatim representations in Alzheimer's patients are not bolstered sufficiently across list repetition to oppose the increasing activation of gist. Other studies have reported similar findings (e.g., Kensinger & Schacter, 1999; Koutstaal & Schacter, 1997; Norman & Schacter, 1997).

The developmental differences that we have discussed provide insight into the memory skills that children, young and older adults, and people with mild cognitive impairment bring to cognitive tasks, suggesting possible strategies for improving performance. As an example, although older people compensate for loss in verbatim memory by reconstructing studied items from gist memory, children do not similarly compensate, despite having some ability to engage in gist-based reconstruction. They do not actively and spontaneously engage in semantic integration to the degree that adults do (as illustrated by results concerning connecting gist across meaningful units, as in the DRM task), and they have a verbatim bias to rely on the literal elements of experience (Reyna & Brainerd, 1991b). However, gist-based strategies can be taught to young children to improve their memory performance (see Bjorklund, 1989).

Reasoning

We now turn to a discussion of interference in reasoning, including representational and retrieval interference and processing interference.

Representational and Retrieval Interference

The processes that we have reviewed in memory tasks are implicated in reasoning tasks as well. Reasoners encode gist and verbatim representations of the problem information into working memory and retrieve stored knowledge from long-term memory. Common reasoning tasks provide fertile ground for exploring interference effects, because they typically require coordination and execution of multiple cognitive processes. Reasoners must first encode relevant task information amid a variety of potentially misleading cues and select one of many potential task representations to act on. Values, principles, or rules must then be retrieved from memory, and finally the selected representation and the retrieved rule must be combined coherently to arrive at a solution. Interference can influence each of these operations and exhibits a clear developmental trend. Representational and retrieval interference are more likely to derail task performance early in development, whereas processing interference from overlapping classes creates low-level bookkeeping errors that are among the last to disappear in development and, thus, are present even in reasoners with accurate logic, memory, and conceptual understanding (Estes, 1976; Reyna et al., 2003). However, the salience of key contextual aspects of the task can render even adults sensitive to interference at each stage.

The research on representational interference in false memory reviewed earlier in this chapter demonstrates the degree to which cognition is dominated by retrieval cues. Representation and retrieval work hand in hand in the sense that retrieval cues increase the probability that particular representations will be retrieved. Retrieval interference operates broadly; the retrieval of knowledge, values, reasoning principles, and other aspects of stored information is sensitive to cues in the environment. Retrieval interference occurs when cognition is derailed by retrieving inappropriate knowledge, values, or reasoning principles (Reyna & Brainerd, 1993, 1994).

Reasoning, judgment, and decision making rely on the ability to retrieve stored information using a variety of contextual cues. *Transfer*, or the ability to apply stored information to problems and situations that do not literally match learning, is crucial for success in educational and professional contexts (Wolfe, Reyna, & Brainerd, 2005). Thus, ideally, reasoners should be able to recognize when stored knowledge is relevant, ignoring interference from misleading cues but remaining alert to relevant cues in superficially different forms (referred to as *cognitive invariance* and *flexibility*, respectively; Reyna & Brainerd, 1995). Misleading cues often reside in the formulation of a task, however, and sensitivity to these framing effects is well documented (Levin, Schneider, & Gaeth, 1998). The wording of a question, for example, can set off a search in memory for the wrong information, and partial matches with the contents of memory may not be detected (Reder, 1987; Reder & Schunn, 1996). In the Moses illusion, when asked "How many animals of each type did Moses take on the ark?" most people answer "two," even though they know that it was Noah who took the animals on the ark (Erickson & Mattson, 1981). Cues in the question (e.g., the word *more*) similarly cause the wrong reasoning principle to be retrieved in Piaget's (1942) class-inclusion task. This task induces a compelling cognitive illusion (i.e., children insist that there are more cows than animals after counting the 10 animals) that persists until age 10, long past the time that children are aware of the correct inclusion relations among classes and their implications for quantitative judgments.

For cognitive illusions to occur, there must be a compelling gist that captures thinking, but there must also be the absence of discrepancy detection (Reyna, 1991). If children were to retrieve their knowledge that cows are a subset of animals and that subsets cannot be more numerous than the sets that include them (the cardinality principle), they would reject the conclusion that there are more cows than animals. Children who exhibit the class-inclusion illusion are nevertheless aware of and respond in accordance with the cardinality principle (e.g., asked if there are more students in their class or in their school, they respond correctly; see, e.g., Brainerd & Kaszor, 1974). Manipulations that draw attention to subset relations (i.e., inclusion hierarchies) in class-inclusion tasks, and thereby encourage retrieval of the cardinality principle, significantly reduce errors in the class-inclusion task (Brainerd & Reyna, 1990b; Reyna, 1991).

The compelling gist in this task is the relation between subsets (e.g., cows and horses), which usurps the queried relation between the subset and the more inclusive set (e.g., cows and animals; Reyna, 1991). Thus, the illusion occurs as a result of the competition between memory representations of relevant set relations, the failure to retrieve relevant knowledge of the cardinality principle, and/or the failure to combine appropriate task representations with the retrieved principle. Manipulations that improve processing accuracy (e.g., tagging members of sets so that class groupings are more salient) improve performance in older, but not younger, children (Brainerd & Reyna, 1990b). It is interesting that performance also improves if the display is removed, making verbatim information about number and their subset relations less salient, and children are forced to respond on the basis of their memory for the gist of the information (Brainerd & Reyna, 1995a). The recurring theme is that salient patterns interfere with appropriate representations that could lead to correct solutions. Even adults suffer interference, taking longer to respond to class-inclusion questions than comparably worded questions that do not involve subset (i.e., inclusion hierarchy) relations (Reyna, 1991). This finding extends to the conjunction fallacy (Tversky & Kahneman, 1983) and its famous illustration, ranking "Linda is a bank teller and is active in the feminist movement" as more likely than "Linda is a bank teller" (see Reyna, 1991; Reyna & Brainerd, 1994). As in instances of false memory, people harbor the correct information in memory, but they fail to retrieve it appropriately in context.

Another illustration of retrieval interference is the effect of "unpacking" descriptions of events: If two descriptions of an event are given, one that implicitly contains subsets of events and the other that explicitly mentions disjunctively related subsets, the explicit description will be given a higher probability assessment (Adam & Reyna, 2005; Reyna, 2004; Reyna & Adam, 2003; Tversky & Koehler, 1994). Asked to assess the probability of death of 20-year-old men, subjects are likely to assess that probability as lower than when asked to assess the probability of death of 20-year-old men from motor vehicle accidents, homicide, AIDS, and all other causes. The explicit mention of causes of death encourages retrieval of plausible ways in which young men might die. Even experts who regularly retrieve knowledge in their domains of expertise are affected by retrieval cues: Reyna and Adam (2003) asked physicians, health educators, and experts in public health aspects of sexually transmitted disease to estimate the probability that an asymptomatic but sexually active young woman had a sexually transmitted disease. Adding a list of examples of sexually transmitted diseases to the identical question—examples well known to health professionals—increased probability estimates for all groups (see also Adam & Reyna, 2005).

When a compelling description leads people away from retrieving the information that they would ordinarily retrieve to make a sound judgment, this is interference. Thus, the image of a healthy young man obscures death from major chronic diseases (the diseases of "old age"), whereas mentioning stereotypical causes of death from risk-taking behaviors such as vehicular accidents and AIDS from unprotected sex makes death seem more plausible. Verbatim matches with stored information are rare in everyday life. Instead, approximate matches, based on gist-based or semantic similarity, must be executed routinely. As the Moses and the class-inclusion illusions illustrate, however, gist-based similarity judgments can produce interference errors.

Processing Interference

Judgments of risk and probability are especially prone to error because they involve overlapping classes, which produce processing interference because of multiple mappings among classes. Conditional probability judgments, with more nested and overlapping classes, are more confusing than simple probability judgments (Wolfe, 1995). Reasoners, especially those who attempt to solve the problem using verbatim quantitative representations, get confused about relations among classes; they focus on target classes, usually in numerators, and hence neglect denominators (Reyna, 2004; Reyna & Brainerd, 1993; Reyna et al., 2003). For example, the pretest probability of a disease is 10%, and a test is available that has an 80% sensitivity (the probability that the test is positive given that a person has the disease) and an 80% specificity (the probability that the test is negative given that a person does not have the disease). Consider that the test is performed with a positive result: What is the probability of disease: 30% or 70%? The correct response is closer to 30%, but most subjects judge it to be more than 70%; only 32% of physicians chose the correct response (Reyna, 2004). Neglecting the denominator creates this illusion (the sensitivity and the posttest conditional probability have the same numerator but different denominators).

The fact that performance is substantially below chance invokes a familiar theme: Contextual cues in the task lead people away from retrieving their relevant knowledge. For example, retrieving general guidance from epidemiology or public health textbooks would have resulted in more accurate performance. Such textbooks remind readers that posttest results skew in the direction of base rates. Retrieving everyday clinical experience should also have produced better performance; positive results, given a low prior probability, mostly turn out to be false alarms. Drawing on that experience would have supported choosing 30% over 70%. Using Bayes's theorem to calculate the posttest probability would certainly have yielded a correct response, and physicians are taught Bayes's theorem as part of their training and are tested on it for certifications. Instead of retrieving or computing the answer, experts relied on their distorted intuitive judgments. Although training in Bayes's theorem had little effect, interventions to reduce processing interference—by disentangling overlapping classes using special notation and other devices—sharply reduced errors among physicians in training (Lloyd & Reyna, 2001). Thus, interpreting diagnostic tests is difficult even for intelligent, well-trained professionals because of processing interference, according to fuzzy-trace theory.

In addition to interpretation of diagnostic test results, interpretation of genetic risk and testing is another common instance of the need to understand conditional probabilities. There are two relevant conditional probabilities: the chance of developing a disease given that one has a defective gene versus the chance of having the defective gene given that one has the disease. If overlapping classes cause processing interference, then it is possible to predict that certain genetic vulnerabilities would be easier to comprehend (i.e., less subject to processing interference) than others. For example, Huntington's disease is an example of virtually one-to-one mapping: If you have the gene, you will develop the disease, and vice versa. Because there is no partial overlap and no ambiguity of reference, there is little processing interference. A disease such as hemochromatosis, however, is asymmetric: If you have the disease, you have the gene, but having the gene does not guarantee developing the disease (because of partial penetrance; see Reyna, Lloyd, & Whalen, 2001). Understanding genetic risk would be of middling difficulty for diseases such as this. The most difficult case is with diseases such as breast cancer, in which most people who develop breast cancer do not have the mutated genes, yet having those genes confers a high risk of developing the disease. Multiple overlapping classes create confusion, yet it is necessary to take account of each of these classes to estimate risk accurately. As Reyna et al. (2001) discussed, patients and physicians have difficulty understanding genetic risk when classes overlap partially. Despite the benefits of genetic counseling, many patients remain unable to assess their own risk and are prone to the sort of error discussed earlier in this chapter of confusing conditional probabilities. Some have even had prophylactic mastectomies to prevent breast cancer, seriously overestimating their genetic risk (Eddy, 1982).

Errors involving conditional probability judgments (and unconditional probability judgments, as in the conjunction fallacy) are systematic, and performance is well below chance. Moreover, the same individuals who evince these systematic errors can perform at high levels with some simple formatting changes. Although judgments must still be thought through, making the classes distinct is sufficient to improve performance. Some researchers have argued that performance is compromised by an overload on working memory capacity or resources, but this explanation has been disconfirmed for this and other judgment illusions (for a review, see Reyna & Brainerd, 1995). Others have argued that errors can be reduced by using frequency representations, as opposed to probabilities, but these explanations, too, have suffered disconfirmation when they were tested directly without confounding factors (e.g., Sloman, Over, Slovak, & Stibel, 2003). Processing (and other kinds of) interference appear to offer a better account of a number of cognitive phenomena that had been explained using disparate conceptual, working memory, or frequentistic approaches (e.g., Reyna, 1992, 1995).

Conclusion

We have reviewed a number of different types of interference—representational, retrieval, and processing, as well as response inhibition—that can explain performance in both memory and reasoning tasks. Response inhibition differs from simple interference in that active self-control is required to suppress a prepotent response. Response impulsivity, the flip side of inhibition, produces reaction without control, causing subjects to say the response that first comes to mind: to recall a reconstructed word without metacognitive review, to respond that Moses took two animals of each type on the ark, and to affirm that there are more cows than animals. As is often the case, this developmental difference corresponds to an individual difference. As children become older, most become increasingly capable of active inhibition, and their cognitive performance improves. Some adults, however, remain less able to control their impulses, and this dimension of individual differences affects their academic performance and their social well-being (Nigg, 2000; Reyna, Adam, Poirier, LeCroy, & Brainerd, 2005).

Such impulsivity also characterizes a number of neuropsychological disorders involving risk and decision making (Bechara, Damasio, Damasio, & Anderson, 1994; Reyna & Farley, 2006). Alzheimer's patients, however, did not differ from younger or older adults in their willingness to respond with a gist-based reconstructed item, thereby allowing them to take advantage of any residual gist-processing ability. The neural integrity and neural redundancy hypotheses, introduced in the first section on memory, imply that gist-processing ability should be more robust than verbatim memory with generalized neural trauma or disease. Consistent with this implication, Alzheimer's patients were able to engage in successful reconstruction more often than verbatim readout. As suggested in connection with children, therapeutic strategies should be explored that encourage those with mild to moderate impairment to compensate for verbatim loss by relying on gist, as older people apparently do spontaneously. Many reasoning and decision-making tasks, as well as memory tasks, can be accomplished with high levels of performance using gist representations of reasoning principles applied to gist representations of the background facts (Reyna et al., 2003). For instance, the gist of the class inclusion task is that the cows must be more numerous than the animals because of their inclusion relation, not because of the exact numbers of cows, horses, and animals.

An advantage of gist representations is their robustness to interference. For example, verbatim memory accuracy goes down over a series of sentence verification trials, because prior judgments interfere with fragile verbatim memories, but gist accuracy remains relatively stable (Brainerd & Reyna, 1993). It makes sense that human information processing would gravitate toward a stable form of information representation. However, gist representations are also a source of interference when they usurp verbatim memories in tasks that require such memories. We have seen that gist-based false memories increase from childhood to adulthood in paradigms such as the DRM list-learning task. Indeed, the increase in verbatim memory accuracy in such tasks (which would enable recollection rejection of false memories) is overcome by the greater increase in gist-based false memories.

As in false memory, an inaccurate response in reasoning often requires the wrong response (or representations supporting it) to be accessible and, simultaneously, the failure to access information that would lead to rejection of that wrong response. An effective recipe for creating cognitive illusions, then, would be a highly accessible gist, such as a compelling image or stereotype, and a scenario that did not cue contradictory principles. The Linda problem, or conjunction fallacy, is an example of retrieval interference. More generally, people make judgments based on the information they retrieve, despite knowing additional or conflicting information that would change their judgments. To the degree that cues distract or misdirect reasoning away from relevant information, this is retrieval interference.

Highly effective illusions combine multiple sources of interference. Processing interference caused by overlapping classes can create initial confusion, which is then exploited by compelling gist representations that seem relevant but are not. In class-inclusion reasoning, children and adults focus on the relations between subsets and respond to superficial cues that the question concerns relative magnitude (e.g., are there *more* cows or animals). Adults eventually reject the compelling gist about subsets and retrieve their knowledge about inclusion relations. Multiple overlapping sets, as in conditional probability judgments, produce more processing interference than partial overlapping sets. Researchers have pointed to improvement in resistance to interference of all kinds—representational, retrieval, and processing—as children develop (Dempster, 1992).

Although we have discussed different kinds of tasks, we have explained performance using a limited set of theoretical concepts: stored knowledge of facts and reasoning principles, verbatim and gist representations of current information, a fuzzy- (gist-) processing preference, retrieval of facts and principles depending on cues in the question or task, and application of retrieved facts or principles to representations to accomplish the task. These theoretical concepts have been applied to memory, reasoning, and judgment tasks (as well as decision-making tasks; see Reyna, 2004; Reyna & Brainerd, 1991a, 1995; Reyna et al., 2003). In many instances, it is possible to use either memory representations or reasoning to answer the question. In class inclusion, for example, it is possible to solve the problems correctly by simply retrieving the inclusion principle; remembering the numbers of cows and horses is immaterial. However, remembering the display and comparing 7 cows with 10 animals also yields the correct answer. In word memory tasks, people can retrieve words from verbatim memory, or they can infer the words by reconstructing gist. At the level of processing, therefore, it is difficult to draw a clear line between memory and reasoning or judgment.

In sum, fuzzy-trace theory offers a process-level account of interference phenomena that differentiates multiple locations in a chain of cognitive processes where interference can intrude. Encoding, representation, retrieval, and processing operations are each susceptible to the effects of interference, and the relative degree to which interference disrupts each of these operations varies with the developmental status of the subject. The theory thus suggests specific ways in which interference could potentially be controlled. By increasing the salience of key retrieval cues in the environment, relevant representations and reasoning principles can be prompted, and attention can be drawn away from inappropriate gists and decision rules. Manipulations that facilitate the memorial segregation of members of overlapping classes can decrease susceptibility to processing interference. Given the developmental trajectory of gist and verbatim memories and the asymmetrical contribution of these representations in patients with Alzheimer's disease, different manipulations may be effective for different developmental groups.

References

Adam, M. B., & Reyna, V. F. (2005). Coherence and correspondence criteria for rationality: Experts' estimation of risks of sexually transmitted infections. *Journal of Behavioral Decision Making, 18,* 169–186.

Balota, D. A., Cortese, M. J., Duchek, J. M., Adams, D., Roediger, H. L., McDermott, K. B., & Yerys, B. E. (1999). Veridical and false memories in healthy older adults and in dementia of the Alzheimer's type. *Cognitive Neuropsychology, 16,* 361–384.

Bechara, A., Damasio, A. R., Damasio, H., & Anderson, S. W. (1994). Insensitivity to future consequences following damage to human prefrontal cortex. *Cognition, 10,* 7–15.

Bjorklund, D. F. (1987). How changes in knowledge base contribute to the development of children's memory. *Developmental Review, 7,* 93–130.

Bjorklund, D. (1989). *Children's thinking: Developmental function and individual differences.* Pacific Grove, CA: Brooks/Cole.

Bjorklund, D. F., & Hock, H. H. (1982). Age differences in the temporal locus of memory organization in children's recall. *Journal of Experimental Child Psychology, 33,* 347–362.

Brainerd, C. J., Holliday, R. E., & Reyna, V. F. (2004). Behavioral measurement of remembering phenomenologies: So simple a child can do it. *Child Development, 75,* 505–522.

Brainerd, C. J., & Kaszor, P. (1974). An analysis of two proposed sources of children's class-inclusion errors. *Developmental Psychology, 4,* 633–643.

Brainerd, C. J., Payne, D. G., Wright, R., & Reyna, V. F. (2003). Phantom recall. *Journal of Memory and Language, 48,* 445–467.

Brainerd, C. J., & Reyna, V. F. (1990a). Gist is the grist: Fuzzy-trace theory and the new intuitionism. *Developmental Review, 10,* 3–47.

Brainerd, C. J., & Reyna, V. F. (1990b). Inclusion illusions: Fuzzy-trace theory and perceptual salience effects in cognitive development. *Developmental Review, 10,* 365–403.

Brainerd, C. J., & Reyna, V. F. (1993). Memory independence and memory interference in cognitive development. *Psychological Review, 100,* 42–67.

Brainerd, C. J., & Reyna, V. F. (1995a). Autosuggestibility in memory development. *Cognitive Psychology, 28,* 65–101.

Brainerd, C. J., & Reyna, V. F. (1995b). Learning difficulty, learning opportunities, and the development of forgetting. *Developmental Psychology, 31,* 252–262.

Brainerd, C. J., & Reyna, V. F. (1998). When things that never happened are easier to remember than things that did. *Psychological Science, 9,* 484–489.

Brainerd, C. J., & Reyna, V. F. (2002). Fuzzy-trace theory and false memory. *Current Directions in Psychological Science, 11,* 164–169.

Brainerd, C. J., & Reyna, V. F. (2005a, October). *Conjoint recognition and the development of recollection and familiarity.* Paper presented at the Cognitive Development Society Fourth Biennial Meeting, San Diego, CA.

Brainerd, C. J., & Reyna, V. F. (2005b). *The science of false memory.* New York: Oxford University Press.

Brainerd, C. J., Reyna, V. F., & Forrest, T. J. (2002). Are young children susceptible to the false-memory illusion? *Child Development, 73,* 1363–1377.

Brainerd, C. J., Reyna, V. F., & Mojardin, A. H. (1999). Conjoint recognition. *Psychological Review, 106,* 160–179.

Brainerd, C. J., Reyna, V. F., Wright, R., & Mojardin, A. H. (2003). Recollection rejection: False-memory editing in children and adults. *Psychological Review, 110,* 762–784.

Brainerd, C. J., Wright, R., Reyna, V. F., & Mojardin, A. H. (2001). Conjoint recognition and phantom recollection. *Journal of Experimental Psychology: Learning, Memory, and Cognition, 27,* 307–327.

Brainerd, C. J., Wright, R., Reyna, V. F., & Payne, D. G. (2002). Dual retrieval processes in free and associative recall. *Journal of Memory and Language, 46,* 120–152.

Budson, A. E., Daffner, K. R., Desikan, R., & Schacter, D. L. (2000). When false recognition is unopposed by true recognition: Gist-based memory distortion in Alzheimer's disease. *Neuropsychology, 14,* 277–287.

Dempster, F. N. (1992). The rise and fall of the inhibitory mechanism: Toward a unified theory of cognitive development and aging. *Developmental Review, 12,* 45–75.

Eddy, D. M. (1982). Probabilistic reasoning in clinical medicine: Problems and opportunities. In D. Kahneman, P. Slovic, & A. Tversky (Eds.), *Judgment under uncertainty: Heuristics and biases* (pp. 249–267). New York: Cambridge University Press.

Erickson, T. D., & Mattson, M. E. (1981). From words to meaning: A semantic illusion. *Journal of Verbal Learning and Verbal Behavior, 20,* 540–551.

Estes, W. K. (1976). The cognitive side of probability learning. *Psychological Review, 83,* 37–64.

Gallo, D. A. (2004). Using recall to reduce false recognition. *Journal of Experimental Psychology: Learning, Memory, and Cognition, 30,* 120–128.

Kensinger, E. A., & Schacter, D. L. (1999). When true memories suppress false memories: Effects of aging. *Cognitive Neuropsychology, 16,* 399–415.

Koutstaal, W., & Schacter, D. L. (1997). Gist based false recognition of pictures in older and younger adults. *Journal of Memory and Language, 37,* 555–583.

Levin, I. P., Schneider, S. L., & Gaeth, G. J. (1998). All frames are not created equal: A typology and critical analysis of framing effects. *Organizational Behavior and Human Decision Processes, 76,* 149–188.

Lloyd, F. J., & Reyna, V. F. (2001). A Web exercise in evidence-based medicine using cognitive theory. *Journal of General Internal Medicine, 16,* 94–99.

Nigg, J. T. (2000). On inhibition/disinhibition in developmental psychopathology: Views from cognitive and personality psychology and a working inhibition taxonomy. *Psychological Bulletin, 126,* 220–246.

Nisbett, R. E., & Ross, L. D. (1980). *Human inference: Strategies and shortcomings of social judgment.* Englewood Cliffs, NJ: Prentice-Hall.

Norman, K. A., & Schacter, D. L. (1997). False recognition in younger and older adults: Exploring the characteristics of illusory memories. *Memory & Cognition, 25,* 838–848.

Piaget, J. (1942). *Classes, relations, et nombres* [Classes, relations, and numbers]. Paris: Vrin.

Reder, L. (1987). Strategy selection in question answering. *Cognitive Psychology, 19,* 90–138.

Reder, L. M., & Schunn, C. D. (1996). Metacognition does not imply awareness: Strategy choice is governed by implicit learning and memory. In L. M. Reder (Ed.), *Implicit memory and metacognition* (pp. 45–77). Mahwah, NJ: Erlbaum.

Reyna, V. F. (1991). Class inclusion, the conjunction fallacy, and other cognitive illusions. *Developmental Review, 11,* 317–336.

Reyna, V. F. (1992). Reasoning, remembering, and their relationship: Social, cognitive, and developmental issues. In M. L. Howe, C. J. Brainerd, & V. F. Reyna (Eds.), *Development of long-term retention* (pp. 103–127). New York: Springer-Verlag.

Reyna, V. F. (1995). Interference effects in memory and reasoning: A fuzzy-trace theory analysis. In F. N. Dempster & C. J. Brainerd (Eds.), *Interference and inhibition in cognition* (pp. 29–61). New York: Academic Press.

Reyna, V. F. (1996). Meaning, memory and the interpretation of metaphors. In J. Mio & A. Katz (Eds.), *Metaphor: Implications and applications* (pp. 39–57). Hillsdale, NJ: Erlbaum.

Reyna, V. F. (2000). Fuzzy-trace theory and source monitoring: An evaluation of theory and false-memory data. *Learning and Individual Differences, 12,* 163–175.

Reyna, V. F. (2004). How people make decisions that involve risk: A dual-processes approach. *Current Directions in Psychological Science, 13,* 60–66.

Reyna, V. F., & Adam, M. B. (2003). Fuzzy-trace theory, risk communication, and product labeling in sexually transmitted diseases. *Risk Analysis, 23,* 325–342.

Reyna, V. F., Adam, M. B., Poirier, K., LeCroy, C. W., & Brainerd, C. J. (2005). Risky decision-making in childhood and adolescence: A fuzzy-trace theory approach. In J. Jacobs & P. Klaczynski (Eds.), *The development of children's and adolescents' judgment and decision-making* (pp. 77–106). Mahwah, NJ: Erlbaum.

Reyna, V. F., & Brainerd, C. J. (1990). Fuzzy processing in transitivity development. *Annals of Operations Research, 23,* 37–63.

Reyna, V. F., & Brainerd, C. J. (1991a). Fuzzy-trace theory and framing effects in choice: Gist extraction, truncation, and conversion. *Journal of Behavioral Decision Making, 4,* 249–262.

Reyna, V. F., & Brainerd, C. J. (1991b). Fuzzy-trace theory and the acquisition of scientific and mathematical concepts. *Learning and Individual Differences, 3,* 27–60.

Reyna, V. F., & Brainerd, C. J. (1993). Fuzzy memory and mathematics in the classroom. In R. Logie & G. Davies (Eds.), *Everyday memory* (pp. 91–119). Amsterdam: North Holland.

Reyna, V. F., & Brainerd, C. J. (1994). The origins of probability judgment: A review of data and theories. In G. Wright & P. Ayton (Eds.), *Subjective probability* (pp. 239–272). New York: Wiley.

Reyna, V. F., & Brainerd, C. J. (1995). Fuzzy-trace theory: An interim synthesis. *Learning and Individual Differences, 7,* 1–75.

Reyna, V. F., & Brainerd, C. J. (1998). Fuzzy-trace theory and false memory: New frontiers. *Journal of Experimental Child Psychology, 71,* 194–209.

Reyna, V. F., & Brainerd, C. J. (2004, July–August). *What theories of memory tell us about the brain: Implications for aging, development and impairment.* Invited plenary address presented at the 112th Annual Convention of the American Psychological Association, Honolulu, HI.

Reyna, V. F., & Farley, F. (2006). Risk and rationality in adolescent decision-making: Implications for theory, practice, and public policy. *Psychological Science in the Public Interest, 1,* 1–44.

Reyna, V. F., & Hamilton, A. J. (2001). The importance of memory in informed consent for surgical risk. *Medical Decision Making, 21,* 152–155.

Reyna, V. F., Holliday, R., & Marche, T. (2002). Explaining the development of false memories. *Developmental Review, 22,* 436–489.

Reyna, V. F., & Kiernan, B. (1994). The development of gist versus verbatim memory in sentence recognition: Effects of lexical familiarity, semantic content, encoding instructions, and retention interval. *Developmental Psychology, 30,* 178–191.

Reyna, V. F., & Kiernan, B. (1995). Children's memory and interpretation of psychological metaphors. *Metaphor and Symbolic Activity, 10,* 309–331.

Reyna, V. F., & Lloyd, F. (1997). Theories of false memory in children and adults. *Learning and Individual Differences, 9,* 95–123.

Reyna, V. F., Lloyd, F. J., & Brainerd, C. J. (2003). Memory, development, and rationality: An integrative theory of judgment and decision making. In S. Schneider & J. Shanteau (Eds.), *Emerging perspectives on judgment and decision research* (pp. 201–245). New York: Cambridge University Press.

Reyna, V. F., Lloyd, F., & Whalen, P. (2001). Genetic testing and medical decision making. *Archives of Internal Medicine, 161,* 2406–2408.

Reyna, V. F., Mills, B., Estrada, S., & Brainerd, C. J. (in press). False memory in children: Data, theory, and legal implications. In M. Toglia & D. Reed (Eds.), *The handbook of eyewitness psychology: Vol. 1. Memory for event.* Mahwah, NJ: Erlbaum.

Reyna, V. F., & Titcomb, A. L. (1997). Constraints on the suggestibility of eyewitness testimony: A fuzzy-trace theory analysis. In D. G. Payne & F. G. Conrad (Eds.), *A synthesis of basic and applied approaches to human memory* (pp. 157–174). Hillsdale, NJ: Erlbaum.

Robinson, K. J., & Roediger, H. L., III. (1997). Associative processes in false recall and false recognition. *Psychological Science, 8,* 231–237.

Roediger, H. L., III, & McDermott, K. B. (1995). Creating false memories: Remembering words not presented on lists. *Journal of Experimental Psychology: Learning, Memory, and Cognition, 21,* 803–814.

Rotello, C. M., Macmillan, N. A., & Van Tassel, G. (2000). Recall-to-reject in recognition: Evidence from ROC curves. *Journal of Memory and Language, 43,* 67–88.

Simon, H. A. (1982). *Models of bounded rationality.* Cambridge, MA: MIT Press.

Sloman, S. A., Over, D., Slovak, L., & Stibel, J. M. (2003). Frequency illusions and other fallacies. *Organizational Behavior and Human Decision Processes, 91,* 296–309.

Titcomb, A. L., & Reyna, V. F. (1995). Memory interference and misinformation effects. In F. N. Dempster & C. J. Brainerd (Eds.), *Interference and inhibition in cognition* (pp. 263–294). San Diego, CA: Academic Press.

Tversky, A., & Kahneman, D. (1983). Extensional versus intuitive reasoning: The conjunction fallacy in probability judgment. *Psychological Review, 90,* 293–315.

Tversky, A., & Koehler, D. J. (1994). Support theory: A nonextensional representation of subjective probability. *Psychological Review, 101,* 547–567.

Tun, P. A., Wingfield, A., Rosen, M. J., & Blanchard, I. (1998). Older adults show greater susceptibility to false memory than young adults: Temporal characteristics of false recognition. *Psychology and Aging, 13,* 230–241.

Wolfe, C. R. (1995). Information seeking on Bayesian conditional probability problems: A fuzzy-trace theory account. *Journal of Behavioral Decision Making, 8,* 85–108.

Wolfe, C. R., Reyna, V. F., & Brainerd, C. J. (2005). Fuzzy-trace theory: Implications for transfer in teaching and learning. In J. P. Mestre (Ed.), *Transfer of learning from a modern multidisciplinary perspective* (pp. 53–88). Greenwich, CT: Information Age Publishing.

Part V

Pathology and Psychopathology

11

Inhibition, Facilitation, and Attentional Control in Dementia of the Alzheimer's Type: The Role of Unifying Principles in Cognitive Theory Development

Mark E. Faust and David A. Balota

A central problem in cognitive science is understanding how the cognitive system, embedded in the environment, modulates the activation or accessibility of information in real time in the direction of thought and action. One attractive method of approaching this problem has been to assume a set of cognitive control processes that work to either enhance or inhibit dedicated task-related processes (e.g., Balota & Faust, 2001; Gernsbacher & Faust, 1991a, 1991b; Hasher, Zacks, & May, 1999; Smith & Jonides, 1999). Given this perspective, it is not surprising that measuring the empirical footprint of inhibitory control processes has been an important goal for many researchers (Dagenbach & Carr, 1994; Dempster & Brainerd, 1995).

Experimental paradigms such as negative priming (Sullivan, Faust, & Balota, 1995; Tipper, 1985), inhibition of return (Faust & Balota, 1997; Posner & Cohen, 1984), Stroop color naming (MacLeod, 1991; Spieler, Balota, & Faust, 1996), task switching (Mayr & Keele, 2000), directed forgetting (Zacks, Radvansky, & Hasher, 1996), and stop-signal processing (Logan, Cowan, & Davis, 1984) have all played a prominent role in this research effort. However, as reflected in the motivation for this volume—to discuss the utility of inhibitory mechanisms in cognition—there are some who now seriously question the utility of inhibition at the level of explaining cognitive processes both within and across groups of subjects (e.g., Burke, 1997; MacLeod, Dodd, Sheard, Wilson, & Bibi, 2003). These recent arguments have been driven by the following:

- the failure to find a consensus inhibitory account of some phenomena consistent with the extant data (e.g., see Neill & Valdes, 1996; for the

The present work was supported by National Institute on Aging Grants PO1 AG03991 and RO1 AG10193.

debate on the interpretation of negative-priming effects, see Tipper, 2001),

- the appearance in the literature of hard-to-dismiss noninhibitory accounts of other phenomena that do have a consensus inhibitory interpretation (e.g., inhibition of return; Pratt, Spalek, & Bradshaw, 1999), and
- lack of a consistent definition of inhibition in the literature.

Although these debates have often focused on the need for specific inhibitory mechanisms in theoretical explanations of processing in a specific task under specific controlled conditions, we argue in this chapter that a broader view of these issues is possible and useful.

Questions About the Utility of Inhibitory Mechanisms

Before detailing the particular theoretical perspective we have taken in our work, it is useful to specify our position on the topic that is the motivation for this volume: to discuss the utility of inhibitory mechanisms in cognition.

First, we consider inhibitory accounts to be useful in a number of empirical domains, and we believe that alternative accounts have not been sufficiently detailed to understand how noninhibitory accounts handle the data. Second, we argue that ultimately, one could raise concerns about the utility of activation mechanisms that are similar to those raised about inhibitory mechanisms. Of course, it is always useful to consider the explanatory power of a mechanism within a particular task, but to question the general utility of activation and inhibition mechanisms in accounting for cognitive behavior seems far too limiting a stance.

Inhibition or Conflict Resolution?

We believe that logical argument and empirical evidence indicate that although there may be alternative accounts of some inhibitory processes, the vast majority of the data are best understood in terms of inhibitory mechanisms. For example, the finding from the simple Stroop color-naming task is that subjects are slower to name the color of a word when it is in an incongruent color name (e.g., the word *red* presented in green) compared with when the color and word are congruent or when a "neutral" stimulus is presented such as a row of *X*s or an unrelated word. One noninhibitory account of the observed behavioral slowing involves a type of conflict resolution in which subjects experience no need to inhibit the word dimension in this task but rather are slower because there is a conflicting dimension, and resolution of the conflict simply takes longer (similar arguments have been made concerning the negative-priming task). We are confused as to how dimension selection might occur in this stage of processing in the 50- to 75-millisecond time frame reported by many studies in the literature (e.g., Spieler et al., 1996) if it does not involve a type of inhibitory control over task-inappropriate information. This resolution-of-conflict approach needs to be specific enough to indicate how the subject selects

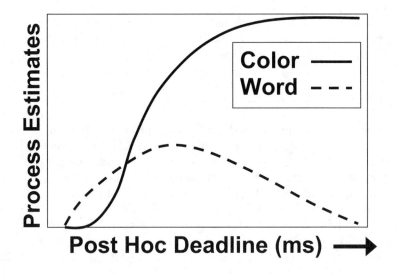

Figure 11.1. Color and word process estimates in the Stroop task as a function of time using the process dissociation procedure (Lindsay & Jacoby, 1994). Process estimates were obtained by gradually increasing the post hoc time deadline for responding (see Spieler et al., 1996, for details). Adapted from "Stroop Performance in Healthy Younger and Older Adults and in Individuals With Dementia of the Alzheimer's Type," by D. H. Spieler, D. A. Balota, and M. E. Faust, 1996, *Journal of Experimental Psychology: Human Perception and Performance, 22,* p. 473. Copyright 1996 by the American Psychological Association.

the appropriate dimension in the face of a strong prepotent pathway without some control of that pathway. Moreover, once one assumes "control" of the prepotent pathway, how does this occur without inhibition?

An inhibitory account that we favor suggests that when the stimulus is presented, multiple pathways are automatically engaged and compete for output. Of course, the greater practice on the word dimension results in early word processing that is initially stronger than the processing of the color dimension. Hence, the word dimension initially pulls attention and must be controlled. We argue that across time, a top-down control signal tied to the representation of task demands begins to exert control over the prepotent word dimension. Figure 11.1 displays the influence of the word and color pathway across time as estimated by Jacoby's process dissociation procedure (Lindsay & Jacoby, 1994) from a study by Spieler et al. (1996). As is evident in the figure, initially there is a strong signal from the word dimension that indeed is suppressed across time. It is this inhibition of partially activated but irrelevant pathways that we argue is fundamental to conflict resolution across many domains.

Such inhibition could be short lived during the act of conflict resolution and may not have lingering effects beyond the act of selection. It is unclear, at least to us, how the time course of conflict resolution occurs without such an inhibitory mechanism. Our analysis of the contributions of the word and color processes during the typical Stroop task (Spieler et al., 1996) leads us to question whether other approaches that fail to modulate strength of processing in the irrelevant pathway, such as that of Cohen, Dunbar, and McClelland (1990), where control processes simply globally enhance the color pathway, can produce the basic pattern depicted in Figure 11.1.

Is There Unequivocal Evidence for Activation Mechanisms?

The current volume emphasizes the discussion of the utility of inhibitory mechanisms to explain aspects of cognitive performance. However, no one is actively questioning the utility of facilitatory processes. In fact, one could argue that facilitatory mechanisms are just as vulnerable to these concerns. For example, for the Stroop facilitation effect, one clearly needs to include some neutral baseline to measure facilitation. In the Stroop task, this typically involves a row of Xs or a noncolor word. How can one be assured that the facilitation in the Stroop task is due to the facilitation of the color response being primed by the word dimension? Is it not possible that the reason one observes facilitation in the Stroop task is because there is inhibition from the neutral noncolor words in color naming? What independent evidence is there that there is facilitation? The answer would seem to depend on the appropriate baseline condition against which to measure facilitation and inhibition. More than 20 years ago, Jonides and Mack (1984) critically reviewed the literature on the selection of an appropriate neutral condition and emphasized the importance of converging evidence. We argue that the vast majority of the paradigms that have measured facilitation and have interpreted the facilitatory effects as reflecting activation mechanisms fall prey to many of the same concerns that have been leveled against inhibitory mechanisms (MacLeod et al., 2003). However, instead of promoting dustbowl empiricism and simply identifying conditions in which behavioral facilitation (benefits) and behavioral inhibition (costs) occur, we believe that the mechanisms of both activation and inhibition are very useful in helping guide cognitive theory.

Aging and Dementia of the Alzheimer's Type: Toward an Attentional Control Framework

The global cognitive deficits associated with dementia of the Alzheimer's type (DAT) provide an opportunity to demonstrate the usefulness of viewing inhibitory and facilitatory processes as meaningful categories of processing that transcend the specifics of the particular process accounts of phenomena associated with specific experimental paradigms and allow a broader picture of the underlying processing deficit. Evidence from broad batteries of neuropsychological tests (Salthouse & Becker, 1998) and from studies of the progression of neurodegeneration (Wenk, 2003) suggests that the global cognitive deficit that marks DAT has at its core impairment of attentional control (Balota & Faust, 2001; Perry & Hodges, 1999). In fact, measures of executive function and attentional control may be the best predictors of progression to clinically diagnosable dementia (Rapp & Reischies, 2005). In this chapter, we present evidence from a variety of experimental tasks suggesting that individuals with

DAT experience a deficit in inhibitory control processes associated with regulation of task-inappropriate information in contrast to a relative preservation of facilitatory processes that activate information related to objects and events in the environment. Our proposed inhibitory control deficit for DAT bears some resemblance to the proposal by Hasher and Zacks and their colleagues (e.g., Hasher et al., 1999) of a similar, albeit less pronounced, deficit in healthy aging.

We begin with presentation of an attentional control framework to motivate the examination of empirical work testing three general processing hypotheses regarding the processing deficits underlying the cognitive decline in DAT. We then discuss the neuropsychology and neuropathology associated with the cognitive decline in DAT. We present a line of research motivated by the attentional control framework addressing three major classes of processing deficits: (a) facilitatory processes associated with stimulus-driven activation of information, (b) inhibitory control over task-inappropriate pathways, and (c) the representation and maintenance of task goals and strategies.

Attentional Control

The environment provides people with multiple objects and events simultaneously toward which they can act in a variety of ways. A large body of research suggests that visual objects and events can initiate a cascade of processes that capture response systems even when there is little or no conscious intention to act (Tipper, 2001). In the case of eating dinner, for example, because of moment-by-moment changes in goals, one might pick up a fork to eat or pick up a cup to drink. This example has important implications. First, a wider range of information is activated by perceptual processes (e.g., cup and fork) than is appropriate given the physical constraints of motor output systems (e.g., pick up the fork). Second, processing pathways associated with multiple objects, events, or stimulus characteristics (e.g., color, form, or motion of an object) compete to drive output systems. Hence, a central function of selective attention is to prevent actions from being inappropriately driven by the most perceptually salient object or event (Diamond, 1990).

Another issue highlighted by the choice to act toward an object at the dinner table involves the role of mental set in representing task demands that differentiate task-appropriate and task-inappropriate information (Norman & Shallice, 1986; Rogers & Monsell, 1995). This perspective stresses the role that the representation of goals and strategies plays in selecting the appropriate action given the current task goal (e.g., pick up the fork with the dominant hand); in avoiding other, less-appropriate actions (e.g., pick up the cup with the dominant hand); and in constraining other possible actions (e.g., it is impolite to pick up the fork and cup simultaneously with different hands).

What this analysis suggests is a global view of everyday cognition where well-learned stimulus-driven processing pathways compete to activate well-learned motor sequences to act toward these objects and events. Control over these processing pathways is required in a variety of situations (e.g., Posner & DiGirolamo, 1998), such as when new or complex actions are required, when error checking is emphasized, or when task goals change. The present discussion centers on attentional control in situations where task-appropriate and task-inappropriate pathways interfere with each other in the sense that they push toward mutually exclusive responses from the same effector (Balota & Faust, 2001).

Attentional Control Framework

Balota and Faust (2001) proposed a theoretical framework for understanding DAT-related changes in attentional control (see Figure 11.2). Central to the attentional control framework is the hierarchical control over low-level perceptual and memory processes that compete for processing resources and access to response systems. Control over processing pathways is most directly exerted by the attentional control system responsible for detecting conflict between

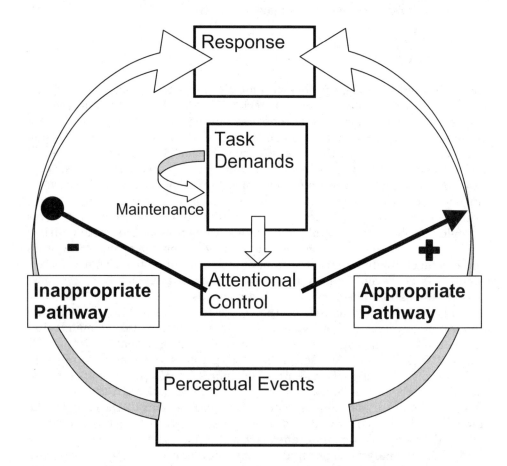

Figure 11.2. An attentional control framework applicable to situations where the task set must regulate potential conflict from task-appropriate and task-inappropriate processing pathways. From *The Handbook of Neuropsychology: Aging and Dementia* (2nd ed., p. 71), by F. Boller and S. Cappa (Eds.), 2001. New York: Elsevier Science. Copyright 2001 by Elsevier. Adapted with permission from Elsevier.

processes (Botvinick, Braver, Barch, Carter, & Cohen, 2001) and for select-ing task-appropriate pathways as well as attenuating processes in task-inappropriate pathways. The notion is that there needs to be a signal that the current configuration of control signals is not appropriate to accomplish the task goals. Hence, when relatively poor performance (i.e., failure to accomplish the task goals) occurs, there is a signal (possibly from the anterior cingulate) that indicates a need for reconfiguration of the attentional control system. This system is in turn controlled by memory representations of the task goals and procedures and strategies for task performance (Cohen, Aston-Jones, & Gil-zenrat, 2004). We propose that the effectiveness of attentional control depends on the ability to regulate the relative strength of task-appropriate and task-inappropriate pathways and the ability to maintain the representation of task demands.

This framework gets much of its inspiration from the supervisory attention system proposed by Norman and Shallice (1986), as well as Baddeley's (1986) proposals regarding executive control of working memory (see also chap. 7, this volume; Engle, Tuholski, Laughlin, & Conway, 1999). We suggest that this framework is useful for understanding performance in a wide range of tasks involving processing of multiple objects or stimuli with multiple dimen-sions (e.g., the form and color of words during the Stroop color-naming task).

With regard to the neural substrates underlying control over low-level processing pathways, a network of frontal and cingulate areas has been found to be related to the selection of appropriate processing pathways and detection of conflict in processing pathways (Cohen et al., 2004; Posner & DiGirolamo, 1998) as well as the maintenance of task demands (Smith & Jonides, 1999). Many of these areas overlap with the areas identified in the studies reviewed later in this chapter as being involved in the neurodegenerative changes in DAT. Consideration of the attentional control framework (Balota & Faust, 2001) and the pattern of neuropsychological and neurodegenerative deficits in DAT might lead one to predict that DAT would lead to impairments in the ability to regulate the processes in task-inappropriate pathways and maintain a stable representation of task demands but would most likely not lead to significant impairments in the automatic activation of information related to perceptual events.

Cognitive Decline in Dementia of the Alzheimer's Type: A Brief Review

DAT is the most common dementing illness, with a prevalence of 3% for the 70- to 74-year-old age range, rising to 24% in the 85- to 89-year-old age range, that represents 60% to 70% of dementia diagnoses overall (Fratiglioni & Rocca, 2001). DAT involves progressive neuropathological changes, including but not limited to the growth of amyloid-containing plaques and neurofibrillary tangles (NFTs). Of particular interest for our discussion are neurodegenerative changes in the cingulate and frontal cortices (Choi, Lim, Monteiro, & Reisberg, 2005; Thompson et al., 2003; Wenk, 2003), areas that have been associated with executive function and attentional control (Botvinick et al., 2001; Posner &

Dehaene, 1994; Smith & Jonides, 1999). NFT-related neuropathology is typically most pronounced in the medial temporal lobe early and spreads along cortico–cortico connections to temporal, parietal, and frontal lobe association cortices (Nagy et al., 1999), with a relative sparing of primary and secondary sensory and motor areas until very late in the progression. It has only recently become possible to image the distribution of amyloid, the primary component in amyloid plaques, in vivo. Positron-emission tomography (PET) studies using newly developed radiotracers that bind to the form of amyloid in amyloid-containing plaques have found marked amyloid depositions in the frontal, posterior temporal, and inferior parietal lobes (Klunk et al., 2004; Verhoeff et al., 2004). The radiotracer binding was greatest in the frontal lobes of DAT patients, in contrast to almost nondetectable binding in the frontal lobes of healthy controls. These results suggest an amyloid-related disease process that is most pronounced in the frontal lobes early in DAT.

The relation of amyloid plaques and tangles to cognitive declines in DAT has been controversial. Whereas most studies have found that NFTs are more strongly associated with dementia severity than are amyloid plaques (e.g., Berg et al., 1998), the density and distribution of amyloid plaques may be better at discriminating DAT and healthy brain aging (e.g., McKeel et al., 2004) and in predicting the relative decline among broad domains of cognitive functioning (e.g., Kanne, Balota, Storandt, McKeel, & Morris, 1998).

DAT is a progressive dementia syndrome involving gradual declines in at least two broad domains of cognitive function, usually including memory, in the absence of other dementing disorders such as stroke, vitamin deficiency, or thyroid malfunction (McKhann et al., 1984). Definite DAT can be determined only by a brain biopsy for DAT-related plaques and NFTs. DAT has been traditionally characterized as primarily involving early impairments of memory, expanding to include impairments in other domains such as language, executive, and perceptual functions. It is now clear that DAT involves impairments in attention and executive function, and there is broad support in the literature suggesting that declines in attention and executive function are present in the earliest stages of DAT (Baddeley, Baddeley, Bucks, & Wilcock, 2001; Balota & Faust, 2001; Parasuraman & Greenwood, 1998; Perry & Hodges, 1999). Recent studies of broad batteries (i.e., including multiple tests across several cognitive domains) of neuropsychological tests indicate that most of the DAT-related variability (i.e., predictive of diagnostic group in the early stages) in scores can be explained by a general factor (Ownby, Loewenstein, Schram, & Acevedo, 2004; Salthouse & Becker, 1998). This finding suggests that early in the progression of DAT, a limited number of cognitive processes common to a wide range of tasks are impaired.

Ownby et al. (2004) also found that memory and verbal tests contributed to prediction of diagnosis above and beyond the ability of the general factor. This finding suggests that early DAT tends to be dominated by a progressive memory impairment and by a general cognitive deficit reflecting a breakdown in attention and executive function. In support of this view, a growing number of studies have reported that performance on tasks of attention and executive control in preclinical populations are the best predictors of later diagnosis of DAT (Amieva et al., 2004; Fabrigoule et al., 1998; Rapp & Reischies, 2005).

It is interesting to note that there is evidence from behavioral genetic studies that also is consistent with the role of early attentional breakdowns in DAT. In particular, there has been considerable work investigating the influence of the apolipoprotein E (*APOE*, related to amyloid regulation in the brain; Lahiri, Sambamurti, & Bennett, 2004) on genetic subtypes as predictors for the development of DAT. There are three allele types of the *APOE* protein: ε2, ε3, and ε4; ε4 carriers have a greater risk of developing the disease than ε2 or ε3 carriers. Work by Greenwood, Lambert, Sunderland, and Parasuraman (2005) showed that healthy control ε4 carriers appear to have deficits in spatial attention tasks compared with ε2 or ε3 carriers, even though these groups do not differ on standard psychometric tasks. Moreover, a recent meta-analysis by Small, Rosnick, Fratiglioni, and Backman (2004) showed that differences in performance on attention and working memory tasks was the strongest discriminator (as reflected by effect size) between ε4 carriers and noncarriers. Small et al. also pointed out that unfortunately, this is the area where there is the least empirical evidence.

In a similar vein, Rosen, Bergeson, Putnam, Harwell, and Sunderland (2002) explored the relation between *APOE* status and the central executive component of working memory. Using an operation span task (Engle et al., 1999) that requires subjects to divide their attention between performing mathematical operations and remembering words, Rosen et al. found that even though the ε4 and non-ε4 individuals did not differ on a set of standardized neuropsychological tests, the ε4 group showed divided attention deficits on the working memory task compared with the non-ε4 group. It is interesting that the ε4 group also showed primacy deficits on the operation span task, which requires divided attention, yet there was no *APOE* group difference for primacy scores from the standard Buschke selective reminding task (Buschke, 1973), which does not require divided attention. Thus, *APOE* genotype was specifically related to attentional deficits in the absence of overall cognitive deficits as measured by standard neuropsychological tests.

More recently, Rosen et al. (2005) reported category fluency deficits in nondemented individuals with the ε4 allele compared with individuals without the ε4 allele. They also found a negative relation between operation span performance and between-cluster retrieval time, suggesting that deficits in attentional capacity in the ε4 group may interfere with the ability to shift attention among categories in the fluency task. Again, the ε4 group exhibited normal performance on standardized neuropsychological tests. Taken together, these studies indicate that subtle aspects of attentional processing may be deficient in nondemented individuals with the ε4 allele and may serve as an early marker for DAT in the absence of deficits in more global measures of cognition.

Facilitatory Processes in Task-Appropriate Pathways

We now turn to an examination of candidate-processing deficits motivated by the attentional control framework (Balota & Faust, 2001). We first consider evidence for a preservation of the processes that allow context (e.g., cues and primes) to activate task-appropriate information. Faust and Balota (1997) used a variant of the spatial cueing procedure developed by Posner and colleagues (e.g., Posner, 1980) and found that the appearance of a peripheral spatial cue facilitated later target detection equivalently for healthy older adults and individuals with DAT. Similarly, Parasuraman, Greenwood, Haxby, and Grady (1992) reported equivalent facilitatory spatial cue effects using a target discrimination task. The ability of individuals with DAT to use a spatial cue to facilitate early perceptual processing seems to be relatively preserved in early DAT (Balota & Faust, 2001).

Another method of probing the ability of the cognitive system to use prior context to facilitate the activation of task-appropriate information is repetition priming, in which prior presentation of pictures or words facilitates subsequent identification on a second presentation. Balota and Duchek (1991) assessed word-naming performance for words that either had or had not been named in a previous block of naming trials. As depicted in Figure 11.3, the results indicated equivalent repetition-priming effects in healthy older adults and individuals with DAT. A similar finding has been reported for repetition priming in picture naming in DAT (Gabrieli et al., 1999) and in lexical decision tasks (Balota & Ferraro, 1996). In general, repetition priming in identification tasks has been found to be preserved in DAT (Russo & Spinnler, 1994).

Semantic priming, the facilitation of word identification when a target word is related to a just-presented word (e.g., *nurse* following *doctor*) in comparison with *word identification*, when a target word is unrelated to a just-presented word (e.g., *nurse* following *chair*), has been argued to involve a component of the automatic spread of activation through semantic memory that facilitates identification of a related target word (Balota, 1983). It has been well documented that DAT results in impaired semantic memory (Greene & Hodges, 1996). Some studies have found evidence in support of disruptions in the organization and structure of semantic knowledge such that concepts, concept attributes, and the links between concepts are lost or degraded because of neural degeneration in critical cortical areas (e.g., Salmon, Butters, & Chan, 1999). Other researchers have suggested that DAT, at least in the early stages, reflects a relative preservation of the structure and organization of semantic knowledge accompanied by a breakdown in controlled attentional processes associated with accessing semantic information (e.g., Balota & Faust, 2001; Chenery, 1996). Studies of semantic priming using brief prime–target intervals (i.e., stimulus onset asynchrony) and/or word naming to assess mechanisms of automatic spreading activation throughout semantic networks have typically found preserved automatic priming in DAT (Balota & Faust, 2001; Chenery, 1996). Some studies of semantic priming have found hyperpriming (i.e., larger priming effects) in DAT groups (e.g., Chertkow, Bub, & Bergman, 1994), but the demonstration of consistent hyperpriming of automatic semantic priming above and beyond general slowing of response remains controversial.

For example, Balota and Duchek (1991) used a word-naming task to assess semantic-priming effects (e.g., naming *organ* following *kidney*). As depicted in Figure 11.3, the results indicated equivalent, or perhaps somewhat increased, semantic priming effects in healthy older adult and DAT groups. Participants in this study named both the prime and target items, and so prime–target

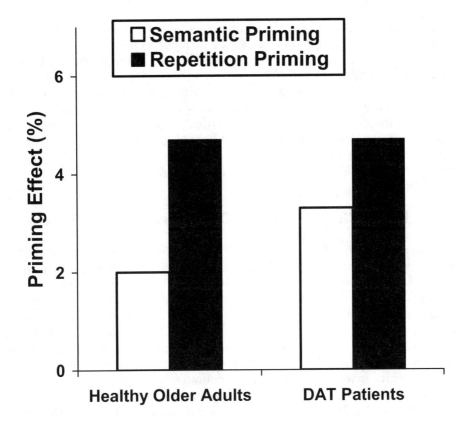

Figure 11.3. Repetition- and semantic-priming effects in word naming (Balota & Duchek, 1991) as a function of group. Priming effects are presented as a mean percentage; that is, the priming differential (i.e., mean response latency for the experimental condition, repetition or related, minus the comparison condition, nonrepetition or unrelated) is expressed as a percentage of the comparison mean. DAT = dementia of the Alzheimer's type. From "Semantic Priming Effects, Lexical Repetition Effects, and Contextual Disambiguation Effects in Healthy Aged Individuals and Individuals With Senile Dementia of the Alzheimer Type," by D. A. Balota and J. M. Duchek, 1991, *Brain and Language, 40,* p. 190. Copyright 1991 by Elsevier. Adapted with permission from Elsevier.

onsets were not under strict control. Studies that have used briefly presented primes and brief stimulus onset asynchronies have also reported preserved automatic semantic priming in DAT (e.g., Balota, Watson, Duchek, & Ferraro, 1999; Hartman, 1991; Ober & Shenaut, 1995). It is interesting that Balota, Black, and Cheney (1992) reported age-related changes in semantic priming at longer stimulus onset asynchronies, and similar findings have been reported for DAT (Ober & Shenaut, 1995), consistent with declines in attentional control over the access to semantic information in DAT (Balota & Faust, 2001; Chenery, 1996). In fact, a meta-analysis (Ober & Shenaut, 1995) indicated that there appears to be relatively little DAT-related change in automatic semantic priming, but semantic-priming effects do appear to increase under conditions that promote attentional control. Moreover, there is some evidence that as DAT progresses in severity, semantic impairments move from problems with attentional control to degradation of representations (e.g., Daum, Riesch, Sartori, & Birbaumer, 1996).

The findings from studies of spatial cueing, repetition priming, and semantic priming converge on a consistent conclusion that the ability of contextual information to drive low-level automatic activation of task-relevant information is relatively well preserved in DAT. This conclusion contrasts with the findings we present in the next section: that tasks that involve informational conflict result in DAT-related declines in performance.

Inhibitory Control Over Task-Inappropriate Pathways

Many words have multiple meanings, and therefore one central task of language comprehension is to use the prior context to enhance the context-appropriate word meanings and suppress the context-inappropriate word meanings (Gernsbacher & Faust, 1991a, 1991b; see also chap. 6, this volume). For example, the word *organ* is a homograph in that the same written form can refer to a musical instrument or a body part. If DAT results in a breakdown in the ability to exert cognitive control over situations where task-appropriate and task-inappropriate information is active, then one might observe DAT-related deficits in how the language comprehension system deals with the multiple interpretations that are often available when a word is presented.

Balota and Duchek (1991) had participants name three different types of sequentially presented (one word at a time) word triplets: concordant (*music–organ–piano*), discordant (*kidney–organ–piano*), and unrelated (*kidney–ceiling–piano*). The basic idea of the experiment was to see how varying the prime words (i.e., the first and second words in each triplet) would affect the size of the semantic-priming effect for naming the target (third) word. For the concordant triplets, the first prime and the target were related to the same meaning of the intervening homograph (*organ*). That is, the first prime should bias the meaning of the subsequent second prime that is consistent with (i.e., related to) the target. The discordant triplets, by contrast, included first primes and targets that were related to different meanings of the intervening homograph. That is, the first prime should bias the meaning of the subsequent second prime that is inconsistent with the target. As presented in Figure 11.4, naming latencies to the third word indicated that both groups produced semantic priming in the concordant condition compared with the unrelated condition. However, only the DAT group produced semantic priming for the discordant condition. This result suggests that individuals with DAT experienced a breakdown in the attentional selection of the appropriate interpretation of the homograph (*organ*) based on context in that there was a decline presumably due to a breakdown in the ability to suppress the context-inappropriate meaning of the intervening homograph.

Faust, Balota, Duchek, Gernsbacher, and Smith (1997) observed a similar DAT-related decline in the ability to use context to suppress the contextually appropriate meaning of a homograph during sentence comprehension. Partici-

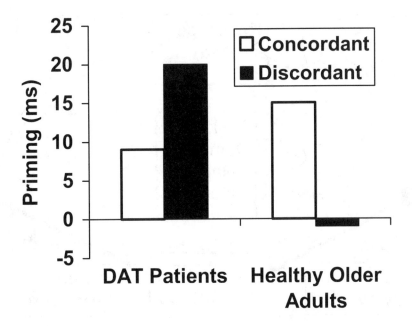

Figure 11.4. Semantic-priming effects (in milliseconds) in naming the third word in a triplet (Balota & Duchek, 1991) as a function of cue (second word) type and group. DAT = dementia of the Alzheimer's type. There were three types of triplet: concordant (*music–organ–piano*), discordant (*kidney–organ–piano*), and unrelated (*kidney–ceiling–piano*). Priming is presented as mean response time for the third word in unrelated triplets minus the concordant or discordant triplet mean. From "Semantic Priming Effects, Lexical Repetition Effects, and Contextual Disambiguation Effects in Healthy Aged Individuals and Individuals With Senile Dementia of the Alzheimer Type," by D. A. Balota and J. M. Duchek, 1991, *Brain and Language, 40,* p. 192. Copyright 1991 by Elsevier. Adapted with permission from Elsevier.

pants made a relatedness judgment to a word (e.g., *ace*) following either a sentence with a sentence-final homograph (e.g., "He dug with a spade") or a sentence that ended with an unambiguous word (e.g., "He dug with a shovel"). The major finding was that individuals with DAT had more difficulty rejecting the word *ace* when it followed the sentence context that ended with the homograph (*spade*). Thus, it appears that individuals with DAT were failing to use the disambiguating sentence context to guide suppression of the context-inappropriate interpretation of the homograph. This result converges with the results obtained by Balota and Duchek (1991), and the results of both studies are consistent with the notion that DAT individuals have difficulty controlling or inhibiting partially activated processing pathways associated with context-inappropriate information. This observation also fits nicely with the attentional control framework (see Figure 11.2), in which the task demands of language comprehension require use of the prior context to select for context-appropriate information and against context-inappropriate information activated in low-level word-recognition processing pathways.

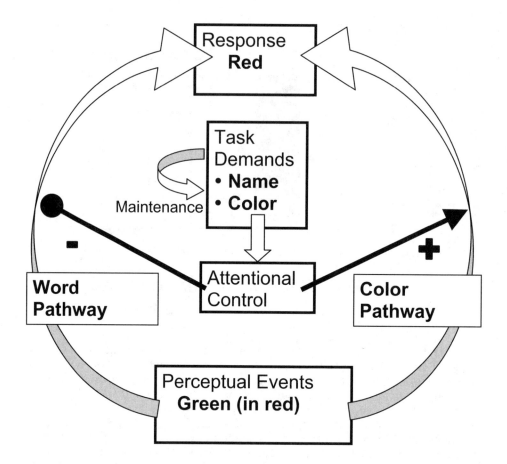

Figure 11.5.   The attentional control framework applied to the Stroop color-naming task. From *The Handbook of Neuropsychology: Aging and Dementia* (2nd ed., p. 71), by F. Boller and S. Cappa (Eds.), 2001. New York: Elsevier Science. Copyright 2001 by Elsevier. Adapted with permission from Elsevier.

The Stroop color-naming task (MacLeod, 1991) has become the gold standard task for studying informational conflict. Figure 11.5 presents a schematic representation of the Stroop task from the viewpoint of the attentional control framework (Balota & Faust, 2001). Of central interest to the current discussion is the proposal that attentional control works to detect conflict between task goals and low-level activation-processing pathways and regulates the relative strength of processing in the word- and color-processing pathways. We do not take a stance on whether this is done dynamically in response to the appearance of conflict within the system or using expectancies to put in place a more stable regulatory regime. In fact, there is evidence that both strategies may be used to control Stroop conflict (e.g., West & Alain, 2000).

Spieler et al. (1996) administered a computerized Stroop color-naming task to younger and healthy older adults and to individuals with DAT. Figure 11.6

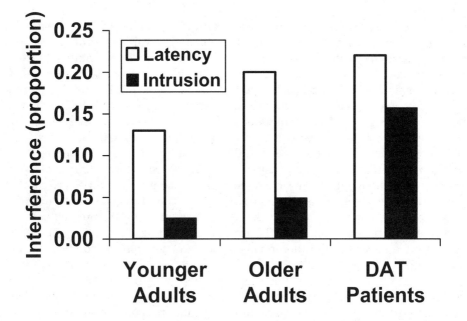

Figure 11.6. Stroop color-naming interference effects (Spieler et al., 1996) for mean response latency and intrusion errors as a function of group. DAT = dementia of the Alzheimer's type. Interference effects are expressed as a proportion of the neutral condition.

presents the Stroop conflict effect (conflict trials minus noncolor word trials) in terms of the difference in proportional latency (i.e., each person's mean latency for a condition divided by his or her overall mean) and the difference in proportion intrusion errors (i.e., saying the word instead of the color). As depicted in Figure 11.6, there was a dissociation in Stroop performance such that healthy older adults produced a larger Stroop conflict effect in color-naming latency compared with younger adults. This finding suggests that the healthy older adults were able to suppress the dominant word pathway but that it took additional time. In contrast, the DAT group did not produce a larger cost in Stroop performance in response latencies but did produce an increase in intrusion rates compared with the healthy older adults. This latter pattern suggests a more complete breakdown in attentional control over the partially active word-processing pathway, leading to the word process inappropriately driving the incorrect response to a much larger extent for the DAT group. Hence, instead of taking more time to suppress the dominant word pathway, the DAT individuals were simply outputting this pathway.

The DAT individuals also produced greater facilitation (not depicted in Figure 11.6). If indeed they were more likely to intrude the word dimension, then one would expect to observe greater facilitation. Because word processing is overall faster than color processing, an increased propensity toward word intrusion errors, presumably because of an increased reliance on the inappropriate word pathway, should result in a speeding up of the congruent condition.

The finding of an increase in Stroop conflict effects is consistent with the findings of many other studies in the literature (e.g., Amieva et al., 2004) and again supports our contention of a general impairment in the ability to exert inhibitory control over partially active, yet task-inappropriate, pathways. It is also consistent with recent studies using newly available brain-imaging techniques to image the degenerative changes associated with DAT in vivo and document the degeneration of cingulate and frontal areas along with connecting cortico–cortico white matter tracts in the cingulate and frontal cortices (e.g., Choi et al., 2005; Thompson et al., 2003). Functional imaging studies have consistently found that activation of the anterior cingulate and prefrontal cortex is associated with monitoring and cognitive control of color–word conflict during the Stroop task (e.g., Kerns et al., 2004). Using dense electrode event-related potential methodology, Markela-Lerenc et al. (2004) found evidence for a prefrontal generator that directly preceded an anterior cingulate generator, suggesting a network for monitoring and then controlling conflict (Cohen et al., 2004).

The attention control framework can also be applied to DAT-related changes in memory. Recent approaches to memory in experimental psychology have stressed the fact that memory and attention are more closely linked than has traditionally been thought (e.g., Cowan, 1995; Oberauer, Lange, & Engle, 2004). To provide an example of the application of the attentional control framework to memory and DAT, we briefly review a recent study of false memory by Balota, Cortese, et al. (1999; see also Watson, Balota, & Sergent-Marshall, 2001). This study used what has come to be called the Deese–Roediger–McDermott (DRM) procedure (Deese, 1959; Roediger & McDermott, 1995), in which a list of words is presented (e.g., *thread, pin, eye, sewing, sharp, point, prick, thimble, haystack, pain, hurt, injection*) that converges on a nonpresented item (e.g., *needle*). This procedure has been found to generate fairly robust false recall of the nonpresented target item (Roediger & Mc-Dermott, 1995), often as high as recall for presented items.

Balota, Cortese, et al. (1999) argued that the false memory generated in the DRM procedure can be viewed as a situation in which low-level memory retrieval processes generate multiple sources of conflicting evidence. The basic idea is that an intact processing system should be able to discriminate between information activated because of truly presented items and information that is active because it is related to the items presented (for a discussion of reality and source monitoring, see Johnson, Hashtroudi, & Lindsay, 1993; for evidence of source deficits in DAT individuals, see Multhaup & Balota, 1997). On the basis of consideration of the attentional control framework (see Figure 11.2), one might expect that individuals with DAT would experience a breakdown in the ability to exert inhibitory control over the activated but nonpresented item (e.g., *needle* in the example), leading to an increased production of false recall. This was, in fact, the finding reported in this study, and the DAT-related increase in false recall held up even after correction for group differences in overall memory performance. Hence, according to this framework, it appears that DAT individuals have difficulty selecting the most relevant pathway (i.e., what was earlier presented in the experiment) in the face of conflict from a partially activated competitor (i.e., the critical nonpresented word).

At this point, one might suggest that if the declines in Stroop and false memory performance in individuals with DAT have a common processing source, then researchers should find evidence for a relation between these two impairments. Sommers and Huff (2003) confirmed our prediction that the same attentional control system that underlies selection in the Stroop task is related to the false memory effect. They found that the size of the Stroop interference effect predicted false memory above and beyond baseline response latencies (i.e., any general slowing across groups; Faust, Balota, Spieler, & Ferraro, 1999). Moreover, Benjamin (2001) provided evidence that if one stresses attentional control at retrieval by using response deadlines, one can also mimic the increased susceptibility to false memory in younger adults (see also Balota, Burgess, Cortese, & Adams, 2002). The important point is that memory breakdowns, the primary diagnostic criteria for DAT, may also reflect attentional mechanisms that may contribute to these memory breakdowns.

Integrity of the Task Set

The attentional control framework also suggests that the quality of the representation of the task set is a critical aspect of control that may be impaired in DAT. In particular, it is likely that although subjects have an understanding of the task goals via instruction, there is variability across individuals in their understanding of what to do to accomplish the goals. Moreover, it is likely that there is variability across time within an individual in the quality of the task set that would be reflected in task set parameters. Multhaup (1995) provided one example of the importance of the task set. This study explored the *false fame effect* (Jacoby, Kelley, Brown, & Jasechko, 1989), the biasing effect of familiarity due to prior presentation during an experiment on fame judgments of famous and nonfamous people. Under typical conditions, when the different sources of familiarity and recollection were not stressed, older adults produced a larger false fame effect than younger adults. However, when the testing procedures were modified so that older adults were explicitly required to directly specify the source of the familiarity, the age-related differences disappeared. Hence, the age-related differences disappeared when subjects were given a more specific retrieval set.

Watson, McDermott, and Balota (2004) also explored the role of the task set in a false memory study comparing healthy younger and older adults. In this study, participants received repeated study tests on the same DRM lists. Half of the participants were directly warned about outputting the critical nonpresented item in a DRM paradigm, whereas the remaining half of the participants did not receive a warning. The interesting finding is that both younger and older adults clearly benefited from the explicit warning. However, even in the nonwarning condition, the younger adults decreased their false recall across trials, whereas the older adults did not. Hence, only the explicit warning helped the older adults avoid outputting the critical nonpresented item. One could consider this an example of explicitly implementing the appropriate task set. Clearly, further work is needed to explore possible ways of implementing the appropriate task across different experimental contexts.

A second issue regarding representation of the task set is the ability to maintain the appropriate task set across time. We believe that this is critical in achieving task goals and that there is considerable variability in maintaining a well-tuned representation across time. It is at least possible that such control states need to be refreshed across time to avoid decay, almost akin to the rehearsal of information in short-term memory. In fact, simple participation in the Stroop task can demonstrate such loss of control when one outputs the word dimension instead of the color dimension. We believe that such slips are due not to random variation but rather likely to a momentary loss of control over attention.

Indeed, there is evidence of breakdowns in the maintenance of attentional control across time in both healthy aging and in early-stage DAT. For example, West (1999) explored the nature of age-related increases in the Stroop interference effect. Across three experiments testing healthy younger and older adults on the Stroop task, older adults produced more numerous and longer lapses of attention leading to intrusion of the conflicting word. De Jong, Berendsen, and Cools (1999) presented a similar view in arguing that interference effects such as those obtained with the Stroop task may be due to transient failures to fully apply inhibitory processes, which they termed *goal neglect*.

Balota et al. (1992, Experiment 1) tested the ability of younger and older adults to maintain an expectancy across time by using a paradigm developed by Neely (1977) that factorially crosses prime–target expectancy and prime–target relatedness. In this study, subjects were given two categories for each block of trials. For example, before a block of trials, subjects might be told that whenever they receive the category *flower*, they should expect to receive types of flowers (e.g., *daisy*, an expected related condition); however, whenever they received the category *body*, they should expect to receive a type of building part (e.g., *door*, an expected unrelated condition). Of course, subjects could also receive unexpected targets (e.g., *iron* for the prime *flower* in the unexpected unrelated condition or *arm* for the prime *body* in the unexpected related condition). Following Neely, Balota et al. varied the cue–target delay. (For simplicity, we collapse across relatedness, which did not modulate the critical comparisons.) The results indicated that both younger and older adults produced an expectancy effect (i.e., targets from expected categories were named faster than targets from an unexpected category) that increased across the short (250-millisecond) and the medium (1,000-millisecond) delays. However, as depicted in Figure 11.7, at the longest (1,750-millisecond) delay, the younger adults continued their trend for an increasing expectancy effect, but the expectancy effect was almost nonexistent for the older adults. This pattern was replicated in a subsequent experiment with a greater range of prime–target intervals. These results suggest that the older adults experienced a decreased ability to maintain an attentional set for an extended time (see also Amrhein, Stemlach, & Goggin, 1991). It is interesting that Johnson, Mitchell, Raye, and Greene (2004) reported that older adults were slower than younger adults to reinstate a just-viewed item and also showed reduced neural activity, as measured by functional magnetic resonance imaging, associated with refreshing the representation of a just-viewed item. These results suggest an age-related decline

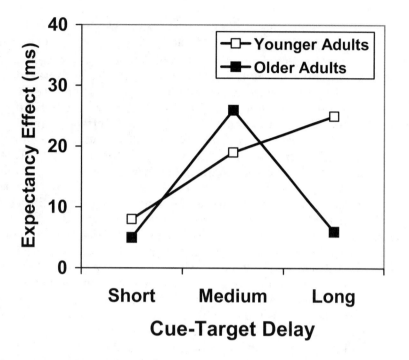

Figure 11.7. Expectancy effects during cued word naming as a function of delay and group. Expectancy effects are computed as mean latency to name a test word from the expected category minus mean latency to name a test word from an unexpected category. Adapted from "Automatic and Attentional Priming in Young and Older Adults: A Reevaluation of the Two-Process Model," by D. A. Balota, S. R. Black, and M. Cheney, 1992, *Journal of Experimental Psychology: Human Perception and Performance, 18,* p. 489. Copyright 1992 by the American Psychological Association.

in control processes responsible for holding the task set in a stable active form across time.

Our interest in the simple maintenance operation and the role of this mechanism in early-stage DAT, and hence its potential as an early marker for DAT, was recently piqued by a study reported by Grady, Furey, Pietrini, Horwitz, and Rapoport (2001). In this study, subjects were presented simple faces to maintain for 1 to 16 seconds and then were presented two faces for a forced-choice matching decision. The interesting pattern in this study was that individuals with early-stage Alzheimer's disease produced a clear decrement in accuracy across delays, but there was no effect of delay in the healthy older individuals. We believe that these data may be symptomatic of a simple breakdown in maintenance of a task set across time. The novel twist in Grady et al.'s experimental procedure was the maintenance of a set across relatively longer delays, on the order of seconds, to maximize the load on the maintenance operation.

Braver, Satpute, Rush, Racine, and Barch (2005) provided more direct evidence of a DAT-related decline in the ability to maintain representations.

They reported a study using a version of the continuous performance task (Servan-Schreiber, Cohen, & Steingard, 1996), in which participants responded to serially presented letters by pressing a target button, with a target response for the letter X but only when it directly succeeds an A. Participants responded by pressing a nontarget button otherwise. A high proportion (70%) of AX letter pairs was presented, encouraging false alarms to AY (with Y indicating any non-X letter) and BX (with B indicating any non-A letter) pairs. Efficient performance on this task requires effective encoding and maintenance of a continuously changing stream of context letters (i.e., the previously presented letter) to discriminate target from nontarget events. The critical manipulation with respect to questions of context maintenance was that the delay between letters was either shorter (1,000 milliseconds) or longer (5,000 milliseconds), leading to differential context maintenance demands.

The results yielded a larger increase in target misses (i.e., a nontarget response following AX pairs) and increasing delay for the individuals with DAT than for the healthy older adults. Of greater interest were the DAT-related changes in false alarms: Whereas the younger adults and the healthy older adults produced an increase in false alarms, with increasing delay for the AY trials, and a decrease in false alarms, with increasing delay for the BX trials (indicating a greater controlling influence of the previous context letter with increasing delay), the DAT individuals produced the converse pattern of changes in errors. That is, as delay increased, individuals with DAT produced a decrease in AY false alarms, consistent with a decline in the use of the context letter to drive the expectation that an X is most likely to follow an A, and an increase in BX false alarms, consistent with a decline in the use of the non-A context letter to recognize the subsequent appearance of the X as a nontarget event. This pattern of results cannot be explained by a general DAT-related decline in memory for the prior items because of the crossover interaction pattern across groups. We take the results of this study as strong support for the proposal that DAT results in a deficit in maintaining the task set over time.

Conclusion

We have presented arguments in favor of the concepts of inhibitory and facilitatory processes as useful building blocks for general theories of cognition. It has been pointed out by those critical of the use of inhibition (e.g., Burke, 1997; MacLeod et al., 2003) that reasonable noninhibitory accounts exist for specific empirical effects (e.g., Stroop, negative priming, and inhibition of return) that have widely accepted inhibitory accounts. Although we are sympathetic to this view, and although we recognize the importance of developing and testing competing models of cognitive processes within task domains, we do feel that it is important to develop more general cognitive frameworks designed to provide a theoretical perspective across a wide range of cognitive tasks. However, we have concerns about the parsimony of noninhibitory explanations proposed by critics of inhibitory accounts of specific empirical effects. More important, our central point is that development of more general models will require inclusion of cognitive control processes that come from two general categories of inhibitory and facilitatory processes.

As a demonstration of this approach, we have presented an attentional control framework (see Figure 11.2) that can be adapted to a variety of situations where the cognitive system must deal with multiple sources of information that compete for response systems. We have presented a brief selective review demonstrating how this framework can be applied to explain the cognitive deficits of groups, such as those with DAT, that have broad yet circumscribed patterns of neurodegeneration. The attentional control framework is based on the assumption that much of the low-level processing of information from the environment involves strongly stimulus driven and relatively automatic activation of internal representations. In a well-learned task environment, low-level stimulus-driven processes associated with multiple sources of information from the environment will come to compete directly for response systems. From this perspective, it appears that competent and appropriate behavior across a wide variety of situations involves control over low-level stimulus-driven processes to reach goals efficiently.

Accordingly, the attentional control framework stresses the importance of representing and maintaining the task set and of using the task set to regulate stimulus-driven processes. Specialized attentional control processes that can act to inhibit or facilitate are proposed as a general set of mechanisms that can provide appropriate control signals across a variety of tasks and situations. Our brief review of cognitive deficits in DAT presented evidence supporting the contention that individuals with DAT experience deficits both in the representation/maintenance of task sets and in inhibitory control over task-inappropriate processing pathways.

From a traditional viewpoint, inhibitory control might be seen to act on the activation of representations, leading to the expectation that the empirical footprint of inhibition would be reduced access to some representations below some baseline control level. We find such a view too constraining, preferring to view the cognitive system in more neural terms as a distributed processing system that relies on pathways of information flow that transmit and transform information as it moves from sensory input to motor output. In this view, inhibitory control can be seen to regulate the signal-to-noise ratio (i.e., task-appropriate and task-inappropriate information processing) through down-regulation of the task-inappropriate processing pathways. This perspective leads us to disagree with some who have, for example, suggested that a model of Stroop performance (Roelofs, 2003) that includes a control parameter that represents the overall strength of processing of the inappropriate (in relation to the task of color naming) word identity does not include inhibitory control processes (MacLeod et al., 2003). To the contrary, we propose that it is exactly this type of down-regulation of information-processing pathways that is proto-typically inhibitory in nature.

Much work remains to be done to move the attentional control framework presented in this chapter to the level of a fully specified theory. Of foremost interest to us is the issue of volitional control. We suspect that inhibitory control processes can be seen as hierarchically organized, ranging from high-level control processes that require volitional initiation to low-level control processes that are more automatic in nature. This view leads to the prediction that within the context of repetitive cognitive tasks, control over inappropriate processing pathways will become relatively automated as participants learn the task.

References

Amieva, H., Lafont, S., Rouch-Leroyer, I., Rainville, C., Dartigues, J. F., Orgogozo, J. M., & Fabrigoule, C. (2004). Evidencing inhibitory deficits in Alzheimer's disease through interference effects and shifting disabilities in the Stroop test. *Archives of Clinical Neuropsychology, 19,* 791–803.

Amrhein, P. C., Stemlach, G. E., & Goggin, N. L. (1991). Age differences in the maintenance and restructuring of movement preparation. *Psychology and Aging, 6,* 451–466.

Baddeley, A. D. (1986). *Working memory.* Oxford, England: Clarendon Press.

Baddeley, A. D., Baddeley, H. A., Bucks, H. A., & Wilcock, G. K. (2001). Attentional control in Alzheimer's disease. *Brain, 124,* 1492–1508.

Balota, D. A. (1983). Automatic semantic activation and episodic memory encoding. *Journal of Verbal Learning and Verbal Behavior, 22,* 88–104.

Balota, D. A., Black, S. R., & Cheney, M. (1992). Automatic and attentional priming in young and older adults: A reevaluation of the two-process model. *Journal of Experimental Psychology: Human Perception and Performance, 18,* 485–502.

Balota, D. A., Burgess, G. C., Cortese, M. J., & Adams, D. R. (2002). The word-frequency mirror effect in young, old, and early-stage Alzheimer's disease: Evidence for two processes in episodic recognition performance. *Journal of Memory and Language, 46,* 199–226.

Balota, D. A., Cortese, M. J., Duchek, J. M., Adams, D., Roediger, H. L., III, McDermott, K. B., & Yerys, B. E. (1999). Veridical and false memories in healthy older adults and in dementia of the Alzheimer's type. *Cognitive Neuropsychology, 16,* 361–384.

Balota, D. A., & Duchek, J. M. (1991). Semantic priming effects, lexical repetition effects, and contextual disambiguation effects in healthy aged individuals and individuals with senile dementia of the Alzheimer type. *Brain and Language, 40,* 181–201.

Balota, D. A., & Faust, M. E. (2001). Attention in dementia of the Alzheimer's type. In F. Boller & S. Cappa (Eds.), *The handbook of neuropsychology: Aging and dementia* (2nd ed., pp. 51–80). New York: Elsevier Science.

Balota, D. A., & Ferraro, F. R. (1996). Lexical, sublexical, and implicit memory processes in healthy young and healthy older adults and in individuals with dementia of the Alzheimer type. *Neuropsychology, 10,* 82–95.

Balota, D. A., Watson, J. M., Duchek, J. M., & Ferraro, F. R. (1999). Cross-modal semantic and homograph priming in healthy young, healthy old, and in Alzheimer's disease individuals. *Journal of the International Neuropsychological Society, 5,* 626–640.

Benjamin, A. S. (2001). On the dual effects of repetition on false recognition. *Journal of Experimental Psychology: Learning, Memory, and Cognition, 27,* 941–947.

Berg, L., McKeel, D. W., Jr., Miller, J. P., Storandt, M., Rubin, E. H., Morris, J. C., et al. (1998). Clinicopathologic studies in cognitively healthy aging and Alzheimer's disease: Relation of histologic markers to dementia severity, age, sex, and apolipoprotein E genotype. *Archives of Neurology, 55,* 326–335.

Boller, F., & Cappa, S. (Eds.). (2001). *The handbook of neuropsychology: Aging and dementia* (2nd ed.). New York: Elsevier Science.

Botvinick, M. M., Braver, T. S., Barch, D. M., Carter, C. S., & Cohen, J. D. (2001). Conflict monitoring and cognitive control. *Psychological Review, 108,* 624–652.

Braver, T. S., Satpute, A. B., Rush, B. K., Racine, C. A., & Barch, D. M. (2005). Context processing and context maintenance in healthy aging and early stage dementia of the Alzheimer's type. *Psychology and Aging, 20,* 33–46.

Burke, D. M. (1997). Language, aging, and inhibitory deficits: Evaluation of a theory. *Journals of Gerontology Series B: Psychological Sciences and Social Sciences, 52B,* P254–P264.

Buschke, H. (1973). Selective reminding for analysis of memory and learning. *Journal of Verbal Learning and Verbal Behavior, 12,* 543–550.

Chenery, H. J. (1996). Semantic priming in Alzheimer's dementia. *Aphasiology, 10,* 1–20.

Chertkow, H., Bub, D., & Bergman, H. (1994). Increased semantic priming in patients with dementia of the Alzheimer type. *Journal of Clinical and Experimental Neuropsychology, 16,* 608–622.

Choi, S. M., Lim, K. O., Monteiro, I., & Reisberg, B. (2005). Diffusion tensor imaging of frontal white matter microstructure in early Alzheimer's disease: A preliminary study. *Journal of Geriatric Psychiatry and Neurology, 18,* 12–19.

Cohen, J. D., Aston-Jones, G., & Gilzenrat, M. S. (2004). A systems-level perspective on attention and cognitive control: Guided activation, adaptive gating, conflict monitoring. In M. I. Posner (Ed.), *Cognitive neuroscience of attention* (pp. 71–90). New York: Guilford Press.

Cohen, J., Dunbar, K., & McClelland, J. (1990). On the control of automatic processes: A parallel distributed processing account of the Stroop effect. *Psychological Review, 97,* 332–361.

Cowan, N. (1995). *Attention and memory: An integrated framework.* New York: Oxford University Press.

Dagenbach, D., & Carr, T. H. (Eds.). (1994). *Inhibitory processes in attention, memory, and language.* San Diego, CA: Academic Press.

Daum, I., Riesch, G., Sartori, G., & Birbaumer, N. (1996). Semantic memory impairment in Alzheimer's disease. *Journal of Clinical and Experimental Neuropsychology, 18,* 648–665.

Deese, J. (1959). On the prediction of occurrence of particular verbal intrusions in immediate recall. *Journal of Experimental Psychology, 58,* 17–22.

De Jong, R., Berendsen, E., & Cools, R. (1999). Goal neglect and inhibitory limitations: Dissociable causes of interference effects in conflict situations. *Acta Psychologica, 101,* 379–394.

Dempster, F. N., & Brainerd, C. J. (Eds.). (1995). *Interference and inhibition in cognition.* San Diego, CA: Academic Press.

Diamond, A. (1990). Developmental time course in human infants and infant monkeys, and the neural bases of inhibitory control in reaching. In A. Diamond (Ed.), *Annals of the New York Academy of Sciences: Vol. 608. The development and neural bases of higher cognitive functions* (pp. 637–676). New York: New York Academy of Sciences.

Engle, R. W., Tuholski, S. W., Laughlin, J. E., & Conway, A. R. A. (1999). Working memory, short-term memory, and general fluid intelligence: A latent variable approach. *Journal of Experimental Psychology: General, 128,* 309–331.

Fabrigoule, C., Rouch, I., Taberly, A., Letenneur, L., Commenges, D., Mazaus, J. M., et al. (1998). Cognitive process in preclinical phase of dementia. *Brain, 121,* 135–141.

Faust, M. E., & Balota, D. A. (1997). Inhibition of return and visuospatial attention in healthy older adults and individuals with dementia of the Alzheimer type. *Neuropsychology, 11,* 13–29.

Faust, M. E., Balota, D. A., Duchek, J. M., Gernsbacher, M. A., & Smith, S. (1997). Inhibitory control during sentence comprehension in individuals with dementia of the Alzheimer type. *Brain and Language, 57,* 225–253.

Faust, M. E., Balota, D. A., Spieler, D. H., & Ferraro, F. R. (1999). Individual differences in information processing rate and amount: Implications for group differences in response latency. *Psychological Bulletin, 125,* 777–799.

Fratiglioni, L., & Rocca, W. A. (2001). Epidemiology of dementia. In F. Boller & S. Cappa (Eds.), *The handbook of neuropsychology: Aging and dementia* (2nd ed., pp. 193–215). New York: Elsevier Science.

Gabrieli, J. D. E., Vaidya, C. J., Stone, M., Francis, W. S., Thompson-Schill, S. L., Fleischman, D. A., et al. (1999). Convergent behavioral and neuropsychological evidence for a distinction between identification and production forms of repetition priming. *Journal of Experimental Psychology: General, 128,* 479–498.

Gernsbacher, M. A., & Faust, M. E. (1991a). Less-skilled comprehenders have less-efficient suppression mechanisms. *Journal of Experimental Psychology: Learning, Memory, and Cognition, 17,* 245–262.

Gernsbacher, M. A., & Faust, M. E. (1991b). The role of suppression in sentence comprehension. In G. B. Simpson (Ed.), *Comprehending word and sentence* (pp. 97–128). Amsterdam: North Holland.

Grady, C. L., Furey, M. L., Pietrini, P., Horwitz, B., & Rapoport, S. I. (2001). Altered brain functional connectivity and impaired short-term memory in Alzheimer's disease. *Brain, 124,* 739–756.

Greene, J. D. W., & Hodges, J. R. (1996). Semantic processing. In R. G. Morris (Ed.), *The cognitive neuropsychology of Alzheimer-type dementia* (pp. 128–148). London: Oxford University Press.

Greenwood, P. M., Lambert, C., Sunderland, T., & Parasuraman, R. (2005). Effects of apolipoprotein E genotype on spatial attention, working memory, and their interaction in healthy, middle-aged adults: Results from the National Institute of Mental Health's BIOCARD study. *Neuropsychology, 19,* 199–211.

Hartman, M. (1991). The use of semantic knowledge in Alzheimer's disease: Evidence for impairments of attention. *Neuropsychologia, 29,* 213–228.

Hasher, L., Zacks, R. T., & May, C. P. (1999). Inhibitory control, circadian arousal, and age. In A. Koriat & D. Gopher (Eds.), *Attention and performance: Vol. XVII. Cognitive regulation of performance: Interaction of theory and application* (pp. 653–675). Cambridge, MA: MIT Press.

Jacoby, L. L., Kelley, C., Brown, J., & Jasechko, J. (1989). Becoming famous overnight: Limits on the ability to avoid unconscious influences of the past. *Journal of Personality and Social Psychology, 56,* 326–338.

Johnson, M. K., Hashtroudi, S., & Lindsay, D. (1993). Source monitoring. *Psychological Bulletin, 114,* 3–28.

Johnson, M. K., Mitchell, K. J., Raye, C. L., & Greene, E. J. (2004). An age-related deficit in prefrontal cortical function associated with refreshing information. *Psychological Science, 15,* 127–132.

Jonides, J., & Mack, R. (1984). On the cost and benefit of cost and benefit. *Psychological Bulletin, 96,* 29–44.

Kanne, S. M., Balota, D. A., Storandt, M., McKeel, D. W., Jr., & Morris, J. C. (1998). Relating anatomy to function in Alzheimer's disease: Neuropsychological profiles predict regional neuropathology 5 years later. *Neurology, 50,* 979–985.

Kerns, J. G., Cohen, J. D., MacDonald, A. W., III, Cho, R. Y., Stenger, V. A., & Carter, C. S. (2004, February 13). Anterior cingulate conflict monitoring and adjustments in control. *Science, 303,* 1023–1026.

Klunk, W. E., Engler, H., Nordberg, A., Wang, Y., Blomqvist, G., Holt, D. P., et al. (2004). Imaging brain amyloid in Alzheimer's disease with Pittsburgh compound-B. *Annals of Neurology, 55,* 303–305.

Lahiri, D. K., Sambamurti, K., & Bennett, D. A. (2004). Apolipoprotein gene and its interaction with the environmentally driven risk factors: Molecular, genetic and epidemiological studies of Alzheimer's disease. *Neurobiology of Aging, 25,* 651–660.

Lindsay, D. S., & Jacoby, L. L. (1994). Stroop process dissociations: The relationship between facilitation and interference. *Journal of Experimental Psychology: Human Perception and Performance, 20,* 219–234.

Logan, G. D., Cowan, W. B., & Davis, K. A. (1984). On the ability to inhibit simple and choice reaction time responses: A model and a method. *Journal of Experimental Psychology: Human Perception and Performance, 10,* 276–291.

MacLeod, C. M. (1991). Half a century of research on the Stroop effect: An integrative review. *Psychological Bulletin, 109,* 163–203.

MacLeod, C. M., Dodd, M. D., Sheard, E. D., Wilson, D. E., & Bibi, U. (2003). In opposition to inhibition. In B. Ross (Series Ed.), *The psychology of learning and motivation* (Vol. 43, pp. 163–214). San Diego, CA: Elsevier Academic Press.

Markela-Lerenc, J., Ille, N., Kaiser, S., Fiedler, P., Mundt, C., & Weisbrod, M. (2004). Prefrontal-cingulate activation during executive control: Which comes first? *Cognitive Brain Research, 18,* 278–287.

Mayr, U., & Keele, S. W. (2000). Changing internal constraints on action: The role of backward inhibition. *Journal of Experimental Psychology: General, 129,* 4–26.

McKeel, D. W., Jr., Price, J. L., Miller, J. P., Grant, E. A., Xiong, C., Berg, L., et al. (2004). Neuropathologic criteria for diagnosing Alzheimer disease in persons with pure dementia of Alzheimer type. *Journal of Neuropathology and Experimental Neurology, 63,* 1028–1037.

McKhann, G., Drachman, D., Folstein, M., Katzman, R., Price, D., & Stadlan, M. (1984). Clinical diagnosis of Alzheimer's disease: Report of the NINCDS–ADRDA Work Group under the auspices of the Department of Health and Human Services Task Force on Alzheimer's disease. *Neurology, 34,* 39–44.

Multhaup, K. S. (1995). Aging, source, and decision criteria: When false errors do and do not occur. *Psychology and Aging, 10,* 492–497.

Multhaup, K. S., & Balota, D. A. (1997). Generation effects and source memory in healthy older adults and in adults with dementia of the Alzheimer type. *Neuropsychology, 11,* 382–391.

Nagy, Z., Hindley, N. J., Braak, H., Braak, E., Yilmazer-Hanke, D. M., Schultz, C., et al. (1999). The progression of Alzheimer's disease from limbic regions to the neocortex: Clinical, radiological and pathological relationships. *Dementia and Geriatric Cognitive Disorders, 10,* 115–120.

Neely, J. H. (1977). Semantic priming and retrieval from lexical memory: Roles of inhibitionless spreading activation and limited-capacity attention. *Journal of Experimental Psychology: General, 106,* 226–254.

Neill, W. T., & Valdes, L. A. (1996). Facilitatory and inhibitory aspects of attention. In M. G. H. Coles & A. F. Kramer (Eds.), *Converging operations in the study of visual selective attention* (pp. 77–106). Washington, DC: American Psychological Association.

Norman, D. A., & Shallice, T. (1986). Attention to action: Willed and automatic control of behavior. In R. J. Davidson, G. E. Schwartz, & D. Shapiro (Eds.), *Consciousness and self-regulation* (pp. 1–18). New York: Plenum Press.

Ober, B. A., & Shenaut, G. K. (1995). Semantic priming in Alzheimer's disease: Meta-analysis and theoretical evaluation. In P. A. Allen & T. R. Bashore (Eds.), *Age differences in word and language processing* (pp. 244–271). Amsterdam: North Holland/Elsevier Science.

Oberauer, K., Lange, E., & Engle, R. W. (2004). Working memory capacity and resistance to interference. *Journal of Memory and Language, 51,* 80–96.

Ownby, R. L., Loewenstein, D. A., Schram, L., & Acevedo, A. (2004). Assessing the cognitive abilities that differentiate patients with Alzheimer's disease from normals: Single and multiple factor models. *International Journal of Geriatric Psychiatry, 19,* 232–242.

Parasuraman, R., & Greenwood, P. M. (1998). Selective attention in aging and dementia. In R. Parasuraman (Ed.), *The attentive brain* (pp. 461–487). Cambridge, MA: MIT Press.

Parasuraman, R., Greenwood, P. M., Haxby, J. V., & Grady, C. L. (1992). Visuospatial attention in dementia of the Alzheimer type. *Brain, 115,* 711–733.

Perry, R. J., & Hodges, J. R. (1999). Attention and executive deficits in Alzheimer's disease: A critical review. *Brain, 122,* 383–404.

Posner, M. I. (1980). Orienting of attention. *Quarterly Journal of Experimental Psychology, 32,* 3–25.

Posner, M. I., & Cohen, Y. (1984). Components of visual orienting. In H. Bouma & D. G. Bouwhuis (Eds.), *Attention and performance: Vol. X. Control of language processes* (pp. 531–556). Hillsdale, NJ: Erlbaum.

Posner, M. I., & Dehaene, S. (1994). Attentional networks. *Trends in Neuroscience, 17,* 75–79.

Posner, M. I., & DiGirolamo, G. J. (1998). Executive attention: Conflict, target detection, and cognitive control. In R. Parasuraman (Ed.), *The attentive brain* (pp. 401–423). Cambridge, MA: MIT Press.

Pratt, J., Spalek, T. M., & Bradshaw, F. (1999). The time to detect targets at inhibited and noninhibited locations: Preliminary evidence for attentional momentum. *Journal of Experimental Psychology: Human Perception and Performance, 25,* 730–746.

Rapp, M. A., & Reischies, F. M. (2005). Attention and executive control predict Alzheimer disease in late life: Results from the Berlin aging study. *American Journal of Geriatric Psychiatry, 13,* 134–141.

Roediger, H. L., & McDermott, K. B. (1995). Creating false memories: Remembering words not presented in lists. *Journal of Experimental Psychology: Learning, Memory, and Cognition, 21,* 803–814.

Roelofs, A. (2003). Goal-referenced selection of verbal action: Modeling attentional control in the Stroop task. *Psychological Review, 110,* 88–125.

Rogers, R. D., & Monsell, S. (1995). Costs of a predictable switch between simple cognitive tasks. *Journal of Experimental Psychology: General, 124,* 207–231.

Rosen, V. M., Bergeson, J. L., Putnam, K., Harwell, A., & Sunderland, T. (2002). Working memory and apolipoprotein E: What's the connection? *Neuropsychologia, 40,* 2226–2233.

Rosen, V. M., Sunderland, T., Levy, J., Harwell, A., McGee, L., Hammond, C., et al. (2005). Apolipoprotein E and category fluency: Evidence for reduced semantic access in healthy normal controls at risk for developing Alzheimer's disease. *Neuropsychologia, 43,* 647–658.

Russo, R., & Spinnler, H. (1994). Implicit verbal memory in Alzheimer's disease. *Cortex, 30,* 359–375.

Salmon, D. P., Butters, N., & Chan, A. S. (1999). The deterioration of semantic memory in Alzheimer's disease. *Canadian Journal of Experimental Psychology, 53,* 108–115.

Salthouse, T. A., & Becker, J. T. (1998). Independent effects of Alzheimer's disease on neuropsychological functioning. *Neuropsychology, 12,* 242–252.

Servan-Schreiber, D., Cohen, J. D., & Steingard, S. (1996). Schizophrenic deficits in the processing of context: A test of a theoretical model. *Archives of General Psychiatry, 53,* 1105–1113.

Small, B. J., Rosnick, C. B., Fratiglioni, L., & Backman, L. (2004). Apolipoprotein E and cognitive performance: A meta-analysis. *Psychology and Aging, 19,* 592–600.

Smith, E. E., & Jonides, J. (1999, March 12). Storage and executive processes in the frontal lobes. *Science, 283,* 1657–1661.

Sommers, M. S., & Huff, L. M. (2003). The effects of age and dementia of the Alzheimer's type on phonological false memories. *Psychology and Aging, 18,* 791–806.

Spieler, D. H., Balota, D. A., & Faust, M. E. (1996). Stroop performance in healthy younger and older adults and in individuals with dementia of the Alzheimer's type. *Journal of Experimental Psychology: Human Perception and Performance, 22,* 461–479.

Sullivan, M. P., Faust, M. E., & Balota, D. A. (1995). Identity negative priming in old adults and individuals with dementia of the Alzheimer type. *Neuropsychology, 9,* 537–555.

Thompson, P. M., Hayashi, K. M., de Zubicaray, G., Janke, A. L., Rose, S. E., Semple, J., et al. (2003). Dynamics of gray matter loss in Alzheimer's disease. *Journal of Neuroscience, 23,* 994–1005.

Tipper, S. P. (1985). The negative priming effect: Inhibitory effects of ignored primes. *Quarterly Journal of Experimental Psychology, 37A,* 571–590.

Tipper, S. P. (2001). Does negative priming reflect inhibitory mechanisms? A review and integration of conflicting views. *Quarterly Journal of Experimental Psychology: Human Experimental Psychology, 54A,* 321–343.

Verhoeff, N. P., Wilson, A. A., Takeshita, S., Trop, L., Hussey, D., Singh, K., et al. (2004). In-vivo imaging of Alzheimer disease beta-amyloid with [11C] SB-13 PET. *American Journal of Geriatric Psychiatry, 12,* 584–595.

Watson, J. M., Balota, D. A., & Sergent-Marshall, S. D. (2001). Semantic, phonological, and hybrid veridical and false memories in healthy older adults and in individuals with dementia of the Alzheimer type. *Neuropsychology, 15,* 254–268.

Watson, J. M., McDermott, K. B., & Balota, D. A. (2004). Attempting to avoid false memories in the Deese/Roediger–McDermott paradigm: Assessing the combined influence of practice and warnings in young and old adults. *Memory & Cognition, 32,* 135–141.

Wenk, G. L. (2003). Neuropathological changes in Alzheimer's disease. *Journal of Clinical Psychiatry, 64,* 7–10.

West, R. (1999). Age differences in lapses of intention in the Stroop task. *Journals of Gerontology Series B: Psychological Sciences and Social Sciences, 54B,* P34–P43.

West, R., & Alain, C. (2000). Effects of task context and fluctuations of attention on neural activity supporting performance of the Stroop task. *Brain Research, 873,* 102–111.

Zacks, R. T., Radvansky, G., & Hasher, L. (1996). Studies of directed forgetting in older adults. *Journal of Experimental Psychology: Learning, Memory, and Cognition, 22,* 143–156.

12

Semantic Short-Term Memory Deficits and Resolution of Interference: A Case for Inhibition?

A. Cris Hamilton and Randi C. Martin

Over the past 10 years, our laboratory has developed a model of short-term memory that includes dissociable semantic and phonological components. The primary motivation for assuming separate semantic and phonological components is the existence of patients who show a double dissociation of these components—that is, some patients who show difficulty maintaining phonological information and others who show deficits in retaining semantic information (Martin & He, 2004). All of these patients have highly reduced memory span (i.e., being able to recall only one or two words compared with the normal span of five words or so). Those showing a phonological short-term memory deficit do not show the standard phonological effects on span, such as effects of phonological similarity or word length, but do show a benefit from semantic information—for example, recalling lists of meaningful words at a much higher level than lists of nonwords. In contrast, patients with a semantic short-term memory deficit do show the standard phonological effects, but fail to show an advantage for words over nonwords. Another test discriminating between the two groups is performance on a recognition probe task in which the participants judge whether a probe word rhymes with a previous list word or is in the same category as a previous list word. Patients with a phonological short-term memory deficit do better on the category than the rhyme probe task, whereas the patients with a semantic short-term memory deficit show the reverse.

Our research has focused on relating these two types of short-term memory deficits to language comprehension and production (for a review, see Martin, 2005). Recently, however, findings from a patient with a semantic short-term memory deficit suggest that this deficit might be due to difficulty in inhibiting irrelevant verbal information. In this chapter, we first review our previous findings on short-term memory and language processing and then present the evidence establishing the inhibition deficit for patient M.L. We then consider how previous findings on language production might be accommodated by an inhibition deficit account. Finally, we consider how neuropsychological data provide important converging evidence for an inhibitory component to cognitive processing.

Phonological and Semantic Components of Short-Term Memory and Their Role in Language Processing

Data from a number of experiments with brain-damaged patients support a distinction between semantic and phonological short-term memory deficits. In addition to the patient data generated in our lab (Martin & He, 2004; Martin, Shelton, & Yaffee, 1994) and those of others (Majerus, Van der Linden, Poncelet, & Metz-Lutz, 2004), several neuroimaging studies provide corroborative data (Martin, Wu, Freedman, Jackson, & Lesch, 2003; Shivde & Thompson-Schill, 2004) indicating that semantic and phonological information in short-term memory are dissociable. Maintenance of semantic information relies on the left frontal lobe, whereas phonological maintenance is thought to depend on more posterior areas in the left parietal lobe.

Another objective of our research has been to determine whether semantic and phonological short-term memory make unique contributions to language processing. In fact, deficits in semantic and phonological short-term memory have very different consequences for language processing. For example, patients with semantic short-term memory deficits have great difficulty in comprehending sentences that require maintenance of multiple semantic representations. Martin and Romani (1994) asked patients to detect anomalies in sentences that were semantically either sensible or anomalous. These sentences included adjective–noun phrases in which the adjectives came either before or after the noun. Patients with semantic short-term memory deficits had difficulty detecting semantic anomalies in sentences such as "She saw the green, bright, shining sun, which pleased her," in which three adjectives preceded the noun. However, these patients performed much better when the three adjectives followed the noun, as in the sentence "The sun was bright, shining, and green, which pleased her." It is important to note that patients with semantic short-term memory deficits did not have difficulty detecting semantic anomalies when only one adjective appeared before a noun, such as in the sentence, "She saw the green sun, which pleased her." In contrast, patients with phonological short-term memory deficits did not show this pattern.

Furthermore, patients with semantic short-term memory deficits have similar problems in production of phrases. Martin and Freedman (2001) used a picture-naming task to elicit phrases and found that patients with semantic short-term memory deficits could not produce adjective–noun phrases such as "short, curly, blonde hair" but were not impaired in producing shorter phrases such as "short hair," "curly hair," or "blonde hair." To account for these findings, Martin and Freedman hypothesized that participants must activate and maintain all of the lexical–semantic representations for a phrase in a lexical–semantic buffer before initiating articulation. Such a proposal is consistent with a phrasal scope of planning at a lexical–semantic level as proposed by

Smith and Wheeldon (1999). Martin and Freedman hypothesized that patients with a semantic short-term memory deficit were unable to maintain these representations simultaneously, instead attempting to produce the utterance in a piecemeal fashion, putting the content words in separate phrases. Thus, Martin and Freedman concluded that semantic short-term memory is important in both the comprehension and production of language, particularly when multiple lexical–semantic representations must be maintained simultaneously. Recent functional neuroimaging data from our lab support the notion that the same brain areas are recruited for both production and comprehension of adjective–noun phrases like those described in this section (Martin, Burton, & Hamilton, 2005).

Our lab has also examined the production of conjoined noun phrases (e.g., a participant producing the response "car and tree" when asked to name simultaneously presented pictures of a car and a tree). Freedman, Martin, and Biegler (2004) manipulated the semantic relatedness of two nouns within a phrase, reasoning that if both nouns were being planned simultaneously, some effect of semantic relatedness (either a facilitative effect or interference) should be observed. They further hypothesized that patients with semantic short-term memory deficits might have particular difficulty with such phrases, given that these phrases would require maintenance of multiple semantic representations. Patients and control participants were asked to name individual pictures or to produce a conjoined noun phrase for two pictures presented simultaneously. Control participants had longer onset latencies for producing conjoined noun phrases describing two semantically related pictures (e.g., producing the phrase "dress and shirt" when presented with pictures of a dress and a shirt) relative to two unrelated pictures (e.g., producing "car and tree" when presented with pictures of a car and a tree). These data are similar to those reported by Smith and Wheeldon (2004). Two patients with semantic short-term memory deficits (M.L. and G.R.) had greatly exaggerated interference effects on this task. In contrast, two patients with phonological short-term memory deficits (E.A. and S.J.D.) had interference effects within the normal range. Freedman et al. explained these exaggerated effects for the patients with semantic short-term memory deficits as a difficulty in selecting between two semantically related representations that resulted from rapid decay of representations in a semantic short-term memory buffer, making selection from similar representations difficult.

Semantic short-term memory appears to be particularly important for language comprehension and production tasks that require maintenance of multiple semantic representations (as is the case in the phrase "green, bright, shining sun"). We have also assumed that these deficits were best characterized by rapid decay of semantic representations that undermines performance on these types of comprehension and production tasks. Likewise, we assumed that patients with phonological short-term memory deficits were plagued by rapid decay of phonological representations in short-term memory with relatively preserved semantic maintenance. However, rapid decay of phonological representations had less severe implications for language production and comprehension.

A Role for Inhibition in Semantic
Short-Term Memory Deficits

Recently, our conceptualization of semantic short-term memory deficits was complicated by new data. These data were collected from M.L., a patient with a semantic short-term memory deficit. Although our lab has assumed that rapid decay of semantic representations was responsible for the semantic short-term memory deficits, Martin and Lesch (1996) reported a curious finding that might be interpreted as inconsistent with such an account. This finding was the paradoxical tendency for patients with semantic short-term memory deficits to produce intrusions during serial recall. That is, although these patients had great difficulty recalling lists of even three words, they nevertheless produced intrusions of words from previously presented lists. In other words, these patients seemed to be extremely susceptible to proactive interference. Such interference effects seemed difficult to reconcile with an account of short-term memory deficits in which overly rapid decay is the principal mechanism underlying the deficit.

In a series of studies (Hamilton & Martin, 2005, 2007), we have more carefully investigated this apparent paradox using a task introduced by Monsell (1978). This task is a variation of a recognition probe task in which a list of letters is presented followed by a probe, and participants indicate whether the probe appeared in the list by making a key press. Monsell's task also manipulated the recency of probes on negative trials. That is, for half of the negative trials, the probe appeared not in the immediate list but rather in the previous list. In the other half of the negative trials, the probe did not appear in the previous two trials (see Table 12.1 for examples). The comparison of recent negative trials to nonrecent negative trials yields a measure of interference. In normal participants, reaction times are longer and accuracy poorer on recent negative trials relative to nonrecent negative trials. Several functional neuroimaging experiments have related resolution of interference in the Monsell task to activity of the left inferior frontal lobe, specifically in Brodmann's

Table 12.1. Recent and Nonrecent Negative Trials, Experiment 1

List items	Probe	Correct response
	Recent negative trial	
cat–spoon–**desk**	cat	Yes
crew–job–ocean	**desk**	No
	Nonrecent negative trial	
duck–rock–**knife**	duck	Yes
cup–phone–arm	moon	No
fog–trash–book	book	Yes
hat–wood–fish	**knife**	No

Note. Words in bold are list words (first column) that are related to probe words (second column).

Area 45 (Jonides, Smith, Marshuetz, Koeppe, & Reuter-Lorenz, 1998; D'Esposito, Postle, Jonides, & Smith, 1999).

A Role for Inhibition in Short-Term Memory

Inhibition and interference resolution are prominent features in some contemporary models of short-term or working memory. For example, Hasher and colleagues (e.g., Hasher & Zacks, 1988) proposed that a critical component of both attentional and short-term memory processes is the ability to inhibit irrelevant information. Specifically, May, Hasher, and Kane (1999) proposed three functions for an inhibitory mechanism, suggesting that inhibition (a) restricts access into working memory to only relevant information, (b) deletes items that were once relevant but are no longer relevant, and (c) restrains the production of prepotent or highly probable responses until they can be adequately evaluated. Relevant to Hasher and colleagues' proposal that an inhibition mechanism deletes no-longer-relevant information is neurophysiological work with monkeys by Miller, Li, and Desimone (1993). Given data from cellular recordings in monkeys, Miller et al. inferred "an active reset process" that "clears out or resets the memory traces of stimuli from one trial to the next" to "avoid cross-trial interference" (p. 1475).

Similar proposals have been advanced by Engle and colleagues, who have claimed that "information maintenance in the face of interference is the critical function of working memory capacity" (Kane & Engle, 2003, p. 48). However, Engle and colleagues have remained largely agnostic regarding the exact mechanism by which interference is resolved. They have reported that a number of tasks, many seemingly unrelated to working memory capacity, nonetheless correlate with working memory performance, presumably because of their engagement of attentional control. For example, the Stroop task (Kane & Engle, 2003), the antisaccade task (Kane, Bleckley, Conway, & Engle, 2001), dichotic listening tasks (Conway, Cowan, & Bunting, 2001), and susceptibility to proactive interference (Rosen & Engle, 1998) are all reported to correlate with measures of working memory. Engle and colleagues have argued that these correlations are attributable to their reliance on controlled attention.

Case Study: M.L.

In this chapter, we summarize data from our investigations of inhibition in a patient, M.L., with a semantic short-term memory deficit. The tasks that we used are commonly assumed to recruit executive functions and to require inhibition. Having established that this patient had a deficit in one task that presumably required inhibition, we asked whether the patient was impaired on other tasks that have been reported to require inhibition.

Patient Background

M.L. was a 62-year-old right-handed man with a left-hemisphere lesion resulting from a stroke in 1990. He had completed 2 years of college and was employed as a draftsman before his stroke. A neurological report included an evaluation of a computed tomography scan and indicated that M.L.'s lesion included the left frontal and parietal operculum, with atrophy noted in the left temporal operculum and mild diffuse atrophy. A magnetic resonance imaging scan of M.L. revealed that his lesion was larger than indicated by the initial neurological report and included not only the left inferior frontal gyrus but also areas in the left middle frontal gyrus. In addition, M.L.'s lesion included areas of the left parietal lobe. The left temporal lobe appeared to be spared.

As reported by Martin and He (2004), M.L. was 77% correct for two-word lists and 10% correct for three-word lists on serial recall tasks. He showed no advantage for recall of words compared with recall of nonwords (Martin & Lesch, 1996). Moreover, he performed better on a probe task requiring detection of rhyming words relative to a probe task requiring detection of semantically related words, the reverse of the pattern shown by patients with a phonological short-term memory deficit. M.L.'s pattern of performance was consistent with a semantic short-term memory deficit. Despite his short-term memory deficit, M.L. had good comprehension of conversational speech on clinical examination. However, his narrative production was characterized by word-finding difficulties and reduced phrase length. It is important to note that M.L.'s repetition of single words was excellent (96% correct), and he showed no apraxia of speech. Thus, M.L.'s difficulties with semantic retention on short-term memory tasks and with spontaneous speech were not attributable to difficulty in comprehending word meanings or producing individual words. In fact, M.L. scored above the mean for control participants on the Peabody Picture Vocabulary Test–Revised (Dunn & Dunn, 1981), a standardized test of word comprehension, using norms for 40-year-old participants, the highest age for which norms are available (Martin & Lesch, 1996). On the Philadelphia Naming Test (Roach, Schwartz, Martin, Grewal, & Brecher, 1996), M.L. scored 98% correct, which was above the mean for control participants (96% correct). He performed at a normal level of accuracy on unspeeded and speeded tasks examining living–nonliving judgments and category judgments (Martin & He, 2004). His reaction times on the living–nonliving judgments were just outside the normal range, but on the category judgments his reaction times were longer than for control participants. Category judgments, however, place some demand on semantic short-term memory, given that participants must retain the category label while deciding whether the exemplar is a member of the category (Martin et al., 1994).

Recent Negatives Task and Proactive Interference

M.L. was tested on a number of versions of the recent negatives task, which assesses proactive interference. The data on these tests appeared in Hamilton and Martin (2005, 2007); we summarize the experiments in this section.

M.L.'s ability to inhibit irrelevant information in short-term memory was tested using a task designed to elicit proactive interference in short-term memory. We used the recent negatives task (Monsell, 1978), in which a list of items is presented serially, followed by a probe. The participant responds yes or no

Table 12.2. Reaction Time and Accuracy for the Recent Negatives Task: Control Participants and Patient M.L.

Participant	Recent negative trials	Nonrecent negative trials	Recent positive trials	Nonrecent positive trials	Interference effect[a]
	Reaction time (milliseconds)				
Control participants	1,006	915	873	872	91
M.L.	2,905	2,174	1,474	1,416	731
	Accuracy (% correct)				
Control participants	95*	99	99	99	
M.L.	63*	88	100	96	

[a]Interference effect is reaction time for recent negative trials minus reaction time for nonrecent negative trials.
*Recent negatives < nonrecent negatives $p < .05$.

according to whether the probe appeared in the list. Half of the trials were recent negative trials; the probe did not appear in the present list but appeared in the immediately preceding list. For the nonrecent negative trials, the negative probe did not appear in the previous two lists. The same manipulation was applied to the positive probes—a recent positive trial included a probe that appeared in the present list as well as the previous list. In a nonrecent positive trial, the probe appeared in the present list but not in the previous two lists. The interference effect was calculated using the contrast of recent negative versus nonrecent negative probes; reaction times were expected to be longer and accuracy lower for the recent negatives than the nonrecent negatives.

This paradigm provided a unique opportunity to decide between the decay and interference accounts of M.L.'s short-term memory deficit. If his deficit was attributable to the rapid decay of representations in short-term memory, then one would predict smaller-than-normal interference effects. If his deficit involved inhibiting no-longer-relevant representations from previous trials, then an exaggerated interference effect would be predicted.

Whereas Monsell's (1978) paradigm used 16 consonants, we modified the paradigm to use 16 words. Words would allow us to also examine semantic and phonological relatedness in determining interference effects. (M.L. was also tested on the same paradigm using letters, and these data were reported in Hamilton & Martin, 2007.) Table 12.2 provides the data for control participants and for M.L. Control participants demonstrated a significant interference effect for reaction time ($M = 91$ milliseconds) and were significantly less accurate on recent negative trials than on nonrecent negative trials (94.7% vs. 98.9% correct). By comparison, M.L. demonstrated an exaggerated interference effect in reaction time for recent versus nonrecent negatives (731 milliseconds). M.L.'s interference effect was 5.9 standard deviations above the mean interference effect for control participants and substantially outside their range. M.L.'s accuracy was much worse on recent negative trials (62.5%) than on nonrecent negative trials (87.5%). This 25% difference was statistically significant and far outside the range for control participants.

To address concerns regarding the comparison of difference scores of participants that show differences in mean reaction times, we also used a more conservative log transformation of untrimmed data.[1] Using log-transformed data, M.L.'s interference effect was well beyond the range of control participants.

Clearly, data from this experiment are not easily accommodated by assuming an abnormally rapid decay of representations in short-term memory. Rather, given these data, the most parsimonious explanation of M.L.'s deficit is that he had an abnormal persistence of activations in short-term memory.

Semantic and Phonological Influences on Proactive Interference

A second series of experiments (Hamilton & Martin, 2007) was conducted to further assess the hypothesis that M.L. experienced an abnormal persistence of representations in short term memory. We wished to replicate the previous finding of abnormal persistence and also to examine the nature of the code that persists (i.e., is it semantic or phonological or both?). To that end, probes were used that shared either semantic or phonological features with a list item. Previous work in our laboratory (Bartha, Martin, & Jensen, 1998) demonstrated that semantic relatedness does elicit proactive interference in short-term memory probe tasks for healthy participants, at least for items in the current list. We therefore examined the role of both semantic and phonological representations in eliciting interference in the recent negatives task for items from the current list and from the previous list.

These experiments provided further insight into the nature of M.L.'s deficit by addressing the level at which M.L. was failing to inhibit previously presented stimuli. If M.L.'s deficit were one of rapid decay of semantic representations, M.L. would be predicted to show little or no proactive interference from semantically related probes. However, he might show normal or exaggerated interference from phonologically related probes. Exaggerated interference from phonologically related probes might be expected if his failure to adequately maintain semantic representations in short-term memory resulted in a greater reliance on phonological information than was the case for control participants. Alternatively, if some type of inhibitory mechanism was failing to operate on semantic representations in short-term memory, M.L. might show interference effects exceeding those for healthy control participants for semantically related probes. Such would be the case if M.L. lacked an "active reset mechanism" that was specific to semantic representations.

Probes were constructed to maximize their phonological or semantic similarity with a single list item. Examples of the related trials appear in Table 12.3.

---

[1] Given the common objections to the use of difference scores in comparing interference effects for subjects showing large differences in mean reaction times (see Verhaeghen & De Meersman, 1998), we also calculated interference using log transformations. The log transformation minimizes the influence of outliers, and the difference between logarithms (used to calculate interference effects) is equivalent to a ratio (Meiran, 1996).

Table 12.3. Phonologically and Semantically Related Trials, Experiment 2

List items	Probe	Correct response
	Phonological—same-list trials	
gun–log–**hair**	**pear**	No
	Phonological previous-list trials	
gun–log–**hair**	tea	No
hub–book–sky	**pear**	No
	Semantic—same-list trials	
gun–bar–**frog**	**toad**	No
	Semantic—previous-list trials	
gun–bar–**frog**	tea	No
hub–book–sky	**toad**	No

Note. Words in bold are list words (first column) that are related to probe words (second column).

On a phonologically related trial, the list item (presented in either the same list or the previous list) shared phonology with the probe word (e.g., list item *hair*, probe word *pear*). Similarly, in semantically related trials, the probe shared semantic features with the previously presented list item (e.g., probe word *toad*, list item *frog*). It was hypothesized that proactive interference would result when a list item presented in the same trial or the immediately previous trial was phonologically or semantically related to a subsequent probe. In this experiment, three-item lists were presented followed by a probe word, and participants judged whether the probe word was in the list. Half of the negative probes were either semantically or phonologically related to previously presented items; the other half were completely unrelated to previously presented items. Half of the related negative probes matched an item in the current list, whereas the other half matched an item in the preceding list. Positive probe trials were also presented, and there were equal numbers of negative and positive trials.

Results for this experiment appear in Table 12.4. Interference effects for each related condition were calculated by subtracting mean reaction times for unrelated negative trials from the related conditions. Control participants showed significant interference effects for both phonologically related (76 milliseconds) and semantically related probes (40 milliseconds), but only when the probe was related to an item in the same list. This finding replicates the semantic interference reported by Bartha et al. (1998) in a similar probe-recognition paradigm. However, these interference effects did not extend to probes that were related to items in previous lists.

In contrast to the results for healthy control participants, M.L. showed large, statistically significant interference on all four related conditions. On the phonologically related same-list trials, M.L. showed a 387-millisecond interference effect. M.L. showed interference effects of 276 milliseconds on the

Table 12.4. Reaction Time and Accuracy for Phonologically and Semantically Related Trials in the Recent Negatives Task: Control Participants and Patients M.L. and E.A.

Participant	Phonological same-list trials	Phonological previous-list trials	Semantic same-list trials	Semantic previous-list trials	Unrelated condition	
					Negative	Positive
Reaction time (milliseconds)						
Control participants	861*	810	825*	790	785	753
M.L.	1,596*	1,485*	1,565*	1,703*	1,209	929
E.A.	1,257	1,255	1,176	1,178	1,206	1,219
Accuracy (% correct)						
Control participants	97*	99	99	99	99	99
M.L.	83	90	95	93	94	92
E.A.	98	100	100	98	99	62

*Related condition versus unrelated condition $p < .05$.

phonologically related previous-list trials, 356 milliseconds on the semantically related same-list trials, and 494 milliseconds on the semantically related previous-list trials.

Again, the most parsimonious explanation for these data from the recent negatives task is that M.L. suffered from abnormal persistence of representations in short-term memory. If M.L.'s deficit was attributable to overly rapid decay of representations in short-term memory, one would predict that M.L. would demonstrate less interference, not the exaggerated interference effects that we found. However, one could conceivably explain these data from the recent negatives paradigm with a rapid decay account. For example, one might suggest that M.L. rapidly lost information from the current list and thus had difficulty distinguishing current and previous list items not because the items from the previous list were overly active in memory, but because the current-list items were too weakly activated. As discussed in the next section, a comparison of serial position functions for positive and negative probes from M.L. and from a patient (E.A.) with a phonological short-term memory deficit is instructive in this regard.

Phonological Short-Term Memory Deficits and the Recent Negatives Task

E.A., a patient with a phonological short-term memory deficit (for a full description and background, see Martin, Shelton, & Yaffee, 1994), was also tested on versions of the recent negatives task. E.A.'s span for list recall was about one item smaller than M.L.'s. For example, when recalling words varying in frequency and imageability, E.A. scored 70% items correct for two-word lists, whereas M.L. scored 97% correct on the two-word lists and 76% correct on the three-word lists. In contrast to M.L.'s exaggerated interference effects, E.A. showed no interference effects. On a task identical to the experiment administered to M.L. (using the same task parameters but different words), E.A. showed no significant difference in accuracy on the recent versus nonrecent negatives, and her reaction time effect was in the wrong direction. E.A.'s overall mean accuracy was similar to M.L.'s, but she was more accurate on negative than positive trials, whereas the reverse was the case for M.L. Although we cannot rule out the possibility that these patterns reflect only differences in the choice of a decision criterion for the two patients, they are consistent with a decay account for E.A. and a persisting activation account for M.L. That is, if information rapidly decays, then the patient should find little match between the probe and the list items, even for the current list, resulting in a preponderance of no responses. If information persists, then a yes response should be likely, particularly for items from immediately preceding lists. The failure to find any effect of the recent versus nonrecent negatives manipulation for E.A. is also consistent with rapid decay of information.

In Experiment 2, E.A. continued to show a preponderance of no responses and failed to show significant interference for any of the related probe conditions (see Table 12.3). Her accuracy data by serial position also support a rapid decay account; she was much more accurate on probes that matched a list item

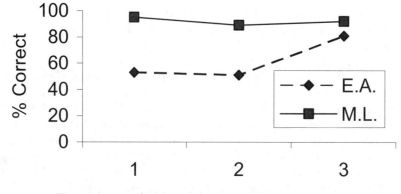

Figure 12.1. Serial position effects on positive trials in Experiment 2 for patients M.L. and E.A.

at the third serial position (81%) than at the first (53%) and second (51%) serial positions (see Figure 12.1). This result suggests that representations decayed so quickly that E.A. could consistently retain only the item in the third serial position. M.L.'s serial position effects were very different (Figure 12.1). For positive trials, M.L.'s accuracy was high and showed no clear serial position effect. He scored 95% for trials in which probes matched items in the first serial position, 89% for the second serial position, and 92% for the third serial position. Thus, although E.A.'s data seem to be best explained by the rapid decay of representations in short-term memory, M.L.'s data suggest that his short-term memory problems were not attributable primarily to rapid decay.

M.L.'s interference on both phonologically related and semantically related trials is somewhat surprising, given that his pattern of short-term memory difficulties was associated with retention of semantic information. However, if his short-term memory deficit were due solely to a rapid loss of semantic information, then no semantic interference would have been predicted. Alternatively, if his short-term memory deficit were due solely to difficulty inhibiting semantic information, then interference from semantically but not phonologically related list items would have been predicted. We observed neither of these patterns. Instead, the results indicate that ML experienced greater than normal interference with both phonological and semantic representations. As reported in Martin et al. (2003), patients labeled as having semantic short-term memory deficits were also somewhat impaired in their retention of phonological information. Although their phonological retention was better than that of patients identified as having phonological short-term memory deficits, they performed below normal on tasks that were thought to tap mainly phonological representations, such as nonword list recall (e.g., Martin & He, 2004; Martin et al., 1994). One hypothesis is that these patients with semantic short-term memory deficits had difficulty inhibiting all types of verbal information. Another possibility is that patients with phonological short-term memory deficits may, in fact, have had a specific deficit resulting in the rapid loss of phonological information that in turn resulted in a more severe deficit on tasks tapping phonological retention.

Other Tests of Inhibition

We tested M.L. on a number of other tasks assumed to involve inhibition (Hamilton & Martin, 2005). However, unlike the recent negatives task, none of these tasks are intended to tap short-term or working memory but are commonly considered to involve executive function. Two of these tasks were demonstrated to load on an inhibition factor in the Miyake et al. (2000) factor analytic study of executive function. We also used two verbal and two nonverbal tasks, thus allowing us to determine whether M.L. had difficulty in both the verbal and nonverbal domains. The tasks we used were the Stroop task, the recent negatives task, a nonverbal Stroop task, and the antisaccade task. Given that previous studies have reported a relation between antisaccade perfor- mance and working memory performance (e.g., Kane et al., 2001), the antisac- cade task was of particular interest in this study. Because of space restrictions, we only summarize these data, but a full account is found in Hamilton and Martin (2005).

STROOP TASK. The Stroop task is widely considered the quintessential mea- sure of inhibitory control. Many theoretical approaches to explaining the Stroop effect involve an inhibitory component (e.g., Cohen, Dunbar, & McClelland, 1990; Posner & Snyder, 1975). MacLeod, Dodd, Sheard, Wilson, and Bibi (2003) argued, however, that inhibition is not necessarily involved. They pointed to Roelofs's (2003) model of the Stroop effect as being the most successful in accounting for the full range of findings, and they claimed that this model has no inhibitory component. However, this model achieves attentional control by allowing the processing network to receive much longer input from the relevant dimension (ink color) than from the irrelevant dimension (word). Roelofs de- scribed the production rule that carries out this function as follows: "If the goal is to say the name of the color, and input is received from a word, THEN block out the word input" (p. 101). It would seem entirely reasonable to consider blocking out the word input to be an example of inhibition.

In our Stroop experiment, participants simply named the color of the stimulus presented on the screen. Stimuli were either color words (*red, green, blue, orange, yellow,* or *purple*) or rows of asterisks. The interference effect was characterized by participants taking a longer time to name the color on incongruent trials (the word *red* appearing in blue) than on neutral trials (a row of asterisks appearing in blue). Twelve congruent trials were also presented. We compared M.L. with 10 control participants on this task.

M.L.'s interference effect was 12.4 standard deviations above the mean interference effect for control participants and well outside the control partici- pants' range. Using transformed onset latencies to address concerns about comparing difference scores for individuals who have large differences in mean reaction times (Verhaeghen & De Meersman, 1998), M.L.'s interference effect was still well outside the range of control participants.

NONVERBAL STROOP TASK. We developed another task to be analogous to the Stroop task with nonverbal stimuli. The nonverbal Stroop task requires the resolution of conflict when the local direction of an arrow and spatial position of the same arrow conflict. For example, when presented a right-pointing arrow on the left half of a display, participants have to indicate which direction the arrow is pointing. Conflict between the direction the arrow is pointing and its spatial position is the source of an interference effect.

Arrows pointing either to the left or to the right were presented on a computer display, and participants were asked to press a key corresponding to each direction. Analogous to the Stroop task, there were congruent trials (e.g., a right-pointing arrow on the right side of the display), neutral trials (either right- or left-pointing arrows appearing in the middle of the display), and incongruent trials (e.g., a left-pointing arrow appearing on the right side of the display). Interference was calculated by subtracting reaction times of neutral trials from reaction times of incongruent trials.

M.L.'s interference effect was well within the range of control participants. Given these data, it appears that resolving response conflict in this nonverbal task was not as difficult as resolving conflict in the verbal Stroop task. Although one might argue that our nonverbal Stroop task differs fundamentally from the classical Stroop task, similar tasks have traditionally been considered to represent a variation of Stroop interference (for a review, see MacLeod, 1991).

M.L.'s normal performance on the nonverbal Stroop task and greatly exaggerated interference effects on both the verbal Stroop and recent negatives tasks suggest that his deficit in inhibition might have been limited to the verbal domain. Testing M.L. on the antisaccade task provided another opportunity to test this possibility. Given that the antisaccade task is a difficult task, with accuracy in the range of 79% to 88% for undergraduate participants (Roberts, Hager, & Heron, 1994), data from this task also allowed us to determine whether M.L.'s difference in performance on verbal and nonverbal Stroop tasks was attributable merely to task difficulty.

ANTISACCADE TASK. The antisaccade task is sensitive to one's ability to inhibit reflexive eye movements toward sudden onsets of stimuli presented in the periphery of the visual field. Instead of making eye movements toward the stimulus, participants are asked to make an eye movement in the opposite direction in order to detect a target presented on the opposite side of the display. Although this task has no obvious short-term or working memory requirements, performance on the antisaccade task has been reported to correlate with working memory ability (Kane et al., 2001; Mitchell, Macrae, & Gilchrist, 2002; Roberts et al., 1994).

We used the antisaccade task reported by Miyake et al. (2000). Participants must resist making a reflexive saccade to the initial cue in order to detect the target on the opposite side of the screen. Given the brief presentation of the target, the target is difficult, if not impossible, to identify if the participant makes an initial saccade to the cue.

M.L.'s accuracy and reaction times were indistinguishable from those of normal control participants. M.L.'s normal level of performance on the antisaccade task would seem contrary to findings from normal participants indicating a relation between antisaccade performance and working memory capacity (Kane et al., 2001).

DISCUSSION OF OTHER TASKS OF INHIBITION. The results from the verbal Stroop task indicate that M.L.'s difficulty with inhibition was not limited to tasks with a short-term memory component. Moreover, it was evident that M.L. was impaired on the verbal tasks (the Stroop and recent negatives tasks) but performed normally on the nonverbal tasks (nonverbal Stroop and antisaccade tasks). These results suggest a distinction between the cognitive and brain mechanisms involved in inhibition in the verbal and nonverbal domains.

The dissociation between Stroop and antisaccade performance is particularly interesting given that the two tasks load on a single factor in factor analytic studies (Miyake et al., 2000). Thus, these data challenge many of the individual differences studies examining these tasks with healthy participants. For example, Kane and Engle (2002) proposed that a single mechanism, localized to the dorsolateral prefrontal cortex, is involved in performance of the antisaccade task and the Stroop task and resolution of proactive interference. In this chapter, we have presented a patient with a deficit in short-term memory (he was unable to reliably recall even three items during serial recall) who performed poorly on the Stroop task as well as on tasks that promote proactive interference but nevertheless had no difficulty with the antisaccade task. Such a pattern of performance seems to indicate that these three tasks do not depend on a single mechanism. We suggest that correlations among these tasks may result from the activity of common neurotransmitter systems, such as dopamine, which vary across individuals. Thus, even though different brain regions may be involved in inhibition tasks, these regions may be modulated by a single neurotransmitter mechanism.

Short-Term Memory Deficits and Inhibition: Implications for Language Processing

Reinterpreting semantic short-term memory deficits as deficits in inhibition forces one to consider the possibility that the associated language deficits may also involve deficits in inhibition. In this section, we provide some speculation as to how an inhibitory deficit might account for the language deficits.

Some of the production deficits described elsewhere are readily accommodated by an inhibition account. For example, Freedman et al. (2004) reported that patients with semantic short-term memory deficits showed unusual interference effects during naming of semantically related pairs of pictures. This difficulty may be attributable to the absence of an inhibitory mechanism that allows selection from among competing items in a phrase. More specifically, inhibition may be especially useful in rapidly selecting from among semantically related representations that are linked within a semantic network. When a semantic representation is activated, it may obligatorily activate related representations that are normally inhibited during selection by some control process originating in the prefrontal cortex. Without this mechanism, related semantic representations stay activated. In the context of naming, increased activation among related items elicited by two semantically related pictures elicits even greater activation, and selection mechanisms are unable to efficiently resolve competition among these representations.

Yet another means of providing an inhibitory deficit account for language production is to assume that the difficulty in production is related specifically to impairments in producing words in the proper order. Several models of serial behavior have proposed the necessity of inhibitory functions in serial ordering. For instance, in Estes's (1972) hierarchical model of serial recall, inhibition is a prominent component. This model assumes that elements to be recalled are connected to control elements and that serial output depends on inhibitory connections between successive elements (and between successive control elements). During output, the control element inhibits all of the following elements under the same control element. Once this control element has been recalled, its activation is set to zero by a self-inhibiting mechanism. This self-inhibition of the first control element allows the second element to have the highest activation, because it is no longer inhibited by Element 1 while it is simultaneously inhibiting Elements 3 and 4. Although this model was created to account for patterns in serial recall of verbal materials, Estes suggested that it could be applied to other domains, including language production.

MacKay (1982, 1987) and Eikmeyer and Schade (1991) presented structurally similar models for language production. In these models, there is a separation between the nodes that represent the sequencing of word classes and the specific lexical elements that are attached to these sequencing elements. In the MacKay (1987) model, lateral inhibition is assumed to occur between the sequential structural elements, such as adjective and noun in the phrase "curly hair," rather than between specific lexical representations.

Dell, Burger, and Svec (1997) proposed another model similar to the MacKay (1982, 1987) model in several respects. Content elements are connected on one side to a plan based on long-term weights and, on the other side, to a structural frame. Although there are no inhibitory links between content elements, Dell et al. stated that one possible mechanism for ordering the activation of the elements in the structural frame would be forward lateral inhibition, as in the Estes (1972) and MacKay approaches. Furthermore, in Dell et al.'s model, activation from the frame to the past is set at zero, which is equivalent to self-inhibition.

Although some production deficits are easily accommodated by an inhibitory deficit account, it is much more difficult to interpret the comprehension deficits associated with semantic short-term memory deficits (Hanten & Martin, 2000; Martin & He, 2004; Martin et al., 1994) using such a framework. The present challenge is to develop paradigms that may determine the relative contributions of inhibition and decay in explaining comprehension deficits.

Conclusion

We have presented evidence from a brain-damaged patient, M.L., that is consistent with a difficulty in inhibition. One major theme of the chapters in this volume is whether it is necessary to postulate an inhibitory component in cognitive function or whether activation or other noninhibitory processes could instead account for resolution of interference. We have argued that it is unlikely that M.L.'s performance on the short-term probe-recognition tasks could be attributed to a failure to sufficiently activate memory representations for the list items. To address the possibility of the involvement of other noninhibitory processes, it would be necessary to spell out exactly what these processes are and to distinguish them from inhibition. In Roelofs's (2003) model of the Stroop effect, interference is minimized by reducing the time that activation from the irrelevant dimension spreads through the network. As discussed in this chapter, such a process would seem to qualify as one involving inhibition, similar to one of the inhibitory processes suggested by Kane et al. (2001) involving restricting access of information into working memory.

Of course, one could postulate other interference resolution mechanisms that do not involve inhibition. For instance, in the recent negatives task, participants might assess the familiarity of the probe by assessing the degree of match between the probe and any activated memory representations. Interference in responding to a recent negative might occur because on such trials a degree of match is detected that is below a yes decision criterion but above a no decision criterion. In such situations, a second process might be invoked that checks for contextual features that provide information about the list in which the (partially) matching item appeared. In resolving interference in the Stroop task, if two different responses are activated (one for the ink color and one for the word) such that a critical difference threshold in activation is not reached, then a boost of activation might be initiated through the system (perhaps only from the relevant dimension) until the difference threshold is achieved. (Such a proposal would seem to be in some ways at odds with the model proposed by Roelofs [2003], in which activation flowing from the irrelevant dimension is minimized.) If these proposals are correct, then M.L.'s deficit might be hypothesized to be in an executive system that, under specific conditions, initiates secondary processes when initial activation does not lead to a response.

At present, we do not have any data that could distinguish between a deficit in inhibition and a deficit in a variety of control mechanisms such as those we have described. An inhibitory deficit would seem to provide a more parsimonious account of our findings. In some domains, convincing evidence of the persistence of inhibition has been demonstrated (Anderson, 2003; Mayr & Keele, 2000), and thus we are convinced that inhibition does play some role in cognitive processes. Whether an inhibitory deficit is the single best account of the pattern of performance demonstrated by M.L. must await further investigation.

References

Anderson, M. C. (2003). Rethinking interference theory: Executive control and the mechanisms of forgetting. *Journal of Memory and Language, 49,* 415–445.

Bartha, M. C., Martin, R. C., & Jensen, C. R. (1998). Multiple interference effects in short-term recognition memory. *American Journal of Psychology, 111,* 89–118.

Cohen, J. D., Dunbar, K., & McClelland, J. L. (1990). On the control of automatic processes: A parallel distributed processing model of the Stroop effect. *Psychological Review, 97,* 332–361.

Conway, A. R. A., Cowan, N., & Bunting, M. F. (2001). The cocktail party phenomenon revisited: The importance of working memory capacity. *Psychonomic Bulletin & Review, 8,* 331–335.

Dell, G. S., Burger, L. K., & Svec, W. R. (1997). Language production and serial order: A functional analysis and a model. *Psychological Review, 104,* 123–147.

D'Esposito, M., Postle, B. R., Jonides, J., & Smith, E. E. (1999). The neural substrate and temporal dynamics of interference effects in working memory as revealed by event-related functional MRI. *Proceedings of the National Academy of Sciences, USA, 96,* 7514–7519.

Dunn, L., & Dunn, L. (1981). *Peabody Picture Vocabulary Test—Revised.* Circle Pines, MN: American Guidance Service.

Eikmeyer, H.-J., & Schade, U. (1991). Sequentialization in connectionist language-production models. *Cognitive Systems, 3,* 128–138.

Estes, W. K. (1972). An associative basis for coding and organization in memory. In A. W. Melton & E. Martin (Eds.), *Coding processes in human memory* (pp. 161–190). Washington, DC: Winston.

Freedman, M., Martin, R., & Biegler, K. (2004). Semantic relatedness effects in conjoined noun phrase production: Implications for the role of short-term memory. *Cognitive Neuropsychology, 21,* 245–265.

Hamilton, A. C., & Martin, R. C. (2005). Dissociations among tasks involving inhibition: A single-case study. *Cognitive, Affective, & Behavioral Neuroscience, 5,* 1–13.

Hamilton, A. C., & Martin, R. C. (2007). Proactive interference in a semantic short-term memory deficit: Role of semantic and phonological relatedness. *Cortex, 43,* 112–123.

Hanten, G., & Martin, R. (2000). Contributions of phonological and semantic short-term memory to sentence processing: Evidence from two cases of closed head injury in children. *Journal of Memory and Language, 43,* 335–361.

Hasher, L., & Zacks, R. T. (1988). Working memory, comprehension, and aging: A review and a new view. In G. H. Bower (Ed.), *The psychology of learning and motivation* (Vol. 22, pp. 193–225). New York: Academic Press.

Jonides, J., Smith, E. E., Marshuetz, C., Koeppe, R. A., & Reuter-Lorenz, P. A. (1998). Inhibition in verbal working memory revealed by brain activation. *Proceedings of the National Academy of Sciences, USA, 95,* 8410–8413.

Kane, M. J., Bleckley, M. K., Conway, A. R. A., & Engle, R. W. (2001). A controlled-attention view of working-memory capacity. *Journal of Experimental Psychology: General, 130,* 169–183.

Kane, M. J., & Engle, R. W. (2002). The role of prefrontal cortex in working-memory capacity, executive attention and general fluid intelligence: an individual-differences perspective. *Psychonomic Bulletin & Review, 9,* 637–671.

Kane, M. J., & Engle, R. W. (2003). Working memory capacity and the control of attention: The contributions of goal neglect, response competition, and task set to Stroop interference. *Journal of Experimental Psychology: General, 132,* 47–70.

MacKay, D. G. (1982). The problems of flexibility, fluency and speed–accuracy trade-off in skilled behaviors. *Psychological Review, 89,* 483–506.

MacKay, D. G. (1987). *The organization of perception and action: A theory for language and other cognitive skills.* New York: Sprague.

MacLeod, C. M. (1991). Half a century of research on the Stroop effect: An integrative review. *Psychological Bulletin, 109,* 163–203.

MacLeod, C. M., Dodd, M. D., Sheard, E. D., Wilson, D. E., & Bibi, U. (2003). In opposition to inhibition. *Psychology of Learning and Motivation, 43,* 163–214.

Majerus, S., Van der Linden, M., Poncelet, M., & Metz-Lutz, M.-N. (2004). Can phonological and semantic short-term memory be dissociated? Further evidence from Landau–Kleffner syndrome. *Cognitive Neuropsychology, 21,* 491–512.

Martin, R. C. (2005). Components of short-term memory and their relation to language processing: Evidence from neuropsychology and neuroimaging. *Current Directions in Psychological Science, 14,* 204–208.

Martin, R. C., Burton, P. C., & Hamilton, A. C. (2005, October). *Left inferior frontal involvement in semantic retention during phrase comprehension and production: Evidence from functional neuroimaging.* Paper presented at the 43rd annual meeting of the Academy of Aphasia, Amsterdam.

Martin, R. C., & Freedman, M. L. (2001). Short-term retention of lexical–semantic representations: Implications for speech production. *Memory, 9,* 261–280.

Martin, R. C., & He, T. (2004). Semantic short-term memory and its role in sentence processing: A replication. *Brain and Language, 89,* 76–82.

Martin, R. C., & Lesch, M. F. (1996). Associations and dissociations between language impairment and list recall: Implications for models of short-term memory. In S. Gathercole (Ed.), *Models of short-term memory* (pp. 149–178). Hove, England: Erlbaum.

Martin, R. C., & Romani, C. (1994). Verbal working memory and sentence comprehension: A multiple-components view. *Neuropsychology, 8,* 506–523.

Martin, R. C., Shelton, J. R., & Yaffee, L. S. (1994). Language processing and working memory: Neuropsychological evidence for separate phonological and semantic capacities. *Journal of Memory and Language, 33,* 83–111.

Martin, R. C., Wu, D., Freedman, M., Jackson, E. F., & Lesch, M. (2003). An event-related fMRI investigation of phonological versus semantic short-term memory. *Journal of Neurolinguistics, 16,* 341–360.

May, C. P., Hasher, L., & Kane, M. J. (1999). The role of interference in memory span. *Memory & Cognition, 27,* 759–767.

Mayr, U., & Keele, S. W. (2000). Changing internal constraints on action: The role of backward inhibition. *Journal of Experimental Psychology: General, 129,* 4–26.

Meiran, N. (1996). Reconfiguration of processing mode prior to task performance. *Journal of Experimental Psychology: Learning, Memory, and Cognition, 22,* 1423–1442.

Miller, E. K., Li, L., & Desimone, R. (1993). Activity of neurons in anterior inferior temporal cortex during a short-term memory task. *Journal of Neuroscience, 13,* 1460–1478.

Mitchell, J. P., Macrae, C. N., & Gilchrist, I. D. (2002). Working memory and suppression of reflexive saccades. *Journal of Cognitive Neuroscience, 14,* 95–103.

Miyake, A., Friedman, N. P., Emerson, M. J., Witzki, A. H., Howerter, A., & Wager, T. D. (2000). The unity and diversity of executive functions and their contributions to complex "frontal lobe" tasks: A latent variable analysis. *Cognitive Psychology, 41,* 49–100.

Monsell, S. (1978). Recency, immediate recognition memory, and reaction time. *Cognitive Psychology, 10,* 465–501.

Posner, M. I., & Snyder, C. R. R. (1975). Attention and cognitive control. In R. L. Solso (Ed.), *Information processing and cognition: The Loyola symposium* (pp. 55–85). Hillsdale, NJ: Erlbaum.

Roach, A., Schwartz, M. F., Martin, N., Grewal, R. S., & Brecher, A. (1996). The Philadelphia Naming Test: Scoring and rationale. *Clinical Aphasiology, 24,* 121–134.

Roberts, R. J., Hager, L. D., & Heron, C. (1994). Prefrontal cognitive processes: Working memory and inhibition in the antisaccade task. *Journal of Experimental Psychology: General, 123,* 374–393.

Roelofs, A. (2003). Goal-referenced selection of verbal action: Modeling attentional control in the Stroop task. *Psychological Review, 110,* 88–125.

Rosen, V. M., & Engle, R. W. (1998). Working memory capacity and suppression. *Journal of Memory and Language, 39,* 418–436.

Shivde, G., & Thompson-Schill, S. (2004). Dissociating semantic and phonological maintenance using fMRI. *Cognitive, Affective, & Behavioral Neuroscience, 4,* 10–19.

Smith, M., & Wheeldon, L. (1999). High level processing scope in spoken sentence production. *Cognition, 73,* 205–246.

Smith, M., & Wheeldon, L. R. (2004). Horizontal information flow in spoken sentence production. *Journal of Experimental Psychology: Learning, Memory, and Cognition, 30,* 675–686.

Verhaeghen, P., & De Meersman, L. (1998). Aging and Stroop effect: A meta-analysis. *Psychology and Aging, 13,* 120–126.

13

Concepts of Inhibition and Developmental Psychopathology

Joel T. Nigg, Laurie Carr, Michelle Martel,
and John M. Henderson

In this chapter, we review the body of work performed in our laboratory and reviewed in the literature that attempts to isolate different kinds of putative inhibitory control in relation to attention-deficit/hyperactivity disorder (ADHD) and, to a lesser extent, other forms of impulsive psychopathology. ADHD is a disorder usually identified in childhood but that is now known to also occur in adults. It is described clinically by two highly correlated but partially distinct symptom domains: inattention–disorganization (e.g., losing things, not paying attention, having difficulty staying on task) and hyperactivity–impulsivity. These domains in turn are used to define a primarily inattentive subtype (ADHD–PI), a primarily hyperactive–impulsive subtype (ADHD–PH), and a combined subtype that involves both inattention and hyperactivity–impulsivity (ADHD–CT). Another type of psychopathology that we discuss is borderline personality disorder, a syndrome marked by unstable and intense interpersonal relationships, extreme anger, fear of abandonment, and self-destructive and impulsive behavior. We also mention conduct disorder (extreme rule breaking and aggressive behavior in childhood) and antisocial personality disorder (extreme rule breaking, aggression, and indifference to the rights of others in adulthood). Finally, we mention substance use disorders (out-of-control use of alcohol or illicit drugs).

We present convergent evidence using multiple approaches to suggest that in parsing psychopathology, it is important to distinguish several kinds of inhibitory control, in particular effortful versus reactive control and motor response suppression versus interference control. We come to the following four conclusions:

1. ADHD is related to problems in the effortful suppression of motor responses independently of a wide range of co-occurring symptoms and disorders.

Work on this chapter was supported by National Institute of Mental Health Grant R01-MH63146 to Joel Nigg, John Henderson, and Fernanda Ferreira.

2. ADHD is not, however, related to problems in the control of interfering information in either perception or attention.

3. At least two distinct kinds of control mechanisms contribute to ADHD, one an effortful process related primarily to symptoms of inattention–disorganization and the other a reactive control process related to symptoms of hyperactivity–impulsivity.

4. Response inhibition is related with only partial specificity to ADHD. Response initiation also has important relations with symptoms of borderline personality disorder and substance use disorders but not symptoms of anxiety or depression.

In this chapter we review evidence for these conclusions and identify the relative strength of these conclusions. (Evidence is very strong for Conclusion 1, for instance, whereas that for Conclusion 2 is more tentative.)

Why is examination of these types of mechanisms in psychopathology important? First, validation of the distinctions among mental disorders (classifications that should be considered open constructs in the process of being validated and revised) is substantially strengthened if the disorders can be related to distinct psychological or physiological mechanisms. Second, studies of within-individual variation in relevant domains of function also contribute to establishing the construct validity of mental disorders. For example, depression resulting from a personal loss that continues for weeks or months may be viewed as a normal healthy response but is considered maladaptive when that depression is incapacitating and persists for years beyond the loss (Wakefield, 1999).

Moreover, the search for within-individual mechanisms is ideally translational in approach. In other words, basic science knowledge is brought to bear in the clinical assessment and measurement of mental disorders. Fundamental insights from cognitive science and cognitive neuroscience, as well as from normal development, temperament, and personality research, have thus been in the forefront of tools used to describe psychopathology. Across disciplines, the construct of inhibition has been among the most widely considered and thus has been as generative and popular in clinical science as in many other fields of psychology. In this chapter we do not attempt to resolve questions about whether operative mechanisms in particular task paradigms are actually inhibitory. Rather, we explore what these paradigms might tell us about each mental disorder and what questions will be important to resolve to enable clinical application of these measures.

With respect to its clinical application, deficits in inhibition have been identified as potentially relevant in disorders as diverse as ADHD, antisocial personality disorder, alcoholism and substance abuse, anxiety and mood disorders, bipolar disorder, borderline personality disorder, obsessive–compulsive disorder, posttraumatic stress disorder, and others. This wide-ranging application may be explained by the fact that theorists addressing these different conditions draw on different fields of basic science (e.g., cognitive psychology vs. personality and temperament) and so invoke different concepts of inhibition to explain disparate clinical difficulties.

Therefore, several conceptual clarifications are needed to evaluate the role of the construct of inhibition in the clinical sciences. We highlight distinct conceptual and theoretical types of inhibition that can guide empirical questions in psychopathology, and we illustrate the yield in applying these approaches. Along the way, we also hope to illustrate how the study of clinical populations and different age groups can provide convergent evidence regarding the likely structure of control abilities.

Conceptual Issues and Framework

Disinhibition often is thought of and used as a synonym for *impulsivity*, but we do not necessarily use it in that way in this chapter. Impulsive behavior is considered to be the result of a breakdown in inhibitory control mechanisms. However, disinhibition must also be considered in the context of other regulatory influences, such as affective processing (e.g., strong reward response) and arousal (e.g., extreme fatigue or excitement). Therefore, the degree to which impulsivity is related to a primary impairment in inhibition is an important empirical and theoretical question. *Impulsivity*, as we define it, specifically means fast and inaccurate (e.g., careless) responding in contexts in which slow, careful responding is necessary for goal success (see Moeller, Barratt, Dougherty, Schmitz, & Swann, 2001). Clinically, impulsive behavior can take several forms, such as speaking before one should (as in ADHD); making sudden, rash decisions, such as a major ill-advised purchase (as in mania); eating or using alcohol or drugs contrary to one's intentions or plans (as in eating disorders or substance abuse); and other behaviors that can harm oneself or others.

These examples illustrate impulsivity on the output end of processing (i.e., molar behavior). One can, for example, metaphorically conceptualize impulsive behavior emanating from frontal brain injury as a "release from inhibition." Such patients may also exhibit impairments in information processing (the input end of processing), because inhibitory processes are a critical aspect of cognitive functioning. For example, the temporal organization of behavior (an element of executive functioning) may depend on the ability to suppress processing steps that are not yet timely. In all, the symptomatic manifestation after a head injury apparently involves breakdowns in cognitive control processes. Yet this metaphor does not necessarily extend to impulsive behavior in psychopathology, which may or may not involve a breakdown in cognitive or neural mechanisms of inhibition.

To capture the various problems seen in different kinds of psychopathology and to describe these problems clearly require additional delineation of different domains or kinds of putative inhibitory control. Table 13.1 provides a schematic summary of the framework that guides our research program (for more details, see Nigg, 2000). We summarize the framework briefly in the following paragraphs.

First, the concept of behavioral inhibition is derived from temperament theory and is closely related to the term *reactive inhibition* that we have adopted

Table 13.1. Conceptual Organization of Inhibition Functions in Cognitive and Temperament and Personality Models

Construct	Cognitive measure	Temperament dimensions	Personality dimensions
Reactive inhibition	Incentive-based tasks	Reactive control Negative emotionality Behavioral inhibition	Neuroticism Introversion
Automatic selection	Negative priming Attentional blink "Pop-out" feature search	?	?
Controlled selection	Conjunction search Change detection	?	?
Interference control	Selective attention Stroop (?)	Effortful control	Conscientiousness Constraint
Executive response Inhibition/suppression	Stop-signal task Go/no-go task	Effortful control	Conscientiousness Constraint

Note. ? = insufficient data to support even a speculative linkage.

in Table 13.1. Kagan and colleagues (e.g., Kagan & Snidman, 2004) established that young children can be classified by their physiological and behavioral responses to entering a room of unfamiliar children, meeting an unfamiliar person, or being offered an unfamiliar object. Children who are behaviorally inhibited exhibit stronger physiological reactions to the situation and are slower to gain physical proximity to or interact with new children (Kagan, Reznick, & Gibbons, 1989; Kagan, Reznick, & Snidman, 1987). Children who are uninhibited exhibit opposite tendencies. This reaction is relatively spontaneous (rather than strategic or effortful) and therefore is a "reactive" type of control, as we explain below. These temperamental types have some predictive validity for later psychopathology in that inhibited preschoolers are somewhat more likely to develop social anxiety disorders later and are less likely to develop externalizing behavior problems (Biederman et al., 1993, 2001) than uninhibited children. Temperament theorists argue that this type of reactive (involuntary) behavioral inhibition in children is governed by subcortical limbic (in particular, amygdalar) activation that overrides exploratory behavior, goal-directed behavior, or other behavior plans (Rothbart & Bates, 1998).

Behavioral inhibition is also referred to as *reactive inhibition* (Rothbart & Bates, 1998) or *reactive control* (Eisenberg & Morris, 2002) to convey its involuntary and affectively driven characteristics. Several related ideas have influenced psychopathology research, but they have in common the idea that reactive inhibition or shutdown of exploratory or goal-directed behavior helps orient a person to unexpected, novel, or potentially threatening information. We herein refer to this type of behavior as *reactive behavioral inhibition*. This temperament is thought to be related to later personality traits (Nigg, 2000; Rothbart & Bates, 1998), including negative emotionality (*neuroticism*, which reflects a tendency to experience anxiety, sadness, and difficulty coping with stress), and to possibly be inversely related to *extraversion* (the tendency to experience positive affect, high energy, social approach, and social dominance). We therefore also consider data on these and related dispositional traits in both adults and children.

Second, a substantial literature considers what we call *interference control*, the ability to control interfering information. Development of this ability continues from childhood into early adulthood (Dempster, 1993), and the efficiency of such control in later decades of life has been extensively studied in the cognitive aging literature (Hasher & Zacks, 1988; Zacks & Hasher, 1994). Interference control has also been studied in the context of psychopathology. For example, the inability to keep unwanted thoughts out of mind is a feature of anxiety conditions, posttraumatic stress disorder, and obsessive–compulsive disorder. Do these disorders reflect a failure of interference control that would normally suppress unwanted thoughts (Eysenck & Calvo, 1992)? Or is the problem simply due to the excess activation of affective response centers, continually intruding into consciousness and interfering with goals and planned behavior? This concept is closely related to the idea of *cognitive inhibition*, or the ability to suppress distracting or irrelevant information from working memory that Harnishfeger (1995) and Hasher and Zacks (1988) described. Despite the close conceptual similarity of interference control and working memory, these functions are not necessarily identical when operationalized with neuropsychological measures. For example, children with ADHD are easily shown to have difficulties on working memory tasks (Martinussen, Hayden, Hogg-Johnson, & Tannock, 2005) yet are not so easily shown to have difficulty on interference control tasks such as the Stroop, flanker, and negative-priming tasks, as we describe later in this chapter.

The degree of distinction between response inhibition and interference control can be disputed. In their groundbreaking efforts to identify the structural relations of various frontal lobe neuropsychological measures, Miyake, Friedman, Emerson, Witzki, and Howerter (2000) noted that Stroop interference and stop-signal reaction time loaded on the same factor when other executive measures were included in a factor analysis. Thus, it may be that interference control and motor inhibition are related but partially distinct control functions, perhaps more closely related to one another than to other executive components. In support of their partial distinction, neuroimaging work suggests that interference control may especially involve the anterior cingulate cortex (Cabeza & Nyberg, 1997), whereas response inhibition may have greater involvement of inferior or orbital prefrontal cortex (Rubia, Smith, Brammer, & Taylor, 2003). Further, in our work we have found that these have distinct external correlates, as we describe in a later section. We therefore find it heuristic to continue to distinguish them.

Third, there is interest in the types of perceptual inhibition processes that may support attention relatively automatically, such as those in negative priming or those referred to by Rafal and Henik (1994). These processes entail the ability to automatically filter irrelevant information when focusing on a goal and the routine ability to filter excess perceptual information in the day-to-day perceptual environment. Several measures fall in this "automatic attentional" inhibition domain, so this domain may or may not be unitary. For purposes of this discussion, however, we group together tasks that appear to assess the relatively automatic filtering of information such as negative priming, attentional blink, and perceptual selection tasks (each described in more detail later in the chapter).

Fourth, *effortful control*, *executive response suppression*, aspects of *cognitive control*, and *deliberate response suppression* all signify the same general ability to suddenly stop a behavior that was prepared and about to be executed. This ability is operationalized as voluntary, deliberate interruption of a prepared motor response. It is therefore a top-down control process presumably mediated by frontal subcortical neural circuits (Rubia et al., 2003). It is distinct from behavioral inhibition (e.g., Kagan, 2003) in that it does not require significant anxiety or fear to be activated. This meaning of response suppression is nearly identical to that offered by Logan (1994) when describing the stop-signal task paradigm. The paradigm consists of two concurrent tasks. For the go task, or primary task, participants must make a speeded choice response (e.g., indicate as quickly as they can whether the letter on the screen is an *X* or an *O*). For the stop-signal task, a tone is administered at varying delays after primary task stimulus onset, signaling participants to withhold their response on that trial. When the tone comes early, it is easy to stop, and when the tone comes at the last possible instant, it is very difficult to interrupt the prepared response. Dozens of clinical studies have used this paradigm to assess response inhibition in psychopathological samples (Nigg, 2001), showing consistent weakness in people with ADHD and, to a lesser extent, in those with some other impulse control disorders, as detailed further in a later section.

This meaning of executive response inhibition can also be related to temperamental or personality traits, which correlate with the ability of children and adults to voluntarily control emotions, speech, and motor actions in the service of a later goal. In the temperament literature, the ability is referred to as *effortful control* (Eisenberg & Morris, 2002; Rothbart & Bates, 1998). These theorists argue that the childhood trait is related to the adult personality trait of *conscientiousness* (Digman, 1990) or *constraint* (Tellegen, 1985). Therefore, once again we are interested in both cognitive measures and measures of personality traits (in adults) or temperament traits (in children) in our search for converging evidence.

The ability to interrupt an unintended (but prepotent) response emerges and develops rapidly during the toddler and preschool years (Diamond, Prevor, Callender, & Druin, 1997; Posner & Rothbart, 2000; Zelazo, Muller, Frye, & Marcovitch, 2003), from early to middle childhood, and into adolescence and adulthood. The ability to strategically control attention continues to develop during childhood from second through sixth grades (Huang-Pollock, Carr, & Nigg, 2002), and the ability to inhibit primary responses likewise improves significantly over the age period from about ages 5 to 7 years and beyond (Carver, Livesey, & Charles, 2001). The ability to suppress responses continues to develop through adolescence (Bedard et al., 2002), presumably aided by ongoing myelination and pruning of frontal cortical neural networks (Benes, 2001).

Table 13.1 summarizes the conceptual structure of types of inhibitory control and example measures in use in our laboratory at Michigan State University. Our work has focused on examining various kinds of measures of deliberate and automatic inhibition mechanisms to evaluate their relation to psychopathology in both children and adults and on seeking convergence of evidence for our conclusions using cognitive (experimental) as well as temperament and personality measures.

In this work, we do not evaluate whether putative measures of inhibition really tap an inhibitory mechanism. Rather, we implement putative measures of inhibition or suppression functions that have a long and rich empirical history in nonpathological samples to evaluate their utility in distinguishing and characterizing types of psychopathology. We do this both with reaction time measures taken from chronometric studies in cognitive psychology and with personality trait measures, in both children and adults, and in both cross-sectional and longitudinal studies. We next summarize key findings in this program of work, noting linkages to the relevant literatures.

Attention-Deficit/Hyperactivity Disorder: Response Suppression and Interference Control as Candidate Mechanisms

Schachar, Tannock, and Logan (1993) introduced Logan's (1994) stop-signal task to developmental psychopathology research. Their finding that children with ADHD had slow stop-signal reaction times has been replicated about two dozen times. A recent meta-analysis (Willcutt, Doyle, Nigg, Faraone, & Pennington, 2005) identified 26 separate studies using the stop-signal task in ADHD, with a composite weighted effect size of $d = .61$ for the estimated stop-signal reaction time. In our lab, we showed that the effect was consistent in children diagnosed with ADHD according to criteria in the fourth edition of the *Diagnostic and Statistical Manual of Mental Disorders* (*DSM–IV*; American Psychiatric Association, 1994) when various comorbid symptoms were controlled (Nigg, 1999). Although this effect held even when antisocial behavior and learning disorder were controlled (Nigg, 1999), it may also occur in other disorders, including conduct disorder (Oosterlaan, Logan, & Sergeant, 1998). It is unclear, however, whether those effects remain when ADHD is statistically partialed out.

A key recent direction with the stop-signal task in ADHD has been to determine whether results can be related to specific types of ADHD or domains of ADHD symptoms. Nigg, Blaskey, et al. (2002) compared children with ADHD–CT (i.e., children who are both inattentive–disorganized and hyperactive–impulsive) and children with ADHD–PI. Compared with controls, the children with ADHD–CT had a clear deficit in stop-signal reaction time ($d = .80$), whereas the ADHD–PI group did not. We also observed a Sex × Group interaction. The two subtypes were completely different in the boys, with the ADHD–PI boys showing normal performance on the task and the ADHD–CT boys showing large deficits in stop-signal reaction times. For girls, however, both ADHD subtypes had slow stop-signal reaction times. This finding, still the sole study of its type in the literature, indicated that the two subtypes are differentiable in terms of executive response suppression for boys but that the picture for girls is less clear.

A second direction has been to look at differential associations of different putative measures of inhibition with ADHD. In the same sample of children, we found no deficit in performance with a paper-and-pencil version of the Stroop interference task, although children with ADHD–CT and ADHD–PI were slower overall in naming colors and words, consistent with the literature (Nigg, Blaskey, Huang-Pollock, & Rappley, 2002). van Mourik, Oosterlaan, and Sergeant (2005) conducted a meta-analysis of the Stroop effect in ADHD and found a composite effect size of about .20 versus controls—in other words, a very small effect that is unlikely to be of clinical significance. However, the paper-and-pencil Stroop task has some methodological weaknesses, such as vulnerability to strategy effects, the establishment of a response set (practice) in each condition, and imprecise reaction time measurement.[1] We therefore followed this study with three additional studies to clarify matters.

---

[1] Some investigators advocate inducing a response bias by administering several color–word trials followed by an interference trial. However, doing so confounds the ability to interrupt a prepotent response (the well-practiced word reading or color naming) with the ability to control interference (the unintended reading of the word). In essence, that task is an amalgam of a go/no-go task and an interference control task.

In the same child sample, we examined a flanker paradigm (Huang-Pollock, Nigg, & Carr, 2005) modeled on that suggested by Lavie (1995; Lavie & Tsal, 1994). In this task, the child looks at a letter in the center of the computer screen and decides as quickly as possible whether it is an L or an N. Flanking this central letter is a circle of distractor letters. They may be competing (an L or N that is the opposite of the correct answer) or noncompeting (other letters, such as A, O, or Y, which may be judged to be irrelevant noise). By varying the number of these distractors, we varied the perceptual load from low (one distractor) to high (six distractors). We had previously shown that we could use this paradigm to differentiate early-maturing perceptual selection from late-maturing cognitive selection in children (Huang-Pollock et al., 2002). When the load is high (too many distractor letters to hold in working memory), we expect perceptual selection (relatively automatic early selection). When the load is low, we expect cognitive selection (relatively deliberate, later selection of elements processed to the point of cognitive control and awareness, which is active in a display with fewer elements). As expected, children experienced interference and exhibited perceptual selection with a large number of letters in the display and late selection with a small number of letters in the display. Yet children with ADHD–CT and ADHD–PI showed normal interference responses in both perceptual and cognitive selection.

We sought to further confirm this dissociation between response inhibition and interference control in ADHD in two studies of adults using different tasks. The first of these studies (Nigg, Butler, Huang-Pollock, & Henderson, 2002) compared 20 adults with ADHD with 20 controls (the majority of participants were women). To get at response inhibition, participants performed the antisaccade task. They viewed a central fixation point (dot) on the computer screen. Their first task was to hold their eyes in place without moving during a variable delay (500–1,000 milliseconds), waiting for a target to appear. Their second objective was to ignore a sudden light onset off to the side. Suppressing this reflex, they moved their eyes in the opposite direction from the light to detect a target that briefly appeared there. They then responded to the target by pressing the appropriate key on the keyboard (up or down arrow). The ADHD group showed clear deficits in both the ability to withhold any eye movements during the variable delay and the ability to suppress reflexive saccades during the antisaccade condition (directional errors), although the second finding was not reliable when comorbid psychological disorders were controlled to assess specificity of effects to ADHD.

To get at cognitive suppression, they completed a computerized priming task with three conditions: facilitation (with instruction to name the same color as the word, e.g., the word *blue* in blue, correct response "blue"), Stroop interference (with instruction to name the same color as the word, e.g., the word *blue* in red ink, correct response "red"), and a negative-priming condition (in which the color to be named is the same as that ignored on the preceding trial—e.g., after responding "red" and ignoring the word *blue*, immediately viewing the word *green* in blue ink and responding "blue"). As expected, there was a main effect of condition, with the fastest response times in the facilitation condition followed by slower response times in the Stroop condition and the slowest of all in the negative-priming condition. However, there was no evidence of a Group × Condition interaction: The ADHD group was slower overall, but the slowing was similar across conditions. Thus, interference control and negative priming were normal in this small sample of adults with ADHD.

Carr, Nigg, and Henderson (2006) sought to replicate this finding in a larger and better characterized sample of adults that included controls ($n = 67$), ADHD-persistent participants (who met full criteria in childhood and adulthood; $n = 72$), and ADHD-residual participants (who experienced partial remission of symptoms and no longer met full criteria; $n = 20$). This sample had more statistical power and was clinically better characterized; structured interviews of the participant and two informants (a parent who knew them well as a child and a spouse or friend who knew them well as an adult) were conducted, and two clinicians reviewed each case and independently agreed that the primary problem was ADHD and not another disorder. These participants completed an antisaccade task that directly measured eye movements using an eye tracker. Latency to target, directional accuracy, and proportion of anticipatory movements were recorded. On the antisaccade task, again, more antisaccade directional errors were observed in the ADHD group than in control participants (18.3% vs. 14.2%) and in the residual group, whereas control participants and the ADHD-residual participants did not differ. In contrast, there was greater difficulty maintaining fixation during a variable delay (anticipation) in both ADHD groups and control participants. This finding could suggest that top-down planned movement control effects are epiphenomenal in that they improve when symptoms improve. In contrast, bottom-up control problems may be core to the disorder, remaining impaired even when symptoms have improved. Alternatively, it may be that maturation of frontal cortices helps resolve both symptoms and planful control problems. Follow-up neuroimaging studies may clarify which interpretation is correct.

To get at cognitive or attentional suppression in this experiment, we used an attentional blink task. This task measures temporal inhibition using a dual-task paradigm with rapid serial visual presentation measuring behavioral data index vigilance and the allocation of attention in time rather than space. Stimuli—for example, all black capital letters—are presented serially and very rapidly (e.g., every 90 milliseconds) at a central fixation point. In the baseline or single-task condition, participants simply confirm or reject the presence of a probe stimulus (e.g., the letter Z). In the dual-task condition, participants must both confirm or reject the presence of a probe and identify a target letter, which appears in a different color (e.g., blue) and can occur in any of several temporal positions before the probe. Accuracy for probes occurring immediately after the target is typically high, because target and probe are thought to be processed together. A dramatic decrement in performance is seen for probes occurring two to three positions after the target, however, a decrement referred to as the *attentional blink*. It is thought that during that attentional blink, resources are committed to processing of the target and are thus temporally insulated from subsequent stimuli. In comparison with normal controls, the ADHD groups missed more probes in both baseline and dual-task conditions, suggesting lower vigilance overall. However, the magnitude and rate of recovery from the attention blink was comparable for all groups, suggesting no specific difficulty with the cognitive or attentional suppression mechanism in ADHD participants. These results suggest that the mechanism of selective attention invoked by this task is essentially spared in ADHD. Nevertheless, findings using this task in children and adults with ADHD have been mixed, with some studies demonstrating exaggerated blink and/or extended recovery times or a temporally shifted blink (Armstrong & Munoz, 2003; Hollingsworth, McAuliffe, & Knowlton, 2001; Li et al., 2004). Differences in paradigms and methods of diagnostic characterization, as well as small samples in some instances, make the results of prior studies difficult to interpret.

In summary, this series of studies suggests that despite differences in operational paradigms and three different samples, we saw consistent replication of an ADHD weakness in response inhibition or effortful response suppression and no consistent evidence of an ADHD weakness in cognitive suppression or interference control. This replicated finding in turn suggests that it is meaningful to distinguish these basic inhibition functions and that only the first one is a good candidate mechanism for dysfunction in ADHD.

Attention-Deficit/Hyperactivity Disorder and Response Inhibition: Specificity Within and Across Disorders

We next consider the question of specificity of inhibition mechanisms to the component symptom domains that make up the ADHD syndrome construct. In the clinical literature, there is considerable theoretical debate about whether ADHD is the product of a unitary neurocognitive problem or of dual deficits. In the second scenario, the hypothesis has been that hyperactive–impulsive symptoms are related to affective, motivational, or reactive processes, such as abnormal reward response. In contrast, inattentive–disorganized symptoms, related to executive control, are thought to be related to problems in effortful response suppression (Nigg, Goldsmith, & Sachek, 2004; Sonuga-Barke, 2002). An alternative view is that response suppression might be related to impulsivity but that other executive functions might be related to inattention–disorganization. Nigg, Stavro, et al. (2005) tested these hypotheses in a slightly larger group using the same adult sample as in Carr et al. (2006; 105 participants with ADHD and 90 control participants). Participants completed the stop-signal task and a battery of other neuropsychological executive measures. The researchers created a latent variable for executive functioning (Stroop interference control had to be dropped because its inclusion worsened model fit), and they created composite symptom scores for inattention and hyperactivity–impulsivity by pooling self and informant ratings of the participant. With executive function as the dependent variable, they entered symptom scores as predictors. Executive function was related only to inattention disorganization (β = .29) and not to hyperactivity–impulsivity (β = .01). Nigg, Stavro, et al. checked this effect for stop-signal response time alone, and the same result held.

As we indicated in opening this chapter, various disorders other than ADHD have also been theorized to relate to disinhibition, largely because of their association with impulsive behavior problems. In exploratory work, Nigg,

Silk, Stavro, and Miller (2005) examined the independent relations of symptoms of ADHD, borderline personality disorder, antisocial personality disorder, anxiety, and mood disorder to stop-signal reaction time. In the same sample of young adults age 18 to 35 years just discussed (which was selected for ADHD, making it a nonrandom sample), both ADHD and borderline personality disorder symptoms were independently related to stop-signal reaction time, whereas other psychopathologies were not.

In summary, we conclude that there was some specificity in that the response inhibition and effortful control or executive problem identified in ADHD in the prior series of studies appeared to be specific to just one aspect of ADHD. It appeared to feed in primarily to the inattention–disorganization component of the disorder and not to the hyperactivity–impulsivity symptom domain, at least by adulthood. In the future, we will examine this question in children, for whom the normative developmental importance of hyperactive–impulsive behaviors is greater. However, there was only partial specificity in relation to other impulse-control disorders. Borderline personality disorder symptoms were also related to response inhibition, although the relation of response inhibition to ADHD held even when a wide range of other symptoms and disorders was statistically controlled.

Temperament and Personality: Convergent Evidence

Temperament (in children) and personality (in children or adults) may provide convergent evidence for the relation of effortful control to ADHD. Table 13.1 provides a heuristic mapping of cognitive measures onto major dimensions of personality or temperament (for further discussion and justification, see Nigg, 2000, 2006). Nigg, John, et al. (2002) looked at personality in a large sample of more than 1,500 adults pulled from three different centers around the country, including adults with ADHD, parents of children with ADHD, parents of children without ADHD, and college students with and without ADHD. Partial correlations were used to isolate relations of traits to symptom domains. They found that inattention–disorganization was uniquely and strongly related ($r = .50$) to low conscientiousness; that hyperactivity–impulsivity was related to low agreeableness (hostility), but this effect was accounted for by co-occurring antisocial behaviors; and that elevated neuroticism (related to negative emotionality) was related to both symptom domains secondarily.

To follow up on these findings, Martel and Nigg (2006) looked at children across maternal and teacher reports of child ADHD symptoms and parent reports of child temperament (after removing overlapping items from the *DSM–IV* symptom lists and the temperament scales). Martel and Nigg found that inattention–disorganization was uniquely related to low resiliency/effortful control, that hyperactivity–impulsivity was uniquely related to low reactive control, and that oppositional defiant symptoms were uniquely related to negative emotionality.

Across these correlational studies of personality and temperament in adults and children, Martel and Nigg (2006) therefore concluded that the results are convergent with the earlier experimental findings. They suggested that effortful inhibitory mechanisms are involved in the inattention–disorganization symptom dimension of the ADHD syndrome and that distinct mechanisms are involved in the hyperactivity–impulsivity symptom dimension.

Utility of Response Inhibition in Predicting Psychopathology

Most of the work on psychopathology and cognitive functioning has been cross-sectional. This fact leaves some question as to whether the presumed cognitive mechanism of inhibition is causal in the disorder or whether it is perhaps simply another symptom of a disorder whose causes lie elsewhere. There are obvious difficulties with attempting to answer this question in any human correlational study, and no ethical experiments exist by which to do so. However, we and others have attempted to investigate this question via functioning in relatives.

Nigg, Blaskey, Stawicki, and Sachek (2004) looked at response inhibition in 386 first-degree relatives of children with ADHD. Gender interactions complicated these results. Slow stop-signal reaction time was observed in the mothers of ADHD girls but not in the relatives of the boys. Thus, the evidence that response inhibition was causal in ADHD in this sample was doubtful, unless it was causal in a subgroup. We therefore divided the ADHD sample into children with impaired stop-signal inhibition (beyond the 90th percentile of the control group) and normal stop-signal inhibition. The relatives of the impaired group had slower stop-signal inhibition than the relatives of the normal ADHD group, and the normal ADHD group relatives did not differ from the relatives of control children. Crosbie and Schachar (2001) conducted a similar analysis, reporting excess ADHD in the relatives of children with slow stop-signal inhibition. Schachar et al. (2005) also found weaker stop-signal response times in unaffected siblings of children with ADHD.

Nigg et al. (2006) looked at the ability of stop-signal reaction time to predict onset of problematic alcohol and drug use in adolescence. They used a longitudinal design in which parental alcoholism and other family characteristics were evaluated beginning in preschool and into the elementary school years. When children were 12 to 14 years old (Study Wave 4), and again when they were 15 to 17 years old (Study Wave 5), they completed the stop-signal task to assess response inhibition. Their alcohol and drug use were assessed annually, and composite measures were created for illicit drugs used and number of alcohol-related problems experienced (e.g., missing school because of drinking, getting in fights while drinking). After controlling for parental alcoholism status, parental antisocial personality, and the child's IQ, age, and other confounds, slow stop-signal reaction time still significantly predicted the extent of these substance-use-related problems in the teenage years.

Table 13.2 summarizes the findings of this program of work across several age groups, samples, and paradigms. It illustrates that measures of putative inhibitory functions in psychopathology yield distinct patterns of results. Thus, distinguishing these various kinds of control mechanisms is necessary to accurately delineate their possible role in the emergence of particular kinds of

Table 13.2. Summary of Results Across All Studies Discussed in the Michigan State ADHD Project

Finding	ADHD children	ADHD adults 1[a]	ADHD adults 2[b]	ID symptom domain	HI symptom domain
Executive response inhibition					
Stop-signal task	Impaired	Impaired	Impaired	Associated	Not associated
Antisaccade task			Impaired		
Interference control (automatized)					
Negative priming		Normal			
Attentional blink			Normal or small weakness		
Perceptual selection	Normal				
Interference control (effortful)					
Stroop interference	Normal				
Flanker task	Normal	Impaired	Impaired		
Personality trait: Conscientiousness				Associated	Not associated
Temperament: Effortful control	Impaired			Associated	Not associated
Temperament: Reactive control	Impaired			Not associated	Associated

Note. Blank cells indicate no data or insufficient data. ADHD = attention-deficit/hyperactivity disorder; ID = inattention–disorganization; HI = hyperactivity–impulsivity.
[a] A convenience sample of 25 college students diagnosed with ADHD and 25 student controls. [b] A well-characterized clinically assessed sample of 195 adults, as discussed in the text.

psychopathology. The table illustrates the broad generativity of a general framework of different kinds of putative inhibitory functions in illuminating psychopathology. In the case of ADHD, only response inhibition is specific to the disorder, and cognitive suppression plays as major a role. Response inhibition, in turn, appears in initial but still-not-replicated studies to be related to the inattention–disorganization symptom domain of ADHD and to have important relations with other kinds of psychopathology in both cross-sectional and longitudinal work.

Future Research Directions

It is important to continue to investigate the specific and distinct associations of potentially distinct types of inhibition measures with different forms of psychopathology over the course of development using both molar behavioral measures (e.g., temperament and personality scales) and experimental laboratory paradigms from cognitive science. A key next step in our own work is to examine the correlations and factor structures of various measures of putative inhibitory control in normal and clinically impulsive samples across the domains of motor control, vision and visual attention, and language processing. From the perspective of cognitive science, an interesting issue is the degree to which inhibitory processes are general domain-independent systems versus the degree to which they are domain specific. For example, it could be that a general inhibition system is functional across domains and that therefore if a deficit in inhibition appears for a particular subgroup (e.g., ADHD) in one domain, it will appear in all domains. Alternatively, it may be that an inhibitory deficit can appear in an ADHD group in one domain (e.g., motor control) but not in another domain (e.g., language processing). Indeed, we have observed some suggestion of domain-specific inhibition in the contrasting results from the antisaccade and attentional blink tasks, the former involving inhibiting a prepotent motor response and the latter involving inhibition of incoming visual information. Our present work is partially devoted to extending this type of analysis to other domains that draw on inhibitory processes, such as ambiguity resolution in language processing.

Conclusion

To the extent that the various measures described in this chapter are measuring the operation of inhibitory mechanisms, our data suggest that it is meaningful to distinguish automatic attentional filtering from strategic response suppression and, further, that it is meaningful to distinguish interference control from response suppression. Across multiple samples and measures, we have found convergent evidence that ADHD is associated with difficulty in strategic response interruption but is not associated with measures of stimulus or response selection, whether these are automatic attentional filtering measures or strategic filtering measures. We suspect that there would be little controversy regarding the assertion that automatic and effortful control mechanisms relate to distinct neural circuits. Alternatively, the field has seen considerable discussion concerning whether strategic interference control mechanisms and response suppression mechanisms involve distinct or similar circuitry. They are probably at least partially related (Barkley, 1997; Miyake et al., 2000; Posner & Rothbart, 2000). Nonetheless, our data, as well as recent meta-analyses, consistently show an ADHD deficit in only one of these two abilities.

When it comes to understanding potential mechanisms that may underlie and help validate the controversial disorder of ADHD, the evidence reviewed in this chapter suggests that the most promising candidate is a strategic or effortful response suppression mechanism. It appears to operate primarily via its effect on the inattention–disorganization symptom domain. The hyperactivity–impulsivity symptom domain is likely under the influence of other, more reactive control processes that are partially distinct from the effortful control processes. This picture in turn suggests that more than one causal stream of influence feeds into the development of the ADHD syndrome.

Overall, this chapter illustrates that both cognitive and personality measures of inhibition can contribute meaningfully to understanding the mechanisms that may be involved in developmental psychopathology. A primary question facing all psychopathology research is to identify the operative dysfunctional mechanisms that are involved in a given disorder. If no such mechanism can be identified, then it can be questioned whether a disorder truly exists (Wakefield, 1999). If a mechanism can be identified, it may provide clues to etiology; for example, it can then be pursued in studies of molecular genetic, toxicological, or psychosocial correlates of the development of the disorder. Whether mechanisms are distinct or shared across different disorders can provide clues to unifying themes that may lead to eventual modification and improved validation of the psychiatric nosology. In addition, translational, multidisciplinary work can also shed light on basic questions of interest to cognitive scientists, such as the underlying architecture of cognitive control mechanisms.

References

American Psychiatric Association. (1994). *Diagnostic and statistical manual of mental disorders* (4th ed.). Washington, DC: Author.

Armstrong, I. T., & Munoz, D. P. (2003). Attentional blink in adults with attention-deficit hyperactivity disorder: Influence of eye movements. *Experimental Brain Research, 152,* 243–250.

Barkley, R. A. (1997). *AD/HD and the nature of self-control.* New York: Guilford Press.

Bedard, A. C., Nichols, S., Barbosa, J. A., Schachar, R., Logan, G. D., & Tannock, R. (2002). The development of selective inhibitory control across the life span. *Developmental Neuropsychology, 21,* 93–111.

Benes, F. M. (2001). The development of prefrontal cortex: The maturation of neurotransmitter systems and their interactions. In C. A. Nelson & M. Luciana (Eds.), *Handbook of developmental cognitive neuroscience* (pp. 79–92). Cambridge, MA: MIT Press.

Biederman, J., Hirshfeld-Becker, D. R., Rosenbaum, J. F., Herot, C., Friedman, D., Snidman, N., et al. (2001). Further evidence of association between behavioral inhibition and social anxiety in children. *American Journal of Psychiatry, 158,* 1673–1679.

Biederman, J., Rosenbaum, J. F., Bolduc-Murphy, E. A., Faraone, S. V., Chaloff, J., Hirshfeld, D. R., & Kagan, J. (1993). A 3-year follow-up of children with and without behavioral inhibition. *Journal of the American Academy of Child and Adolescent Psychiatry, 32,* 814–821.

Cabeza, R., & Nyberg, L. (1997). Imaging cognition: An empirical review of PET studies with normal subjects. *Journal of Cognitive Neuroscience, 9,* 1–26.

Carr, L., Nigg, J. T., & Henderson, J. (2006). Attentional versus motor inhibition in adults with attention deficit hyperactivity disorder. *Neuropsychology, 20,* 430–441.

Carver, A. C., Livesey, D. J., & Charles, M. (2001). Further manipulation of the stop-signal task: Developmental changes in the ability to inhibit responding with longer stop-signal delays. *International Journal of Neuroscience, 111,* 39–53.

Crosbie, J., & Schachar, R. (2001). Deficient inhibition as a marker for familial ADHD. *American Journal of Psychiatry, 158,* 1884–1890.

Dempster, F. N. (1993). Resistance to interference: Developmental changes in a basic processing mechanism. In M. L. Howe & R. Pasnak (Eds.), *Emerging themes in cognitive development: Vol. 1. Foundations* (pp. 3–27). New York: Springer-Verlag.

Diamond, A., Prevor, M. B., Callender, G., & Druin, D. P. (1997). Prefrontal cortex cognitive deficits in children treated early and continuously for PKU. *Monographs of the Society for Research in Child Development, 62*(4), 1–205.

Digman, J. M. (1990). Personality structure: Emergence of the five-factor model. *Annual Review of Psychology, 41,* 417–440.

Eisenberg, N., & Morris, A. S. (2002). Children's emotion-related regulation. In R. V. Kail (Ed.), *Advances in child development and behavior* (Vol. 30, pp. 189–229). Amsterdam and Boston: Academic Press.

Eysenck, M. W., & Calvo, M. G. (1992). Anxiety and performance: The processing efficiency theory. *Cognition and Emotion, 6,* 409–434.

Harnishfeger, K. K. (1995). The development of cognitive inhibition: Theories, definitions, and research evidence. In F. N. Dempster & C. J. Brainerd (Eds.), *Interference and inhibition in cognition* (pp. 175–204). New York: Academic Press.

Hasher, L., & Zacks, R. T. (1988). Working memory, comprehension, and aging: A review and a new view. In G. H. Bower (Ed.), *The psychology of learning and motivation: Advances in research and theory* (Vol. 22, pp. 193–224). San Diego, CA: Academic Press.

Hollingsworth, D. E., McAuliffe, S. P., & Knowlton, B. J. (2001). Temporal allocation of visual attention in adult attention deficit hyperactivity disorder. *Journal of Cognitive Neuroscience, 13,* 298–305.

Huang-Pollock, C. L., Carr, T. H., & Nigg, J. T. (2002). Development of selective attention: Perceptual load influences early versus late attentional selection in children and adults. *Developmental Psychology, 38,* 363–375.

Huang-Pollock, C. L., Nigg, J. T., & Carr, T. H. (2005). Deficient attention is hard to find: Applying the perceptual load model of selective attention to attention deficit hyperactivity disorder subtypes. *Journal of Child Psychology and Psychiatry, 46,* 1211–1218.

Kagan, J. (2003). Behavioral inhibition as a temperamental category. In R. J. Davidson, K. R. Scherer, & H. H. Goldsmith (Eds.), *Handbook of affective sciences* (pp. 320–331). New York: Oxford University Press.

Kagan, J., Reznick, J. S., & Gibbons, J. (1989). Inhibited and uninhibited types of children. *Child Development, 60,* 838–845.

Kagan, J., Reznick, J. S., & Snidman, N. (1987). The physiology and psychology of behavioral inhibition in children. *Child Development, 58,* 1459–1473.

Kagan, J., & Snidman, N. (2004). *The long shadow of temperament.* Cambridge, MA: Harvard University Press.

Lavie, N. (1995). Perceptual load as a necessary condition for selective attention. *Journal of Experimental Psychology, 21,* 451–468.

Lavie, N., & Tsal, Y. (1994). Perceptual load as a major determinant of the locus of selection in visual attention. *Perception and Psychophysics, 56,* 183–197.

Li, C.-S., Lin, W.-H., Chang, H.-L., & Hung, Y.-W. (2004). A psychophysical measure of attention deficit in children with attention-deficit/hyperactivity disorder. *Journal of Abnormal Psychology, 113,* 228–236.

Logan, G. D. (1994). A user's guide to the stop signal paradigm. In D. Dagenbach & T. Carr (Eds.), *Inhibition in language, memory, and attention* (pp. 189–239). San Diego, CA: Academic Press.

Martel, M., & Nigg, J. T. (2006). Control, resiliency, negative emotionality, and ADHD in children. *Journal of Child Psychology and Psychiatry, 47,* 1175–1183.

Martinussen, R., Hayden, J., Hogg-Johnson, S., & Tannock, R. (2005). A meta-analysis of working memory impairments in children with attention-deficit/hyperactivity disorder. *Journal of the American Academy of Child and Adolescent Psychiatry, 44,* 377–384.

Miyake, A., Friedman, N. P., Emerson, M. J., Witzki, A. H., & Howerter, A. (2000). The unity and diversity of executive functions and their contributions to complex "frontal lobe" tasks: A latent variable analysis. *Cognitive Psychology, 41,* 49–100.

Moeller, F. G., Barratt, E. S., Dougherty, D. M., Schmitz, J. M., & Swann, A. C. (2001). Psychiatric aspects of impulsivity. *American Journal of Psychiatry, 158,* 1783–1793.

Nigg, J. T. (1999). The ADHD response inhibition deficit as measured by the stop task: Replication with *DSM–IV* combined type, extension, and qualification. *Journal of Abnormal Child Psychology, 27,* 391–400.

Nigg, J. T. (2000). On inhibition/disinhibition in developmental psychopathology: Views from cognitive and personality psychology and a working inhibition taxonomy. *Psychological Bulletin, 126,* 200–246.

Nigg, J. T. (2001). Is ADHD an inhibitory disorder? *Psychological Bulletin, 127,* 571–598.

Nigg, J. T. (2006). Temperament and developmental psychopathology. *Journal of Child Psychology and Psychiatry, 47,* 395–422.

Nigg, J. T., Blaskey, L. G., Huang-Pollock, C., & Rappley, M. D. (2002). Neuropsychological executive functions and ADHD *DSM–IV* subtypes. *Journal of the American Academy of Child and Adolescent Psychiatry, 41,* 59–66.

Nigg, J. T., Blaskey, L. G., Stawicki, J. A., & Sachek, J. (2004). Evaluating the endophenotype model of ADHD neuropsychological deficit: Results for parents and siblings of children with *DSM–IV* ADHD combined and inattentive subtypes. *Journal of Abnormal Psychology, 113,* 614–625.

Nigg, J. T., Butler, K. M., Huang-Pollock, C. L., & Henderson, J. M. (2002). Inhibitory processes in adults with persistent childhood onset ADHD. *Journal of Consulting and Clinical Psychology, 70,* 153–157.

Nigg, J. T., Goldsmith, H. H., & Sachek, J. (2004). Temperament and attention-deficit/hyperactivity disorder: The development of a multiple pathway model. *Journal of Clinical Child and Adolescent Psychology, 33,* 42–53.

Nigg, J. T., John, O. P., Blaskey, L. G., Huang-Pollock, C. L., Willcutt, E. G., Hinshaw, S. P., & Pennington, B. (2002). Big Five dimensions and ADHD symptoms: Links between personality traits and clinical symptoms. *Journal of Personality and Social Psychology, 83,* 451–469.

Nigg, J. T., Silk, K., Stavro, G., & Miller, T. (2005). An inhibition perspective on borderline personality disorder. *Development and Psychopathology, 17,* 1129–1150.

Nigg, J. T., Stavro, G., Ettenhofer, M., Hambrick, D., Miller, T., & Henderson, J. M. (2005). Executive functions and ADHD in adults: Evidence for selective effects on ADHD symptom domains. *Journal of Abnormal Psychology, 114,* 706–717.

Nigg, J. T., Wong, M. M., Martel, M., Jester, J. M., Puttler, L. I., Glass, J. M., et al. (2006). Poor response inhibition as a predictor of problem drinking and illicit drug use in adolescents at risk for alcoholism and other substance use disorders. *Journal of the American Academy of Child and Adolescent Psychiatry, 45,* 468–475.

Oosterlaan, J., Logan, G. D., & Sergeant, J. A. (1998). Response inhibition in AD/HD, CD, comorbid AD/HD+CD, anxious, and control children: A meta-analysis of studies with the stop task. *Journal of Child Psychology and Psychiatry, 39,* 411–425.

Posner, M. I., & Rothbart, M. K. (2000). Developing mechanisms of self-regulation. *Development and Psychopathology, 12,* 427–441.

Rafal, R., & Henik, A. (1994). The neurology of inhibition: Integrating controlled and automatic processes. In D. Dagenbach & T. H. Carr (Eds.), *Inhibitory processes in attention, memory, and language* (pp. 1–51). San Diego, CA: Academic Press.

Rothbart, M. K., & Bates, J. E. (1998). Temperament. In W. Damon (Series Ed.) & N. Eisenberg (Vol. Ed.), *Handbook of child psychology: Social, emotional, and personality development* (Vol. 3, pp. 105–176). New York: Wiley.

Rubia, K., Smith, A. B., Brammer, M. J., & Taylor, E. (2003). Right inferior frontal cortex mediates response inhibition while medial prefrontal cortex is responsible for error detection. *NeuroImage, 20,* 351–358.

Schachar, R. J., Crosbie, J., Barr, C. L., Ornstein, T. J., Kennedy, J., Malone, M., et al. (2005). Inhibition of motor responses in siblings concordant and discordant for attention deficit hyperactivity disorder. *American Journal of Psychiatry, 162,* 1076–1082.

Schachar, R. J., Tannock, R., & Logan, G. D. (1993). Inhibitory control, impulsiveness, and attention deficit hyperactivity disorder. *Clinical Psychology Review, 13,* 721–739.

Sonuga-Barke, E. J. S. (2002). Psychological heterogeneity in AD/HD—A dual pathway model of behaviour and cognition. *Behavioural Brain Research, 130,* 29–36.

Tellegen, A. (1985). Structure of mood and personality and their relevance to assessing anxiety, with an emphasis on self-report. In A. H. Tuma & J. D. Maser (Eds.), *Anxiety and the anxiety disorders* (pp. 681–706). Hillsdale, NJ: Erlbaum.

van Mourik, R., Oosterlaan, J., & Sergeant, J. A. (2005). The Stroop revisited: A meta-analysis of interference control in AD/HD. *Journal of Child Psychology and Psychiatry, 46,* 150–165.

Wakefield, J. C. (1999). Mental disorder as a black box essentialist concept. *Journal of Abnormal Psychology, 108,* 465–472.

Willcutt, E. G., Doyle, A. E., Nigg, J. T., Faraone, S. V., & Pennington, B. F. (2005). Validity of the executive function theory of ADHD: Meta-analytic review. *Biological Psychiatry, 57,* 1336–1346.

Zacks, R. T., & Hasher, L. (1994). Directed ignoring: Inhibitory regulation of working memory. In D. Dagenbach & T. H. Carr (Eds.), *Inhibitory processes in attention, memory, and language* (pp. 241–264). San Diego, CA: Academic Press.

Zelazo, P. D., Muller, U., Frye, D., & Marcovitch, S. (2003). The development of executive function: Cognitive complexity and control—Revised. *Monographs of the Society for Research in Child Development, 68*(3), 93–119.

Part VI

Network Models

14

Uses (and Abuses?) of Inhibition in Network Models

Daniel S. Levine and Vincent R. Brown

It has been established for close to a century that the brain has inhibitory as well as excitatory neural connections (Eccles, 1968; Sherrington, 1925). About 20% of cortical synapses use the neurotransmitter gamma-aminobutyric acid (GABA), which is virtually always inhibitory (for a review, see Gottlieb, 1988), and modulatory transmitters (dopamine, serotonin, acetylcholine, and norepinephrine) have been found to be inhibitory at some synapses. Because neural inhibition is so ubiquitous, it is natural to suppose that some set of important cognitive functions might require inhibitory neural signals for their performance. This chapter explores what some of those cognitive functions might be.

We start with a review of some classical results on inhibition in the nervous system and some long-standing hypotheses about what roles such inhibition might play in system dynamics. Then we review several previous computational models of cognitive tasks that include inhibition and discuss some of the implications of these models for cognitive psychology. After that, we note that the implications of the computational models that we discuss are in many respects quite different from what has come to be known among psychologists as *cognitive inhibition*, whose existence is debated elsewhere in this volume (notably in chaps. 1, 5, 8, and 9). As an illustration of the differences between what we call *computational inhibition* and classical cognitive inhibition, we review a homophone disambiguation paradigm that appears to refute the "classical" form of cognitive inhibition (Gorfein, Berger, & Bubka, 2000; Gorfein, Brown, & DeBiasi, in press; see also chap. 6, this volume), and we present our own neural network model of those same homophone data in which inhibitory connections (at the choice level but not at the representation level) are included.

What Researchers Know About Neural Inhibition

Perhaps the first idea for a role of inhibition in cognitive psychology arose from the observations of 19th-century physicists Helmholtz (1924/1962) and Mach (1886/1959, chap. 10; cf. Ratliff, 1965) that edges or contours between light and dark portions of a scene tend to be enhanced relative to the light or dark interiors of the scene.[1] They explained this phenomenon by means of networks of retinal cells, each excited by light within a central area and inhibited by light within a surrounding area, which leads to sharpening of luminance differences between adjacent loci. Subsequently, receptive fields with that structure were isolated experimentally in the compound eye of the horseshoe crab limulus (Hartline & Ratliff, 1957) and in the mammalian retina (Kuffler, 1953). In the case of the horseshoe crab, this process was verified to be a result of direct mutual inhibition between receptors, leading to an increase in one cell's firing to the bright side of an edge and decreased firing to the dark side of the edge. In the case of the mammalian retina, a similar type of mutual inhibition is exerted indirectly through a feed-forward network. Both are examples of what is called *lateral inhibition*.

Lateral inhibition is mutual inhibition, directly or indirectly, between neurons or nodes at the same level of processing. The lateral inhibition process has also been invoked to explain contrast enhancement in other sensory modalities besides vision, such as audition and touch (e.g., von Bekesy, 1969), and in motor responses (Sherrington, 1906/1947). There are also examples in the brain, and in network models, of *top-down inhibition*—that is, inhibition by a brain region representing a higher level of processing exerted on neurons or nodes in another region representing a lower level of processing. Top-down inhibition is the type that best fits theories of executive inhibition that other researchers have suggested (e.g., chaps. 5 and 8, this volume). However, although top-down inhibition is believed to play some roles in high-level categorization, we suggest in later sections that executive processes might be better modeled by selective top-down facilitation (i.e., priming) of a lateral inhibitory lower level network.

There is neurophysiological as well as psychological evidence that inhibition can play at least two other significant roles besides contrast enhancement. These roles are stabilization and choice making, as detailed in the next section within a neural modeling context.

Inhibition in Neural Network Models

Some early uses of inhibition in neural networks are reviewed in chapters 2 and 4 of Levine (2000) and in Levine and Leven (1991), and we sketch them in this section. First, we note that our use of the term *neural network* encompasses much more than the type of three-layered feed-forward networks (Rumelhart & McClelland, 1986) that are the most widely known. Our usage includes a wide variety of network architectures: Some require training and others are self-organizing; some are strictly feed forward and others use recurrent connections; some are tailored toward engineering applications and others mimic detailed properties of brain regions (cf. Golden, 1996). Neural network modeling has been an active research area since the late 1960s and by now

---

[1]The Mach band phenomenon that Mach observed has also been modeled without inhibition (see Purves, Williams, Nundy, & Lotto, 2004; Ross, Morrone, & Burr, 1989; Yellott, 1989).

has made contact with virtually every branch of cognitive psychology, as well as animal learning, psychiatry, and some branches of social psychology (Levine, 2002).

Some of the earliest neural network modelers connected networks more or less at random and simply studied their resulting activity patterns mathematically. The first attempts at random net modeling included only excitatory connections and no inhibitory ones. The absence of inhibition in model networks, which is unrealistic from the standpoint of known neuroanatomy, also led to unrealistic patterns of activity. The excitatory nets developed by Beurle (1956) and Ashby, von Foerster, and Walker (1962) tended to approach one of two extremes of activity: maximal activity, leading to saturation of the entire net, or quiescence. The intermediate level of activity found in actual brains was not attained by these nets. Griffith (1963a, 1963b, 1965) introduced inhibition within this random net framework and showed that stable intermediate levels of network activity became possible when inhibition was added.

More generally, inhibition can prevent a network of neurons from "blowing up"—that is, reaching levels of electrical activity that could be damaging to the network. Some mathematical results on networks with the shunting form of lateral inhibition (Grossberg, 1973; Sperling & Sondhi, 1968; Wilson & Cowan, 1972), to be explained in later sections, show that network activity levels can remain within a reasonable range despite the input of arbitrarily intense stimuli. Moreover, in some cases, the activities can remain at those reasonable levels without distorting the relative intensities among stimulus features or attributes, which is a property that facilitates recognition of the same object under variable illumination conditions.

Walley and Weiden (1973) related the contrast-enhancing property of lateral inhibition to its choice-making property. On the basis of an earlier proposal of Broadbent (1958), Walley and Weiden developed a theory and mathematical model of lateral inhibition as a basis for selective attention. They noted that in cell columns in the cerebral cortex, the largest neurons (pyramidal cells) often synapse on smaller interneurons that in turn inhibit other pyramidal cells in neighboring columns. Their model included a hierarchy of such lateral inhibitory interactions from the primary sensory cortex up to the association cortex, which can be a basis for selectivity at different levels of abstraction.

The idea of lateral inhibition has played a prominent role in many quantitative cognitive models of visual attention and of memory. LaBerge and Brown (1989) developed a theory for classic visual attention tasks involving a target and a flanker. Their mechanism relied on a "filter" that amplified target activity and suppressed flanker activity. LaBerge and Brown identified this filter with the reticular nucleus of the thalamus, which receives localized inputs from spatial and shape regions of the cortex and then sends inhibitory collaterals back to cortical areas that are neighbors of the areas from which it receives signals. Reeves and Sperling (1986) developed an attentional gating model to simulate data on processing of sequentially presented stimuli. The Reeves–Sperling model was based on a temporal analog of the spatial center-surround organization in the visual system. The lateral inhibition idea has also been proposed in semantic space. Barnhardt, Glisky, Polster, and Elam

(1996) argued for a center-surround model of attentional retrieval to explain their lexical-decision data from what is known as the *rare-word paradigm*, although they did not simulate this model computationally.

Hence, lateral inhibition can provide a basis for many different types of cognitive choices, all of which have been modeled in neural networks. These choices include those among competing sensory percepts; competing attributes of the same percept; competing meanings of a word, as in our homophone model; competing behavioral plans or (as in the reticular formation model of Kilmer, McCulloch, & Blum, 1969) behavioral modes; and competing decision rules.

In addition to lateral inhibition (which is a form of inhibition of excitatory neurons), many brain pathways include disinhibition (inhibition of inhibitory neurons). As described in the next section, this disinhibition releases a previously inhibited neural signal pattern, which can be a mechanism for rapid changes of behavioral set when a context changes.

Selective Disinhibition and Quick Release in the Brain

A series of articles by Roberts (1976, 1986), one of the discoverers of the inhibitory neurotransmitter GABA, suggested cognitive and behavioral roles for disinhibition (i.e., inhibition of inhibitors). When active, some GABA neurons inhibit certain complex patterns of neural activity that involve large numbers of neurons and may relate to specific behavioral tendencies. These GABA neurons are in turn inhibited by neurons that use some other transmitter, such as acetylcholine, dopamine, or norepinephrine. Inhibition of GABA causes release of a neural activity pattern that has already been programmed and leads to some set of behaviors.

This process is mediated, in Roberts's (1976, 1986) theory, by areas of the brain that send "command signals" that may determine which of several possible behaviors is expressed. These areas are in widely scattered areas of the brain (e.g., cerebellum, brain stem, basal ganglia, and cerebral cortex) and even in the spinal cord. Different centers control a wide variety of neural processes, both cognitive and motor. Roberts speculated that disinhibition provides an efficient way to keep behavior flexible. If contexts change and radically different sets of behaviors become necessary, the brain does not have to generate the required behavior pattern anew each time. Rather, the pattern can be stored permanently, inhibited most of the time, and disinhibited by signals representing the appropriate context for its release.

A particularly important disinhibitory region that has been drawing much attention, and that has formed the basis for models of high-level cognitive tasks, is the one at the basal ganglia. There are two sets of parallel pathways from the cortex (particularly the motor and prefrontal cortex) via the basal ganglia to the thalamus and then back to the cortex. One is called the *direct pathway* and involves two inhibitory links (therefore sending net excitation); the other is called the *indirect pathway* and involves three inhibitory links (therefore sending net inhibition). These two pathways are widely regarded as respectively a "go" pathway and a "stop" pathway for motor actions (Bullock

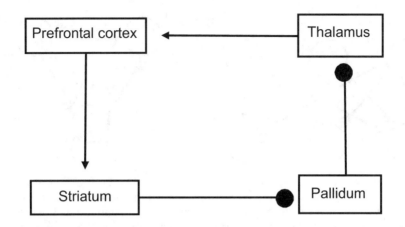

Figure 14.1. Schematic of the disinhibitory direct pathway that runs from the prefrontal cortex via two basal ganglia regions (striatum and pallidum) to the thalamus and then back to the cortex. Arrows denote excitation, and filled circles denote inhibition.

& Grossberg, 1988). In other words, the basal ganglia system is regarded as a *gating system*: a brain network that selects sensory stimuli for processing and motor actions for performance (Frank, Loughry, & O'Reilly, 2001).

The disinhibitory link from the striatum to the pallidum (both part of the basal ganglia) to the thalamus (Figure 14.1) plays the role of allowing (based on contextual signals) performance of actions whose representations are usually held in check. Prefrontal basal ganglia–thalamic loops such as those shown in Figure 14.1 have formed the basis for computational models of numerous cognitive tasks, including the Wisconsin Card Sorting Test (Amos, 2000; Monchi & Taylor, 1998); the Iowa Gambling Task (Levine, Mills, & Estrada, 2005; Wagar & Thagard, 2004); sequence learning (Berns & Sejnowski, 1998); and saccadic eye movement control (Brown, Bullock, & Grossberg, 2004).

In general, what cognitive functions are facilitated by mutually inhibitory neural structures? In the following section, we look at some mathematical theorems about networks with lateral inhibition that can help one understand the cognitive significance of this type of neural architecture.

A Theoretical Framework for Lateral Inhibition Networks

Grossberg and his colleagues developed a particularly important set of mathematical results on lateral inhibition (e.g., Cohen & Grossberg, 1983; Ellias & Grossberg, 1975; Grossberg, 1973; Grossberg & Levine, 1975). The networks in these articles consist of a set of arbitrarily many nodes at the same level connected by recurrent lateral inhibition (see Figure 14.2 for a schematic of the difference between recurrent and nonrecurrent inhibition). The dynamics of inhibition between nodes are shunting rather than subtractive. In subtractive inhibition, the incoming signal is linearly weighted, and an amount proportional to that signal is subtracted from the activity (or firing frequency) of the

A
B

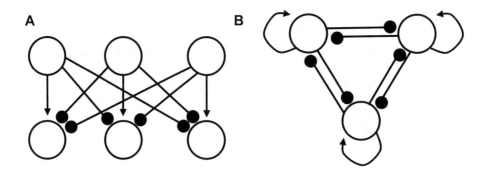

Figure 14.2. A. Nonrecurrent (feed-forward) lateral inhibition. B. Recurrent lateral inhibition. Each of these nodes is usually interpreted as a population of neurons, such as a cortical column, so the self-excitation in B simply means that cells in the same column excite each other.

receiving node. In shunting inhibition, the amount subtracted is also proportional to the activity of the receiving node. Thus, the inhibiting node acts as if it divides the receiving node's activity by a given amount—that is, as if it shunts a given fraction of the node's activity onto another, parallel pathway.

In addition to shunting (multiplicative) inhibition, recent lateral inhibitory models often include shunting excitation, whose strength is proportional to the difference of a node's activity from its maximum possible level. This is in contrast to additive excitation, the opposite of subtractive inhibition, which simply adds an amount proportional to the excitatory signal to the activity of a receiving node. Shunting interactions in neural networks have been suggested by experimental results on the effects of a presynaptic neuron on the conductances of various ions across the postsynaptic membrane (cf. Freeman, 1983; Hodgkin, 1964).

Grossberg's (1973) network was defined by differential equations that combine shunting lateral inhibition from each node to all others, shunting lateral excitation from each node to itself, and passive decay, as shown in Figure 14.3.

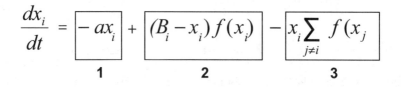

$$\frac{dx_i}{dt} = \boxed{-ax_i} + \boxed{(B_i - x_i)f(x_i)} - \boxed{x_i \sum_{j \neq i} f(x_j)}$$

$$\quad\quad\quad\;\; 1 \quad\quad\quad\;\; 2 \quad\quad\quad\quad\;\; 3$$

Figure 14.3. Form of the equations for shunting lateral inhibition used in Grossberg and Levine (1975). A differential equation is an *update rule*. The left-hand side represents the derivative of the activity x_i of the ith node. The right-hand side represents the three influences on this activity. First term (1): decay back to baseline. Second term (2): shunting self-excitation. Third term (3): shunting lateral inhibition from other nodes. Long-term behavior (which competitors "win," whether it is winner-take-all) depends on function, f; initial data; and biases, B_i. A negative term denotes a decay or inhibitory influence; a positive term denotes an excitatory influence.

Grossberg (1973) proved theorems about the stable long-term behavior of the node activities x_i in the cases where the values B_i, each of which represents the attentional bias toward the feature represented by the ith node, are all equal. These theorems were generalized by Grossberg and Levine (1975) to arbitrary attentional biases, by Ellias and Grossberg (1975) to a network where excitatory and inhibitory nodes are separate (which is biologically more realistic), and by Cohen and Grossberg (1983) to a more general system of equations that includes those of Figure 14.3 as a subcase.

In all of these versions of Grossberg's network (except some subcases of Ellias & Grossberg, 1975, which show oscillatory dynamics), the node activities x_i approach steady-state values as time becomes large. If the initial (Time 0) values of these activities represent the incoming sensory pattern stored by the network, the steady-state values represent the pattern as transformed by recurrent interactions between nodes.

As Figure 14.3 indicates, there is considerable variation in the network's steady-state values, depending on the values of the equation's parameters and the choice of the function f in the equation, which is called the *signal function* and represents an input–output signal (playing the same role as the activation function in Rumelhart & McClelland, 1986). Some choices of signal function (those that grow faster than linearly) incline the network toward winner-take-all steady states whereby all but one of the nodes has zero activity at large times. In contrast, a linear signal function leads to a steady state that faithfully represents the original input pattern, which might include noise as well as meaningful signals. For processing complex stimuli, the goal is to be able to maintain multiple relevant representations yet suppress irrelevant noise. To be able to simultaneously enhance contrast, suppress noise, and avoid a winner-take-all outcome, the best choice of f turns out to be a sigmoid (S-shaped) function, which is a compromise between faster than linear, linear, and slower than linear functions.[2] However, in our homophone models, which involve only two representations, for simplicity we use a linear rather than a sigmoid activation function.

Some theorems by Grossberg (1973) and Grossberg and Levine (1975) show that in the winner-take-all case, the competition between nodes is biased in favor of nodes that have the highest attentional bias values B_i, indicating some kind of expectation-driven or motivation-driven (possibly top-down from another layer) priming signal in favor of the stimuli coded by those particular nodes. But there is also a competing bias in favor of representations that have the highest input values, indicating stimulus-driven priming in favor of more-intense stimuli. There is no clear intuitive result about which of these biases, if either, produces the winning node in which contexts. We mention these results mainly to indicate the richness and variability of the potential dynamics of these types of lateral inhibitory network, which have enabled them to be components of many multilevel networks that can reproduce data in perception,

---

[2] Rumelhart and McClelland (1986) favored a sigmoid activation function for an entirely different reason; namely, it enabled those nodes that had not yet "made up their minds" what items to represent to have greater changes in their connection weights during learning.

categorization, memory, word recognition, and other cognitive processes (for reviews, see Levine, 2000, 2002).

What Does This All Mean for Cognitive Psychology?

The type of inhibition discussed in the previous section, and also the type of inhibition used in our homophone model, is recurrent lateral inhibition between nodes at the same level. Nonrecurrent (feed-forward) inhibition is not explicitly considered further in this chapter, although in some cases it can perform functions similar to the contrast enhancement and selection functions of recurrent lateral inhibition that we emphasize. Top-down inhibition will be discussed later in the context of executive function.

Lateral inhibition is one of many examples of a neural organizing principle first suggested by psychological data and later verified by neurophysiological data. Other examples include Hebbian or associative learning, top-down facilitation, error correction, and (possibly) opponent processing (Hebb, 1949). Yet in each case, the conception of the principle has undergone some modification as the neuroscientific knowledge became more precise.

In the case of lateral inhibition, both recurrent and nonrecurrent forms (see Figure 14.2) have been found to occur (e.g., recurrent in the cortex and nonrecurrent in the retina). And there are still controversies about some purported instances of lateral inhibition in the brain; for example, not all investigators believe that it occurs within the striatum.

Yet there are enough results from both neuroscience and neural network theory to give a sense of what is and is not entailed when inhibitory neural processes are invoked to explain cognitive data. As MacLeod, Dodd, Sheard, Wilson, and Bibi (2003) noted, "neural inhibition" does not imply "cognitive inhibition," as has commonly been conceived. From the psychological viewpoint, the effect of neural inhibition is simply an influence from one process that tends to decrease either the likelihood or the intensity of another process. As our review of models suggests, neural inhibition can be a substrate for a number of valuable cognitive properties, including selection of stimuli or responses, contrast enhancement, and stabilization of network activity. We now discuss some psychological processes that are commonly considered part of cognitive inhibition but not implied by the inhibitory network viewpoint we have described.

Inhibition Need Not Be Total Suppression

Walley and Weiden (1973) noted that several other investigators argued against inhibitory processes in attention on the ground that the nonattended representations can be reactivated when the context changes. Gorfein (2001) and MacLeod et al. (2003) presented analogous arguments against inhibitory processes in other cognitive functions, including meaning selection and memory. Yet the lateral inhibition networks of Grossberg (1973) and Grossberg and Levine (1975) are compatible with the contextual reactivation data, because those networks are not necessarily winner-take-all networks. Lateral inhibition networks do tend to produce clear winners at any given time—that is, stimuli, meanings, or other representations whose activities are larger than those of their competitors. But in many cases, the activity of the losing representations remains significantly above 0. Hence, the losers can later become winners, temporarily or permanently, if primed by a changed context.

If such a lateral inhibitory network is embedded in a larger multilayer network (as is required to model any complex cognitive function), the ability of previously suppressed nodes to recover under changed contexts is even greater. For example, if a one-level network such as that depicted in Panel B of Figure 14.2 is embedded in a larger network, inhibited nodes in one subnetwork can be selectively disinhibited by contextual signals from another subnetwork, as occurs at the basal ganglia gate (Frank et al., 2001; see also Figure 14.1). This process again can cause a previously inhibited node to become active and even possibly to reach an activation level higher than those of its competitors, although previous inhibition might slow that process. Our homophone disambiguation network includes this ability for the node with highest activation to change with context.

There Is No Executive System Whose Exclusive Purpose Is Inhibition

One of the meta-functions that clinicians and behavioral neuroscientists often ascribe to the prefrontal cortex is behavioral inhibition (e.g., Davidson & Rickman, 1997). This is a natural conclusion from the observation that prefrontal damage often leads to emotional impulsiveness. However, this emphasis on inhibition of emotions carries an implicit bias seemingly founded in Cartesian dualism, with perhaps some influence from Hullian drive-reduction theory (Hull, 1943), which is the bias that the highest possible human functioning takes place when primitive, emotional, animal-like behaviors are inhibited. This assumption is not congruent with the clinical observation that damage to the brain's emotional pathways stunts effective decision making (Damasio, 1994). As described more fully in Eisler and Levine (2002), the prefrontal executive facilitates as much as it inhibits lower-level neural activity. It regulates the excitatory–inhibitory balance and selects activity patterns to either facilitate or inhibit on the basis of task appropriateness. Hence, we believe that top-down inhibition is part of what the executive does but should not be considered as an isolated overarching function. Instead, the overarching top-down executive function is selection among lower-level alternatives, of which facilitation and inhibition are equally important components.

Prefrontal executive inhibition is also invoked as an explanation for some data from cognitive tasks such as the Wisconsin Card Sorting Test. Anderson and Levy (in chap. 5, this volume) note that "perseverative behavior in memory tasks is largely what motivated the original inhibitory deficit hypothesis of frontal lobe dysfunction" (p. 91). However, the neural network model of Levine and Prueitt (1989), based on a theoretical formulation by Nauta (1971), simulated the perseverative behavior of frontal patients on the Wisconsin Card Sorting Test as a reduced influence of current rewards or penalties on choices between competing categorization rules. The representations of these rules in the Levine–Prueitt network are connected by mutual lateral inhibition; each one is increased in activation by habit (i.e., previous use of a particular rule) and by reward (e.g., the experimenter saying "right") and decreased by penalty (e.g., the experimenter saying "wrong"). In frontal patients, there is still mutual inhibition between rule representations, but both reward and penalty influences are much weakened, leaving habit as the dominant influence on interrule competition. Hence, the patient perseveration data can be explained as a deficit in the selective influence of reward or penalty, without resort to a generalized deficit in inhibition.

As Anderson and Levy (chap. 5, this volume) discuss, several common disorders of human executive functioning have often been described as deficits in cognitive inhibition. These conditions include anxiety disorders, dementia of the Alzheimer's type, and even normal aging (see chap. 8, this volume), as well as effects of prefrontal cortex damage. However, the network approach advocated in this chapter suggests that these executive disorders are characterized not so much by deficits in inhibition as by deficits in response selection, more in line with the argument advanced by MacLeod et al. (2003). At the neural level, a generalized deficit of inhibition could lead to excessive, epileptic-like electrical activity as suggested by the early random net models without inhibition discussed earlier in this chapter. Also, an excess of excitatory as compared with inhibitory activity in the sensory cortex would lead to vivid hallucinations and an inability to distinguish those hallucinations from reality, such as occurs in positive symptoms of schizophrenia. (For a review of some evidence and a network analysis, see Hestenes, 1992.) None of these types of neural responses are characteristic of anxiety disorder, dementia, normal aging, or prefrontal executive syndromes (American Psychiatric Association, 1994).

The perseveration results for patients with prefrontal lesions suggest an alternative to a generalized inhibitory deficit as a characterization of patients with any of these conditions: anxiety disorder, dementia, or prefrontal executive syndromes. We propose that, as in Levine and Prueitt's (1989) perseveration network, these conditions are characterized by intact inhibitory connections but with abnormal relative activations of mutually inhibiting representations, the precise nature of the abnormality being different for each syndrome.

In chapter 8 in this volume, Lustig, Hasher, and Zacks point to data on older versus younger adults that argue for a selective deficit in cognitive inhibition with aging. They review data showing that performance of many cognitive tasks leads to increased activity of some areas (e.g., left prefrontal) and decreased activity of others (e.g., posterior cingulate and medial frontal) and that older adults show the increases but not the decreases. It is possible that the changes in aging lead to selective impairment of inhibitory connections within the executive system (although in chap. 9 in this volume, Burke and Osborne propose that some of the deficits attributed to inhibition are actually at the perceptual level). However, this is not the same as saying that the executive system's function is primarily inhibitory. The neural transmitters to which Lustig et al. ascribe inhibitory function (acetylcholine and catecholamines) are actually inhibitory at some loci and excitatory at others. It may be that specific types of receptors for these transmitters are the key to these age differences, but the results are inconclusive, and more research is needed to determine the relative contribution of excitation versus inhibition to these processes.

The modeling perspective suggests that top-down influences are not purely inhibitory in other cognitive domains as well, such as visual attention. Reynolds, Chelazzi, and Desimone (1999) examined single-cell responses in the inferotemporal cortex of monkeys who either were or were not attending to a stimulus outside the cell's typical receptive field. They found that attention can facilitate bottom-up signals from the primary visual cortex. Grossberg (2004) cited this result in support of his well-known ART (adaptive resonance theory) network (Carpenter & Grossberg, 1987), in which a higher level of nodes regulates the pattern processing of a lower level by a combination of facilitation and suppression. He contrasted his model with other computational models of visual processing in which top-down influences are purely suppressive (Mumford, 1992; Rao & Ballard, 1999).

Inhibition Is Not Greatest When There Is Most "Need" for It

Some arguments against cognitive inhibition are leveled at the assumption that inhibition would be greatest when the representation to be inhibited is strongest and therefore there is more "need" for active inhibition. This idea goes back to Wundt (1902) and the concept of reactive inhibition (see chap. 1, this volume). For example, as Gorfein et al. (in press) noted,

> According to inhibition–suppression views, inhibition is necessary in the service of discourse processes whenever there is a conflict between the interpretation of the ambiguous word and the context, and in general the greater the conflict the greater the need to inhibit the competing meaning [as characterized by Simpson & Adamopoulos, 2001].

Gorfein et al. (in press) then argued against inhibition–suppression theories on the basis of a primacy effect they observed in homophone disambiguation. The data arise from the ambiguous word paradigm (Gorfein et al., 2000) consisting of three successive phases in which the subject must choose between dominant and subordinate meanings of a homophone. On the first phase, the subordinate meaning is primed; on the second phase, the dominant meaning is primed; and on the third phase, neither meaning is primed. As Figure 14.4 shows, the percentage of time that the dominant meaning is chosen increases, naturally, from the first to the second phase and then decreases again on the third phase: The decrease is not back to the first-phase levels but is statistically significant. This primacy effect is not explained by some inhibition–suppression accounts that would predict, as Simpson and Adamopoulos (2001) stated, that previous priming of the subordinate meaning would increase the need to inhibit the subordinate meaning when the dominant meaning is later primed on the second phase. This inhibition of the subordinate meaning should carry over to the third phase, leading to a greater than baseline proportion of dominant responses in the third phase, contrary to the observed results.

These data do in fact refute one property that is frequently attributed to cognitive inhibition—namely, the tendency of inhibition to increase when there

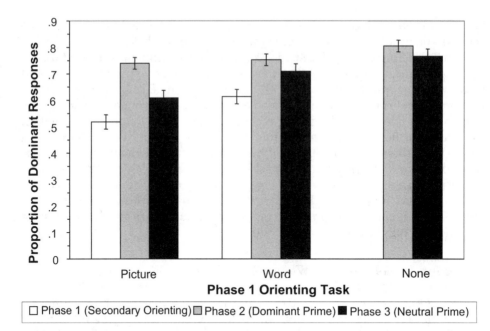

Figure 14.4. Proportion of dominant responses to homophones as a function of form of presentation in the Phase 1 orienting task. The data are averages of the word association and spelling response. Error bars represent 1 standard error on either side of the mean. Adapted from chapter 6, this volume, Figure 6.2.

is more conflict. However, the form of inhibition theory based on equations such as those in Figure 14.3, which we term *computational inhibition*, and its typical cognitive consequences are consistent with the primacy effect found by Gorfein and his colleagues (Gorfein et al., 2000, in press; chap. 6, this volume). For rather than inhibition increasing with the activity of the inhibited node, these equations show that, all other things being equal, the strength of inhibition from node i to node j increases with activity of the inhibiting node i and is counteracted by activity of the inhibited node j. In the case of our neural network homophone model, this can be interpreted as saying that priming a subordinate meaning buffers the choice of that meaning against inhibitory competition from the opposite choice.

Moving from the general to the specific, we now review the homophone data of Gorfein et al. (2000) and present our neural network model of those data. The network we have constructed uses only the minimum amount of inhibition that seems to be needed to reproduce the experimental effects.

Our neural network model incorporates much of the design of the original computational model of the same data described in Gorfein et al. (in press; cf. chap. 6, this volume). As stated previously, we do not treat inhibition as a type of active (conscious or unconscious) suppression that is largest when it needs to be largest. Hence, our model of the word ambiguity data differs from another neural network model of similar data by Norman and O'Reilly (2003), in which inhibition is largest when there is most need for it. Specifically, the

Table 14.1. Summary of Cognitive Effects of Our Computation Inhibition Framework and of Aspects of Classical Cognitive Inhibition That Do Not Occur in the Framework

Cognitive effects arising from computational inhibition	Effects not arising from computational inhibition
Selective attention between stimuli	Total suppression of inhibited representations
Selective attention between attributes	Executive control with inhibition as its primary function
Response selection	Stronger inhibition of stronger representations ("punishing competitors")
Contrast enhancement	
Stabilization of network activity	

Norman–O'Reilly model is based on "punishing competitors"—that is, inhibiting representations of inappropriate responses in proportion to their ability to compete with the desired response.[3]

Table 14.1 summarizes several cognitive predictions, all discussed in preceding sections, of our theoretical framework for lateral inhibition neural networks. The left-hand column of Table 14.1 lists effects that arise from the modeling framework that we call *computational inhibition*. The right-hand column lists some effects that are sometimes considered part of cognitive inhibition but are not predicted by our framework.

Modeling the Primacy Effect in Homophone Disambiguation

Our neural network simulations reproduce a class of experiments on the disambiguation of English homophones with one of the pair clearly dominant (e.g., *sun–son, hair–hare, none–nun*). The sequence of experiments is described in detail in Gorfein et al. (in press), and all experiments are telescoped into one for the purposes of simulation, as they were in the activation-selection model of Gorfein et al. (in press).

All variations of the task are divided into three phases in which the same homophone is interpreted, except for control homophones, which were presented only during the last two phases. Early in the first phase, the subordinate meaning of the homophone is primed either by a picture that depicts the

---

[3] It is likely to be useful for models of other cognitive processes to include selective inhibition of the strongest representations. For example, in the categorization model of Carpenter and Grossberg (1987), once the input has been shown to mismatch the prototype of the most likely category, a new search of prototypes is initiated, and the previously tested category is selectively disabled. This idea of inhibition in the service of efficient search is also seen in the inhibition of previously attended locations in visual processing, termed *inhibition of return* (Posner & Cohen, 1984).

subordinate meaning of the homophone or by another word related semantically to that meaning. Early in the second phase, the dominant meaning is primed (by a word, not a picture). Neither meaning is primed at any time during the third phase. The choice of dominant or subordinate meaning is tested toward the end of each of the three phases by asking the subject either to spell the ambiguous homophone or to generate a word associated with the homophone. In a control condition, homophones were not presented during the Phase I subordinate meaning orienting task but only during the last two phases.

Figure 14.4 shows the proportion of times subjects chose the dominant meaning in each phase. As noted earlier, priming the dominant meaning in Phase 2 increased the proportion of dominant responses from Phase 1 to Phase 2 for both versions (picture and word) of Phase 1 subordinate priming. And for both versions, the history of subordinate priming in Phase 1 led to a small but significant decrease in the dominant response proportion from Phase 2 to Phase 3. This decrease was greater in the picture condition than in the word condition, presumably because processing the picture demanded more cognitive effort (i.e., depth of processing) and therefore led to activation of more attributes of the subordinate meaning than did processing the associated word. By *attributes* we mean abstract features that combine to represent the meaning of a word (Bower, 1967).

Figure 14.5 shows the neural network used to simulate the data of Figure 14.4. Equations are given in Appendix 14.1. The network includes lateral inhibition, but only at the highest (choice) level—that is, between the nodes in Figure 14.5 labeled "dominant choice" and "subordinate choice." To be consistent with the absence of cognitive inhibition in the Gorfein–Brown activation-selection model, our neural network model includes no direct inhibitory link between the representations of the two meanings themselves; the nodes in Figure 14.5 labeled "dominant meaning" and "subordinate meaning" are not directly connected to one another.

The network includes representations of the sound itself (e.g., *s&n*), of the two meanings (the dominant one such as *sun* and the subordinate one such as *son*), of 50 attributes of each meaning, and of the actual choice made. The picture versus word conditions in the experiment were simulated by having more attributes of the subordinate meaning primed by the picture. A preselected number of attributes (more in the picture condition than in the word condition) of the subordinate meaning in Phase 1 were given an excitatory signal representing priming. The same priming signal was given in Phase 2 to a number of attributes of the dominant meaning equal to the number of attributes primed in the word condition in Phase 1. Neither meaning was given an excitatory signal in Phase 3.

The only inhibitory connections in the model were lateral inhibitory connections at the choice stage. The proportion of dominant responses was simulated toward the end of each of the three phases by dividing the activity of the dominant choice node by the sum of the dominant and subordinate choice node activities. At this stage, the chosen meaning was determined by which of the choice nodes had the larger activity (usually the subordinate in Phase 1 and usually the dominant in Phase 2). After the choice, a selected number of the attributes (not the same ones as previously primed) of the chosen meaning

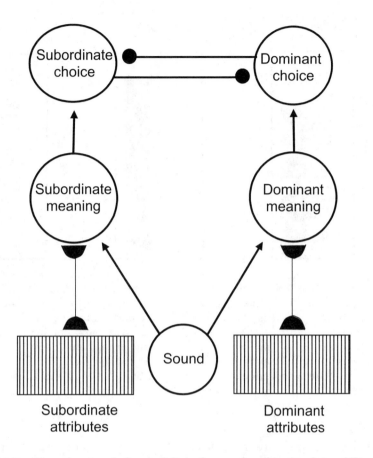

Figure 14.5. Neural network for modeling the word ambiguity data of Figure 14.4. Semicircles denote modifiable connections.

were activated, and the weights in both directions of the connections between those attributes and the meaning were allowed to change.

Figure 14.6 illustrates two simulations of our model network on this three-phase task under three different conditions. The graphs on the left represent the three phases in succession of the "picture" condition of Figure 14.4. The graphs in the middle represent the three phases in succession of the "word" condition of Figure 14.4. The graphs on the right represent Phases 2 and 3 (there was no Phase 1 in this case) of the "none" condition of Figure 14.4. Moving from picture to word to none, the number of attributes of the subordinate meaning primed in Phase 1 changed from 12 to 4 to 0, whereas the number of attributes of the dominant meaning primed in Phase 2 remained at 4 for all three conditions.

As in the data shown in Figure 14.4, the picture condition led to a smaller percentage of dominant responses on all phases and a greater dip in the percentage of dominant responses between Phases 2 and 3. Thus, some of the qualitative properties of the data of Gorfein et al. (in press) have been reproduced.

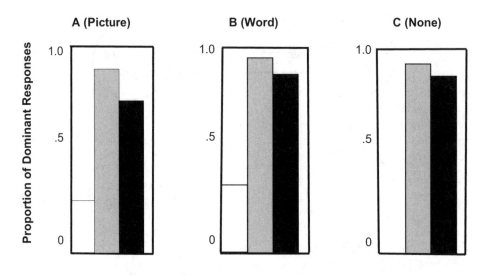

Figure 14.6.   Proportion of dominant responses in our network simulation as measured by the ratio of dominant meaning node activation to the sum of dominant and subordinate meaning node activations. In all three parts of this figure, four attributes of the dominant meaning are primed in Phase 2 (gray bars; dominant prime). The number of attributes of the subordinate meaning primed in Phase 1 (white bars; secondary orienting) is 12 in Panel A, corresponding to the picture condition of Figure 14.4; 4 in Panel B, corresponding to the word condition; and 0 in Panel C, corresponding to the none condition. Black bars represent Phase 3 (no prime).

We also ran some preliminary simulations of the network of Figure 14.5 with the lateral inhibition removed. These indicated that without inhibition, the tendency to choose the dominant or subordinate meaning is relatively insensitive to the number of subordinate meaning attributes primed in the first phase. Depending on the settings of the other parameters, either the response graph was the same over a wide range of numbers of attributes, or there were two possible response graphs, one for a few or no attributes and one for many attributes. Hence, without inhibition, the type of graded response seen when comparing the picture and word conditions in the experimental data of Figure 14.4 and in the model graphs of Figure 14.6 was not seen in the network.

Our model is still undergoing refinement, because it does not yet reproduce all of the qualitative properties of the data shown in Figure 14.4. For example, the experimental participants showed more tendency to choose the dominant meaning on Phase 2 if they had not experienced the priming of the subordinate meaning in Phase 1, as indicated by the greater height of the gray bar on the none condition than on the word condition in Figure 14.4. This height difference does not occur in the simulations shown in Figure 14.6.

The difference in our model's behavior with and without inhibition at the choice level argues that this type of lateral inhibition facilitates graded responses to the amount of priming experienced. Yet there are still two open issues about levels of network inhibition. First, we deliberately included inhibition in our network only at the end closest to the output, as shown in Figure 14.5. This instantiates our belief that there is no suppression of the nonchosen meaning at the representation stage, only at the output stage. Further, simulation studies can be done to test our intuition that no improvement would be made to the model by also including inhibition at the representation stage. Second, it can be argued that the choice of whichever meaning has the highest activation (in any model based on selective activation) presupposes an implicit neural inhibition at the choice level, not included in the actual model equations.

Conclusion

MacLeod et al. (2003; cf. chap. 1, this volume) argued for a strong distinction between neural inhibition and cognitive inhibition, saying that whereas neural inhibition is an incontrovertible fact, it does not imply cognitive inhibition. Moreover, they argued, many results from attention and memory that have been explained using cognitive inhibition can be explained as well or better by other processes, such as selective rehearsal or conflict resolution. The cognitive concept of inhibition that these authors discussed was explained as being composed of three subprocesses—suppression, restraint, and blocking:

> *Suppression* pertains to the prevention of a process from beginning or from continuing once begun, encompassing both psychological and physiological processes. *Restraint* refers to a mental state in which behavior is difficult to initiate or is curtailed. *Blocking* represents the classical psychoanalytic sense wherein a process, seen as instinctual, is kept from coming into consciousness (in psychoanalytic theory, by the activity of the superego). (MacLeod et al., 2003, p. 164)

Because of this set of connotations that many psychologists associate with the term *inhibition* (their description is derived from a 1958 dictionary of psychology), MacLeod et al. advocated avoiding the use of the term *inhibition* in the way we have used it in this chapter as simply a process causing a decrease in the activity of some other process from its baseline level. Rather, they preferred to use the term *interference* for that general type of interaction. The rehearsal and resolution processes they invoked can be generated by *interference* but not *inhibition* in the way these authors used the terms.

We have no particular disagreements with the explanations of data by MacLeod et al. (2003); in fact, Vincent R. Brown has developed computational models based on activation and selection without inhibition in the sense that MacLeod and his colleagues used (Gorfein et al., in press; chap. 6, this volume). Yet from the perspective of neural network modeling, where the boundary between neural and cognitive entities is still often fuzzy, we argue that it can be useful to have some degree of a common vocabulary across disciplines. This is why, in line with most neuroscientists and most other neural network theorists, we continue to use the word *inhibition* for network connections that contribute negative amounts to the change in activity of the node receiving the signal, such as the connections represented by the filled circles in Figure 14.5.

In this interdisciplinary spirit, we suggest that it might be possible to reinvent the term *cognitive inhibition* to mean the effects listed on the left-hand side of Table 14.1 and not to include the effects listed on the right-hand side of that table. The items listed on the right-hand side of Table 14.1 carry traditional baggage that is tied to Freudian notions of impulse control and repression but has little support in data from modern cognitive psychology and therefore should be dropped. The neural network definition of inhibition, which codifies what MacLeod and his colleagues (2003) called *interference,* has a much different set of connotations for cognitive psychologists. These connotations, listed on the left-hand side of Table 14.1, include its roles in enhancing perceptual contrast, stabilizing and shaping system responses, and making choices at all levels. In general, inhibition is not making the representation that is inhibited go away, as the earlier psychoanalytic interpretations suggested. Nor is there a part of our mental makeup that is specifically inhibitory in its function. Rather, inhibition and activation are complementary operations that should be conceived of as partners as much as opponents. The interplay between activation and inhibition facilitates adaptation of perceptual, attentional, and memory processes to current stimulus contexts and current task requirements.

Appendix 14.1

Equations Used in the Neural Network Simulations

Our simulations of the network depicted in Figure 14.5 were based on the variables shown in Table 1. If $I(t)$ represents the actual sound presentation inputs and $I_{1i}(t)$ and $I_{2i}(t)$ represent priming inputs to the various attribute nodes (the timing of the inputs is discussed below), the differential equations for the interacting node activities and connection weights are as follows:

$$\frac{ds}{dt} = -s + (1-s)I(t)$$

$$\frac{dm_1}{dt} = -m_1 + (1-m_1)\,(.5s + \sum_{i=1}^{50} a_{1i}w_{1i})$$

$$\frac{dm_2}{dt} = -m_2 + (1-m_2)\,(s + \sum_{i=1}^{50} a_{2i}w_{2i})$$

$$\frac{da_{1i}}{dt} = -a_{1i} + (1-a_{1i})I_{1i}(t)w_{1i},\ i = 1, ..., 50$$

$$\frac{da_{2i}}{dt} = -a_{2i} + (1-a_{2i})I_{2i}(t)w_{2i},\ i = 1, ..., 50$$

$$\frac{dc_i}{dt} = -c_i + (1-c_i)\,(m_i + c_i) - 3c_1c_2,\ i = 1,2$$

$$\frac{dw_{1i}}{dt} = 50I_{1i}(t)m_1,\ i = 1, ..., 50$$

$$\frac{dw_{2i}}{dt} = 50I_{2i}(t)m_2,\ i = 1, ..., 50$$

The version of the model with no lateral inhibition used the same equations (1), except that in the equation for the choice node c_i, the last negative term was dropped, leading to

$$\frac{dc_i}{dt} = -c_i + (1-c_i)\,(m_i + c_i),\ i = 1,2$$

In the simulations whose graphs are shown in Figure 14.6, the duration of each of the three phases was 6 time units. The sound input $I(t)$ was turned on

Table 1. Variables Used in Simulation of Network

Variable	Explanation
s	Activity of the node representing the sound, common to the two homographs.
$m_i, i = 1, 2$	Activities of the nodes representing subordinate and dominant meanings, respectively.
$a_{1i}, i = 1, 50$	Activities of the nodes representing the attributes of the subordinate meaning.
$a_{2i}, i = 1, 50$	Activities of the nodes representing the attributes of the dominant meaning.
$c_i, i = 1, 2$	Activities of the nodes for subordinate and dominant choices, respectively.
$w_{1i}, i = 1, 50$	Connection weights between the 50 subordinate attribute nodes and the subordinate meaning node.
$w_{2i}, i = 1, 50$	Connection weights between the 50 dominant attribute nodes and the dominant meaning node.

(with Intensity 1) for a period of 0.5 units at the beginning of the first phase while the subordinate attributes were primed in either the picture or word condition. The sound was again turned on toward the end of each of the three phases while the meaning choice was tested; this occurred during the interval between 4.0 and 4.5 time units into each phase. Hence,

$$I(t) = 1 \text{ if } t \; \varepsilon \; [0.0, 0.5] \text{ or } [4.0, 4.5] \text{ or } [10.0, 10.5] \text{ or } [16.0, 16.5]$$
$$0 \text{ otherwise.}$$

The inputs I_{1i} and I_{2i} to the attribute nodes were turned on (with Intensity 1) during two distinct periods. In the case of I_{1i}, representing inputs to the attribute nodes corresponding to the subordinate meaning, a number of the attributes (12 in the picture condition, 4 in the word condition, and 0 in the none condition) were randomly chosen to be primed during the interval (0.0, 0.5) at the start of the first phase. If we relabel the attributes so that the primed ones are the ones with the smallest indices, for $1 \le i \le 12$,

$$I_{1i}(t) = 1 \text{ if } t \; \varepsilon \; [0.0, 0.5] \text{ and (condition = picture)}$$
$$1 \text{ if } t \; \varepsilon \; [0.0, 0.5] \text{ and } 1 \le i \le 4 \text{ and (condition = word)}$$
$$0 \text{ otherwise.}$$

In addition, eight attributes, distinct from the primed ones, received inputs during the testing interval of each of the three phases, which occurred between 4.0 and 4.5 time units into each phase. If we label those eight additional attributes with numbers 13 to 20, this means that for $13 \le i \le 20$,

$$I_{1i}(t) = 1 \text{ if } t \; \varepsilon \; [4.0, 4.5] \text{ or } t \; \varepsilon \; [10.0, 10.5] \text{ or } t \; \varepsilon \; [16.0, 16.5]$$
$$0 \text{ otherwise.}$$

None of the other subordinate attributes were ever activated—that is, for $21 \le i \le 50$, $I_{1i}(t) = 0$ for all t.

The inputs I_{2i} to the attribute nodes corresponding to the dominant meaning followed similar patterns, except that independently of condition (picture, word, or none), the priming always took place on the second phase just before the testing interval. There were always four primed attributes of the dominant meaning and eight additional attributes activated during the testing intervals. Hence, for $1 \le i \le 4$,

$$I_{2i}(t) = 1 \text{ if } t \; \varepsilon \; [9.0, 9.5]$$
$$0 \text{ otherwise.}$$

For $5 \le i \le 12$,

$$I_{2i}(t) = 1 \text{ if } t \; \varepsilon \; [4.0, 4.5] \text{ or } t \; \varepsilon \; [10.0, 10.5] \text{ or } t \; \varepsilon \; [16.0, 16.5]$$
$$0 \text{ otherwise.}$$

For $13 \le i \le 50$,

$$I_{1i}(t) = 0 \text{ for all } t.$$

References

American Psychiatric Association. (1994). *Diagnostic and statistical manual of mental disorders* (4th ed.). Washington, DC: Author.

Amos, A. (2000). A computational model of information processing in the frontal cortex and basal ganglia. *Journal of Cognitive Neuroscience, 12,* 505–519.

Ashby, W. R., von Foerster, H., & Walker, C. C. (1962, August 11). Instability of pulse activity in a net with threshold. *Nature, 196,* 561–562.

Barnhardt, T. M., Glisky, E. L., Polster, M. R., & Elam, L. (1996). Inhibition of associates and activation of synonyms in the rare-word paradigm: Further evidence for a center-surround mechanism. *Memory & Cognition, 24,* 60–69.

Berns, G. S., & Sejnowski, T. J. (1998). A computational model of how the basal ganglia produce sequences. *Journal of Cognitive Neuroscience, 10,* 108–121.

Beurle, R. L. (1956). Properties of a mass of cells capable of regenerating pulses. *Philosophical Transactions of the Royal Society of London, Series B, 250,* 55–84.

Bower, G. (1967). A multicomponent theory of the memory trace. In K. W. Spence & J. T. Spence (Eds.), *The psychology of learning and motivation* (Vol. 1, pp. 229–325). New York: Academic Press.

Broadbent, D. E. (1958). *Perception and communication.* London: Pergamon.

Brown, J. W., Bullock, D., & Grossberg, S. (2004). How laminar frontal cortex and basal ganglia circuits interact to control planned and reactive saccades. *Neural Networks, 17,* 471–510.

Bullock, D., & Grossberg, S. (1988). Neural dynamics of planned arm movements: Emergent invariants and speed–accuracy properties during trajectory formation. *Psychological Review, 95,* 49–90.

Carpenter, G. A., & Grossberg, S. (1987). A massively parallel architecture for a self-organizing neural pattern recognition machine. *Computer Vision, Graphics, and Image Processing, 37,* 54–115.

Cohen, M. A., & Grossberg, S. (1983). Absolute stability of global pattern formation and parallel memory storage by competitive neural networks. *IEEE Transactions on Systems, Man, and Cybernetics, 13,* 815–826.

Damasio, A. (1994). *Descartes' error: Emotion, reason, and the human brain.* New York: Grosset/Putnam.

Davidson, R. J., & Rickman, M. (1997). Behavioral inhibition and the emotional circuitry of the brain: Stability and plasticity during the early childhood years. In L. A. Schmidt & J. Schulkin (Eds.), *Extreme fear, shyness, and social phobia: Origins, biological mechanisms, and clinical outcomes* (pp. 67–87). New York: Oxford University Press.

Eccles, J. C. (1968). *The physiology of excitable cells.* Baltimore: Johns Hopkins University Press.

Eisler, R., & Levine, D. S. (2002). Nurture, nature, and caring: We are not prisoners of our genes. *Brain and Mind, 3,* 9–52.

Ellias, S. A., & Grossberg, S. (1975). Pattern formation, contrast control, and oscillations in the short-term memory of shunting on-center off-surround networks. *Biological Cybernetics, 20,* 69–98.

Frank, M. J., Loughry, B., & O'Reilly, R. C. (2001). Interactions between frontal cortex and basal ganglia in working memory: A computational model. *Cognitive, Affective, and Behavioral Neuroscience, 1,* 137–160.

Freeman, W. J. (1983). Experimental demonstration of "shunting networks," the "sigmoid function," and "adaptive resonance" in the olfactory system. *Behavioral and Brain Sciences, 6,* 665–666.

Golden, R. M. (1996). *Mathematical methods for neural network analysis and design.* Cambridge, MA: MIT Press.

Gorfein, D. S. (2001). An activation-selection view of homograph disambiguation: A matter of emphasis? In D. Gorfein (Ed.), *On the consequences of meaning selection: Perspectives on resolving lexical ambiguity* (pp. 157–173). Washington, DC: American Psychological Association.

Gorfein, D. S., Berger, S. A., & Bubka, A. (2000). The selection of homophone meaning: Word association when context changes. *Memory & Cognition, 28,* 766–773.

Gorfein, D. S., Brown, V. R., & DeBiasi, C. (in press). The activation-selection model of meaning: Explaining why the son comes out after the sun. *Memory & Cognition.*

Gottlieb, D. I. (1988, March). GABAergic neurons. *Scientific American,* 82–89.

Griffith, J. S. (1963a). A field theory for neural nets: I. Derivation of the field equations. *Bulletin of Mathematical Biophysics, 25,* 111–120.

Griffith, J. S. (1963b). On the stability of brain-like structures. *Biophysical Journal, 3,* 299–308.

Griffith, J. S. (1965). A field theory for neural nets: II. Properties of the field equations. *Bulletin of Mathematical Biophysics, 27,* 187–195.

Grossberg, S. (1973). Contour enhancement, short term memory, and constancies in reverberating neural networks. *Studies in Applied Mathematics, 52,* 213–257.

Grossberg, S. (2004, May). *Linking brain to mind.* Tutorial lecture series presented at the Eighth International Conference on Cognitive and Neural Systems, Boston University.

Grossberg, S., & Levine, D. S. (1975). Some developmental and attentional biases in the contrast enhancement and short-term memory of recurrent neural networks. *Journal of Theoretical Biology, 53,* 341–380.

Hartline, H. K., & Ratliff, F. (1957). Inhibitory interaction of receptor units in the eye of limulus. *Journal of General Physiology, 40,* 357–376.

Hebb, D. O. (1949). *The organization of behavior.* New York: Wiley.

Helmholtz, H. L. F. von. (1962). *Helmholtz's treatise on physiological optics* (3rd ed., J. P. C. Southall, Ed. & Trans.). New York: Dover Publications. (Original work published 1924)

Hestenes, D. O. (1992). A neural network theory of manic–depressive illness. In D. S. Levine & S. J. Leven (Eds.), *Motivation, emotion, and goal direction in neural networks* (pp. 209–257). Hillsdale, NJ: Erlbaum.

Hodgkin, A. L. (1964). *The conduction of the nervous impulse.* Springfield, IL: Charles C Thomas.

Hull, C. L. (1943). *Principles of behavior.* New York: Appleton.

Kilmer, W., McCulloch, W. S., & Blum, J. (1969). A model of the vertebrate central command system. *International Journal of Man–Machine Studies, 1,* 279–309.

Kuffler, S. (1953). Discharge patterns and functional organization of mammalian retina. *Journal of Neurophysiology, 16,* 37–68.

LaBerge, D., & Brown, V. (1989). Theory of attentional operations in shape identification. *Psychological Review, 96,* 101–124.

Levine, D. S. (2000). *Introduction to neural and cognitive modeling* (2nd ed.). Mahwah, NJ: Erlbaum.

Levine, D. S. (2002). Neural network modeling. In H. Pashler & J. Wixted (Eds.), *Stevens' handbook of experimental psychology* (3rd ed., Vol. 4, pp. 223–269). New York: Wiley.

Levine, D. S., & Leven, S. J. (1991). Inhibition in the nervous system: Models of its roles in choice and context determination. *Neurochemical Research, 16,* 381–395.

Levine, D. S., Mills, B. A., & Estrada, S. (2005, August). Modeling emotional influences on human decision making under risk. *IEEE: Proceedings of International Joint Conference on Neural Networks,* pp. 1657–1662.

Levine, D. S., & Prueitt, P. S. (1989). Modeling some effects of frontal lobe damage: Novelty and perseveration. *Neural Networks, 2,* 103–116.

Mach, E. (1959). *The analysis of sensations and the relation of the physical to the psychical* (C. M. Williams, Trans.). New York: Dover. (Original work published 1886)

MacLeod, C. M., Dodd, M. D., Sheard, E. D., Wilson, D. E., & Bibi, U. (2003). In opposition to inhibition. *Psychology of Learning and Motivation, 43,* 163–214.

Monchi, O., & Taylor, J. (1998). A hard wired model of coupled frontal working memories for various tasks. *Information Sciences Journal, 113,* 221–243.

Mumford, D. (1992). On the computational architecture of the neocortex: II. The role of cortico-cortical loops. *Biological Cybernetics, 66,* 241–251.

Nauta, W. J. H. (1971). The problem of the frontal lobe: A reinterpretation. *Journal of Psychiatric Research, 8,* 167–187.

Norman, K. A., & O'Reilly, R. C. (2003). Modeling hippocampal and neocortical contributions to recognition memory: A complementary-learning-systems approach. *Psychological Review, 110,* 611–646.

Posner, M., & Cohen, Y. (1984). Components of visual orienting. In H. Bouma & D. Bouwhuis (Eds.), *Attention and performance* (Vol. 10, pp. 531–556). Hillsdale, NJ: Erlbaum.

Purves, D., Williams, M., Nundy, S., & Lotto, R. (2004). Perceiving the intensity of light. *Psychological Review, 111,* 142–158.

Rao, R. P., & Ballard, D. H. (1999). Predictive coding in the visual cortex: A functional interpretation of some extra-classical receptive-field effects. *Nature Neuroscience, 2,* 79–87.

Ratliff, F. (1965). *Mach bands: Quantitative studies of neural networks in the retina.* San Francisco: Holden-Day.

Reeves, A., & Sperling, G. (1986). Attention gating in short-term visual memory. *Psychological Review, 93,* 180–206.

Reynolds, J. H., Chelazzi, L., & Desimone, R. (1999). Competitive mechanisms subserve attention in macaque areas V2 and V4. *Journal of Neurophysiology, 19,* 1736–1753.

Roberts, E. (1976). Disinhibition as an organizing principle in the nervous system—the role of the GABA system: Application to neurologic and psychiatric disorders. In E. Roberts, T. N. Chase, & D. B. Tower (Eds.), *GABA in nervous system function* (pp. 515–539). New York: Raven Press.

Roberts, E. (1986). What do GABA neurons really do? They make possible variability generation in relation to demand. *Experimental Neurology, 93,* 279–290.

Ross, J., Morrone, M., & Burr, D. (1989). The conditions under which Mach bands are visible. *Vision Research, 29,* 699–715.

Rumelhart, D. E., & McClelland, J. L. (Eds.). (1986). *Parallel distributed processing* (Vols. 1–2). Cambridge, MA: MIT Press.

Sherrington, C. S. (1925). Remarks on some aspects of reflex inhibition. *Proceedings of the Royal Society Series B, 105,* 332–362.

Sherrington, C. S. (1947). *The integrative action of the nervous system.* New Haven, CT: Yale University Press. (Original work published 1906)

Simpson, G. B., & Adamopoulos, A. C. (2001). Repeated homographs in word and sentence contexts: Multiple processing of multiple meanings. In D. S. Gorfein (Ed.), *On the consequences of meaning selection: Perspectives on resolving lexical ambiguity* (pp. 157–173). Washington, DC: American Psychological Association.

Sperling, G., & Sondhi, M. M. (1968). Model for visual luminance detection and flicker detection. *Journal of the Optical Society of America, 58,* 1133–1145.

von Bekesy, G. (1969). Similarities of inhibition in the different sense organs. *American Psychologist, 24,* 707–719.

Wagar, B. M., & Thagard, P. (2004). Spiking Phineas Gage: A neurocomputational theory of cognitive–affective integration in decision making. *Psychological Review, 111,* 67–79.

Walley, R. E., & Weiden, T. D. (1973). Lateral inhibition and cognitive masking: A neuropsychological theory of attention. *Psychological Review, 80,* 284–302.

Wilson, H. R., & Cowan, J. D. (1972). Excitatory and inhibitory interactions in localized populations of model neurons. *Biophysical Journal, 12,* 1–24.

Wundt, W. (1902). *Grundzüge der physiologischen Psychologie* [Fundamentals of physiological psychology] (5th ed.). Leipzig, Germany: Engelmann.

Yellott, J. (1989). Constant volume operators and lateral inhibition. *Journal of Mathematical Psychology, 33,* 1–35.

Part VII

Overview and Commentary

15

Is It Time to Inhibit Inhibition? Lessons From a Decade of Research on the Place of Inhibitory Processes in Cognition

Thomas H. Carr

What's the fuss in this book all about? A major goal of cognitive science is to account for the control of goal-directed thoughts and actions and to explain in mechanistic terms the objective success or failure of such performances, as well as the subjective sense of choice and responsibility that is so much a part of the phenomenology of being human. As Logan and Bundesen (2003) put it, we want to understand "the clever homunculus"—a term that literally means "the smart little man in the head" and stands for the core locus of central or executive control that seems to reside somewhere in the mind and brain.

Understanding executive control presents a host of thorny problems, not the least of which is what appears to be the extremely limited capacity of the clever homunculus to pay attention and take explicit account of multiple pieces of information. The problems only grow worse when one thinks about the demanding and complicated lives of clever homunculi out there in the real world. How is it that people can actually succeed in choosing a task, planning how to do it, and executing it effectively, even under extremely stressful conditions that are known to create serious obstacles to retrieving and deploying task-relevant knowledge (e.g., many things to do, complex environments with lots of information both relevant and irrelevant, unfamiliar stimuli and events that present new challenges, rewards and punishments hanging on the outcomes of one's actions)? A standard answer appears in a timeworn joke (folk psychology is not always wrong psychology). A tourist trying to find his way around Manhattan appeals to an old New Yorker: "Please, sir, how do I get to Carnegie Hall?" The old man looks him up and down and says, "Practice, practice, practice."

One of the proposed consequences of all this practice is to eliminate the need for the clever but limited homunculus as much as possible by making task performance automatic. And there is considerable evidence for this solution to the problems caused by the limits of executive control: Practice can improve dual-task performance, reduce the impact of number of stimuli, and improve the ability to ignore irrelevant stimuli. But automaticity has its own limits. It introduces new paths to fragility of performance (Beilock & Carr, 2001; Beilock, Carr, MacMahon, & Starkes, 2002), including the possibility that automated responses may usurp appropriate responses that require more time and effort to construct and execute (Reason, 1979). And sometimes one must go forward even though one has not had much time to practice, and hence automaticity is not an option. Again, automated responses to stimuli present in the environment may vie to take over, whether or not they are the appropriate responses given the goal, and there is no single practiced response that can gain ascendancy over the host of practiced and unpracticed possibilities. If there is only one affordance provided by the stimulus situation, there is no problem of choice, but if there are many affordances—and there almost always are—then executive control must earn the big bucks researchers believe it deserves.

There is another and quite different standard answer to the question posed by the problem of executive control. Basically, this second answer is that bigger is better and so is more powerful: If one cannot eliminate the need for control through practice, then one can go to the other extreme and maximize control's capabilities. A bigger working memory capacity for keeping perceptual, memory, and response codes activated can result in more effective task-relevant control, because the information needed for the task is more likely to remain available in the contents of working memory. Alternatively, a more powerful mechanism for inhibiting unwanted perceptual, memory, and response codes—even if they were activated automatically—can result in more effective task-relevant control, because such powerful inhibition reduces the cognitive clutter created by a large working memory capacity that allows for much chaff to be mixed in with the grain that is needed for accurate and efficient task performance. So big working memories would keep lots of grain (but might also keep lots of chaff), whereas powerful inhibition would throw out lots of chaff, leaving mostly grain. Wouldn't it be nice to have both, if practice-based automaticity is not enough to solve the problem of executive control?

The Place of Inhibitory Processes in Cognition

These issues supply the context in which the discussions in this volume take place. To solve the problems of executive control, we need to investigate and establish the strengths, weaknesses, and interactions among three components of control by which real-time cognitive performances are implemented. These three components are automated structures built up through practice; effortfully maintained structures held in working memory; and judiciously applied processes of inhibition that protect working memory from unwanted, irrelevant, and detrimental perceptual inputs, retrievals from memory, and response computations. The inhibitory processes might block unwanted representations from entering working memory, or they might cull them from working memory after they have arrived and been detected. So the research agenda should focus on practice-based automaticity, working memory capacity, inhibitory power, and the relations among them.

The Really Complicating Question: Are There Any Such Things as "Inhibitory Processes"?

One might imagine that the account just set out describes a complicated-enough agenda for research on cognitive control. But the really complicating question, addressed head-on in this volume, is a more epistemological one, taxing the evidentiary limits of how cognitive science does its business: Are there even such things as "inhibitory processes" to begin with? This is an inflammatory question at present, but it is not a new one.

In a classic treatment of attention, Pillsbury (1908) described three views of the role that attention might play in real-time cognitive processing. Attention might facilitate information that is wanted or inhibit information that is unwanted, or it might do both. The last seems to be the position that was favored by the black sheep of the Pillsbury flour family—Pillsbury himself—but he made it clear that the issue could not be decided on the evidence then available. Debate over whether attention is facilitatory, inhibitory, or both has lasted to the present day, and the issue apparently still cannot be decided on the basis of the evidence that is available. Although there is now little argument that attention facilitates representations and processes toward which it is directed, opinion remains divided over whether inhibition has a place.

During the past 2 decades, the pendulum has swung erratically back and forth between yes and no. When Dagenbach and Carr (1994) wrote their introduction to a volume touting inhibitory processes in theories of attention, memory, and language, the popularity of inhibition as a theoretical construct was high and rising. Among several reasons Dagenbach and Carr offered for this popularity was a desire to integrate cognitive psychology with neuroscience:

> Finally, this being the Decade of the Brain, we might speculate that the desire to have what is known about the way the nervous system works reflected in our cognitive models may be a relevant factor in renewed interest in inhibitory processes. (p. xiii)

In chapter 1 of this volume, MacLeod reminds readers that trends toward importing inhibition from theories of brain to theories of mind have been seen before. MacLeod resurrected an objection to such a trend from the late 1800s, that theories at the level of cognitive computation do not need to instantiate the same architectures or processes as theories at the level of neural anatomy and physiology. MacLeod mentions Breese (1899), who was derisive toward such copying or matching: "What does inhibition in psychology mean? Most psychologists have presupposed that its meaning in psychology is practically the same as in physiology. They begin with illustrations of neural inhibition and end with illustrations of inhibition among ideas" (p. 6). MacLeod builds on Breese by asking whether a concept of inhibition is necessary in a psychological theory of attentional selection or is only sufficient—an ideological bow to the better established understanding that at the level of physiology, cells in the nervous system do interact with one another in both of the ways entertained by Pillsbury (1908) for psychological processes of selection.

MacLeod sets the tone for this volume with a skeptical stance on this question of necessity. He suggests that in building psychological theory, researchers should start by denying inhibitory processes to the mind and should introduce them only if they absolutely cannot get along without them. This strategy for building theory is endorsed in chapter 9 of this volume by Burke and Osborne, who quote from MacLeod, Dodd, Sheard, Wilson, and Bibi (2003): "In most cases where inhibitory mechanisms have been offered to explain cognitive performance, non-inhibitory mechanisms can accomplish the same goal" (p. 203). In establishing their position, Burke and Osborne do not go as far as MacLeod et al., who followed up on the quote from Breese by saying, "Yet we would no more expect to find cognitive inhibition because there is neural inhibition than we would expect to find cognitive glia or cognitive ion channels because their neural counterparts demonstrably exist" (p. 165). What could a theorist who favors inhibition possibly say in response to that?

The Reality of Cognitive Glia

One possible response can be derived from the work of Potts, St. John, and Kirson (1989), who reported data consistent with just such a notion—that there could be *cognitive glia* (i.e., the cognitive equivalent of glial cells in the brain that move in and out between neurons, either inhibiting or facilitating the ability of neurons to establish connections with one another). Potts et al. asked people to read short narrative passages presenting new information about an esoteric topic, including new vocabulary words that participants would not have encountered before reading the passage. Afterward, participants were tested for two kinds of priming. Episodic priming between one of the new vocabulary words in a passage and an immediately following word or phrase provided an index of whether an episodic representation of having read the passage was established in memory. Semantic priming between one of the new words and a word not in the passage but related to the meaning of the new word provided an index of the extent to which the new knowledge gained from the passage was integrated or brought into contact with already-existing representations of knowledge in semantic memory. The important manipulation was whether participants were told in advance of reading that the passages were true accounts taken from encyclopedias or fictional accounts invented for the experiment. Both groups of participants evidenced episodic priming. The striking result was that the occurrence of semantic priming depended on the instructions. Participants who were told that the passages were fictional showed episodic priming but no semantic priming, whereas participants told that the passages were encyclopedic truth showed semantic priming in addition to episodic priming. Potts et al. concluded that belief of truth or fiction controlled the deployment of a segregation-versus-integration mechanism that either allowed the new knowledge gleaned from the passage to be integrated into the knowledge base of semantic memory or kept it segregated as an episodic memory of an isolated event.

Why should I raise this example of instruction-induced integration versus segregation of new learning in the context of MacLeod et al.'s (2003) comparison between cognitive inhibition and cognitive glia? Work by Hatton (2004) and others has shown that glia serve exactly the sort of role at the cellular level that Potts et al. (1989) observed at the cognitive level: Glia move physically over short time frames to facilitate or interfere with the establishment of new, integrating connections between individual neurons. Thus, although this analogy is (extremely) abstract, it might not be quite so ridiculous as MacLeod et al. suggested for one to propose that there are cognitive glia in some way, shape, or form. And if one might be willing to entertain, by analogy to neural glia, the existence of cognitive glia that regulate the establishment of new, integrating connections between ideas, why not be even more willing to entertain the possibility of inhibition among ideas by analogy to inhibition among neurons? After all, the latter analogy already has a long history, and it seems much less preposterous.

The Default Conception

Asking such a question amounts to identifying the major underlying theme running through this volume: What should be the default conception regarding inhibitory cognitive processes? This theme plays out in three big issues:

1. Do we need a concept of inhibition?
2. What standards of evidence should be applied? That is, how do researchers know an inhibition when they see one in the data?
3. Perhaps most fundamentally, what initial stance should researchers take, and why? That is, should they start from a skeptical point of view and embrace inhibitory processes only if they cannot get along without them, putting the burden of proof on those who posit inhibition to show that it is not something else? Or should they assume that inhibitory processes are a likely reality and build them into theory and interpretation of data until these processes are proved not to exist, putting the burden of proof on those who propose alternatives as substitutes?

Inhibitophiles and Inhibitophobes

Investigators starting from these two positions were in combat—well, in collegial competition—throughout the conference that was the basis for this volume. At one point during the meeting, Gordon Logan assigned them category memberships: "inhibitophiles" and "inhibitophobes." It is a useful organizing distinction.

If one is an inhibitophile, then there are two big questions one must be prepared to address. First, there is a need to determine whether inhibition is all of a piece—a single mechanism, a general processing capability—or is implemented by multiple mechanisms with domain-specific duties and separable task involvements. Theory is loose on this point at present.

Second, one must determine how such a question can be answered. Two basic approaches are showcased in this volume. One is the psychometric approach, examining correlations among task performances to show whether all tasks that might involve inhibition correlate with one another or whether there might be clusters of tasks with strong within-cluster correlations and independence between clusters. One example is an article by Friedman and Miyake (2004). The other approach is the computational or "isolable subsystems" approach (Posner, 1985), analyzing tasks into component mechanisms and comparing reaction times and error rates across task conditions to isolate the individual mechanisms. Examples can be found in chapters 2, 4, 6, and 12 in this volume. Often, in psychology, these two approaches live almost completely independent lives, but in the study of inhibitory processes, they live side by side. The two approaches can serve each other as converging operations; each has its own strengths and weaknesses, and together they are stronger than either by itself. Chapters 7 and 8 in the present volume and more recent work by Hambrick, Helder, Hasher, and Zacks (2005) meld the two approaches.

If one is an inhibitophobe, one has another set of questions to answer. The first is whether the list of alternative processes is enough. That is, once one has run the gamut of possible noninhibitory explanations for the various phenomena to which inhibition has been applied—sensory degradation, discrimination problems that lead to selection failure, breadth and strength of associations in the knowledge base, competition and retrieval interference when multiple representations are activated—is there still variance left to be explained? And what about parsimony? Is a long list of separate mechanisms, each applied in a different situation, really to be preferred?

It seems clear that if one is to successfully answer either set of questions—the inhibitophile's or the inhibitophobe's—one must engage in careful task analysis and thorough empirical testing of alternative process explanations. This is one of the major messages of the contributions to this volume. Systematic methodologies for discriminating among the various proposed processes and for determining whether two task performances, each of which looks sort of like it depends on inhibition, involve the same processes or different processes, are absolutely crucial at this juncture in developing theories of the place of inhibitory processes in cognition. Anderson and Levy in chapter 5 deal directly with this problem, as do Dagenbach et al. in chapter 3, Burke and Osborne in chapter 9, and Friedman and Miyake (2004). These analyses enlist to varying degrees the two approaches already talked about—the computational approach for isolating individual processes and the psychometric approach for measuring covariation versus independence between performances as an index of whether the performances rely on the same or different processes.

Confessions of an Inhibitophile: Brain and Mind Together

So far I have tried to strike a balanced pose, but now is the time for confession. In truth, I am an inhibitophile. Having outed myself, I can pose the final question that I think inhibitophobes need to address: Why can't you get on board? If the brain uses inhibition, and we know it does, why should you deny it to the mind?

Perhaps the urge to pose this question is simply the cross one bears as a Posner-trained cognitive scientist. It has become something of a reflex for me to try to think in terms of structurally isomorphic theories of brain and mind. The great contribution Posner made in marrying theories of cognition with theories of brain anatomy and physiology has been picking the right "grain size" at which to characterize both mental processes and localization of brain function to permit mapping back and forth between one and the other (Carr, 2005; Mayr, Awh, & Keele, 2005; Posner, 1985; Posner & Raichle, 1995). The product of this enterprise, when it is worked out well, is a multilevel theoretical description of great beauty and great utility, allowing data about cognition to support inferences about brain and data about brain to support inferences about cognition.

I close this chapter with two examples of work bringing cognitive–behavioral and neural evidence to bear in concert. The first is chapter 8 by Lustig, Hasher, and Zacks, who found evidence in functional magnetic resonance imaging data collected by Gazzaley, Cooney, Rissman, and D'Esposito (2005) that the brain deploys inhibitory processes at the level of cognitive operations and representations—that is, inhibition among ideas. Gazzaley et al. measured activation in face-specific and scene-specific processing areas of the brain in three different conditions: (a) a condition in which participants engaged in passive viewing of a series of pictures, some of which were faces and some of which were scenes; (b) a condition in which participants were to remember the faces and ignore the scenes; and (c) a condition in which participants were to remember the scenes and ignore the faces.

What Gazzaley et al. (2005) found were age differences in the pattern of results across these three conditions, and these age differences were important to Lustig et al.'s theory described in chapter 8 that cognitive aging differentially influences inhibitory processes. For all participants, "remember" activation for either type of stimulus was greater than the passive viewing activation for that type of stimulus. Furthermore, for young adults, "ignore" activation for either type of stimulus was less than the passive viewing activation for that type of stimulus. However, for older adults, there was no difference between "ignore" activation and passive viewing activation.

Lustig et al. have drawn what seems to an inhibitophile to be a very straightforward conclusion: Young adults inhibit ignored stimuli, but older adults do not inhibit them. Older adults do attend to stimuli they want to remember, but they do not actively inhibit those they want to ignore.

The second example introduces a second recommendation. Not only should neural evidence be brought to bear in concert with cognitive–behavioral evidence, but formal and simulation modeling of the processes at each level of analysis will help immensely to clarify the theoretical descriptions at each level and to establish the presence or absence of correspondence between them. In the second closing example, Logan and Schall (2005) combined skills—Logan's skills in cognitive modeling of stop-signal reaction time in the stop-signal task and Schall's skills in drawing strong process inferences about single-cell neural data recorded from monkeys in tasks of the type commonly used by cognitive psychologists, including Logan's stop-signal task. In the stop-signal task, participants perform a forced-choice discrimination among a set of stimuli, responding as rapidly and accurately as possible by pressing a button to indicate the stimulus that has been presented. On some trials, at a random time ranging from a few hundred milliseconds before presentation of the target stimulus to a few hundred milliseconds afterward, a signal occurs telling the participant to stop—to withhold the key-press response indicating which target was presented. Logan developed a formal mathematical model of the processes involved in this task that instantiates a particular architecture: a race between a stream of processing that identifies the target and releases the key press indicating the decision and a stream of processing that detects the stop signal and generates an inhibitory message that interrupts the stream of target processing. The assumption is made that beyond some critical point in the stream of target processing, the decision has been made, the key to press has been chosen, and a ballistic command— beyond stopping—has been sent off from motor processes to the fingers. Hence, the time relative to target presentation at which the stop signal must be presented for the participant to be able to reliably stop the imperative key press provides an estimate of stop-signal reaction time—the time needed to generate the inhibitory signal and communicate it to target processing in advance of the point of no return when the ballistic command is sent from motor cortex to the fingers.

Application of this model to the behavioral stopping data—how likely at each delay of the stop signal relative to the target presentation it was that the participant would succeed in stopping—produces a range of individual differences in stop-signal reaction time. This range has already been shown to distinguish participants of the same age with attention-deficit/hyperactivity disorder (ADHD) from those without it (people with ADHD need more time to generate a successful stop command) and also to distinguish older adults from younger adults (older adults also need more time to generate a successful stop command). In both cases, it has been concluded that the group with the longer stop-signal reaction time shows a deficit in the particular inhibitory process tapped by this experimental paradigm.

What was new in the collaboration between Logan and Schall (2005) was that monkeys were taught the stop-signal task, and single-cell recordings from the monkeys' frontal cortices were inspected in search of cells whose firing patterns corresponded to the stop commands identified via application of Logan's formal model to the monkeys' behavioral reaction time data. Clear differentiation was observed between cells whose firing corresponded to the key-press response to the imperative target and cells whose firing corresponded to successful withholding of response on stop trials. Logan and Schall drew what is again, to an inhibitophile, a straightforward conclusion: that they had identified a particular type of inhibitory process—the stop command—and furthermore that they had, through the application of a formal model of stopping, identified the neural locus of the processing mechanism that generates the inhibition, isolating it to a particular class of cells.

How Will Researchers Make Further Progress?

These two examples lead to my final point. One of the examples was from neuroimaging of human task performance, and the other was from single-cell recording of monkey task performance followed by analysis of the data in the context of a formal model of the cognitive processes that the neural activity might be supporting. Together they suggest that if researchers are, at this crucial point in the development of research on inhibitory processes, to finally go beyond Pillsbury (1908), they will do so armed with two tools that Pillsbury did not possess. The first is the ability to combine cognitive–behavioral evidence with neural evidence gained from functional imaging of people and more invasive techniques applied to appropriate animal models. The second is the construction and application of formal mathematical and real-time simulation models of the cognitive processes and the unfolding of the neural activity as an aid to thought, hypothesis generation, and hypothesis testing.

The ultimate message of this volume, then, is the enormous utility of converging methods. We have reached a time in which cognitive–behavioral, neural, and formal methods are all mature and able to integrate with one another. Taking advantage of this nexus will provide the next big step forward in understanding the nature and interactions among the mechanisms responsible for executive control and implementation of real-time cognitive performance.

References

Beilock, S. L., & Carr, T. H. (2001). On the fragility of skilled performance: What governs choking under pressure? *Journal of Experimental Psychology: General, 130*, 701–725.

Beilock, S. L., Carr, T. H., MacMahon, C., & Starkes, J. L. (2002). When attention becomes counterproductive: Divided versus skill-focused attention in performance of sensorimotor skills by novices and experts. *Journal of Experimental Psychology: Applied, 8*, 6–16.

Breese, B. B. (1899). On inhibition. *Psychological Monographs, 3*, 1–65.

Carr, T. H. (2005). On the functional architecture of language and reading: Tradeoffs between biological preparation and cultural engineering. In U. Mayr, E. Awh, & S. W. Keele (Eds.), *Developing individuality in the human brain: A tribute to Michael I. Posner* (pp. 17–44). Washington, DC: American Psychological Association.

Dagenbach, D., & Carr, T. H. (1994). *Inhibitory processes in attention, memory, and language.* San Diego, CA: Academic Press.

Friedman, N. P., & Miyake, A. (2004). The relations among inhibition and interference control functions: A latent-variable analysis. *Journal of Experimental Psychology: General, 133*, 101–135.

Gazzaley, A., Cooney, J. W., Rissman, J., & D'Esposito, M. (2005). Top-down suppression deficit underlies working memory impairment in normal aging. *Nature Neuroscience, 8*, 1298–1300.

Hambrick, D. Z., Helder, L., Hasher, L., & Zacks, R. T. (2005, November). *The relationship between inhibition and working memory: A latent-variable approach.* Paper presented at the annual meeting of the Psychonomic Society, Toronto, Ontario, Canada.

Hatton, G. I. (2004). Dynamic neuronal–glial interactions: An overview 20 years later. *Peptides, 25*, 403–411.

Logan, G. D., & Bundesen, C. (2003). Clever homunculus: Is there an endogenous act of control in the explicit task cuing procedure? *Journal of Experimental Psychology: Human Perception and Performance, 29*, 575–599.

Logan, G. D., & Schall, J. (2005, March). *As above, so below: Behavioral and neural inhibition in the stop-signal task*. Paper presented at the Conference on the Place of Inhibitory Processes in Cognition, Arlington, TX.

MacLeod, C. M., Dodd, M. D., Sheard, E. D., Wilson, D. E., & Bibi, U. (2003). In opposition to inhibition. In B. H. Ross (Ed.), *The psychology of learning and motivation* (Vol. 43, pp. 163–214). San Diego, CA: Academic Press.

Mayr, U., Awh, E., & Keele, S. W. (Eds.). (2005). *Developing individuality in the human brain: A tribute to Michael I. Posner*. Washington, DC: American Psychological Association.

Pillsbury, W. B. (1908). *Attention*. New York: Macmillan.

Posner, M. I. (1985). *Chronometric explorations of mind* (2nd ed.). Hillsdale, NJ: Erlbaum.

Posner, M. I., & Raichle, M. E. (1995). *Images of mind*. New York: Scientific American.

Potts, G. R., St. John, M. F., & Kirson, D. (1989). Incorporating new information into existing world knowledge. *Cognitive Psychology, 21,* 303–333.

Reason, J. (1979). Slips of action. In G. Underwood & R. Stephens (Eds.), *Consciousness in models of human information processing* (pp. 67–89). London: Academic Press.

Author Index

Page numbers in italics refer to listings in the references.

Kunda, Z., 7, *21*
Kupfer, D. J., 150, *161*
Kurland, D. M., 125, *140*

LaBerge, D., 283, *302*
Lacey, S. C., *162*
Lafont, S., *234*
Lahiri, D. K., 221, *236*
Lambert, C., 221, *236*
Lange, E., 228, *237*
Langley, L. K., 172, *181*
Larish, J. F., 60, *61,* 149, *160,* 166, *181*
Laughlin, J. E., 126, *140,* 219, *235*
Lavie, N., 56, *61,* 267, *275*
Leahy, M. M., 11, *20*
LeCroy, C. W., 205, *209*
Leighton, E., 158, *161*
Lenartowicz, A., 146, *161*
Lesch, M. F., 240, 242, *257*
Leslie, A. M., 6, *21*
Letenneur, L., *235*
Leven, S. J., 282, *302*
Levin, I. P., 202, *209*
Levine, D. S., 282, 283, 285–290, *301, 302*
Levy, B. J., 83, *101*
Levy, J., *238*
Lewis, G. H., 151, *160*
Li, C.-S., *275*
Li, K. Z. H., 151, *160,* 170, 172, *181*
Li, L., 173, *181,* 243, *257*
Liberman, N., 7, *20*
Light, L. L., 109, *123,* 167, *179*
Lim, K. O., 219, *235*
Lin, W.-H., *275*
Lindenberger, U., 170, *179, 181*
Lindsay, D. S., 215, 228, *236*
Lissner, L. S., 69, *77*
Livesey, D. J., 265, *275*
Lloyd, F. J., 185, 189, 199, 204, *209, 210*
Loess, H., 118, *123*
Loewenstein, D. A., 220, *237*
Loftus, E. F., 104, *122*
Logan, G. D., 4, 18, *21,* 37, 39, 41, *43, 44,* 60,
   61, 67, *77,* 110, *123,* 133, *141,* 149, *159,*
   160, , 166, *181,* 213, *236,* 264–266, *274–*
   277, 307, 313, 314, *315*
Long, D. L., 133, *141*
Lotto, R., 282n1, *303*
Loughry, B., 285, *301*
Lowe, D. G., 9, *21,* 64, 67, 68, *77*
Luce, P. A., 177, *181*
Luchins, A. S., 8, *21*
Lupianez, J., 73, *77*
Lustig, C., 146–148, 153, 156–157, *160, 161,*
   169, 172, *180, 181*
Lykken, D. T., 150, *160*

MacDonald, A. W., III, *236*
MacDonald, P. A., 64, 66, *77*
Mach, E., 281, *302*
Mack, R., 15, *21,* 216, *236*
MacKay, D. G., 167, 171, 176, 177, *179, 181,*
   254, *256*
MacLeod, A. M., *161*
MacLeod, C. M., 3, 5, 11, 14–18, *21,* 73, *76,*
   77, 125, 127, 139, *141,* 164, 178, *181,* 213,
   216, 226, 232, 233, *236,* 252, *256,* 288,
   290, 297, 298, *302,* 309–311, *315*
MacLeod, M. D., 17, *22,* 84, *101*
MacMahon, C., 308, *315*
Macmillan, N. A., 195, *210*
MacQueen, G. M., 68, *78*
Macrae, C. N., 252, *257*
Madden, D. J., 155, *161,* 172, *181*
Majerus, S., 240, *256*
Malley, G. B., 73, *77*
Malone, M., *277*
Manly, T., 151, *161*
Marche, T., *210*
Marcovitch, S., 265, *277*
Marful, A., 83
Marian, D. E., 171, *181*
Mari-Beffa, P., 73, *77*
Markela-Lerenc, J., 228, *236*
Marrington, S., 151, *161*
Marshuetz, C., 243, *256*
Martel, M., 270, *275*
Martin, E., 103, *123*
Martin, N., 244, *257*
Martin, P. Y., 151, *161*
Martin, R. C., 12, *21,* 239–242, 244–246, 249,
   251, 254, *255–257*
Martinussen, R., 264, *276*
Mathews, A., 7, *23*
Mathis, K. M., 17, 18, *22,* 63, 64, 68, 75, *77*
Mattson, M. E., 202, *208*
Mauthner, N., 6, *22*
May, C. P., 3, *21,* 75, *76, 77,* 125, 128, 138,
   141, 146, 148–153, 155, 158, *160–162,*
   163, 165, 166, 168–170, *180, 181,* 213,
   236, 243, *257*
Maylor, E. A., 177, *181*
Mayr, S., 74, *76,* 168, *179*
Mayr, U., 30–35, 37–41, 43, *44,* 46–49, 52, *61,*
   87, 94, 96, *100, 101,* 213, *236,* 255, *257,*
   313, *315*
Mazaus, J. M., *235*
McAuliffe, S. P., 269, *275*
McAvoy, M., 157, *160*
McCandliss, B. D., 130, *140*
McCartney, H. J., 56, *61*
McClelland, J. L., 216, *235,* 251, *255,* 282,
   287, 287n2, *303*
McCoy, S. L., 172, *183*

Subject Index

About the Editors

David S. Gorfein, PhD, began his research career as a social psychologist, but within a few years his interests came to emphasize learning and memory and ultimately basic processes in language, exploring how people handle ambiguity. A fellow of the American Psychological Association, he has previously edited three books, including *Human Memory and Learning: The Ebbinghaus Centennial Conference* (1987), with Robert R. Hoffman; *Resolving Semantic Ambiguity* (1989); and *On the Consequences of Meaning Selection: Perspectives on Resolving Lexical Ambiguity* (American Psychological Association, 2001).

Dr. Gorfein grew up in the Bronx, and really could not tear himself away from his neighborhood team, the New York Yankees. He received his BA from City College of New York in 1956 and his PhD from Columbia University in 1962. For 10 years, he was a faculty member at the New College in Florida before moving back to New York to serve as chair at Adelphi University, a position he held for 18 of his 21 years there. In 1996, he "retired" to the University of Texas at Arlington to continue his research and supervise research students. He has a lifelong love of the stage, from the folk clubs of Greenwich Village in the 1960s to the Shakespearean Festival of Stratford, Ontario, today.

Colin M. MacLeod, PhD, has focused his research on attention, learning, and memory, exploring the underpinnings of conscious and unconscious processes. A fellow of the American Psychological Association, the Association for Psychological Science, and the Canadian Psychological Association, he has served as editor of both the *Canadian Journal of Experimental Psychology* and *Memory & Cognition*. His previous edited books include *Neuroplasticity, Learning, and Memory* (1987), with Norton W. Milgram and Ted L. Petit; *Intentional Forgetting: Interdisciplinary Approaches* (1998), with Jonathan M. Golding; and *Dynamic Cognitive Processes* (2005), with Nobuo Ohta and Bob Uttl.

He grew up in Montréal, Québec, Canada, making him a lifelong fan of the Montréal Canadiens. He received his BA from McGill University in 1971 and then moved to Seattle, receiving his PhD from the University of Washington in 1975, where he had the honor of being the first graduate student of the late Thomas O. Nelson. For 25 years, he was a faculty member at the University of Toronto at Scarborough, before moving to the University of Waterloo in 2003, the year his son Nathan was born. Along with his research, his other lifelong devotion has been popular music, as a result of which he has far too many LPs and CDs.